MAX WEBER ON POWER AND SOCIAL STRATIFICATION

To the memory of my dear mother, Julia

Max Weber on Power and Social Stratification

An Interpretation and Critique

CATHERINE BRENNAN
Department of Sociology
Massey University
New Zealand

Routledge
Taylor & Francis Group

LONDON AND NEW YORK

First published 1997 by Ashgate Publishing

Reissued 2018 by Routledge
2 Park Square, Milton Park, Abingdon, Oxon, OX14 4RN
711 Third Avenue, New York, NY 10017

Routledge is an imprint of the Taylor & Francis Group, an informa business

Publisher's Note
The publisher has gone to great lengths to ensure the quality of this reprint but points out that some imperfections in the original copies may be apparent.

Disclaimer
The publisher has made every effort to trace copyright holders and welcomes correspondence from those they have been unable to contact.

A Library of Congress record exists under LC control number: 97073613

ISBN 13: 978-1-138-32542-5 (hbk)
ISBN 13: 978-1-138-32543-2 (pbk)
ISBN 13: 978-0-429-45039-6 (ebk)

Contents

v

Foreword

The fact that scholarly devotion to the writings of Max Weber shows no sign of abating should not occasion much wonderment. Sociology is a discipline that is founded upon an unusually narrow intellectual base - principally the accomplishment of Marx, Weber and Durkheim. Beyond the corpus of ideas produced by this dazzling triumvirate all other contributions appear somewhat meagre. Now the original base itself has become subject to erosion following the virtual demise of socialism and with it the Marxist legacy which provided most of its philosophical fibre. With the credibility of Marx's system of ideas so badly dented, it is understandable that the classical tradition would be correspondingly reoriented in the direction of Weber and Durkheim. Weber's work is bound to be seen as especially pertinent in this respect, since it has commonly and very plausibly been viewed as both a refutation of Marx's system and a theoretical alternative to it. At the close of the millennium, with socialism everywhere in retreat and capitalism everywhere in the ascendancy, it really does seem as if the long drawn out contest between Marxism and Weberian sociology has been settled decisively in Weber's favour.

Anyone anticipating a celebration of this viewpoint in Dr Brennan's book will be in for a surprise. Far from being an exercise in Weberian triumphalism, the following pages gnaw away relentlessly at some of the most hallowed tenets of the master's work. The core of the problem as Dr Brennan sees it, and the recurring theme of her book, is that despite Weber's reputation as the theorist of social action *par excellence*, his conception of action is restricted almost exclusively to the conduct of elites. Only elites are capable of meaningful action: the masses are merely fodder to be acted upon. It might be thought that Weber is here bluntly stating a factual condition, not necessarily giving it his moral imprimatur. But Dr Brennan argues that his entire theoretical stance rules out the possibility of non-elites being conceived of as actors in their own right. Capitalist entrepreneurs and charismatic leaders are among the few figures endowed with the rational attributes which enable them to act in the full Weberian sense: workers, citizens, ordinary people, are merely the *means* of other's actions.

Dr Brennan teases out the many and various ramifications of Weber's notion of action - or, more correctly, inaction - in his analyses of social stratification, bureaucracy, and democratic politics. In each case she identifies the inadequacies of an approach which effectively devalues the moral capacities of unsung individuals and which systematically underrates the potential for concerted 'action from below'.

Other writers have found fault with Weber's open or tacit approval of elitism, particularly in his pronouncements on political leadership. Few, however, have pursued the point to so many other aspects of his work or have rested their case on the wealth of direct textual support that Dr Brennan has accumulated. Committed Weberians will certainly find a great deal here to disagree with; but only the most churlish will fail to admire the erudition and exegetical prowess of such a splendid piece of iconoclasm.

Frank Parkin

Acknowledgements

This book is the outgrowth of a doctoral dissertation written under the supervision of Jack Barbalet in the Department of Sociology at the Australian National University. The Australian National University provided the ideal social environment conducive to a life of serious reflection. Gianfranco Poggi made valuable critical comments on the thesis version of the book. Needless to say, any shortcomings that are apparent are my own responsibility.

I wish to express my sincere thanks to Heather Hodgetts for preparing the word-processed text. I am deeply indebted to Heather for her practical help, thoughtfulness and forbearance throughout the preparation of this book.

Special thanks are due to Judy Lawrence for preparing the index.

I am very grateful to the Department of Sociology, Massey University for a research grant which contributed towards the production of this book.

I would like to extend a heartfelt thanks to my dear friends in Australia, New Zealand and Ireland for their constant encouragement and unfailing commitment to me. I am particularly grateful to my dear friend and colleague, Mary Murray, for being so exceedingly kind and supportive when it was most needed. Mary has shown me that generosity of spirit amongst scholars still makes for a society worth living in.

Finally, words are not sufficient to express how deeply indebted I am to my dear family in Ireland. Without their unconditional love, this book would never have seen the light of day.

Introduction

Max Weber is one of the great figures on the landscape of modern social thought. He is rightfully known as one of the 'founding fathers' of sociology. He has influenced the development of many sub-fields within the discipline such as the sociology of religion, urban sociology, the sociology of law, economic sociology, political sociology and the sociology of social stratification. This book will explore Weber's sociology of social stratification. The sociology of social stratification is essentially concerned with the study of structural social inequalities.

In order to clarify the focus of this book, it is first of all necessary to briefly comment on the development of the study of structural social inequalities. In the form of modern industrial capitalism, the economy emerged as a structurally independent sub-system within society. Society now progressed under the imperative of economic growth and the increase of wealth. It was under these historical conditions that what is usually called 'civil society' was identified for the first time as a distinct social sphere separate from the state by the moral philosophers of the Scottish Enlightenment in the second half of the eighteenth century.[1] 'Civil society' was thematized as that particular sphere which is constituted and held together by the production, distribution and consumption of goods as well as the organization of social labour. Analogously, economic value was recognized as a structurally scarce resource in civil society. Consciousness of the scarcity of economically produced value meant, in turn, that social inequality was understood and experienced as the partaking of some in, and the exclusion of others from, partaking in this form of value. If the disparity of judicial rights pertaining to noble and commoner was one of the primary forms of inequality characteristic of feudal society, the unequal distribution of economic value became the principal factor that stratified civil society. Social inequality acquired a strictly material meaning.

Of particular relevance also is that the Scottish moral philosophers influenced

1

Hegel's conceptualization of civil society (*bürgerliche Gesellschaft*).[2] Hegel argues in the *Philosophy of Right* that civil society is the creation of the modern world. He observes, for instance, that the ancient Greeks lived almost exclusively as family members and as citizens or dependent subjects of a highly controlled political community. No social space existed for forms of association detached from the ties of family and state. It was only in the modern world that a vast middle-ground, civil society, emerged as the social counterpart of the production, exchange and consumption of goods at the economic level. Hegel outlines the laws of the internal dialectic of civil society eventuating in the formation of classes and special interest groups.

Marx identifies civil/bourgeois society as a class society *per se*. The class structure of bourgeois society is such that two classes, the bourgeoisie and the proletariat, directly confront one another. For Marx, the economic structure of society is always the starting-point from which it is ultimately possible to unravel the significance of the whole superstructure of religious and other ideas as well as of political institutions. That is to say:

> Definite individuals who are productively active in a definite way enter into these definite social and political relations. *Empirical observation must in each separate instance bring out empirically ... the connection of the social and political structure with production.* (1976a, p.41; emphasis added)

Through such empirical observation, Marx brought to light the fact that the owners of the means of production also monopolize the sources of ideological domination and wield political power in bourgeois society.

If Marx is usually acknowledged as the theorist of class and class conflict within that part of the sociological tradition concerned with social stratification, Max Weber is most often regarded to have presented a definitive statement of his conception of social stratification in the essay, 'The Distribution of Power Within the Political Community: Class, Status, Party' (1978a, pp.926-40). The exact dating of this essay is uncertain. But it undoubtedly derives from the period between 1915 and 1919, that is, up to five years before Weber's death in 1920. The essay remained unpublished during his lifetime. In fact, Weber never completed it. It was found among the papers he left upon his death. It was published for the first time in the 1920s under the direction of Weber's widow, Marianne. A restatement and suggestions for the extension of some of the central ideas in 'Class, Status, Party' can be found in a later chapter and section of *Economy and Society*: 'Status Groups and Classes' (1978a, pp.302-7) and 'Parties' (1978a, pp.284-8).

The central thesis which Weber develops in 'Class, Status, Party' bears on the fact that '"classes", "status groups", and "parties" are phenomena of the distribution of power within a community' (1978a, p.927). Classes, status groups and parties are bases of the aggregation of power.[3] For Weber, the study of social stratification revolves around the analysis of the distribution of economic, social and political power within various societies in different historical periods. As a matter of fact, Weber's contention that not only classes but also status groups and parties are phenomena of the distribution of power, can be partly understood as a response to the vulgar Marxism current in Germany at the time he was writing. Weber vehemently opposed what he deemed to be the economic determinism intrinsic to this form of Marxism. For the salient point is that:

> The explanation of everything by economic causes *alone* is never exhaustive in any sense whatsoever in *any* sphere of cultural phenomena, not even in the economic sphere itself. (Weber 1949, p.71; emphasis in original)

In the context of social stratification, the unequal distribution of power between various groups within a society is not necessarily accounted for in economic terms. Social and political factors may be more relevant in explaining power differentials in certain societies. For example, Weber argues that power differentials in feudal society are, first and foremost, explicated in terms of the unequal distribution of the primary resource, social honour. The uneven distribution of social honour is, in turn, usually associated with the unequal distribution of economic resources and a rights-based system of inequality.

Of paramount importance also is that Weber's understanding of classes, status groups and parties as bases of the aggregation of power does not constitute a theory of social stratification. Weber did not hand down to us a fully-fledged theory of social stratification in the sense of a set of consistent and systematically related statements. Quite the contrary. He considered society as an historical process analyzed by the open-ended nature of concepts. Concepts are intrinsically historical and must, therefore, be continually criticized and reconstructed. Accordingly, Weber's treatment of social stratification involves an historically oriented analysis of power relations in different societies.[4]

In the context of this very brief commentary on the development of the study of social stratification, the next crucial stage is represented by the American appropriation of the classical European ideas of Marx and Weber. American sociology took over the European concepts of class, status, party and power without the European experience out of which they grew. These concepts were, thereby, deprived of their roots and subsequently grafted onto the completely different American experience.[5]

To fully appreciate the American appropriation of the classical European tradition, it is important to remember that the development of the study of social inequality in Europe was inextricably intertwined with the rise of social movements struggling for human rights and economic well-being. These social movements emerged as a response to the growing awareness and experience of social inequality in industrial capitalist societies in the nineteenth century. Marx's class analysis of bourgeois society contributed to this developing consciousness among the working-class. The labour movement fought for better working

3

conditions such as the shortening of the work-day, a guaranteed minimum wage, the abolition of child labour, and the right to organize.

In the United States, on the other hand, the study of social inequality from the 1920s onwards was mainly confined to academic circles.[6] It was from the outset heavily institutionalized. This being the case, many American theorists were predisposed towards developing a consensus theory of social stratification like structural-functionalism. The structural-functionalist theory is succinctly summed up by Davis and Moore:

> Starting from the proposition that no society is 'classless', or unstratified, an effort is made to explain, in functional terms, the universal necessity which calls forth stratification in any social system. (1967, p.47)

In contrast to the historically oriented study of power relations undertaken by Weber, many American stratification theorists set out to develop a consistent and systematic structural-functional theory of universal validity.

It is against the backcloth of structural-functionalism that the American appropriation of Weber's views on social stratification is comprehensible. This American appropriation is distinguished by a shift from the notion that classes, status groups and parties are bases of the aggregation of power within historical societies to the so-called ahistorical, three-dimensional theory of social stratification consisting of class, status and power. Even though this American theory of social stratification is held to be three-dimensional, the social dimension (i.e., status stratification) is usually given primacy.

In fact, many American stratification theorists have created an image of Weber as the representative of stratification by status.[7] What is more, this Americanized Weber is presented as a comprehensive alternative to Marx's theory of class and class conflict. Many American stratification theorists are primarily interested in status and status ranking. The function of a position is always the contribution of a part or unit to the whole. A position is always occupied by an individual. Prestige allocated to a position accrues to an individual serving as the basic symbol of his social standing or social status. The inordinate stress on the position of the individual within a framework of normative hierarchization typifies the American misappropriation of Weber. Status is the prestige allocated to different functions or roles and roles are performed by individuals.

In the process of appropriating Weber's ideas on social stratification, many American theorists also reduced power as such to a mere internal dimension of social stratification. 'Power' becomes synonymous with 'party'. In other words, power is simply identified as a political phenomenon. But Weber was quite explicit about the fact that not only parties but also classes and status groups are phenomena of the distribution of power. Given many American stratification theorists' interest in status ranking in terms of a common value system, it is not surprising that the centrality of power in Weber's analysis of social inequality was ignored. Indeed, the end-result of this American misappropriation of Weber is such that political power is studied in relative conceptual isolation from status stratification. Political power is treated as part of the subject-matter of political science or political sociology within the academic division of labour. In sum, then, the Weber that emerges from American stratification theory is one who, as Parkin pointedly remarks, 'has been thoroughly de-Marxified and so rendered fit to assume duties as the ideological champion of the classless society of American capitalism' (1979, p.604).

In the light of this very brief commentary on the rise of the study of social inequality, it is obvious that Weber's conception of social stratification has undergone a peculiar transmutation in the process of being integrated into American stratification theory. Indeed, Weber's ideas have been analyzed, modified and misappropriated to such an extent that Weber himself is often lost in the commentaries. The difficulty is that many American stratification theorists have reduced Weber's intentions to their own interests. Weber's views on social stratification are lost in putative deductions. Similarly, Burger observes in the course of his evaluation of Weber's rendition of social stratification that:

> ...despite the vigor of Weber's intellectual and scientific legacy, the secondary literature does not contain a single account which brings into the open the *analytic structure* underlying Weber's statements, i.e., the systematic assumptions and conceptualizations embodied in them. (1985, p.11; emphasis added)

Given this state of affairs, it is the principal objective of this book to retrieve the essential form and significance of Weber's ideas on social stratification. Although Weber is usually reputed to have presented a definitive account of his conception of social stratification in 'Class, Status, Party', this book will show that relevant statements are scattered throughout his varied writings. An internal reconstruction of Weber is undertaken by clarifying the inconsistencies and contradictions in his thought on social stratification, whilst simultaneously acknowledging its intrinsic unity. This internal reconstruction involves a textual analysis of some of Weber's key writings.[8] Textual exegesis is a crucial component of theoretical work. Despite the apparently gratuitous tediousness associated with textual exegesis, it is a mode of exposition which must be employed to dissect the 'analytic structure' underpinning the Weberian thesis that '"classes", "status groups", and "parties" are phenomena of the distribution of power within a community' (1978a, p.927).

One further preliminary clarification is necessary. Although the employment of gender-neutral language is *de rigueur* in much contemporary sociological writing, the use of 'sexist' language is quite deliberate throughout this book. Utilizing gender-neutral language would, in my view, simply efface the real sense of gender in Weber's sociology, including his sociology of social stratification. When Weber reflects upon structural social inequalities in both feudal and modern society, he is analyzing how various groups of *men* experience the unequal distribution of power. Women's experience of power differentials in these societies is inaccessible to sociological analysis in Weber's writings. Women are outcasts in Weber's sociology of social stratification. They are hidden from Weber's sociological gaze.

Chapter 1 will focus on the epistemological-methodological principles grounding Weber's study of social stratification. The principal objective is to clarify the Weberian understanding of scientific knowledge. For Weber regards his historically oriented analysis of power inequalities in various societies as scientific. Chapter 2 will examine the sociological principles underpinning Weber's treatment of social stratification. Weber's credentials as an action theorist will be critically scrutinized. Once the epistemological-methodological and sociological principles presupposed in Weber's writings on social stratification have been clarified, the third chapter will consider various key concepts crucial for understanding the Weberian analysis of power differentials in historical societies. These include: power, resistance, domination and discipline. The remainder of the book will explore some of Weber's historically oriented studies of power inequalities. Weber's view of classes as phenomena of the distribution of economic power within the modern capitalist market-economy is assessed in Chapter 4. Weber's conception of mediaeval status groups (i.e., estates) as bases of the aggregation of power is appraized in Chapter 5. Chapter 6 will concentrate on Weber's understanding of the unequal distribution of political power between responsible political leaders, democratic parties and the electoral masses within the confines of the German nation-state.

Notes

1 Of particular importance are works like Adam Ferguson's *Essay on the History of Civil Society*, first published in 1767, and John Millar's *The Origin of the Distinction of Ranks*, first published in 1779.

2 For instance, Avineri (1974, p.141) notes that there is evidence that during his years in Berlin Hegel had been reading Ferguson's *Essay on the History of Civil Society*.

3 Similarly, Toennies (1967, pp.12-21) makes a distinction between classes, estates and parties.

4 In a somewhat similar vein, Marx apprehended society as an historical totality which related immediately to praxis. Therefore, it is not surprising that he never gave a clear and consistent definition of the concept of class.

5 For an interesting discussion of the process by which Weber was channelled into the mainstream of American sociology, see Horowitz 1961, pp.344-54; Honigsheim 1968, pp.135-50; Hinkle 1986, pp.87-104; Roth 1992, pp.449-59.

6 See Gordon 1963.

7 Cf. Wenger 1980, pp.357-78; Parkin 1979, pp.601-5.
8 I use the standard English translations of Weber's writings throughout this book. Since most Weber-users around the world use these translations, Sica's (1993, p.840) point that a case could be put forward for an hermeneutic study of Weber that concentrated primarily on the English translations, is quite valid.

1 Values and social-scientific knowledge

In this chapter I explore the epistemological-methodological principles underpinning Weber's study of social stratification in the modern capitalist market-economy, the feudal estate order and the German nation-state. It is important to examine Weber's epistemological-methodological writings to gain an understanding of his idea of scientific knowledge. For Weber regards his study of social stratification as scientific. In the first section of the chapter I focus attention on Weber's concern with cognition as a method of constituting knowledge. Values are deemed central to the process of cognition. It is argued that Weber's application of the logical principle of value-relevance means that only those empirical phenomena are selected for a scientific investigation in which, according to the social scientist, cultural values are embodied. In this particular section I also investigate how Weber grounds the thesis of the objectivity of criteria for truth in the social sciences. The second section of the chapter comprises an examination of the scientific concept, the ideal-type, constructed by Weber to engage in a scientific analysis of selected empirical phenomena. The final section revolves around an evaluation of Weber's contentious principle of value-freedom.

1.1 Value-relevance

In view of the fact that Weber belongs within the neo-Kantian tradition, he argues that problems of ontology are dependent upon epistemology.[1] The fundamental problem concerns the means by which humans acquire knowledge of empirical reality. How can humans attain knowledge of the 'life' confronting them as a 'stream of immeasurable events...' (Weber 1949, p.84; see also pp.72, 111)?[2] According to Weber, empirical reality cannot be apprehended independently of the human mind perceiving. It cannot be conceptualized separately from humans being conscious of it. The phenomena comprising empirical reality are 'given in our consciousness' (Weber cited in Burger 1976, p.61). Viewed in this light, human knowledge is not a reproduction of empirical reality in the mind. In this same connection, Weber writes that:

> *Reflective knowledge,* even of one's own experience, *is nowhere and never* a literally 'repeated experience' or *a simple 'photograph' of what was experienced;* the 'experience', when it is made into an 'object', acquires perspectives and interrelationships which were not 'known' in the experience itself. (1949, p.178, emphasis added; see also p.92)

It is impossible to 'analyze reality "without presuppositions"' (Weber 1949, p.78). It is reasonable to assume, then, that Weber regards human knowledge as a selective mental representation of empirical reality.

In fact, Weber is, as Burger (1976, pp.61-3) states, much more precise about the selective intellectual processing of empirical reality, the end-result of which is 'scientific' knowledge. This selective intellectual processing involves three essential steps: immediate experience, concrete facts and scientific concepts. In the first place, what is immediately 'given in our consciousness' is 'experience'. Weber explains that:

> ...the 'object of immediate experience' is ... constituted by the totality of our 'perceptions' in connection with the undifferentiated 'feelings' and 'desires' that are associated with them ... 'The object of immediate experience' in this sense cannot be the object of a *proposition*—that is, an empirical explanation of facts. In which case, it remains irrelevant to all empirical knowledge. (1975a, p.160, emphasis in original; see also pp.130-36, 148, 151, 161-70, 176-81; 1949, p.158)

The distinction made between immediately experienced reality and empirical knowledge is a logical disjunction. The totality of '"feelings"' and '"desires"' comprising the '"object of immediate experience"' has 'the character of relative "vagueness"' (Weber 1975a, p.178). Emotions, sensations and the like make up the formless substance immediately 'given in our consciousness'. This being the case, Weber purports that the *'leaden diffuseness of "immediate experience"* must be broken...' (1975a, p.162; emphasis added), if 'factual' knowledge of this experience is to be procured. Sensations, feelings and so forth cannot be 'known' as they are 'experienced'. That is to say, 'the actual *"desire"* is never "experienced" in the same way that one becomes "aware of" the *objects* of desire...' (Weber 1975a, p.132; emphasis in original). As soon as human beings become '"aware of"' their feelings, desires and so on, they cannot help but do so in terms of categories. When humans have ideas of their feelings, desires and the like, they classify them. For Weber, human knowledge is 'related to a categorically formed reality...' (1949, p.188; see also pp.177-8).[3] Stated otherwise, when a human being reflects upon his raw experience, a pre-

9

objectified, subjective experience *'becomes* an "object", a "complex of observed facts"...' (Weber 1975a, p.131; emphasis in original). When a wage-labourer in a modern capitalist factory reflects upon his raw experience, upon the fact, for instance, that his employer is very wealthy whilst he remains poor, a subjective experience is changed into 'a "complex of observed facts"'. The wage-labourer may begin to think in terms of categories like social equality and justice.

The final step in the selective intellectual processing of immediately given reality bears on a scientific analysis of the constituted facts through the construction of concepts. These concepts are, according to Weber, 'primarily analytical instruments for *the intellectual mastery of empirical data...*' (1949, p.106, emphasis added; see also pp.60, 68). A scientific concept is a specific arrangement of facts in the human mind. In this regard, Burger (1976, p.62) discerns that Weber is not always sufficiently consistent about the point that the 'content' of 'scientific' knowledge is 'facts'.[4] Weber, for instance, states that 'valid *judgments* always presuppose the *logical* analysis of what is concretely and immediately perceived, i.e. the use of *concepts*' (1949, p.107; emphasis in original). Weber is saying here that 'science' pertains to the 'logical analysis' of immediate experiences, feelings and so on.[5] The crucial issue, though, is that the transformation of raw experience into facts represents the vital intermediate step in the development of scientific knowledge.

Pertinent to the issue at hand here also is that although all scientific knowledge is knowledge of facts, a complete representation of facts cannot be the purpose of a scientific investigation. Facts are infinitely varied (Weber 1949, p.78). Moreover, the 'finite human mind' (Weber 1949, p.72) is only capable of analyzing a finite part of the infinitely many facts. This being the case, science concentrates on a partial representation of these facts. Scientific knowledge entails only a knowledge of those facts which are relevant to the goals of a scientific investigation of a specific type.

Regarding the constitution of the facts of the social sciences, it is first of all important to understand that human individuals make value-judgements about certain phenomena.[6] When a human individual makes a value-judgement about a particular phenomenon, it is removed from the sphere of that which is merely 'experienced' and 'felt'. Weber explains that:

> In contrast to mere 'emotional contents', we ascribe 'value' to an item if and only if it can be the content of a commitment: that is, a consciously articulated positive or negative 'judgment', something that appears to us to 'demand validity'... it is the *determinateness of content* which removes the object of the value judgment from the sphere of that which is merely 'felt'. (1975a, pp.182-3, emphasis in original; see also 1949, pp.1, 10, 150)

Weber is stressing the cognitive dimension of value-judgements in contrast to mere emotions and feelings which are indeterminate and, hence, incommunicable.[7] Certain phenomena, then, are detached from immediately given reality and become discursively accessible, because humans make value-judgements about them. And these phenomena, by the same token, become subjectively meaningful for the humans who assign value to them. In effect, valuation (*Wertung*), on Weber's interpretation, provides a necessary criterion by means of which the inexhaustibility of immediately experienced reality is overcome, and meaningful social facts are constituted (Weber 1975a, p.185).[8]

Put another way, Weber is conveying the idea here that *Kultur* is a finite segment of the infinite manifold that is *Realität*. Culture represents a finite slice of *Realität* invested with meaning and value by human beings. When workers, for example, in the modern capitalist market-economy challenge the juristic precision of modern rational law because of its failure to serve their needs and, further, demand 'a "social law" to be based upon such emotionally colored ethical postulates as "justice" or "human dignity"...' (Weber 1978a, p.886)—they are making a value-judgement. These workers are making clear their preference for a substantive law as opposed to a strictly formal law.

However, Weber goes on to say that '"valuation" is the normal *psychological* transitional stage for "intellectual understanding"' (1975a, p.184; emphasis in original). The 'immediate valuation of the "attitude-taking subject"' (Weber 1949, p.158) such as the wage-labourer is a 'practical' rather than a strictly 'scientific' means of surmounting the diffuseness and infinity of immediately given reality. But the social scientist's fundamental goal in a scientific investigation, on Weber's interpretation, is 'the analysis of facts' (1949, p.60; see also pp.59, 63). Stated otherwise, scientific knowledge 'can be produced only by "objectification": i.e., by artificially divorcing the object from the primordial subject who "understands and evaluates"' (Weber 1975a, p.133).

Seen in this light, what social scientists require is a principle of selection which enables them to select facts in order to analyze them, without taking a positive or negative stance towards them. Value-relevance (*Wertbeziehung*) is such a principle. Value-relevance establishes an interrelationship between empirical phenomena and certain values without evaluating them. According to Weber:

> ...'relevance to values' refers to the philosophical interpretation of that specifically scientific 'interest' which determines the selection of a given subject-matter and the problems of an empirical analysis. *In empirical investigation, no 'practical evaluations' are legitimated by this strictly logical fact.* (1949, p.22, emphasis added; see also pp.72-85, 143-63; 1975a, pp.157-8, 181-6; 1977)[9]

More pointedly, the application of the logical principle of value-relevance means that only those empirical phenomena are selected for a social-scientific investigation in which, according to social scientists, cultural values are embodied.[10] Weber writes, for example, that:

11

The 'interpretation' of 'Faust' or of 'Puritanism' or of some specific aspect of 'Greek culture' in *this* sense is an inquiry into those 'values' which 'we' *can* find 'embodied' in these objects. (1975a, p.181; emphasis in original)[11]

Those empirical phenomena in which for social scientists cultural values are incorporated, provide a wide-ranging group of cultural phenomena (social facts) appropriate for a social-scientific inquiry. And given that those empirical phenomena which for social scientists embody cultural values, were constituted in the first instance by individuals like capitalist entrepreneurs, wage-labourers, feudal knights and charismatic leaders making value-judgements about them— these evaluating individuals are part of any social-scientific investigation (see Weber 1949, pp.150-51).

Therefore, the fact that cultural values are for social scientists embodied in certain empirical phenomena, represents a valid means of overcoming the infinite diversity of existing empirical phenomena. Such cultural values are contained in a finite number of the innumerable concrete phenomena. Weber affirms that:

> Order is brought into this chaos only on the condition that in every case only a *part* of concrete reality is interesting and *significant* to us, because only it is related to the *cultural values* with which we approach reality. Only certain sides of the infinitely complex concrete phenomenon, namely those to which we attribute a general *cultural significance*—are therefore worthwhile knowing. (1949, p.78, emphasis in original; see also pp.76-84)[12]

Moreover, when Weber asserts that only those empirical phenomena are 'worthwhile knowing' to which social scientists assign 'a general *cultural significance*', he is underlining the fact that these phenomena are of general interest. They are 'cultural' phenomena. Western feudalism, modern capitalism and the modern nation-state, for instance, are all designated as 'cultural' phenomena—'*only* because and *only* insofar as their existence and the form which they historically assume touch directly or indirectly on our *cultural interests...*' (Weber 1949, p.81; emphasis in original). And of course, such phenomena will continue to be of 'general *cultural significance*' only so long as the cultural values embodied in them, relate to the collective interests of the society of which the social scientist is a member. Accordingly, Weber declares that the social scientist 'must understand how to relate the events of the real world consciously or unconsciously to universal "cultural values" and to select out those relationships which are significant for us' (1949, pp.81-2).

Of particular relevance also is that social scientists can find a large number of cultural values of general significance contained in empirical phenomena. What is more, new general cultural values are always being discovered. According to Weber, the reason for this lies in the fact that:

> Life with ... its store of possible meanings is inexhaustible. The *concrete* form in which value-relevance occurs remains perpetually in flux, ever

12

subject to change in the dimly seen future of human culture. (1949, p.111, emphasis in original; see also pp.84, 159)

And owing to the possibility of new general cultural values being constantly found, 'a systematic science of culture', on Weber's interpretation, 'would be senseless in itself' (1949, p.84; see also p.72). For instance, the key cultural value of general significance in the feudal estate order in the West, social honour, is an obsolete value in modern capitalist society. But this is not to say that Western feudalism no longer relates in a direct or indirect way to 'our cultural interests' in modern capitalist society. Indeed, one reason for Weber's (1978a, pp.1099-1102) analysis of Western feudalism was to unravel the causes which hampered capitalist development in this social structure.

For all this, there is, in my view, an apparent inconsistency inherent in Weber's notion of general cultural values being continually subject to historical change. Weber speaks, for example, of '*meta*historical values' (1975a, p.111; emphasis in original) and of value-analysis having a status 'beyond history' (1949, p.147). He also alleges that:

The belief which we all have in some form or other, in the *meta-empirical validity of ultimate and final values,* in which the meaning of our existence is rooted, is not incompatible with the incessant changefulness of the concrete viewpoints, from which empirical reality gets its significance. (1949, p.111; emphasis added)

Weber is stating in this instance that transcendental values exist alongside general cultural values. He, however, never indicates how such transcendental values could be congruent with general cultural values.[13]

Pertinent to the general impetus of the present discussion also is that although there are a large number of cultural values of general significance embodied in empirical phenomena, there are no logical principles, as Burger (1976, p.81) underscores, enjoining the social scientist to adopt some of these cultural values as opposed to others. In this respect, Weber himself purports that 'it is due to the evaluative ideas with which he unconsciously approaches his subject matter' that the social scientist 'has selected from an absolute infinity a tiny portion with the study of which he *concerns* himself' (1949, p.82, emphasis in original; see also p.151; 1975a, pp.181-2). That is to say, the social scientist is 'free' to choose a particular cultural value of general significance from the broad category of such cultural values and, concomitantly, a particular constellation of empirical phenomena from the wide-ranging category of such phenomena (see Weber 1975a, p.273). He is 'free' to make a particular group of empirical phenomena the embodiment of a particular cultural value of general significance.[14] Put somewhat differently, the social scientist is 'free' to construct an 'historical individual', that is, 'an "entity" synthetically produced by a *value* relation' (Weber 1975a, pp.183-4; emphasis in original). Weber makes particular constellations of empirical phenomena like modern capitalism and the modern nation-state the embodiment of a particular cultural value of general significance, namely, instrumental rationality. Modern capitalism and the modern nation-state are 'historical individuals' 'synthetically produced' by reference to instrumental rationality.

The fact that only those empirical phenomena are deemed appropriate social facts for a social-scientific investigation in which, according to the social scientist, a specific cultural value of general significance is incorporated, signifies for Weber that 'all knowledge of cultural reality ... is always knowledge from *particular points of view*' (1949, p.81; emphasis in original). Admittedly, the empirical phenomena which for the social scientist embody particular cultural values, were constituted in the first instance by human individuals evaluating them. But 'logically', on Weber's (1949, pp.82-4, 159) reading, this does not imply that the particular configuration of empirical phenomena ('the object') dictates the particular cultural value which will be employed. The adoption of a particular cultural value of general significance by the social-scientific investigator himself ('the subject') has, for logical reasons, precedence. It is in this sense that Weber maintains that 'all evaluative ideas are "subjective"' (1949, p.83; see also pp.72, 82, 84, 110, 152, 159). He goes so far as to say that:

> ...the values to which the scientific genius relates the object of his inquiry may determine, i.e., decide the 'conception' of a whole epoch, not only concerning what is regarded as 'valuable' but also concerning what is significant or insignificant, 'important' or 'unimportant' in the phenomena. (1949, p.82; emphasis added)

The fact that Weber himself relates objects of his research such as modern capitalism and the modern nation-state to instrumental rationality, has had a major influence on many social scientists' understanding of the development of modern Western society. When Weber relates modern capitalism and the modern nation-state to instrumental rationality, he is reflecting upon the rationalization of the modern West. The process of rationalization has not only become an integral component of contemporary sociological discourse, but also of the layperson's language.

So far it has been established that, on Weber's interpretation, the social scientist's choice of a particular cultural value of general significance to which he relates a particular configuration of social facts, is for logical reasons strictly subjective. However, Weber does concede that, empirically, the social-scientific investigator's choice is subject to other influences. To begin with, he affirms that there is a close relation between value-choices and socio-historical conditions. This is tantamount to saying that 'the choice of the object of investigation' is 'determined by the evaluative ideas which dominate the investigator and his age' (Weber 1949, p.84). Seen in this light, the number of cultural values of general significance from which the social scientist can choose is limited in any particular

14

society at any particular period of history. Moreover, the fact that the value adopted by the social scientist is a cultural value of general significance, suggests that it must in some way relate to the collective interests of the society of which the social scientist is a member. Instrumental rationality, as already noted, is one such key cultural value of general significance adopted by Weber, to which he relates the principal objects of his scientific study of social stratification. Weber states that 'the fate of our times is characterized by rationalization and intellectualization and, above all, by the "disenchantment of the world"' (1970, p.155). On this account, Habermas misreads Weber when he depicts his concern with the process of rationalization as 'a private philosophy of history from whose visual angle Weber interprets the whole development of society' (1971a, p.62).

In addition to the social scientist's value-choices being influenced by the evaluative ideas prevailing in the particular society in which he lives at a particular period of history, I would suggest that the role of the social-scientific community of which the social scientist is a member must also be taken into account. For the value-choices of other social scientists of the past and present tend to influence the social scientist's selection of a particular cultural value of general significance. For instance, Weber's adoption of another general cultural value, namely, the nationalist value of promoting the 'power-political interests' (1980, p.438) of the German nation-state, was not only a value related to the collective concerns of German society in the nineteenth and early twentieth centuries. It was also a value to which many German scholars like the nationalist historian, Treitschke (1978), related the objects of their research.

Once the social scientist has opted for a particular cultural value of general significance to which he relates a particular constellation of empirical phenomena, he proceeds to the next stage, that is, the social-scientific analysis of the selected group of social facts. Whilst engaged in the social-scientific analysis of these facts, the general cultural value which provided the justification for their selection, is presupposed by the social scientist. The social-scientific analysis of the relevant facts includes the study of the activity of those human individuals, who in the first instance constituted these social facts by evaluating them.

It is important at this stage to mention that certain assumptions about the nature of humankind underpin Weber's idea of a social/cultural science. To begin with, Weber declares that 'we are *cultural beings*, endowed with the capacity and the will to take a deliberate attitude towards the world and to lend it *significance*' (1949, p.81; emphasis in original). It is Weber's contention that the human subject is the constructor of his own set of values and, hence, meanings. It is only through the exercize of choice on the part of the human subject that values (and meanings) come into being. The 'origin' of values (and meanings) inheres not in 'the world' itself, but in the 'faculty of choice' (i.e., 'the will') which the human subject as a cultural being (*Kulturmensch)* exercizes, when he commits himself to certain values.[15] Weber explains that:

The fate of an epoch which has eaten of the tree of knowledge is that it must know that we cannot learn the *meaning* of the world from the results of its analysis, be it ever so perfect; it must rather be in a position to create this meaning itself. (1949, p.57; emphasis in original)

It is useless, then, for the modern individual to search for objective values (and meanings). The unitary view of the world as a meaningful cosmos which prevailed in the Christian-feudal era in the West, is no longer relevant in modern rationalized society. It is in this sense that Weber understands modern society in the West to be characterized by a 'loss of meaning'.[16] In this same connection, Weber affirms that 'former illusions' like the 'way to true being', the 'way to true God' and so forth 'have been dispelled' (1970, p.143) in modern rationalized society in the West. Whilst the idea of constituting/positing values was inconceivable to the pre-modern (traditional) individual, the onus is on the modern individual himself to endow the world with meaning. The sacredness of tradition in the feudal estate order in the West, for example, meant that values could not be constituted/posited by an individual like the feudal knight. Rather, the feudal knight could only 'find' values by adhering to the customary. Modern individuals like capitalist entrepreneurs, on the other hand, must 'create' their own values. They must bestow meaning and significance on a segment of reality.

In fact, Weber's apprehension of the human individual as a 'cultural being' 'endowed with the capacity and the will to take a deliberate attitude towards the world and to lend it significance', attests to his philosophical commitment to modern rationalized society.[17] The inner-worldly asceticism of the Protestant believer epitomizes this cultural/value-implementing being (see Weber 1976a). And of course, the sociological embodiment of this particular kind of being is the rational actor. The impeccably rational actor represents a sociological extension of the human subject as a cultural being of freedom and purpose.[18]

Another important feature of the idea of the human individual as a 'cultural being', has to do with the fact that Weber, as Benhabib astutely observes, 'makes no clear distinction between *intersubjectively* shared cultural values and ideals ... and the individual choice of values by the person' (1981, p.361; emphasis in original).[19] When Weber speaks of 'cultural values', he is referring to values that pertain to the collective concerns of the society of which the social scientist is a member. It is obvious that such values in their orientation extend beyond the isolated human individual. But, on the other hand, the conception of the cultural being suggests that the human individual is solely responsible for the creation of values. It is in this sense that life for the human individual in modern rationalized society becomes 'a series of ultimate decisions through which the soul ... chooses its own fate, i.e., the meaning of its activity and existence' (Weber 1949, p.18). Values are created and actively upheld by the human subject in modern rationalized society. Weber is in this instance espousing the neo-Kantian principle of moral autonomy which arguably promotes an overinflated individualism. This

16

being so, Weber cannot even begin to conceptualize the constitution of an intersubjectively shared system of cultural values.[20] The same problem is manifest, as we shall see in the following chapter, in a limited idea of 'the social' in Weber's sociology of action.

Weber's conception of the charismatic leader provides a good illustration of the fact that he does not make a clear distinction between intersubjectively shared cultural values and the individual's choice of a particular value Weber believes that the charismatic leader is entirely responsible for the creation of values. This kind of leader draws his values/ mission/cause from within himself. Weber writes that 'the mission and the power of its bearer is *qualitatively delimited from within, not by an external order*' (1978a, p.1113; emphasis added). On this account, the charismatic leader in the German nation-state was likewise exclusively responsible for the constitution of the nationalist value, that is, the promotion of the 'power-political interests' of the German nation-state. But it is clear, on the other hand, that this nationalist value extended beyond the charismatic leader in the sense that it was a general cultural value bearing on the collective interests of German society in the nineteenth and early twentieth centuries.

One final issue must be addressed, that is, the problem of objectivity in the social sciences. How does Weber ground the thesis of the objectivity of criteria for truth in the social sciences, whilst simultaneously dismissing an objective system of values? Weber's answer is given in the following statement:

> ...the choice of the object of investigation and the extent or depth to which this investigation attempts to penetrate into the infinite causal web, are determined by the evaluative ideas which dominate the investigator and his age. In the *method* of investigation, the guiding 'point of view' is of great importance for the *construction* of the conceptual scheme which will be used in the investigation. In the mode of their *use*, however, the investigator is obviously bound by the norms of our thought just as much here as elsewhere. For scientific truth is precisely what is *valid* for all who seek the truth. (1949, p.84, emphasis in original; see also p.51; 1975a, p.148)

Weber is stating here that the social scientist's adoption of a particular cultural value of general significance, determines which particular constellation of social facts is selected as the object of a social-scientific investigation, the limits to which this investigation is pursued, and the construction of the conceptual apparatus which will be employed in the investigation.

Regarding the manner in which the constructed conceptual apparatus is utilized, though, Weber maintains that the social scientist's value choice is not relevant. The social scientist's selection of a specific cultural value of general significance is subjective in the sense that it represents an extra-scientific starting-point for a social-scientific inquiry. This being so, Weber contends that

17

objective validity, that is intersubjectively valid objective truth in the realm of social science, refers to the methodical procedures which are applied after the value-related selection of the object of scientific investigation. Objective validity in the sphere of social science is a property of method, since it is assumed that consensus concerning a proposition can be attained through scientific methods.[21]

As a matter of fact, two presuppositions, according to Weber, underpin all scientific procedures. To begin with, 'all scientific work presupposes that the rules of logic and method are valid; these are the general foundations of our orientation in the world...' (Weber 1970, p.143). Essentially, Weber is saying that 'the rules of logic and method' grounding all scientific activity are universally binding and *a priori*. These rules are not made by any particular culture and, furthermore, they are not peculiar to any particular historical period. Weber augments this argument when he affirms that:

> ...a systematically correct scientific proof in the social sciences, if it is to achieve its purpose, must be acknowledged as correct even by a Chinese—or—more precisely stated—it must constantly *strive* to attain this goal, which perhaps may not be completely attainable due to faulty data. (1949, p.58, emphasis in original; see also pp.40, 59)

Despite the fact, then, that different social researchers select different cultural values of general significance and, thereby, different constellations of social facts, the same rules of logic and method are used in the social-scientific analysis of these facts. In other words, 'the criterion of scientific knowledge is to be found in the *"objective" validity of its results...*' (Weber 1949, p.51; emphasis added).

In addition to the rules of logic and method, Weber purports that 'science further presupposes that what is yielded by scientific work is important in the sense that it is "worth being known"' (1970, p.143). Weber is in this instance speaking of scientific truth (empirically valid truth) as a value.[22] The pivotal point is that belief in the value of scientific truth:

> ...cannot be proved by scientific means. It can only be *interpreted* with reference to its ultimate meaning, which we must reject or accept according to our ultimate position towards life. (Weber 1970, p.143; emphasis in original)

Weber is explaining that the scientist's adoption of the value of empirically valid truth is his personal decision, since intersubjectively valid objective truth is unattainable in the realm of values. Opting for the value of empirically valid truth is an extra-scientific point of departure for a scientific investigation.

Another related point is that 'the belief in the value of scientific truth is the product of certain cultures and is not a product of man's original nature' (Weber 1949, p.110; see also pp.55, 58; 1975a, p.116). Belief in the value of empirically valid truth is, according to Weber, a cultural value. It obviously follows that the universally valid rules of logic and method can only be utilized by scientists who, in the first place, believe in the value of empirically valid truth. In the last analysis, then, Weber's key contention is that although the rules of logic and method used in all scientific investigations are universally valid, the community of scientists which believes in the value of empirically valid truth is not found in all cultures.

Weber's argument for the irrelevance of values to the scientific explanation of the selected group of social facts ('the object') is, I would argue, not wholly tenable.[23] Weber himself comes close to conceding that values influence the scientific investigation of the selected configuration of social facts, when he states that values determine 'the extent or depth to which this investigation attempts to penetrate into the infinite causal web...' (1949, p.84). Values determine how far the social scientist should proceed in the causal explanation of a selected group of social facts. On this account, it is apparent that the social scientist can never give a complete causal explanation of these facts. Weber does, indeed, state that 'an *exhaustive* causal investigation of any concrete phenomena in its full reality is not only practically impossible—it is simply nonsense' (1949, p.78; emphasis in original). Causal explanations in the social sciences can only be given from particular value-standpoints. And, therefore, such explanations cannot produce results of universal validity. The fact that values determine how far a scientific inquiry extends into 'the infinite causal web' results, as Rossi (1971, p.76) points out, in 'conditional' rather than 'deterministic' causal explanations.

In light of the preceding discussion, it might be reasonably assumed that the influence of values cannot be confined to the initial stages of a social-scientific inquiry. In effect, if the social scientist must decide on a particular cultural value of general significance before he can even commence his scientific research, the results of his research will undoubtedly be influenced by this value-choice in a direct or indirect manner. But this is precisely what Weber is reluctant to concede openly. Instead, he maintains that 'an "absolute and unconditionally valid" knowledge' is possible in the case of causes (1949, p.159).

For example, Weber's adoption of the nationalist value, the promotion of the 'power-political interests' of the German nation-state, profoundly influences the results of his scientific investigation of the unequal distribution of political power within this nation-state. To take a particular case, Weber's notion of political responsibility is not a neutral, technical term. Quite the contrary. The more responsible political leader is the one most passionately devoted to advancing the interests of national power. The syndicalist's commitment to the promotion of the value of proletarian brotherhood, on the other hand, is deemed to be 'irresponsible' and, therefore, 'apolitical' by Weber. Furthermore, Weber's commitment to the nationalist value influenced the results of his empirical study of the situation of East Elbian rural labourers in the 1890s (1979, pp.177-205). A major part of the study was concerned with the inflow of Polish agricultural workers into East Elbe to replace the German workers who were migrating to the cities in Western Germany. Although this influx of Polish labour was leading to the development of a dynamic, capitalist, agricultural economy, Weber's primary conclusion in the study was the crucial importance of preserving the

German character of the East Elbian region.

One final issue pertinent to Weber's grounding of the thesis of objective validity in methodological procedures in the sphere of social science, has to do with his assertion that the scientific investigator is 'bound by the norms of our thought...' (1949, p.84). But it is not at all clear, as Oakes (1982, pp.613-15) indicates, which 'norms of our thought' the scientific investigator is supposedly bound by. Given Weber's understanding of 'cultural' values and, further, his conception of the human individual as a 'cultural being' *(Kulturmensch)* implementing values, it does not seem possible to identify meta-historical, cognitive norms which occupy the status of transcendental presuppositions underpinning all social-scientific inquiries. What is more, the identification of such meta-historical, cognitive norms would be totally opposed to Weber's logical principle of value-relevance, whereby the social scientist's own choice of a particular cultural value of general significance is the logically necessary precondition for the selection of the object appropriate for a scientific investigation. Owing to the ambiguities intrinsic to Weber's advocacy of objective validity as a property of method in the realm of social science, the only reasonable conclusion is that it is not possible to accept Weber's logical principle of value-relevance whilst simultaneously rejecting methodological relativism.

1.2 Ideal-type

Bearing in mind the ambivalence built into Weber's espousal of methodological objectivity in the sphere of social science, he goes on to argue that the particular constellation of social facts selected by the social scientist can only be subject to scientific analysis through the construction of an ideal-type. That is to say, the ideal-type, on Weber's reading, makes it possible to attain objectively valid knowledge of the selected group of social facts. The creation of the ideal-type is predicated upon the synthesis of various aspects of the selected configuration of social facts. Thus, the crucial issue, as Hekman (1983, pp.31-3) points out, bears on the identification of the criteria governing this synthesis.

It is against this background that Weber introduces his definition of the ideal-type:

> An ideal type is formed by the one-sided *accentuation* of one or more points of view and by the synthesis of a great many diffuse, discrete, more or less present and occasionally absent *concrete individual* phenomena, which are arranged according to those one-sidedly emphasized viewpoints into a unified *analytical* construct. (1949, p.90, emphasis in original; see also pp.84, 105; 1975a, p.168)

It is quite clear from this definition that one criterion guiding the unification of selected 'concrete individual phenomena' into an ideal-type is the point of view (i.e., value-choice) of the social scientist. The social scientist's adoption of a particular cultural value of general significance decides what particular aspects of the selected social facts can be logically combined into a 'unified *analytical* construct'. Expressed another way, the "'unity'" of the ideal-type, in Weber's view, 'is constituted by the selection of those aspects which are "essential" from the point of view of specific *theoretical goals*' (1975a, p.168; emphasis added). It is in this sense that Weber describes social phenomena like Christianity, Germany, modern capitalism, Western feudalism and the modern nation-state as '*individualized value-concepts*' (1949, p.160; emphasis in original).

The other major criterion guiding the synthesis of diverse features of selected social facts into an ideal-type is the logic intrinsic to this concept itself (see Weber 1949, p.90; 1978a, p.20). Various aspects of the selected social facts are unified into an ideal-type because they are logically congruent. In this light, ideal-types are not formed in an haphazard manner. There are logically constructed concepts, that is, scientific concepts. More to the point, Weber is primarily interested in defining the logic of the social scientist's explanation of meaningful social facts.

Given Weber's criteria for the construction of an ideal-type, he, then, considers its attributes in more detail (see Weber 1949, pp.42-6, 89-106, 164-88; 1975a, pp.186-91; 1975b, pp.32-6; 1978a, pp.19-22).[24] Weber designates the ideal-type as 'a thoroughly *synthetic* construct' (1975a, p.168; emphasis in original) which does not reproduce reality. 'It is not a *description* of reality but it aims to give unambiguous means of expression to such a description' (Weber 1949, p.90; emphasis in original). In other words, the ideal-type is a 'mental construct' (ibid.). The expression, 'mental construct', is of paramount importance since the ideal-type relates to a thought or idea, in principle, embodied in social reality. The ideal-type '*brings together certain relationships and events of historical life* into a complex, which is conceived as an internally consistent system' (ibid., emphasis added).[25] Weber continues that this 'mental construct' 'cannot be found empirically anywhere in reality' in its pure conceptual form (ibid.). Rather, empirical reality, or aspects of it, come close to the ideal-type in varying degrees. Expressed another way, the ideal-type is an 'utopia' with which empirical reality can be compared for the purpose of explicating some of its significant features (see Weber 1949, pp.90-93).

Weber suggests, for example, that abstract economic theory provides 'an illustration of those synthetic constructs which have been designated as *"ideas"* of historical phenomena' (1949, p.89, emphasis in original; see also p.90; 1975b, pp.33-4). Abstract economic theory gives us an ideal picture of events on the capitalist commodity-market. This ideal commodity-market could only be found in a society organized on the basis of an exchange economy, free competition and rigorously rational conduct. The ideal-type of abstract economic theory does not describe the components which the capitalist commodity-market has in common in 'empirical' reality, but the components which it has in common in an

21

'imaginary' one. The deviation of the ideal-type from 'empirical' reality must constantly be kept in mind. This relationship between the ideal-type and 'empirical' reality 'is problematical in every individual case' (Weber 1949, p.103). When it has been established in a particular case that an ideal-type like abstract economic theory corresponds with 'empirical' reality, or aspects of it, this ideal-type can be utilized as a 'description' of 'empirical' reality. This is what Weber regards as the 'descriptive' use of an ideal-type. To keep this example, if the ideal-type of abstract economic theory leads to a more precise understanding of non-capitalist components of an economy organized principally on the basis of free competition, '*it fulfills its logical purpose*, even though, in doing so, it demonstrates its divergence from reality' (Weber 1949, p.102; emphasis added).[26]

In effect, then, the social scientist, on Weber's reading, 'faces the task of determining in each individual case, the extent to which this ideal-construct approximates to or diverges from reality...' (1949, p.90). And the social scientist must explain these approximations to and divergences from the ideal-type causally (Weber 1949, p.43). However, the fact that the ideal-type is not an hypothesis means that it cannot be disproved by an 'empirical' case that is opposed to it. Quite the contrary. A correctly constructed ideal-type, according to Weber, can only be discarded, if the value-standpoints which guided its construction become obsolete. Therefore, ideal-types like modern capitalism and the modern nation-state cannot be dispensed with as long as a cultural value like instrumental rationality which guided their construction, remains of general significance. Furthermore, Weber's primary interest in instrumental rationality guided his construction of the ideal-type of Western feudalism in the sense that this particular constellation of social phenomena in the Middle Ages was deemed by Weber to lack rationality. Western feudalism was understood by Weber as the negative of the rational. It was one major variant of traditional domination as opposed to legal-rational domination.

It should also be remembered that the logical principle of value-relevance is such that it is not necessary for Weber in the course of constructing an ideal-type like Western feudalism to take into account the points of view of those (e.g., the feudal knights) who, in fact, historically contributed to the formation of the feudal estate order. For the cultural values the social scientist himself adopts, have precedence in the construction of the ideal-type of Western feudalism. In other words, 'the object of interpretation is not whatever those who historically participated in the production of the "valued" object subjectively "felt" from their own point of view' (Weber 1975a, p.182).

Another point especially pertinent here is that it is not possible to construct an exhaustive system of ideal-types in the social sciences analogous to the system of concepts/models found in the natural sciences. Weber's key contention is that in contrast to the exhaustive system of concepts found in the natural sciences, the social sciences are characterized not only by 'the transiency of *all* ideal types *but*

22

also at the same time the inevitability of *new* ones' (1949, p.104; emphasis in original). The reason why such an exhaustive system of concepts cannot be established in the social sciences, resides in the fact that the construction of ideal-types is bound to cultural values of general significance adopted by the social scientist. Different value-standpoints result in the creation of different ideal-types. Furthermore, the fact that 'the cultural problems which move men form themselves ever anew and in different colors...' (Weber 1949, p.84; see also pp.91, 104-6, 111)—entails the emergence of new cultural values and, thereby, the construction of new ideal-types.[27] It goes without saying, then, that the ideal-types constructed by Weber to engage in a social-scientific analysis of the selected constellations of social facts pertaining to the unequal distribution of power in the modern capitalist market-economy, the feudal estate order and the German nation-state, do not constitute an exhaustive theoretical system. For example, Weber constructs the ideal-type of class to undertake a social-scientific analysis of the unequal distribution of economic power within the modern capitalist market-economy. The estate group is another ideal-type created by Weber to gain a social-scientific understanding of the unequal distribution of social power within the feudal estate order.

Regarding the ideal nature of the ideal-type, the vital point is that the ideal-type appertains to a 'logical' rather than a 'moral' utopia.[28] Weber proclaims that:

> ...the *elementary duty of scientific self-control* and the only way to avoid serious and foolish blunders requires a sharp, precise distinction between the logically comparative analysis of reality by ideal-types in the logical sense and the *value-judgment* of reality on *the basis of ideals.* An 'ideal type' in our sense ... has no connection at all with *value-judgments,* and it has nothing to do with any type of perfection other than a purely *logical* one. (1949, pp.98-9; emphasis in original)

The ideal-type is labelled 'ideal' because it is very rare, indeed, that any of the components of the 'pure' type can be found in 'empirical' reality in their 'pure', conceptual form.[29] The ideal-type is a tool employed as 'a purely ideal *limiting* concept with which the real situation or action is *compared* and surveyed for the explication of certain of its significant components' (Weber 1949, p.93; emphasis in original).

This being the case, it is obvious that Weber's ideal-typical mode of concept formation exemplifies, from an ethical standpoint, a profound anti-utopian scepticism. This is tantamount to saying that Weber does not appraize 'empirical' reality in the light of some ethical ideal which 'should' be realized. He argues that:

> ...the idea of an ethical *imperative*, of a 'model' of what 'ought' to exist is to be carefully distinguished from the analytical construct, which is 'ideal' in the strictly logical sense of the term. (1949, pp.91-2; emphasis in original)

Owing to the 'scientific' nature of ideal-types, they cannot be used to derive an 'ought' from the 'empirical' world. Quite simply, then, Weber is stipulating that 'from the logical point of view ... the normative "correctness" of these types is not essential' (1949, p.43).[30]

Finally, the distinction established by Weber between 'individual' and 'generic' ideal-types must be considered. Concerning this distinction, it is imperative to accentuate the fact that there is no difference, according to Weber, in the way an 'individual' ideal-type and a 'generic' ideal-type is constructed.[31] Firstly, Weber avers that:

> The *empirical material* which underlies the concepts of sociology consists to a very large extent, though by no means exclusively, of the same concrete processes of action which are dealt with by historians. (1978a, p.19, emphasis added; see also p.13)

That is, the order of social facts from which the concepts (ideal-types) of both sociology and history are formed, is constituted by social actors' ascription of value and, thereby, meaning to certain phenomena. Both the sociologist and the historian select a particular configuration of these meaningful social facts on the basis of a particular value-standpoint (theoretical goal). Secondly, the two basic principles guiding the synthesis of various aspects of the selected meaningful social facts into 'general' and 'individual' ideal-types—are the particular value-standpoints adopted by the sociologist and historian respectively, and the logic used by these social-scientific investigators. Owing to the fact that there is no difference in the way 'individual', historical ideal-types and 'general', sociological ideal-types are formed, the difference between them, as Hekman (1983, p.42) states, is essentially a question of delineating ideal-types of different levels of abstraction and complexity.[32]

In respect of the 'individual' ideal-type, Weber defines it as:

> ...a mental construct for the scrutiny and systematic characterization of *individual* concrete patterns which are significant in their *uniqueness*, such as Christianity, capitalism, etc. (1949, p.100, emphasis added; see also 1978a, p.19)

It is clear from this definition that the theoretical goal guiding the synthesis of varied characteristics of a selected group of social facts into an 'individual' ideal-type, is the interest in uniqueness. In the course of combining diverse features of the selected constellation of social facts into an 'individual' ideal-type, the theoretical goal adopted by the social scientist relates to conserving the particularity of these facts. The creation of all 'individual' ideal-types is contingent upon this interest in uniqueness.

Of particular relevance also is that Weber's reference to '*individual* concrete patterns which are significant in their *uniqueness*' does not, as Burger (1976, pp.130-31) emphasizes, refer literally to just one social phenomenon. 'Individual' ideal-types like modern capitalism, Western feudalism and the modern nation-state are employed to characterize several social phenomena and not only one. The reason why a social phenomenon such as Western feudalism is considered as an 'individual' ideal-type, lies in the fact that the configuration of social facts comprising it, represents from the standpoint of the social scientist, a class of social phenomena peculiar to a particular society in a particular historical period. This is not to say, though, that an 'individual' ideal-type can only be applied to the analysis of social phenomena existing in the past. The salient point is that this kind of ideal-type is created by the social scientist to analyze a particular group of social phenomena. Interestingly enough, most of the major concepts employed by Weber in his social-scientific analysis of the nature of social stratification in modern capitalism, the feudal estate order and the German nation-state are 'individual' ideal-types. These include: class, estate group and modern democratic party.

In the case of 'general' ideal-types, on the other hand, the configuration of social facts that is of interest to the social scientist is not confined to one specific society in one specific historical period. Rather, the theoretical goal of the social scientist in this instance is such that the social facts which are deemed relevant to a scientific investigation, can be drawn from many societies and many historical periods. It is in this sense that sociology, on Weber's interpretation, 'seeks to formulate type concepts and generalized uniformities of empirical process' (1978a, p.19). The sociologist is interested in the regularities of social conduct. On this score, Weber contends that:

> As in the case of every generalizing science the abstract character of the concepts of sociology is responsible for the fact that, compared with actual historical reality, they are *relatively lacking in fullness of concrete content*. To compensate for this disadvantage, sociological analysis can offer a greater precision of concepts. (1978a, p.20; emphasis added)

Although 'general' ideal-types are 'relatively lacking in fullness of concrete content', this is not to say that these types (as opposed to 'individual' ideal-types) do not relate to a thought or idea, in principle, embodied in concrete social reality. For Weber (1949, p.93), both 'individual' and 'general' ideal-types are 'genetic' concepts in the sense that they are both formed to elucidate existing social facts. The fundamental difference between them inheres in the fact that 'individual' ideal-types are principally constructed to explicate social facts in a particular society in a particular historical period, whereas the historical context of social facts is only one of the relevant factors in the creation of 'general' ideal-types.[33] This having been said, Weber does not often construct 'general' ideal-types to undertake a social-scientific analysis of the unequal distribution of power in modern capitalism, the feudal estate order and the German nation-state. The ideal-types of value-rational action, traditional action, affectual action, traditional domination, charismatic domination and the charismatic leader, comprise some of the principal 'general' ideal-types used by Weber in his scientific study of social stratification.

1.3 Value-freedom

Weber's principle of value-freedom has always been a bone of contention amongst his interpreters.[34] To begin with, Weber reasons that:

> The constant confusion of the scientific discussion of facts and their evaluation is still one of the most widespread and also one of the most damaging traits of work in our field. The foregoing arguments are directed against this confusion, and not against the clear-cut introduction of one's own ideals into the discussion. An *attitude of moral indifference* has no connection with *scientific* 'objectivity'. (1949, p.60, emphasis in original; see also 1977, p.115)

Two fundamental points are made in this passage. Firstly, Weber admonishes us not to confuse the normative and the scientific. The former is 'concerned with *practical* evaluations regarding the desirability or undesirability of social facts from ethical, cultural or other points of view' (Weber 1949, p.10, emphasis in original; see also p.150; 1977, p.171). The latter concentrates on the causal explanation of social facts. In effect, the differentiation of the normative from the scientific is a 'logical disjunction' (Weber 1949, p.2).[35]

The second fundamental point made in the quoted passage from Weber is that value-judgements must not be ignored. Rather, such judgements must be made explicit.[36] Value-freedom, then, is much more than a methodological principle. In fact, the doctrine of value-freedom acquires the status of an ethical imperative. Weber did not wish us to avoid making evaluations. Quite the contrary. He enjoined us, as Dawe remarks, to confront and affirm our value-judgements and, in this manner, 'to preserve the possibility of moral consciousness, moral choice and moral action' (Dawe 1971, p.62). Weber was intent on securing the autonomy of the normative sphere, given that the social sciences were endangering this autonomy. In this respect, Weber argues that:

> The social sciences, which are strictly empirical sciences, are the least fitted to presume to save the individual the difficulty of making a choice, and they should therefore not create the impression that they can do so. (1949, p.19; see also pp.53-4)

Social science cannot be used as a court of appeal to justify normative claims. Weber's own commitment to a value-free social science presupposes the freedom to pursue the value of scientific truth (empirically valid truth), without being impeded by other values irrelevant to the scientific investigation. Indeed, Weber tried to formulate an ethical code around the idea of science as a vocation.[37]

Even though value-free social science cannot be employed to validate value-judgements, this is not to say that scientific knowledge is irrelevant in the treatment of such judgements. As a matter of fact, Weber (1949, pp.52-3) contends that value-judgements can be subject to scientific criticism. In other words, it is one of the major purposes of the social sciences to establish the most appropriate means for the realization of values, and the consequences that ensue from their realization. Expressed more precisely, the scientific criticism of value-judgements is, according to Weber, 'oriented primarily in terms of the categories "end" and "means"' (1949, p.52). The question of the suitability of the means for the attainment of a given end can be subject to scientific analysis.

Weber (1949, pp.20-21) formulated a logical scheme for the scientific criticism of value-judgements. The logical steps involved in this scientific procedure include: the elucidation of the basic axioms from which the value-judgements are derived, the deduction of the consequences resulting from these axioms, the determination of the factual consequences that follow from the realization of a certain practical evaluation, and the discovery of new axioms which the exponent of a practical evaluation did not take into account. For Weber, the fact that no evaluations are made in the course of engaging in a criticism of value-judgements, confirms the scientific nature of the whole procedure. No practical evaluations are made concerning whether a positive or negative stance should be taken towards certain values. The scientific criticism of value-judgements simply supplies empirical knowledge as a foundation for the informed choice of the means for the achievement of a preselected end. This line of criticism is unable to tell you what you ought to do, but what you can do. It is in this context that Weber proclaims that:

> If you take such and such a stand, then, according to scientific experience, you have to use such and such a *means* in order to carry out your conviction practically. (1970, p.151, emphasis in original; see also p.147)

Although the scientific criticism of value-judgements makes it possible to choose the most appropriate means for the attainment of a preselected end, the difficulty, in my view, is that such criticism is merely technical (see Weber 1949, p.53). It is simply descriptive. The clarification of value-judgements is limited to investigating their internal consistency.[38] Weber writes that:

> ...the scientific treatment of value-judgments may not only understand and empathically analyze the desired ends and the ideals which underlie them; it can also 'judge' them critically. This criticism can of course have only a dialectical character, i.e., it can be no more than a formal logical judgment of historically given value-judgments and ideas, a testing of the ideals according to the postulate of the internal *consistency* of the desired end. It can, insofar as it sets itself this goal, aid the acting willing person in attaining

self-clarification concerning the final axioms from which his desired ends are derived. (1949, p.54; emphasis in original)

Scientific knowledge is complete, once the empirical coherence of the relevant value-judgements has been established. This form of knowledge is logically precluded from asking whether the espousal of these judgements is objectionable or approvable. It is not concerned with advocating certain values at the expense of negating others. In this connection, Weber contends that:

Only on the assumption of a belief in the validity of values is the attempt to espouse value-judgments meaningful. However, to *judge* the *validity* of such values is a matter of *faith*. (1949, p.55; emphasis in original)

The question concerning whether the individual expressing value-judgements should or should not abide by them, 'is his personal affair; it involves *will and conscience, not empirical knowledge*' (Weber 1949, p.54, emphasis added; see also 1973a, pp.591-2; 1978b, p.387). Values are merely posited, they cannot be known. In other words, Weber is a decisionist in the normative realm, because intersubjectively valid objective truth is unattainable regarding the desirability or undesirability of expressing a value-judgement. The making of a value-judgement is deemed a pre-rational (and, hence, irrational) decision.[39]

Owing to Weber's advocacy of the principle of value-freedom, it is logically impossible, for example, to consider capital's use of wage-labour as a mere tool of rational profit-making activity in the modern market-economy as unjust or exploitative. The expression of a value-judgement concerning the injustice of treating workers as a means of making a profit does not involve empirical (i.e., scientific) knowledge. It simply involves a personal commitment to ethical values such as social justice and human dignity. Weber's value-free pattern of sociological thinking is such that it is *a priori* impossible to acquire intersubjectively valid objective truth concerning the desirability or undesirability of utilizing workers as a mere means of rational profit-making activity. Similarly, Weber (1978a, p.886) contends that when workers object to the legal formalism of modern rational law by demanding substantive justice, they are solely expressing their personal commitment to certain ethical values. The workers' evaluation of legal formalism as unjust is an extra-scientific question. Weber, in his role as a value-free social scientist, does not recognize the existence of rationally validated ethical principles that could support the workers' claims.

Another questionable feature of Weber's scientific criticism of value-judgements has to do with the fact that the relevance of scientific knowledge to value-judgements can only be rendered in terms of a relation of means to ends. The ambiguity lies in Weber's equation of ends and value-judgements. Ends (goals, aims, desires and the like) are, as Giddens (1979a, p.94) points out, traits of the individual personality. However, a value-judgement relates, as Weber himself indicates, to a practical evaluation concerning the desirability or undesirability of social facts from ethical, cultural and other standpoints. More to the point, Weber affirms that a value-judgement 'may ... be under certain circumstances *the consciousness of a certain ... concrete kind of imperative'* (1949, p.150; emphasis added). Accordingly, the individual's expression of a value-judgement can involve the making of a personal commitment to ethical imperatives, ethical rules and so forth. It obviously follows that such imperatives and rules are not attributes of the individual personality as such. But, on the other hand, Weber also speaks of a value-judgement as a 'thoroughly concrete, *highly individually structured and constituted "feeling" and "preference"...'* (1949, p.150; emphasis added). In this instance, Weber's rendering of a value-judgement is much closer to characteristics of an individual personality like ends and goals.

In light of the aforesaid, it could be argued that Weber restricts the role of a value-free social science to the production of knowledge which can be used technically. In this respect, Habermas (1971a, p.63) observes that Weber's espousal of a value-free social science contradicts the 'hermeneutic intention' of the socio-cultural sciences which was continually underlined by Weber in his epistemological-methodological writings. Weber states quite explicitly that:

> Our aim is the understanding of the characteristic uniqueness of the reality in which we move. We wish to understand on the one hand the relationships and the cultural significance of individual events in their contemporary manifestations and on the other the causes of their being historically *so* and not *otherwise.* (1949, p.72; emphasis in original)

But Weber's value-free social science is arguably a mere technique for the calculation of the means requisite for the attainment of a preselected end. The placement of a value-free social science within a technocratic model, implies that the role of social science can easily be reduced to the technical control of human individuals. Weber does, indeed, understand technique in its broadest sense as 'rational action in general: in all spheres, including the political, social, educational, and propagandist manipulation and domination of human beings' (1949, p.35). For instance, he (1978a, p.150) points out that scientific disciplines of the factory like the Taylor system emerged as a means of exercizing increased control over the workers. The control of human beings is, as we shall see in the following chapter, also built into Weber's sociology of action.

Bearing in mind Weber's understanding of value-free social science, it is important to consider a more specific case such as the relationship holding between value-free social science and political action.[40] Weber says that 'a feeling of responsibility' is one of the 'pre-eminent qualities' that a politician should possess (1970, p.115; see also 1949, p.10). Therefore, if a politician in the German nation-state, for example, is expected to act in a responsible manner, he must consider the relevant social facts in the course of making an informed decision. Value-free social science has a role to play in facilitating the making of such a decision. Scientific criticism can help the politician to attain clarity about the value-judgements he makes. Social scientists in their role as technical experts can act as counsellors for the politician. They can expose the politician's most profound convictions to scrutiny and, thereby, advize him on the means to be employed for the attainment of a particular political end.[41] Social scientists, of course, can only advize the politician as to what he can do, not regarding what he ought to do. It is Weber's contention that for an 'acting, willing person' like the politician, 'the act of choice itself is his own responsibility' (1949, p.53; see also p.19). The role of social scientists is to impart technical knowledge which can, then, further responsible political action on the part of the politician.[42]

Viewed in this light, it is quite clear that the social scientist is logically debarred from appraizing the normative validity of the politician's evaulations. The scientific treatment of politics signifies that the issue of whether the politician in the German nation-state ought or ought not stand by a certain evaluation, cannot be subject to intersubjective validation. Rather, 'what the cause in the service of which the politician strives for power and uses power, looks like is a *matter of faith*' (Weber 1970, p.117; emphasis added). Weber is a decisionist in the sense that valuation in the sphere of politics is ultimately a question of a pre-rational (and, hence, irrational) decision. In this same connection, Habermas reasons that the 'scientization of politics' within the Weberian schema, implies that 'political action cannot rationally justify its own premises' (1971b, p.63). Rationality in the choice of means for the promotion of a certain value like the interests of national power, and avowed irrationality in the case of the judgement of the validity of this same value, belong together.[43]

One final issue pertinent to the general impetus of the present discussion is that ineluctable value-conflict is the outcome of the fact that intersubjectively valid, objective truth is unattainable in the case of the assessment of value-judgements.[44] Weber speaks of 'an irreconcilable death-struggle' between values (1949, p.17), and 'the struggle that the gods of the various orders and values are engaged in' (1970, p.148). He also states that 'the highest ideals, which move us most forcefully, are always formed only in the struggle with other ideals which are just as sacred to others as ours are to us' (1949, p.57). Expressed more pointedly, 'fate, and certainly not "science" holds sway over these gods and their struggles' (Weber 1970, p.148). There is no rational way, in Weber's view, of deciding whether individuals expressing different value-judgements should or should not adhere to them. For all values are equally valid. Value disputes are not open to rational resolution. It goes without saying, then, that a collective value-system achieved by way of a rationally arrived-at public consensus is within a Weberian framework an impossibility.

Another related point is Weber's observation that there is an intrinsic connection between the process of rationalization and the intensification of value-conflict in modern society. Weber contends that:

...the rationalization and the conscious sublimination of man's relations to the various spheres of values, external and internal, as well as religious and secular, have then pressed towards making conscious the *internal and lawful autonomy* of the individual spheres; thereby letting them drift into those tensions which remain hidden to the originally naive relation with the external world. (1970, p.328, emphasis in original; see also 1949, p.57)

Weber is referring here to the differentiation of several value-spheres in modern society. These include: the economic sphere, the political sphere, the aesthetic sphere, the erotic sphere and the intellectual sphere (see Weber 1970, pp.323-59). Since each of these value-spheres is, according to Weber, 'governed by different laws' (1970, p.123; see also 1949, p.15), value-conflict is unavoidable in modern society. In a word, modern society for Weber exists without normative foundations.

That said, I would suggest that Weber does offer a solution to the problem of inescapable value-conflict that logically follows from his espousal of normative irrationalism. It is a political solution.[45] The interminable conflict between the individuals and groups making different evaluations is overcome, according to Weber, by the imposition of the will of a particular individual personality on that of others. Value conflict is overcome by having recourse to an arbitrary subjective decision based on personal conviction. It is only the most powerful individual who can 'impose' his values by subduing those less powerful or powerless individuals and groups espousing different values. Weber regarded the responsible charismatic leader in the German nation-state as such a powerful individual. To anticipate what I shall say later in the book, Weber reasoned that a charismatic plebiscitary leader dedicated to the value of advancing the 'power-political interests' (1980, p.438) of the German nation-state, with an independent power base in the votes of the electorial masses, was the means of transcending the capital-labour conflict built into the capitalist society of Weimar Germany. This leader, by virtue of his commitment to the interests of national power, had the capacity to secure national unity in the face of the relentless struggle between capitalist entrepreneurs devoted to rational profit-making activity and workers dedicated to fulfilling human needs. In effect, Weber's proposed solution to the incessant conflict between the individuals and groups making different value-judgements points in the direction of political absolutism, that is, political dictatorship. An enforced consensus, that is, order is brought about by compelling compliance with the more powerful will.

In this first chapter I have examined the fundamental epistemological-methodological principles underlying Weber's study of structural social inequalities in modern capitalism, the feudal estate order and the German nation-state. What distinguishes Weber as a neo-Kantian is his idea of human knowledge as a selective mental representation of empirical reality. Empirical reality cannot be analyzed without preconceptions. As to social-scientific knowledge, Weber argues that the application of the logical principle of value-relevance means that only those empirical phenomena are selected for analysis in which, according to the social scientist, cultural values are embodied. In the case of the scientific study of social stratification, in particular, Weber makes specific constellations of empirical phenomena such as modern capitalism and the modern nation-state the embodiment of general cultural values like instrumental rationality. Moreover, when Weber analyzes the configuration of social facts that is Western feudalism, his interest in instrumental rationality is still presupposed. Weber's crucial interest in instrumental rationality and, concomitantly, the process of rationalization, is one of the main threads running through the discussion in the remainder of the book. Furthermore, the importance of the ideal-typical mode of concept formation for Weber's study of social stratification cannot be overemphasized. Weber undertakes a scientific analysis of the social facts pertaining to the unequal distribution of power in the modern capitalist market-economy, the feudal estate order and the German nation-state only through the construction of ideal-types. This book basically revolves around an examination of these conceptual representations of power inequalities. Finally, the ethically neutral nature of Weber's study of social stratification will be accentuated in the study. Because Weber is primarily interested in 'an *empirical science* of *concrete* reality' (1949, p.72; emphasis in original), he concentrates on the distribution of economic, social and political power. Weber, in his role as a value-free social scientist, cannot make evaluations regarding the desirability or undesirability of the unequal distribution of economic, social and political resources from an ethical standpoint. For normative questions concerning the nature of social stratification in any society cannot be adjudicated rationally within a Weberian framework.

Notes

1   It is part of the accepted scholarly wisdom that Weber's epitstemological-methodological reflections grew out of the neo-Kantian debate in nineteenth century Germany. However, Hennis (1988, pp.107-45) underscores Weber's intellectual debt to the nineteenth century Historical School of Political Economy.
2   Cf. Bruun 1972, pp.98-143; Kocka 1985, pp.140-42. The following discussion of Weber's epistemology is especially indebted to Burger (1976, pp.57-72).
3   See Burger 1976, p.65; Weiss 1985, p.120.
4   See also Hekman 1983, p.34.
5   Weber (1975a) contrasts 'immediately experienced reality' and 'scientific concept formation' quite frequently, without referring to the transitional stage of categorically formed constructs.

6 'Cultural sciences', 'social sciences' and 'history' are employed interchangeably by Weber in his epistemological-methodological writings.

7 In this connection, Weiss speaks 'of the necessary "communicability" of socially established interpretations of meaning' (1986, p.47). See also Schluchter 1981, p.18.

8 Or as Hekman adroitly remarks, 'the "facts" of the social sciences are constituted by the meaning bestowal of social actors' (1983, p.29).

9 Cf. Benhabib 1981, pp.359-61; Hirst 1976a, pp.60-65; Hirst 1976b, pp.407-8; Herva 1988, pp.143-56; Bruun 1972, pp.78-144; Hekman 1983, pp.26-30; Oakes 1982, pp.598-608. See, esp., Burger (1976, pp.77-93) who engages in an incisive analysis of Weber's rendition of value-relevance. The following treatment of value-relevance is indebted to Burger.

10 Value-relevance, value-relatedness and value-reference can be used interchangeably.

11 The crucial Weberian difference between 'value-judgement' and 'value-relevance' is also accentuated by Portis 1979, p.143; Aron 1970, p.194; Strauss 1953, p.40.

12 It is worthy of note that Shils' and Finch's translation of Weber in this instance could mislead, because it implies that the 'concrete reality' confronting the social scientist only becomes 'culture' when the social scientist relates it to values. But it has already been made clear that those empirical phenomena which for social scientists embody cultural values, were constituted in the first place by individuals adopting a positive or negative stance towards them. In other words, the 'concrete reality' to which the social scientist relates values, has already been constituted as *Kultur* by evaluating individuals.

13 Cf. Brand 1977, pp.3-7; Giddens 1979a, pp94-5.

14 Given the importance of values in Weber's epistemological-methodological writings, it is noteworthy that he does not discuss the nature of values. See Brunn 1972, pp.28-30; Strauss 1953, p.39; Portis 1986, p.196.

15 See Eisen 1979, pp.203-18; Hirst 1976a, pp.60-62; Kronman 1983, pp.14-22. Kronman, in fact, speaks of Weber's *'will-centred* conception of personhood' (1983, p.21; emphasis in original).

16 Cf. Habermas 1984a, pp.243-7.

17 See also Benhabib 1981, p.359.

18 Weber's notion of the rational actor is discussed in the following chapter.

19 Cf. also Oakes 1982, pp.602-8; Burger 1976, pp.97-102; Bruun 1972, pp.127-31; Hekman 1983, p.28; Weiss 1986, p.42.

20 See also Cohen 1972, p.67; Habermas 1974a, p.271; Voegelin 1952, p.14; Turner and Factor 1984, pp.26-7; Barker 1980, p.236.

21 Cf. Oakes 1982, pp.589-615; Simey 1965, p.53; Sewart 1978, pp.326-30; Goddard 1973, pp.15-17; Butts 1975, p.196.

22 See also Hekman 1983, pp.158-60.

23 Cf. Oakes 1982, pp.608-15; Rossi 1971, pp.74-6; Portis 1979, p.414.

24 Cf. Burger 1976, pp.115-40; Bruun 1972, pp.201-39; Weiss 1986, pp.43-63; Hearn 1975, pp.531-61; McIntosh 1977, pp.265-79; Parkin 1982, pp.27-34; Käsler 1988, pp.180-84.

25 Similarly, Marianne Weber (1988, p.676) states that Weber's ideal-types are underpinned by a comprehensive knowledge of history rather than being what she calls 'speculative intellectural systems'.

26 Weber, in fact, used this ideal-type of abstract economic theory as far back as 1898 in a course of lectures given at the University of Heidelberg (see Hennis 1988, pp.120-21).

27 Similiarly, Marianne Weber (1988, p.678) states that Weber's ideal-types were intended to be transient rather than fixed concepts.

28 See Wilson 1976, pp.301-4; Weiss 1986, pp.60-65; Hearn 1975, pp.532-7.

29 Weber, for example, describes economic history as made up of ideal-types. The components of these ideal-types 'are derived from experience and *intensified* to the point of pure rationality only in a process of thought...' (1975b, p.34; emphasis in original).

30 Given Weber's conception of the ideal-type as a mere 'logical' utopia, Hearn (1975, pp.531-61) sets out to reconstruct the ideal-type in accordance with the assumptions of the dialectic. That is to say, he wants to specify the methodological procedures which make it possible to prove that normative prescriptions are, in fact, ingrained in the real historical possibilities of the society under examination.

31 Cf. Burger 1976, pp.130-35; Hekman 1983, pp.39-43; Sahay 1972, pp.36-8.

32 However, the following interpreters maintain that Weber's 'individual' and 'generic' ideal-types are incompatible: Rex 1971, pp.17-36; Watkins 1953, pp.23-43; Parsons 1949, pp.601-10.

Another reading of Weber argues that the construction of 'general', sociological ideal-types is an ancillary procedure for historical, causal analysis proper. See, e.g., Whimster 1980, pp.352-76; Roth 1976, p.307; Lukács 1972, p.392.

33 In a similar vein, Marianne Weber (1988, pp.677-8) observes that while history is primarily concerned with analyzing individual events, sociology studies typical events and attempts to create general concepts and formulate universal rules for the constantly occurring course of social action.

34 Shils and Finch in their translation of Weber (1949, pp.1-47), employ the term 'ethical neutrality'. 'Freedom from value-judgement' is another term frequently used.

35 The differentiation of the normative from the scientific underscores, as Hennis (1988, p.144) points out, Weber's intellectual indebtedness to the German Historical School of Political Economy. It was this school that first developed the distinction between 'what is' and 'what ought to be'.

36 Cf. Braude 1964, pp.396-9; Burger 1977a, pp.165-75; Gouldner 1975, pp.3-26; Schluchter 1979a, pp.65-116.

37 See Lassman and Velody 1989, pp.159-204.

38 Cf. Hirst 1976a, pp.54-6; Giddens 1979a, pp.89-90; Turner and Factor 1984, pp.37-8.

39 On the history of the concept of decision, see Habermas 1974a, pp.253-82.

40 Cf. Schluchter 1979a, pp.65-116; Habermas 1971b, pp.62-80; Mommsen 1984, pp.441-4; Portis 1986, pp.136-44; Burger 1977a, pp.165-75.

41 On this score, Roth (1965, pp.213-23) misinterprets Weber when he assumes the separability of science and politics in Weber's work.

42 Given Weber's understanding of the social scientist as a technical expert, it is not surprising when he speaks: 'of the inevitable disillusionment with an almost superstitious veneration of science as the possible creator or at least prophet of social revolution, violent or peaceful, in the sense of salvation from class rule' (1978a, p.515).

43 It is worthwhile noting that the contemporary German philosopher, Karl-Otto Apel (1979, pp.307-50), is deeply concerned with the deficiencies inherent in what he aptly calls 'the Western complementarity-system of value-free rationality and pre-rational value-decisions'. Weber is one major exponent of this complementarity system.

44 For an assessment of Weber's notion of value-conflict, see Brubaker 1984, pp.61-90; Habermas 1984a, pp.243-54; Gronow 1988, pp.319-31.

45 See Dawe 1971, pp.43-6; Landmann 1976, pp.187-8; Münch 1988, pp.43-5.

2 Sociology of action

In this chapter I examine Weber's fundamental concept of social action. It is essential to critically evaluate this ideal-typical concept in order later to assess Weber's understanding of class action, estate action and political action. Weber's account of action has given rise to diverse interpretations. My own contribution to this debate concentrates primarily on the irony of labelling Weber an action theorist. I argue that Weber's pattern of thinking is such that the majority of what are called social actors in modern society do not act at all. They are simply a 'means' of action. Another central argument which I develop in the second section of the chapter, bears on Weber's espousal of the teleological model of action. The fact that this model merely involves a contingent intersubjectivity, attests to Weber's extremely limited understanding of the nature of the social in modern society. My third crucial argument in the last section revolves around the paradox of freedom built into Weber's sociology of action. Weber's advocacy of a particular notion of modern empirical freedom results in the radical stratification of individuals into the free and the unfree in modern society.

2.1 Social action

The concept of action is the most elementary unit of analysis in Weber's sociology. The beginning of Weber's fourfold typology of action can be detected in an early research report dealing with changes in the lives of agricultural labourers in seven major provinces of eastern Germany. The research report was prepared for the *Verein für Sozialpolitik* in 1892.[1] Weber mentions the '*action of individuals*' in the first part of *Roscher and Knies: The Logical Problems of Historical Economics*, published in 1903 (1975a, p.80; emphasis in original). In the second part of *Roscher and Knies*, published in 1905, he speaks of 'purposeful human action' (1975a, p.96). Weber reflects in a more explicit way on the concept of social action in his article, 'Some Categories of Interpretive Sociology', published in 1913 (1981a, pp.151-80). However, it was in the later Part I of *Economy and Society*, written between 1918 and 1920, that Weber engaged in the most incisive analysis of social action.[2] Roth aptly describes *Economy and Society* as 'the sum of Max Weber's scholarly vision of society' (1978, p.xxxiii). It encapsulates the bulk of Weber's previous substantial research in one form or another.

To begin with, Weber declares that:

> We shall speak of 'action' insofar as the acting individual attaches a subjective meaning to his behavior—be it overt or covert, omission or acquiescence. Action is 'social' insofar as its subjective meaning takes account of the behavior of others and is thereby oriented in its course. (1978a, p.4; see also 1981a, p.159)

The concept of action logically precedes and is, therefore, presupposed by the more specific concept of social action. Action in contradistinction to behaviour is oriented towards meaning and constitutes an intentional and reflexive act. Social action like all specifically meaningful human action is oriented towards subjective meaning. In addition, social action is oriented towards the other. It is only where such an orientation is constitutive of the kind and direction of action that Weber is prepared to call it social.

Zweckrational action is the most fundamental form of meaningfully oriented social action in modern society. This particular ideal-type of social action represents a sociological extension of the human subject as a free being endowing the world with meaning which, as already shown, is presupposed in Weber's epistemology. *Zweckrational* action is:

> ...determined by expectations as to the behavior of objects in the environment and of other human beings; these expectations are used as 'conditions' or 'means' for the attainment of the actor's own rationally pursued and calculated ends... (Weber 1978a, p.24)

This type of action, according to Weber, involves not only an appraizal of the cost and consequences of the alternative means available for the attainment of a given end. The alternative ends are also rationally assessed. And *zweckrational* action tends to produce individuals who are calculating, methodical and internally motivated.[3]

Given Weber's definition of *zweckrational* action, it is apparent that this type of action can only be deemed meaningful in a very specific sense. In this respect, Huff (1984, p.47) points out that Weber does not consider meaning *per se* as an exclusive component of social relations. Weber himself observes that:

> ...there is no sense in which the property of being 'meaningful'—the property of 'meaning' or 'signifying' something—is a feature peculiar to 'social' life; its

defining property. (1977, p.111)

To the contrary, social action can only be regarded as meaningful in so far as it embodies purpose. There must be meaningful interpretation of social action in terms of motives and intentions. The social is constituted by purposive interaction among conscious individual agents.[4] Or as Weber puts it:

> ...*processes* or *conditions*, whether they are animate or inanimate, human or non-human, are ... *devoid of meaning if they cannot be related to action in the role of means or ends* but constitute only the stimulus, the favoring or hindering circumstances. (1978a, p.7, emphasis added; see also 1949, p.52)

Meaningfully oriented social action involves purposeful action where the means and ends are rationally taken into account and assessed. In so far as action cannot be analyzed in terms of means and ends, it lacks meaning and is, therefore, irrational.[5]

On this score, Warriner (1969, pp.501-11) misconstrues Weber when he contends that Weber's understanding of social action allows for a conceptual distinction between action and its meaning. On Warriner's interpretation, meaning is not an intrinsic component of social action. The essential point, though, is that the separation of action and its meaning is constitutive of merely reactive behaviour within a Weberian framework.

As a matter of fact, Weber concedes that 'the line between meaningful action and merely reactive behavior to which no subjective meaning is attached, cannot be sharply drawn empirically' (1978a, p.4). Owing to the ideal-typical nature of Weber's concept of meaningfully oriented social action, it is an artificial construction which aims not to reproduce social reality, but rather a thought construct with which concrete reality can be compared. By comparison with the ideal-type of means-end rational action, it is possible to apprehend how actual action is influenced by irrational factors like emotions and tradition. Weber argues that when measured against the ideal-type of means-end rational action, it is evident that:

> In the great majority of cases actual action goes on in a state of inarticulate half-consciousness or actual unconsciousness of its subjective meaning. (1978a, p.21)

The behaviour of individuals is mainly determined by impulse or habit. The majority of individuals in the concrete situation do not act on their own motives. The irony of labelling Weber an action theorist, in my view, inheres in the fact that within his theoretical framework the majority of individuals do not act at all, they simply behave. They are irrational. Most individuals are defined out of Weber's action schema. They are located below the level of sociological detection.[6] In other words, Weber's action schema involves what Barker (1985, p.98) aptly calls 'a radical bifurcation of humanity'. It is the fate of the mass of human beings to merely engage in reactive behaviour. Only outstanding individuals act.

Weber, in fact, concedes that:

> Sociology ... is by no means confined to the study of social action; this is only ... its central subject matter, that which may be said to be decisive for its status as a science. (1978, p.24; see also pp.12-13)

It is the study of social action (and, especially, *zweckrational* action) which renders sociology scientific. However, a substantial part of what Weber (1978a, p.4) calls 'sociologically relevant behavior' lies between meaningfully oriented social action and merely reactive behaviour. For example, traditionalism grounded in traditional action and charisma grounded in affectual action, 'stand on the indefinite borderline of social action' (Weber 1978a, p.24).

Taking account of the fact that an ideal-type relates to a thought or idea, in principle, embodied in social reality, the preponderance of the ideal-type of means-end rational action in Weber's typology of social action is connected with 'the preeminent *factual significance* of this sense of "consciously purposive" action in empirical reality...' (Weber 1975a, p.188; emphasis added). *Zweckrational* action represents the basic form of meaningfully oriented social action in modern society.

What is darkly ironic, however, about the process of rationalization in modern society is that it:

> ...proceeds in such a fashion that the *broad masses of the led merely accept or adapt themselves* to the external technical resultants which are of practical significance for their interests ... whereas the substance of the creator's ideas remain irrelevant to them. This is meant when we say that rationalization and rational organization revolutionize 'from the outside'... (Weber 1978a, p.1117; emphasis added)

The process of rationalization results in a situation whereby the vast majority of individuals do not in reality rationally take into account and weigh means and ends. According to Weber, the activity of most individuals in modern society lacks subjective meaning. Most individuals simply accept or adapt to the external social environment. As a matter of fact, 'primitive' individuals had a much better understanding of the socio-economic conditions determining their mode of life, when compared with supposedly 'civilized' people living in modern society (see Weber 1981a, p.178). Most individuals in modern society have less need or the chance to act rationally. In effect, Weber's line of reasoning is such that only individuals like capitalist entrepreneurs and responsible charismatic leaders think in a purposive-rational manner, that is, consciously act on their own motives in modern society.[7] The majority of individuals in modern society are simply a 'means' of action.

Pertinent to the issue at hand here also is that the ethically neutral nature of

Weberian social science, implies that the sociologist is logically precluded from questioning the normative validity of the rational actor's motives. The irony of labelling Weber an action theorist is reinforced because the ultimate foundations of *zweckrational* action are not amenable to rational justification. In other words, the ultimate foundations of purposive-rational action are irrational.

In line with the present discussion, yet another salient point is that although means-end rational action may be purposive, the results of this form of action often tend to undermine the very purposes which initiated it. That is to say, even those individuals who act have not complete control over the end-results. Weber is underlining the fatefulness of human intention. The fatefulness of human intention is elucidated in what Weber calls 'the paradox of unintended consequences', that is, 'the relation of man and fate, of what he intended by his acts and what actually came of them' (1951, p.238). The juxtaposition of means-end rational action and the self-defeating nature of this form of action creates the Weberian 'iron cage'.[8]

Weber claims, that the birth of modern capitalism was an unintended consequence of Christian ethics (1970, p.149). The essential point is that:

> The Puritan *wanted* to work in a calling; we are *forced* to do so. For when asceticism was carried out of monastic cells into everyday life, and began to dominate worldy morality, it did its part in building the tremendous cosmos of the modern economic order. (Weber 1976a, p.181; emphasis added)

The Puritan worked in a calling for what he perceived as the greater glory of God. He regarded himself as a tool of the Divine. However, the moral order of modern industrial capitalism resides precisely in the enforcement of Puritan action without the benefit of the Puritan religious ethic. The capitalist entrepreneur is a man 'dominated by the making of money, by acquisition as the ultimate purpose of his life' (Weber 1976a, p.53).

'The paradox of unintended consequences' is not just applicable to the economic order of modern industrial capitalism. Weber concedes that it 'is fundamental to all history' (1970, p.117). The unintended effects that flow from substantive rationalization are especially pertinent in Weber's studies of the various world religions. Weber declares that:

> Not ideas, but material and ideal interests, directly govern men's conduct. Yet very frequently the 'world images' that have been created by 'ideas' have, like switchmen, determined the tracks along which action has been pursued by the dynamic of interest. (1970, p.280)

In the various world religions it is material and ideal interests which directly govern men's conduct. Yet, the unintended result is that ideas help to define the social situation in which interests are pursued. The fatefulness of human intention is especially acute in modern society, because the rationalization of action in an

40

instrumental sense is carried through in such a comprehensive manner.

Weber's explication of 'the paradox of unintended consequences' raises another interesting question: Does the paradox dispel the notion that social phenomena are comprehensible only in so far as they are the resultants of the actions of individuals? From the foregoing inquiry into Weber's understanding of meaningfully oriented social action, it was established that action is only intelligible in so far as it embodies the purposes of individuals interpreted in a means-end rational fashion. However, Turner maintains that 'the paradox of unintended consequences' underscores the fact that Weber 'cannot be adequately treated as a subjectivist sociologist whose analysis is caught within a "problematic of the subject"' (1981, p.35). On the contrary, Weber's famous paradox produces a 'deterministic' sociology in which the key issues are compulsion, fate and irony. Human intention is, according to Turner, 'determined by the fateful working out of objective constraints' (1981, p.45). In like manner, Merquior argues that the focus on unintended effects disproves the claim that Weber's social action approach can be reduced to what he calls 'a shallow rhetoric of motives and purposes' (1980, p.170).

In contradistinction to Turner (1977, pp.1-16; 1981) and Merquior (1980), other interpreters, especially Marxist scholars, contend that Weber's sociology of action involves subjective reductionism. Weber apparently lacks a clear notion of objective, structural constraints. According to Hirst (1976a, p.80), the idea of social totality is abolished. In a similar vein, Lukács claims that within Weber's sociology of action 'the whole of objective social reality is dissolved into subjectivity' (1972, p.393). And Hindess (1977, pp.157-89; 1987, pp.137-53) asserts that Weber is an exponent of 'theoretical humanism', that is, he reduces the social realm to the will and consciousness of human agents.

Another version of the argument relates to the interpretation of the concept of meaning as merely a psychological problem of recreating mental states. It is supposedly essential to know psychic or psychological motives in order to evaluate social action.[9] But Weber purports that 'interpretive sociology ... is not part of a "psychology"' (1981a, p.154). The 'use of the results of psychology is something quite different from the investigation of human behavior in terms of its subjective meaning' (Weber 1978a, p.19). More pertinently, the analysis of subjective meaning entails an understanding of the 'complex of meaning' within which it belongs (Weber 1978a, p.9). That is to say, Weber is concerned with subjective meaning rendered as a cultural phenomenon. Meaning is associated with a specific kind of action in a specific culture.[10] Weber was particularly interested in subjective meaning understood in means-end rational terms in modern society. In this case, the apprehension of subjective meaning cannot be discovered by merely probing the mind of the individual actor. Weber maintains that:

...it is quite obvious that rational reflection upon both the means required to achieve the purpose of a concrete 'action' and the possible consequences of the contemplated act would have no place in the world of unobjectified 'experience'. (1975a, p.131; see also p.154; 1981a, p.157)

Hence, meaningfully oriented social action does not take place in a vacuum. To the contrary, the setting of goals and the choice of means are embedded in the framework of a socio-historical context of meanings.

In view of the fact that Weber is identified as an exponent of both a 'subjectivist' and 'deterministic' sociology, the key issue, in my view, is that Weber's action perspective attempts to combine the analysis of goals/intentions with the analysis of the course and consequences of social action. Weber states that:

> Sociology ... is a science concerning itself with the interpretive understanding of social action and thereby with a causal explanation of its course and consequences. (1978a, p.4)

Within a Weberian framework the course and consequences of social action can be equated with social collectivities, that is, stable patterns of interaction between individual agents. No matter how objective and compelling a social collectivity or social structure may appear to be, it ultimately originates from the activity of individuals with particular subjective meanings. As Schluchter (1981, p.34) puts it, social structure and social actor are mediated through subjective meaning.[11]

Given that within the Weberian schema only individual human beings 'act', courses of action/social collectivities such as states, associations, business corporations:

> ...must be treated as *solely* the resultants and modes of organization of the particular acts of individual persons, since these alone can be treated as agents in a course of subjectively understandable action. (Weber 1978a, p.13; emphasis in original) [12]

Social collectivities denote particular kinds of continuing collective activities undertaken by a number of individuals. In Weber's view, 'a "state", for example, ceases to exist in a sociologically relevant sense whenever there is no longer a probability that certain kinds of meaningfully oriented social action will take place' (1978a, p.27). Organizations like the state only have reality in so far as they operate through individuals investing their actions with subjective meaning. The state ceases to exist when individuals no longer orient themselves towards it.

Bearing in mind that social collectivities originate from the activities of individual agents with particular subjective meanings, Weber nevertheless concedes that these agents often act in a manner which has been laid down before they enter a social relationship. In this regard, he observes that:

> Within the realm of social action *empirical uniformities* can be observed, that is, courses of action that are repeated by the actor or (simultaneously)

occur among numerous actors since the subjective meaning is meant to be the same. *Sociological investigation is concerned with these typical modes of action.* (1978a, p.29; emphasis added)

These 'empirical uniformities' may comprise structural constraints which predetermine individual conduct. That is to say, social action occurs in the context of an already constituted social world. The modern capitalist economy, for example, generates the subjective orientations requisite for its functioning. This economy presents itself to the individual 'as an unalterable order of things in which he must live' (Weber 1976a, p.54). Both the entrepreneur and the wage-labourer are compelled 'to conform to capitalistic rules of action' (ibid.). The only other alternative is economic ruin. Therefore, the activities which 'give rise to' the modern capitalist economy are themselves in a sense 'generated' by it. In this respect, courses of action like the modern state and the modern capitalist economy can be regarded as a series of objective constraints that human agents 'adapt to'.

Interpreted in this light, it would seem that Weber's sociology of action comprises a series of analytical tensions between choice and determinism, subjectivity and objectivity, social action and social structure, atomism and holism and so on. The crucial question is: How is it possible for a social collectivity to 'originate' from the activity of individual agents with particular subjective meanings, whilst this same collectivity is perceived as 'generating' the subjective orientations indispensable for its functioning? Does Weber's understanding of the relationship holding between social action and social collectivities support voluntarism and reification simultaneously?

The answer, I would suggest, resides in the fact that although social collectivities can confront individuals as objective constraints to which they have no kind of meaningful relationship, such collectivities in so far as they exist historically, can only be reproduced through social action. In other words, social collectivities can only continue to exist and, further, be transformed by virtue of human agency. Human agency does not simply refer to the conduct of single individual actors like the charismatic leader. On this score, Kalberg bequeaths the important insight that 'Weber never viewed social life as an "endless drift" of solitary action-orientations' (1994, p.30). Rather, as Kalberg continues, it is 'the diverse ways in which individuals act *in concert...*' that interests Weber (ibid., emphasis in original). In a somewhat similar vein, Poggi argues that it is only a 'collective actor' (in the Weberian sense, that is, a number of discrete individuals oriented towards and driven by shared interests) who 'can exercise leverage upon existing constraints, modify their bias, replace them' (1983, p.37). By altering existing social collectivities, social actors contribute to the making/creation of new ones. Thus, an action perspective must play a major role in explaining the genesis of any emerging course of action/social collectivity.

The fact that social collectivities can only continue to exist by virtue of human agency (i.e., reproduction and transformation), is further underscored in Weber's treatment of functionalism. Weber accepts 'the sociological significance of the functional point of view for preliminary orientation to problems' (1978a, p.17). It is 'functionally necessary' to know what kind of action is needed for survival. Moreover, it is imperative to be aware of the kind of action indispensable for the maintenance of a certain cultural type. It is only, then, that one can analyze how the relevant action-type arose and what motives determine it. The crucial point, in Weber's view, is that 'it is only this analysis itself which can achieve the sociological understanding of the actions of typically differentiated human (and only human) individuals' (1978a, p.18). The action perspective must always be accorded primacy over the functional point of view.

In the last analysis, though, Weber's endeavour to link social action and courses of action/social collectivities remains, I would argue, problematic in the context of modern society. Given Weber's master ideal-type of *zweckrational* action, it follows, as we shall see later, that most individuals within the modern capitalist market-economy and the modern nation-state do not act in a purposive-rational manner. This being so, the majority of individuals in modern society do, indeed, confront courses of action/social collectivities like the capitalist economy and the state as a series of objective constraints to which they have no kind of meaningful relationship. Because the majority of individuals in modern society (e.g., wage-labourers, the electoral masses) are not impeccably rational actors calculating the most efficient means for the achievement of a particular goal, they cannot within the Weberian action schema contribute directly to the reproduction and/or transformation of existing courses of action/social collectivities.[13] Most individuals in modern society are merely a 'means' of action. That said, it might be reasonably assumed that all individuals who orientate themselves to courses of action/social collectivities contribute to their reproduction/transformation, even if it involves nothing more than unthinking acquiesence in the present situation.

Thus far, the irony of labelling Weber an action theorist has been underlined. It is now necessary to focus closer attention on the predominance of means-end rational action in Weber's classification of ideal-types of social action. In fact, the preponderance of means-end rational action in Weber's sociology accentuates his commitment to modernity. Or as Benhabib (1981, p.367) puts it, this type of action is the theoretical and practical legacy of the disenchanted world-view of modernity. Weber himself affirms that:

> It is ... our first concern to work out and to explain genetically the special peculiarity of Occidental rationalism, and within this field, that of the modern Occidental form.(1976a, p.26; see also p.78; 1970, p.155)

Weber is underscoring the singularity of Western civilization. He claims that European and American socio-economic life has been rationalized in a particular manner and in a particular sense. The study of this specific process of rationalization is deemed 'one of the chief tasks of our disciplines' (Weber 1949, p.34). Western rationalism is the hermeneutic starting point.[14]

Weber does concede that rationalism is not peculiar to the Occident. He declares that 'rationalizations of the most varied character have existed in various departments of life and in all areas of culture' (1976a, p.26; see also 1970, p.293; 1978a, p.30). What is distinctive about the modern West is the unrelenting march of rationalization understood in an instrumental sense. *Zweckrationalität* indiscriminately facilitates the calculated pursuit of any goal, whatever its significance, worth or value. This form of rationality treats all substantive beliefs and values with complete indifference. Value-neutrality is built into *Zweckrationalität*. The calculability of means and procedures, then, for the achievement of well-defined goals is for Weber the unique feature of modern Western rationalism.[15]

In light of the aforesaid, it is not surprising that Weber regards *Zweckrationalität* as the paradigm of the ideal-type of meaningfully oriented social action. He states that:

> The construction of a purely rational course of action ... serves the sociologist as a type (ideal type) which has the merit of clear understandability and lack of ambiguity. (1978a, p.6)

The ideal-type of *zweckrational* action enables Weber to demonstrate a lack of purposive-rationality in real life. It allows him to assess the significance of irrational factors. Weber labels certain types of social action like traditional and affectual action irrational simply because they cannot be analyzed under the aspect of *Zweckrationalität*.

Since action is identified as 'rational' only if it involves acting in an instrumental fashion, all action which deviates from the ideal-type of *Zweckrationalität* will, by definition, be considered as irrational. Weber writes that:

> ...in every explanation of 'irrational' processes—i.e., those where either the 'objectively' correct conditions of the instrumentally rational action had been unheeded or, what is different, the subjective instrumentally rational considerations of the actor had been largely ruled out ... it is necessary, above all, to determine how the rational ideal-typical limiting case of pure instrumental and correct rationality *would have proceeded*. (1981a, p.154; emphasis in original)

By utilizing words like 'necessary' and 'correct' in this passage, the ideal-type of means-end rational action could easily acquire an *a priori* status. Weber is in danger here of equating the historical process of rationalization in the West with rationality as such.[16]

The historical, individual nature of the ideal-type of *zweckrational* action can easily be corroborated by showing how closely connected this form of action is with the rationality of economic action in modern capitalist society.[17] Interestingly enough, Weber clarifies the nature of interpretative sociology by referring to marginalist economics. He writes that:

> Sociology, just like history, at first explains things 'pragmatically' from the rational relationships of behaviour. This is for example how economic science proceeds, with its rational construction of 'economic man'. Interpretative sociology does just the same. (cited in Therborn 1980a, p.294)

Apprehending social action within modern capitalist society as rational is intertwined with the characterization of the rationality of economic action:

> 'Economic action' is any peaceful exercise of an actor's control over resources which is in its main impulse oriented towards economic ends. 'Rational economic action' requires instrumental rationality in this orientation, that is, deliberate planning. (Weber 1978a, p.63)

Rational economic action is distinguished by an instrumental rationality in the selection of means and ends. More particularly, capitalist economic action 'rests on the expectation of profit by the utilization of opportunities for exchange...' (Weber 1976a, p.17).

In this connection, Clarke (1982, pp.225-6) correctly purports that whatever contributes to increased economic calculation, must inevitably also be rational. The designation of religious beliefs (e.g., the Protestant ethic), modern law, the modern state and so forth as rational is linked with capitalist economic rationality. Conversely, traditional action and affectual action can only be described as irrational because they impede the full development of economic rationality. Undoubtedly, then, the motives and purposes constituting meaningfully oriented social action within the Weberian schema are imposed by modern capitalism. Furthermore, Weber quite correctly suggests that *Zweckrationalität* is more and more becoming an universal force to be reckoned with:

> ...under today's conditions of existence the approximation of reality to the theoretical propositions of economics has been a *constantly increasing* one. It is an approximation to reality that has implicated the destiny of ever-wider layers of humanity. And it will hold more and more broadly, as far as our horizons allow us to see. (1975b, p.33; emphasis in original)[18]

Although Western *Zweckrationalität*, especially in the form of rational economic action, is embracing 'ever-wider layers of humanity', this form of rationality cannot be equated with rationality as such.[19]

To further corroborate the fact that Weber identifies certain modes of action as irrational simply because they cannot be assessed under the aspect of *Zweckrationalität*, an inquiry into the nature of the ideal-type of traditional action is called for. Weber alleges that traditional action is 'determined by ingrained habituation' (1978a, p.25). Weber goes on to say that:

> Strictly traditional behavior ... lies very close to the borderline of what can justifiably be called meaningfully oriented action, and indeed often on the other side. For it is very often a matter of almost automatic reaction to habitual stimuli which guide behavior in a course which has been repeatedly followed. (1978a, p.25; see also 1970, p.296)

From the vantage point of *Zweckrationalität,* traditional action is meaningless and irrational. The individual's conduct is determined by habit. What Weber calls traditional action does not involve means and ends being rationally taken into account and assessed. It is the negative of the rational. Such behaviour can 'be interpreted in terms of subjective motives only in fragments' (Weber 1978a, p.17).

The reduction of traditional action to habit can in turn be subcatergorized as usage and custom. The continual occurrence of a certain mode of behaviour can be called usage when it 'is based on nothing but actual practice' (Weber 1978a, p.29). Usage, in turn, will be deemed a custom 'if the practice is based upon long standing' (ibid.). Individuals adhere to the customary simply by 'unreflective imitation' (Weber 1978a, p.319). From the foregoing, it is apparent that Weber perceives traditional action as static. He refers to 'the inertia of the customary' (1978a, p.321). Human agents (e.g., feudal knights) committed to traditionalism do not reason in a purposive-rational manner, they merely engage in habituated forms of activity.

As a matter of fact, Weber goes so far as to use a biological analogy in his treatment of traditional action. He argues that deviation from the customary 'seems to act on the psyche of the average individual like the disturbance of an organic function' (1978a, p.320; see also p.17). It is not far-fetched to suggest that Weber is stating here that instinctive (i.e., non-social) factors may be important in the understanding of traditional action.[20]

For all this, Weber does concede that 'attachment to habitual forms can be upheld with varying degrees of self-consciousness and in a variety of senses' (1978a, p.25). For instance, the Swiss population 'by virtue of old tradition' was well-informed about political issues (1978a, p.1456). Similarly, Weber observes that a *'true aristocracy* ... with the benefits of a stable tradition ... can achieve very great political successes in the leadership of a state' (1994, p.108; emphasis in original). We shall also see later that the various estates in the feudal social order often consciously championed tradition in the course of attempting to acquire and express social honour. Indeed, the feudal estate order can be appropriately described as a modality of traditional action. If tradition is regarded as a value worthy of respect, it moves very close to what Weber calls value-rational action.

With regard to purely affectual (especially emotional) action, it is 'determined by the actors' specific affects and feeling states...' (Weber 1978a, p.25). It is

Weber's (1978a, p.30) contention that the triumph of *Zweckrationalität* is at the expense of emotional values. For emotions and feelings are disruptive of the methodical pursuit of goals by the employment of the most efficient means. Emotionalism would, for example, deflect sober capitalist entrepreneurs from the calculated pursuit of profit.

Contrary to Weber, I would argue that *Zweckrationalität* is inescapably emotionally tinged. 'Hard' emotions like aggression buttress instrumentally rational action. An impeccably rational actor like the capitalist entrepreneur is a self-reliant, calculating, aggressive individual who uses others as a means simply for the achievement of his own goals. The rational actor solely oriented to the attainment of his own egoistic ends, cannot relate to others in a compassionate, caring way. Rather than the onset of *Zweckrationalität* driving emotions and feelings out of the individual self, then, it suppresses the so-called 'soft' emotions like compassion and caring.

All affectual action is, of course, deemed irrational by Weber because it is not constituted in terms of means and ends. He states that this type of action:

> ...stands on the borderline of what can be considered 'meaningfully' oriented, and often it, too, goes over the line. It may, for instance, consist in an uncontrolled reaction to some exceptional stimulus. (1978a, p.25; see also p.28)

The passionate devotion of followers to a charismatic leader, for instance, comprises affectual action. However, when this form of action involves a 'conscious release of emotional tension', that is sublimination, it is, according to Weber (1978a, p.25), in the process of being rationalized. McIntosh (1983, p.82) makes the pertinent point, though, that affectual action may be regarded as rational in its own right. In other words, an emotional act is rational to the extent that it accurately expresses (objectifies) the emotion/feeling which motivates it.[21]

Finally, in the context of the discussion of the preponderance of means-end rational action in Weber's typology of social action, the distinction between *zweckrational* and *wertrational* action must be considered. According to Weber, *wertrational* action is 'determined by a conscious belief in the value for its own sake of some ethical, aesthetic, religious, or other form of behavior, independently of its prospects of success...' (1978a, pp.24-5). Such action is distinguished by its unambiguously self-conscious formulation of the ultimate values governing the action, and the consistently planned orientation of its course to these values.

Weber's differentiation of *zweckrational* from *wertrational* action is, as Albrow (1987, pp.168-70) indicates, drawn directly from the Kantian idea of reason. That is to say, Kant's hypothetical and categorical imperatives are sociologized respectively as means-end rational action and value-rational action. The conditional, hypothetical imperative, in Kant's view, involves knowledge of means which, in turn, entails knowledge of laws. Moreover, the utilization of these laws for the acheivement of any individual end/purpose 'is an objective principle valid for every rational being' (Albrow 1987, p.168). Acquiring a knowledge of means for the attainment of an end is essentially a technical problem. The categorical imperative, on the other hand, is a moral issue. The morality of an action, according to Kant, lies in following rules such as those of duty and moral obligation. Moral action is 'conformity to law in general' (Kant cited in Korner 1955, p.134). The morality of action does not inhere in the desires of the individual nor in the repercussions that flow from a certain line of action.

In a similar vein, Weber declares that:

> ...value-rational action always involves 'commands' or 'demands' which, in the actor's opinion, are binding on him. It is only in cases where human action is motivated by the fulfillment of such unconditional demands that it will be called value-rational. (1978a, p.25)

This kind of action is concerned with rules/principles which the actor has adopted and to which he attempts to conform. Action is evaluated in terms of rules which it is expected to express. Moreover, Weber underlines the fact that the meaning of value-rational action 'does not lie in the achievement of a result ulterior to it, but in carrying out the specific type of action for its own sake' (1978a, p.25). This type of action cannot be characterized in terms of means and ends, it 'supposedly must go to pieces on the problem of the justification of means by ends' (Weber 1970, p.122).[22] Although value-rational action cannot be assessed in instrumental terms, Weber claims that it is not inadequate at the level of meaning. To the contrary, it 'makes sense and expresses a kind of dignity' (1970, p.119). Weber's account of value-rational action attests to the fact that he does, after all, broaden the concept of meaning. Social action motivated by the fulfillment of unconditional demands is meaningful.

The difference between means-end rational action and value-rational action is, in fact, not always clear-cut in Weber's writings. In respect of means-end rational action, the rational actor usually chooses ends in the light of a 'rational consideration of alternative means to the end, of the relations of the end to secondary consequences, and finally of the relative importance of different possible ends' (Weber 1978a, p.26). In this instance, consideration of means has a major influence on the rational actor's decision concerning the ends of his action. However, Weber also concedes that the:

> ...choice between alternative and conflicting ends and results may well be determined in a value-rational manner. In that case, action is instrumentally rational only in respect to the choice of means. (1978a, p.26)

The rational actor makes a choice between alternative ends on the basis of some value. In this regard, Habermas (1984a, p.70) speaks of Weber's concept of purposive-rational action as involving an 'instrumental rationality of means' and a

49

'rationality of choice' in deciding upon ends in accord with values.[23]

Weber also mentions that:

> ...the actor may, instead of deciding between alternative and conflicting ends in terms of a rational orientation to a system of values, simply take them as *given subjective wants* and arrange them in a scale of consciously assessed relative urgency. (1978a, p.26; emphasis added)

In this case, ends are not taken into account and evaluated in a methodical, calculating manner at all. They simply relate to the rational actor's 'given subjective wants'. The rational actor's subjective wants are appraized against the yardstick of the economic principle of marginal utility in modern capitalist society.

Yet another relevant point made by Weber is that commitment to a particular value may require the individual to act in an instrumental way. The ideal-type of personality, for example, is:

> ...a concept which entails a constant and intrinsic relation to certain ultimate 'values' and 'meanings' which are forged into purposes and thereby translated into rational-teleological action. (Weber 1975a, p.192)

For Weber, a great personality like the charismatic leader in the German nation-state renders his actions consciously consistent with the ultimate value of promoting the interests of national power. The leader may also have to calculate the most efficient means for the realization of his ultimate value. The modern party bureaucracy is, for instance, used as a tool by Weber's charismatic leader to actualize his ultimate value.[24]

The fact that the realization of a value may be contingent upon the calculation of the most efficient means, leaves Weber trapped in a net of agonizing contradictions. For *Wertrationalität,* as Bologh (1990, pp.126-30) observes, tends to degenerate into mere expediency. *Wertrationalität* which is concerned with adhering to a value for its own sake, ends up requiring in practice what it opposes in principle, namely, the subordination of the value to the calculation of the relative costs and benefits of the alternative means available for its actualization.

All things considered, then, Weber's typology of social action testifies, in my view, to the patent one-sidedness of *Zweckrationalität.* The social actor is construed as a creature of pure, instrumental reason. All action which transcends the calculation of means and procedures is irrational. The impeccably rational actor treats all substantive beliefs and values with complete nonchalance. Moreover, Weber eliminates affectual (i.e., the so-called 'soft' emotions) and traditional traits from the rational actor so that he may employ calculation to control the social world.

From the preceding discussion, it should not come as a surprise that Weber also develops a specific method of inquiry for the analysis of purposive-rational action. This action-type is especially amenable to rational understanding. Weber purports that:

> The immediately 'most understandable kind' of meaning structure of an action is, after all, action subjectively, rigorously, and rationally oriented towards means that are (subjectively) held to be unequivocally adequate for the attainment of (subjective) unequivocally and clearly comprehended ends. (1981a, p.154)

The logical limit of the ability to rationally understand social reality resides where this reality is no longer the product of the activity of rational actors. We can understand what individuals are doing when they attempt to attain certain ends by selecting the most appropriate means on the basis of the facts of the situation. The understanding of such instrumentally rational action possesses, according to Weber, 'the highest degree of verifiable certainty' (1978a, p.5). Rational understanding is subdivided into logical and mathematical understanding. Weber affirms that 'the highest degree of rational understanding is attained in cases involving the meanings of logically or mathematically related propositions' (1978a, p.5).

Owing to the fact that only *zweckrational* action can be subject to rational understanding within the Weberian schema, all other forms of conduct defy such understanding. Even in the case of the impeccably rational actor, Weber concedes that:

> ...'conscious motives' may well, even to the actor himself, conceal the various 'motives' and 'repressions' which constitute the real driving force of his action ... Then it is the task of the sociologist to be aware of this motivational situation and to describe and analyze it, even though it has not actually been concretely part of the conscious intention of the actor; possibly not at all, at least not fully. (1978a, pp.9-10)

Ironically enough, Weber is saying here that 'motives' and 'repressions' embedded in the subconsciou/unconscious may account for the rational actor's conduct. It obviously follows that these subconscious/unconscious motives and repressions are only understandable in terms of the degree of their deviation from the master ideal-type of *zweckrational* action.

In the case of affectual action characteristic of the followers of a charismatic leader, for instance, feelings and emotions are only understandable as an empathic re-experiencing or reliving. Weber postulates that 'empathic or appreciative accuracy is attained when, through sympathetic participation, we can adequately grasp the emotional context in which action took place' (1978a, p.5). Empathy does not involve 'objectified knowledge'. It is merely a matter of 'pure experience' (Weber 1975a, p.166). Similarly, traditional action is not amenable to rational understanding. Weber, for example, considers the lord's interest in the direct consumption rather than the rational accumulation of wealth in the feudal estate order as thoroughly irrational. Seen in this light, Weber (1978a, p.6) argues that all irrational modes of behaviour must be treated as elements of deviation from the conceptually pure type of purposive-rational action. Affectual and traditional action can only be rendered as the negative of *Zweckrationalität*.

With regard to value-rational action, values which are very different from those found in modern capitalist society are even difficult to grasp empathically. Weber declares that:

> ...many ultimate ends or values towards which experience shows that human action may be oriented, often cannot be understood completely, though sometimes we are able to grasp them intellectually. The more radically they differ from our own ultimate values, however, the more difficult it is to understand them empathically. (1978a, pp.5-6)

For example, it is exceedingly difficult for us in modern capitalist society to fully appreciate the significance of social honour as one of the core values governing knightly conduct in the feudal estate order in the West. For the feudal notion of social honour is now obsolete.

Taking account of the fact, then, that most individuals do not act in an instrumental fashion within the Weberian schema, the sociologist can only proceed by showing the extent of deviation of actual conduct from *zweckrational* action. *Zweckrational* action 'serves as an ideal type, enabling us to assess the significance of ... *irrational* action' (Weber 1981a, pp.152-3; emphasis in original). Although Weber (1978a, p.22) admits that the ideal-type of fully meaningful action is a 'marginal case', he still postuates means-end rational action as the basis for sociological understanding. The only rationale for attributing meaning is on the basis of similarity to *zweckrational* action. Moreover, identifying the course of deviation of actual conduct from the conceptually pure type of *zweckrational* action depends, as Parkin puts it, 'on the observer having greater insight into the subjective state of the actor than the actor had himself' (1982, p.27). Weber's approach is arguably elitist, given that one can assume that it is only the sociologist who is fully conscious of the conceptually 'true' course of action. Otherwise, he could not detect a deviation from it.[25]

In sum, the preceding discussion accentuates the fact that *zweckrational* action acquires almost an *a priori* status. Weber misunderstands himself when he alleges that it is important to avoid the error 'which confuses the unavoidable tendency of sociological concepts to assume a rationalistic character with a positive valuation of rationalism' (1978a, p.18; see also 1981a, pp.152, 161). The heart of the matter is that *zweckrational* action is used as the anchor point against which all other forms of action are deemed rational or irrational. It is true that *Zweckrationalität* has, as Habermas indicates, 'deeply marked the self-understanding of the modern era' (1984a, p.10). But the difficulty, I would suggest, is that Weber articulates the prevailing form of rationality within modern society, without being sufficiently critical of it.[26] In view of the fact that sociology is an *empirical science* of concrete *reality*' (Weber 1949, p.72; emphasis in original), it is basically concerned with 'what is'. Weberian sociology logically precludes one from judging the normative validity of purposive-rational action. For the employment of normative criteria is deemed to be 'unscientific'.

Hitherto, the discussion of Weber's notion of rationality has been limited to *zweckrational and wertrational* action. However, Weber speaks of 'the complexity of the only superfically simple concept of the rational' (1976a, p.194). It is, thus, important to briefly mention the other forms of rationality to be found in Weber's writings. In fact, Weber's classification of the ideal-types of rational action refers to what Levine (1981, pp.10-12) aptly calls forms of 'subjective' rationality. One can identify 'subjective' rationality in the mental processes of actors. This kind of rationality applies to action that is conscious and deliberate.

Levine (1981, pp.12-15) identifies another major category of rationality in Weber's writings, namely, 'objectified' rationality.[27] 'Objectified' rationality, according to Levine, refers to action that employs objectively correct means in line with available scientific knowledge, and/or has undergone some process of external systematization. In this respect, Weber argues that:

A subjectively 'rational' action is not identical with a rationally 'correct' action, i.e., one which uses the objectively correct means in accord with scientific knowledge. (1949, p.34; see also 1981a, p.154)

Levine suggests that four forms of 'objectified' rationality can be teased out of Weber's writings: instrumental rationality, substantive rationality, formal rationality and conceptual rationality. Instrumental rationality which underpins the modern capitalist market-economy and the modern state involves, according to Weber, 'the methodical attainment of a definitiely given and practical end by means of an increasingly precise calculation of adequate means' (1970, p.293). Substantive rationality refers to '"valid" norms' against which the 'empirically given' is assessed (Weber 1970, p.294). This 'objectified' form of rationality is, for instance, central to Weber's study of the feudal estate order. Formal rationality entails a methodical ordering of activities by reference to universally valid rules, regulations or laws. This type of rationality pervades the modern capitalist market-economy and the modern legal-rational state. Finally, conceptual rationality ('rational intellectualism'), as exemplified in modern science, involves 'an increasing theoretical mastery of reality by means of increasingly precise and abstract concepts' (Weber 1970, p.293).[28] These four forms of 'objectified' rationality have, as Levine (1981, p.14) observes, their counterparts in the forms of 'subjective' rationality: instrumental rationality/means-end rationality, substantive rationality/value-rationality, formal rationality/propensity for actors to secure order by the establishment of fixed rules, regulations or laws, and conceptual rationality/rational understanding.[29]

2.2 The teleological model of action

When the predominance of means-end rational action in the classification of types of social action is taken into account, it is obvious that Weber starts from a teleological model of action.[30] To repeat an earlier quotation, means-end rational action is:

> ...determined by expectations as to the behavior of objects in the environment and of other human beings; these expectations are used as 'conditions' or 'means' for the attainment of the actor's own rationally pursued and calculated ends. (Weber 1978a, p.24; see also 1981a, p.159)

The solitary, rational actor is oriented towards his own calculated ends. He is aggressively individualistic. An orientation towards others is considered necessary by this actor only as a means for the attainment of his own goals. The rational actor is willing to co-operate with others only to the extent that it is compatible with his own set goals. I would urge the view, then, that the teleological model of action informing Weber's notion of *zweckrational* action, can never take on more than a contingent intersubjectivity. It admits of an orientation to the other only marginally. It serves monological action. Weber affirms that 'one of the most important aspects of the process of "rationalization" of action is ... deliberate adaptation to situations in terms of self-interest' (1978a, p.30). Or as Habermas puts it, the teleological model of action entails social action only to the extent of 'the interlacing of egocentric calculations of utility' (1984a, p.101). In point of fact, this conception of the social is constitutive of modern capitalist society. Capitalist entrepreneurs oriented to their own calculated end of profit are aware of the other, the wage-labourers, only to the degree that these labourers can be wielded as tools for the attainment of their goal. Similarly, the responsible charismatic leader in the modern nation-state is aware of the electoral masses only to the extent that they can be used as a means for acquiring votes.

Value-rational action is arguably also social in the most limited sense. Such action is characterized by the 'consistently planned orientation' to ultimate values (Weber 1978a, p.25). More precisely, value-rational action presupposes independent, isolated, autonomous individuals espousing individually chosen values. The Puritan, for instance, 'rationally routinized all work in this world into serving God's will and testing one's state of grace' (Weber 1970, p.332). Because the Puritan was motivated by the unconditional demand of serving God's will, this meant, according to Weber, renouncing salvation as a goal attainable by everyone. Grace was particularized since the Puritan was interested solely in proof of his own membership among God's elect, by fulfilling his duty in a vocation. The end-result is what Weber (1970, p.333) adroitly calls a 'standpoint of unbrotherliness', a lack of a sense of community.[31]

Since the social is symptomatic of the interplay of self-seeking interests, it is not surprising that Weber's understanding of the ideal-type of a social relationship is likewise circumscribed:

> The term 'social relationship' will be used to denote the behavior of a plurality of actors insofar as in its meaningful content, the action of each takes account of that of the others and is oriented in these terms. (1978a, p.26)

The defining principle of a social relationship is that there must, at least, be a minimum of mutual orientation of the action of each individual to that of other individuals.[32] Although a minimum of mutual orientation is indispensable for a social relationship, Weber argues that there need not be reciprocity/solidarity. It is not necessary for the subjective meaning to be the same for all the individuals mutually oriented in a given social relationship. An associative relationship represents the most rational type of a social relationship. Such a relationship involves 'a rationally motivated adjustment of interests or a similarly motivated agreement, whether the basis of rational judgment be absolute values or reasons of expediency' (Weber 1978a, p.41). The purest examples of associative relationships are: rational free-market exchange, the pure voluntary association based on self-interest, and the voluntary association of individuals oriented to a set of common values. In accordance with Weber's rendering of the social, the actors in a free-market exchange or in a voluntary association like a rational sect are mutually oriented to each other only to the degree that it contributes to the achievement of their own egoistic ends. Quite simply, associative relationships promote instrumental collectivism.

It is not surprising that the other ideal-type of a social relationship, namely a communal relationship, is held to be irrational. According to Weber:

> A social relationship will be called 'communal' if and so far as the orientation of social action—whether in the individual case, on the average, or in the pure type—is based on a subjective feeling of the parties, whether affectual or traditional, that they belong together. (1978a, p.40)

A communal relationship involves intersubjectively meaningful conduct. Communal relationships include: a religious brotherhood, a feudal estate group, a national community and so forth. It is affection or tradition rather than reasons of expediency that bring individuals together in a communal relationship. But both affectual and traditional action are categorized as irrational within Weber's action-typology. Hence, a communal relationship grounded in affection or tradition is likewise irrational. What is more, a communal relationship is based on a mere 'subjective feeling', it is not grounded in 'objective knowledge'. In a word, communal relationships promote communal collectivism.

However, given the ideal-typical nature of a communal relationship like the feeling of 'belonging together' among the members of the knightly estate group in the feudal social order in the West, it is not surprising that an actual communal relationship 'may involve action on the part of some or even all of the participants which is to an important degree oriented to considerations of expediency' (Weber 1978a, p.41). Conversely, an actual associative relationship such as the co-operation between capitalist entrepreneurs in a class-conscious organization can include emotional elements.

Weber's rendering of subjective meaning further underscores the fact that the teleological model of action informing *zweckrational* action involves nothing more than a contingent intersubjectivity. Behaviour becomes action to the extent that it acquires subjective meaning. Action, in turn, becomes social action in so far 'as its subjective meaning takes account of the behavior of others and is thereby oriented in its course' (Weber 1978a, p.4). It is apparent here that Weber belongs within the tradition of the modern philosophy of consciousness. Subjective meaning precedes the definition of social action. Subjective meaning is such for a pure consciousness.[33] Meaning, for instance, is autonomously created and chosen by the charismatic leader in the modern nation-state. This autonomous creation of meaning would appear to contravene Weber's other assertion, namely, the fact that subjective meaning entails an understanding of the 'complex of meaning' within which it belongs. As a matter of fact, Weber declares that he wants to draw 'a sharp distinction between subjectively intended and objectively valid "meanings"...' (1978a, p.4; see also 1981a, p.179; 1972, pp.158-63). However, the distinction between subjective meaning and objective meaning is not always clear-cut in Weber's writings.

Weber's rather limited understanding of subjective meaning itself is further corroborated by the fact that it is not a product of language-communication. Habermas aptly describes Weber's concept of subjective meaning as 'a (precommunicative) action intention' (1984a, p.280). If meaning were a product of language-communication, it would already involve 'the other', it would be intrinsically intersubjective.[34] True, Weber does speak of a language-community:

A *language* community is constituted, in the rational limiting case, of numerous individual instances of social action that are oriented towards the expectation of reaching an 'understanding' of an intended meaning with another person. (1981a, p.167; emphasis in original)

The root of the problem, as Habermas (1984a, p.95) points out, is that the teleological model of action treats language as one of several media employed by the rational actor in pursuit of his own calculated ends. The rational actor in his capacity as a speaker tries to get his opponent to form or to hold beliefs, goals, intentions and so on that are advantageous to him. It goes without saying that language-communication interpreted in an instrumental sense, is a very important medium wielded by rational actors like capitalist entrepreneurs in pursuit of their own egoistic ends.

The teleological model of action informing *zweckrational* action and, more particularly, the pre-communicative nature of subjective meaning attest, then, to the fact that Weber's conception of the social is very limited. Weber's location within the tradition of the modern philosophy of consciousness accounts for the fact that the individual creates his own universe of meaning and, thereby, is completely autonomous. Each individual must achieve his own self-realization and internal liberation. A major *lacuna* in this notion of the autonomous individual, as Rasmussen (1973, p.13) suggests, is that it makes the self simply problematic to itself. It does not problematize the self's relation with the other, nor does it make the other problematic to the self. Pertinent to the issue at hand here also is Wuthnow's point that Weber's emphasis on subjective meaning was 'filtered through a very formalized, socially constructed set of cultural categories', namely, Puritanism (1987, p.136). The Puritan *Weltanschauung* is such that serious introspection is demanded. The Puritan is trapped in a lonely subjectivity. He is obsessed with acquiring evidence of his own membership among God's elect. Accordingly, a meticulous analysis of his own thoughts and feelings is required.

In sum, then, Weber's location within the tradition of the modern philosophy of consciousness and, moreover, the Puritan influence, corroborate the fact that the communicative dimension of subjective experience is not treated.[35] Identity is not intersubjectively defined. The self-reliant, autonomous individual does not acquire an identity in the course of his encounter with the other. This type of individual is at the very heart of Weber's sociology of action.

It is against this backcloth that Habermas (1979a, pp.185-205; 1979b, pp.1-68; 1984a) sets out to develop a concept of communicative action in order to untangle those aspects of the rationality of action which were neglected by Weber. Rationalization entails not only the extension of means-end rationality, but also of a form of rationality proper to the medium of social interaction. Whereas purposive-rational action is characterized by an instrumental orientation towards success, communicative action has as its distinguishing feature the fact that the actions of the participants are coordinated through their orientation towards mutual understanding and agreement. As such, communicative action refers to the enculturation process in general, that is, the process by which intersubjectivity is made possible within a society. For Habermas, communicative action does not posit a self-sufficient, solitary subject. Quite the contrary. It begins from the idea of a symbolically structured life-world in which the actor's identity is formed.

It is of decisive importance to point out that the communicative model of action does not equate action with communication. Habermas contends that:

Language is a medium of communication that serves understanding, whereas actors, in coming to an understanding with one another so as to coordinate their actions, pursue their particular aims. In this respect the teleological structure is fundamental to *all* concepts of action. (1984a, p.101; emphasis in original)

Even though the teleological structure is built into all concepts of social action, these concepts are nonetheless differentiated according to how the coordination among the goal-directed actions of different participants is specified (Habermas 1984a, p.101). Such coordination among purposive-rational actors involves the merging of self-seeking interests. In the case of communicative action, Habermas argues that coordination means 'reaching understanding in the sense of a cooperative process of interpretation' (1984a, p.101). In short, participants in communicative action pursue their individual goals under the condition that agreement can be accomplished among speaking and acting subjects.

Although the communicative model of action implies social action to the extent of reaching mutual understanding and agreement, Habermas does concede that relations of power can be 'surreptitiously incorporated in the symbolic structures of the systems of speech and action' (1974a, p.12; see also 1984a, p.288). An individual agent, for instance, may induce another to act in a way beneficial to his own success by the manipulation of language.

All in all, Habermas' key argument that the process of rationalization extends to a form of rationality proper to the medium of social interaction, underlines Weber's circumscription of the rationality of action and, more particularly, his rather limited notion of the social. Habermas wants to 'bring to consciousness the dignity of modernity, the dimension of a nontruncated rationality' (1984b, p.15). This is tantamount to saying that Habermas initiates a transition from the paradigm of the philosophy of consciousness to the paradigm of mutual understanding. It is this transition which makes possible an extended understanding of the social. The social need no longer involve merely a contingent intersubjectivity. One can conceptualize a notion of the social that is truly intersubjective.

2.3 Social action and freedom

The question of human freedom is important in both Weber's epistemological-methodological and sociological writings. Weber is opposed to the metaphysical view of freedom.[36] He writes that:

...for this reason concern on the part of history to judge of historical actions as responsible before the conscience of history or before the judgment seat of any god or man and all other modes of introducing the philosophical problem of 'freedom' into the procedures of history would suspend its character as an empirical science just as much as the insertion of miracles into its causal sequences. (1949, p.123)

Taking account of the fact that history, sociology, economics and so on are empirical disciplines concentrating on what is, a philosophical analysis of freedom is irrelevant. Weber refers, for example, to the 'Rights of Mankind' as 'extremely rationalized fanaticisms' (cited in Mommsen 1984, p.392). These 'rights' are grounded in Natural Law. Natural Law is based upon the supposition that a metaphysical order must be approximated. The heart of the matter is that a metaphysical rendering of freedom lies 'beyond any "observational experience"' (Weber 1975a, p.198). Such a notion of freedom is not subject to empirical verification. It is entirely transcendental.

Yet, on the other hand, Weber is impelled to acknowledge the fundamental historical significance of the so-called idealist interpretation of freedom for modern man. It is:

...a gross self-deception to believe that without the achievements of the age of the Rights of Man any one of us, including the most conservative, can go on living his life. (Weber 1978a, p.1403; see also p.1209; 1978b, p.281)

The most fundamental 'right of man', namely freedom of conscience, was first espoused by the Protestant sects. This inalienable personal right guarantees all individuals 'freedom from compulsion, especially from the power of the state' (Weber 1978a, p.1209). The moral autonomy of the individual is secured. In fact, Weber goes so far as to say that '*only radical idealism* could create this' (cited in Mommsen 1984, p.393; emphasis in original).[37] In this same connection, Apel perspicaciously observes that 'freedom of conscience as moral autonomy is confused with private arbitrariness of decision' (1979, p.312). The root of the problem lies in the methodical solipsism of the modern philosophy of consciousness since Descartes. The confusion of freedom of conscience as moral autonomy with private arbitrariness of decision is especially relevant in Weber's sociology of action. The rational actor is dedicated to the pursuit of his own egoistic ends.

Bearing in mind Weber's rather ambivalent attitude towards a metaphysical conception of freedom, he contends that:

Every purely rational interpretation of a concrete historical process obviously and necessarily *presupposes* the existence of 'freedom of the will' in every sense of this expression which is possible within the domain of the empirical. (1975a, p.194; emphasis in original)[38]

In point of fact, Weber's empirical idea of 'freedom of the will' lines up with the predominance of means-end rational action in his action-typology. Weber invites us to:

Consider all other possible forms of the 'problem' of 'freedom of the will' which have no bearing upon the meaning of purposefully rational action. They lie beyond the domain of history and are of no historical significance at all. (1975a, p.194)

Freedom is intrinsically linked with purposive-rational action. An action can be deemed free only when the means, the ends and the secondary results are all rationally taken into account and appraised. Freedom and calculability are directly proportional to each other. The freer the actor is, the more his actions conform to the logic of means and ends. Or as Weber puts it:

Consider the sense in which an actor's 'decision' is 'more free' than would otherwise be the case—i.e., based more extensively upon his own 'deliberations', which are upset neither by 'external' constraints nor by irresistible 'affect'. If the actor's 'decision' is 'more free' in this sense, then, other things being equal, his motivation can be more completely understood in terms of the categories of 'means' and 'ends' than would otherwise be the case. (1975a, p.191; see also 1949, pp.124-5)

The condition in which the actor chooses his own means and ends constitutes what Levine (1981, p.16) appropriately calls freedom in the subjective sense of 'autonomy'.[39] Moreover, Weber's action-typology (*zweckrational, wertrational,* affectual and traditional action) pertains to his ideological evaluation of the relative freedom of different kinds of action.

Weber's association of the highest degree of empirical freedom with purposive-rational action is further underscored in his criticism of Knies' notion of freedom (Weber 1975a, pp.95-101, 120-9). Knies divides action into free, irrational, concrete action and nomologically, that is, causally determined action. Weber's response is to insist that 'incalculability' is not peculiar to human action. The essential point is that '"incalculability" ... is the principle of the "madman"' (Weber 1975a, p.125; see also 1949, p.124). Indeed, Weber goes so far as to say that the calculability of natural processes is 'not susceptible to the same degree of certainty' as the calculation of the action of a person (1975a, p.121).[40]

The fact that the empirical interpretation of freedom is inextricably connected with *zweckrational* action also exemplifies its historical character. In effect, Weber is referring to the nature of freedom in modern capitalist society. Weber states that modern freedom 'arose from a unique, never to be repeated set of circumstances' (1995, p.109). These included: overseas expansion, the peculiar socioeconomic structure of 'early capitalism' in Western Europe, 'the conquest of life by science', and the development of certain ideal values like the 'rights of man' (1995, pp.109-10). The historical origins of modern freedom attest, by and large, to the emergence of bourgeois freedom. Basic 'rights of man' such as inviolability of individual property, freedom of contract and vocational choice, according to Weber, 'made it possible for the capitalist to *use things and men freely...*' (1978a, p.1209; emphasis added). Freedom of contract, for instance, enables the capitalist entrepreneur to use the wage-labourer as a means for the making of a profit.

Taking account of the fact that empirical freedom is grounded in *zweckrational* action, Weber (1975a, pp.191-8; 1978a, pp.9-13) also propounds what Mayrl (1985, pp.108-24) aptly calls a non-deterministic causality of freedom.[41] In the social sciences the principle of causality is applied independently of the notion of necessary condition. It obviously contravenes Weber's association of empirical freedom with purposive-rational action to suppose that the ultimate purpose of the causal interest in the social sciences could be the subsumption of a concrete social event under some general law as a representative case. Weber declares that:

> Where the *individuality* of a phenomenon is concerned, the question of causality is not a question of *laws* but of concrete causal *relationships*, it is not a question of the subsumption of the event under some general rubric as a representative case but of its imputation as a consequence of some constellation. It is in brief a *question of imputation* ... of those components of a phenomenon the individuality of which is culturally significant. (1949, pp.78-9, emphasis in original; see also p.168)

Causal analysis in social science reveals what Zaret (1980, p.1185) adroitly calls 'the serial causality of an event'. It is concerned with the correlation of concrete social effects with concrete social causes. In this instance, the establishment of a causal relationship by the subsumption of social phenomena under universal laws, would inevitably destroy the individuality and uniqueness of social events and, hence, their cultural significance. Weber's non-deterministic social causality derives from concrete social reality.

As a matter of fact, Weber's non-deterministic social causality replaces the notion of necessity with the category of objective possibility (Weber 1949, pp.164-88). Objective possibility refers to 'the propositions regarding what "would" happen in the event of the exclusion or modification of certain conditions...' (Weber 1949, p.173). It also involves 'the continuous reference to "empirical rules"' (ibid.).[42] The social phenomenon under investigation is reconstructed as an ideal-typical sequence of events without, however, those factors to which causal significance has been attributed. It is, then, that what actually occurred is compared with the constructed type. The sole function of the judgement of objective possibility is to establish beyond a reasonable doubt that the social event in question would not have occurred, if the social factors to which causal significance has been attributed, had not been present.[43] In short, Weber's category of objective possibility enables one to distinguish between essential and non-essential factors in explaining a certain social outcome.

Weber's (1976a) study of the Protestant ethic provides us with a good example of how the principle of objective possibility operates. To prove beyond a reasonable doubt that the Protestant ethic is a key to the understanding of modern capitalism, we assume that a certain development of religious thoughts and actions (i.e., Calvinism) had not occurred. On this basis, an attempt is made to construct a hypothetical sequence of actions which might have occurred, given the knowledge of the historical situation and the empirical regularities of social action. The end-result might be that Western history would have taken a different course, if Calvinism had not developed. And so it is possible to ascribe causal significance to the onset of Calvinism to the extent that our theoretical construct has shown a different development due to its hypothetical non-occurrence.

In this same connection, Weber conceived the idea of casting light on the development of Western capitalism by concentrating on cases where capitalism failed. Hence, his great comparative studies of the Eastern religions (Weber 1951, 1958). It was through the category of objective possibility that Weber was able to prove the causal adequacy of the Protestant ethic as an important factor in promoting the development of modern rational capitalism in the West. His comparative studies of the Eastern religions made more plausible the thesis that one of the reasons why modern rational capitalism developed in the West, was the uniqueness of Judeo-Christianity among world religions. The study of the Eastern religions contributed towards eliminating them as plausible explanations and, thereby, increasing the credibility of Weber's own interpretation.

Following the application of the category of objective possibility, Weber argues that it is necessary to establish causal adequacy at the level of meaning. In other words:

A correct causal interpretation of typical action means that the process which is claimed to be typical is shown to be both adequately grasped on the level of meaning and at the same time the interpretation is to some degree causally adequate. (Weber 1978a, p.12)

When Weber mentions 'adequacy at the level of meaning' (or 'subjective adequacy'), he is referring to a level of knowledge deemed sufficient for the explanation of a course of action by the individual actor or by the observer. The available knowledge 'seems to the actor himself or to the observer an adequate ground for the conduct in question' (Weber 1978a, p.11).

Weber goes on to say that:

...the interpretation of a sequence of events will on the other hand be called *causally* adequate insofar as, according to established generalizations from experience, there is a probability that it will actually occur in the same way. (1978a, p.11; emphasis in original)

More pertinently, causal explanation is based on the probability which is always calculable in some sense, 'that a given observable event (overt or covert) will be followed or accompanied by another event' (Weber 1978a, p.12). Although causal adequacy is based on empirical generalizations concerning the conduct of others, the crucial point is that such generalizations must ultimately be grounded in meaningfully adequate explanations. Weber affirms that:

> It is customary to designate various sociological generalizations, as for example 'Gresham's Law', as 'laws'. These are in fact typical probabilities confirmed by observation to the effect that under certain given conditions an expected course of social action will occur, which is understandable in terms of the typical motives and subjective intentions of the actors. (1978a, p.18)

If an expected course of action is not comprehensible in terms of the typical motives and subjective intentions of rational actors (i.e., adequate on the level of meaning), it inevitably follows, according to Weber, that sociological generalizations are inane, no matter how high the probability that a certain course of action might occur.

In fine, then, a non-deterministic causality of freedom can only be rendered meaningful if it relates to action in the role of means and ends. A non-deterministic social causality and purposive-rational action belong together. Conversely, adequacy on the level of meaning can only have causal significance from a sociological standpoint, in so far as it can be proved that a probability exists that action actually follows the course which has been deemed meaningful.[44]

Another important point relates to the fact that Weber's rendition of freedom is such that domination is the precondition of freedom. Domination is built into purposive-rational action.[45] To repeat an earlier quotation once again, means-end rational action is:

> ...determined by expectations as to the behavior of objects in the environment and of other human beings; *these expectations are used as 'conditions' or 'means' for the attainment of the actor's own rationally pursued and calculated ends...* (Weber 1978a, p.24; emphasis added)

The paradox of freedom in Weber's sociology of action is such that the freer the rational actor is, the more he uses other human beings as tools for the achievement of his own calculated ends. Weber envisages a social world in which most individuals are not autonomous, they are not free to select means and ends. To the contrary, their unfreedom is the *sine qua non* of the freedom of the few free individuals. Or as Habermas aptly puts it, 'by virtue of its structure, purposive-rational action is the exercise of control' (1971b, p.82). Rational control of 'others' is the most efficient means at the disposal of the rational actor in his endeavour to secure his own egoistic ends. *Zweckrational* action is synonymous with imperious conduct. The prototypes of rational agents like the capitalist entrepreneur and the responsible charismatic leader, achieve freedom by subverting the freedom of the majority of those individuals who engage in reactive behaviour rather than act on their own motives. The precondition for the overinflated autonomy of rational agents in modern society is the subjugation of the mass of human beings. It is *a priori* impossible for the rational actor to secure his freedom by developing the freedom of others. In this regard, Lukács observes that 'in contemporary bourgeois society individual freedom can only be corrupt and corrupting because it is a case of unilateral privilege based on the unfreedom of others' (1974, p.315).

In light of the aforesaid, it is evident that freedom rendered in an instrumental sense is an individual rather than a social attribute. In view of the fact that Weber belongs within the tradition of the modern philosophy of consciousness, freedom is such for a pure consciousness. It is solely the individual's responsibility to achieve liberation of the self. Or as Levine indicates, Weber holds on 'to an ideal of the human universe as one constituted by heroically rational, free, autonomous monads' (1981, pp.22-3). And because Weber's conception of the social is symptomatic of nothing more than a contingent intersubjectivity, he could not envisage freedom in the context of communal relations. In this respect, Weber states that 'all rational action somehow comes to stand in tension with the ethic of brotherliness' (1970, p.339). Any conduct which extends beyond the subjectivity of self-interest is within the Weberian action framework devoid of rationality, it is not free. The only freedom that Weber recognizes is what Lukács (1974, p.315) astutely calls the 'freedom of the egoist'. Notions of solidarity, community and so forth are alien to Weber's view of freedom grounded in *zweckrational* action.

Habermas' answer to Weber's aggressively individualistic approach to freedom is the view that personal freedom and societal freedom belong together. Against the backcloth of the communicative model of action, Habermas avers that:

> Freedom, even personal freedom, freedom of choice in the last instance, can only be thought in internal connection with a network of interpersonal relationships, and this means in the context of the communicative structures of a community, which ensures that the freedom of some is not achieved at the cost of the freedom of others. (1986a, p.147)

Juxtaposing personal freedom and freedom at the level of society creates a false dilemma. For the individual, in Habermas' view, can only be free when all are free. What is more, all can only be free in community, in solidarity.[46] On this score, Lukács is incorrect, in my view, to affirm that the transcendence of bourgeois freedom entails the abandonment of individual freedom. Lukács advocates 'the conscious subordination of the self to that collective will that is destined to bring real freedom into being', that is, subordination to the Communist Party (1974, p.315). But the heart of the matter is that individual freedom and societal freedom are implicated in each other. It is not a question of one submitting to the other. The freedom of the individual is mediated through the freedom of society and vice versa.

Of particular significance also is that Weber's understanding of modern empirical freedom is distinguished by a profound anti-utopian scepticism. Weber stipulates that:

> ...the idea that it might be possible to eliminate the 'domination of man over man' by a socialist society or by whatever kind, or by a most sophisticated democractic system is utopian throughout. (cited in Mommsen 1977, p.393)

Weber in his role as the value-free social scientist simply establishes the nature of modern empirical freedom. He identifies what constitutes freedom in modern society. The social scientist is, of course, logically debarred from questioning the normative validity of modern freedom. Only the empirical nature of freedom is subject to rational deliberation. The "'domination of man over man'" is a verified fact. The notion of a society free of domination is simply inconceivable.

Finally, it is worthy of note that, on Weber's reading, modern empirical freedom is itself restricted. This is tantamount to saying that purposive-rational action is prescribed by objective conditions. The rational actor in pursuit of his goals is subject to structural constraints. Weber concedes that:

> Even the empirically 'free' actor—i.e., who acts on the basis of his *deliberations*—is teleologically bound by the means which, varying with the circumstances of the objective situation, are nonequivalent and knowable. The belief in 'freedom of his will' is of precious little value to the manufacturer in the competitive struggle or to the broker in the stock exchange. He has the choice between economic destruction and the pursuit of very specific maxims of economic conduct. (1975a, p.193, emphasis in original; see also pp.96, 186-7, 202; 1976a, pp.54-5)

Impeccably rational actors like the capitalist manufacturer and the stock broker in pursuit of the end of profit, must work under conditions not freely chosen. They are motivated by the necessity of adhering to systemic exigencies. Otherwise, they will face economic ruin. Similarly, 'the dominated persons, acting with formal freedom, rationally pursue their own interests as they are forced upon them by objective circumstances' (Weber 1978a, p.943). The wage-labourer, for example, in modern capitalism must, 'under the compulsion of the whip of hunger', offer his services to the capitalist entrepreneur in order to survive (Weber 1981b, p.277).[47]

The limitations imposed on modern empirical freedom are reinforced by the fact that the rational actor uses his own self as a tool. On this account, Weber writes that:

> The dealers in a market ... *treat their own actions as means* for obtaining the satisfaction of the ends defined by what they realize to be their own typical economic interests... (1978a, p.30; emphasis added)

Besides treating his workers as a means of rational profit-making activity, the capitalist entrepreneur treats himself likewise.

In light of the discussion in this chapter, it is obvious that Weber's treatment of social action is seriously inadequate. Most individuals in modern society are hidden from Weber's sociological gaze except as a 'means' of action. Weber's ideal-type of means-end rational action has not much relevance in the modern, mundane world of ordinary individuals where emotion, habit and irrationality hold sway. This modern, mundane world is held to be of sociological interest by Weber because of its deviation from the ideal-type of purposive-rational action. The end-result of Weber's sociological line of reasoning is such that only 'extraordinary' individuals like capitalist entrepreneurs and charismatic leaders act and attain their freedom by subverting the freedom of 'ordinary' individuals in modern society. In a similar vein, individuals engaged in habituated forms of activity in a pre-modern society like the feudal estate order, are deemed to be acting irrationally by Weber. Finally, the idea of the social built into *zweckrational* action is such that action can never take on more than a contingent intersubjectivity in modern society. Social action simply involves the interlacing of self-seeking interests. In sum, then, the limitations built into Weber's action framework will be one of the main threads running through the fabric of the discussion in the following chapters.

Notes

1   Cf. Sica 1990, pp.105, 107.

     It should also be noted that Weber's concern with action represents a continuation of the *Handeln* tradition associated with the German Historical School of Political Economy. See Hennis 1988, pp.129-40.

2   It is important to note that Part II of Roth's and Wittich's translation of *Economy and Society* is the earlier part. It was written between 1910 and 1914. If this important chronological fact is not kept in mind, the direction of Weber's thought is reversed.

3   *Zweckrational* action, means-end rational action, purposive-rational action and instrumentally rational action will be used interchangeably in this study.

4   Cf. McIntosh 1983, pp.71-4; Hirst 1976a, pp.66-74; Kronman 1983, pp.22-8; Turner and Factor 1994, p.31.

5   It is also important to note Weber's other point that in no case does meaning 'refer to an objectively "correct" meaning or one which is "true" in some metaphysical sense' (1978a, p.4).

6   Cf. Hirst 1976a, pp.70-74; Turner 1986, pp.123-7; Udéhn 1981, pp.131-47; Eisen 1979, pp.203-18. See, esp., Sica's (1990) exemplary study of Weber's failure to deal with *das Irrationalitätsproblem* in his writings.

7   In a somewhat similar vein, Andreski (1984, p.66) suggests that rationalization in the sense of scientific and technical progress creates a

division of labour in modern society. One crucial aspect of this division of labour is differentiation with regard to the amount of skill and knowledge which individuals possess, and the amount of reasoning which they actually do.

8   It is interesting to remember that Weber's 'paradox of unintended consequences' is akin to Simmel's notion of the 'tragedy of culture'. In a similar vein, Stark (1967, p.261) equates Weber's 'paradox' with the 'negative heterogony of purposes'. Cf. also Turner 1981, pp.3-28.

9   Cf. Abel 1948, pp.211-18; Abel 1967, pp.334-6; Torrance 1974, pp.145-53; Runciman 1972, pp.42-4.

10 Cf. Huff 1984, pp.62-8; Käsler 1988, pp.176-80; Scaff 1988, pp.1-30; Munch 1975, pp.60-62; Burger 1977b, p.131.

11 See also Hekman 1983, pp.49-59; Poggi 1983, pp.34-9; Weiss 1986, pp.72-83; Kalberg 1994, pp.30-49.

12 Another interesting point is that Weber very rarely uses the term 'society' in *Economy and Society*. Instead, he describes 'society' as 'the general structures of human groups' (1978a, p.356). The holistic notion of 'society' is not in line with Weber's understanding of the individual acting on his own motives.

13 In this connection, it is interesting to note that Parsons (1964) and Parsons et al. (1953) attempt to go beyond Weber by assimilating the concept of action to a theory of the social system. Society conceptualized as a system develops at a level which completely transcends human action. Habermas (1984a), on the other hand, suggests that we choose the theory of action as 'the superordinate point of view'. He wishes to keep open the possibility of social change through action. In addition, he argues that it is only by retaining the theory of action as 'the superordinate point of view' that language can be introduced at all. Societies, it is true, can be regarded as systems. But the pertinent point is that the development of societies always rests on structures which are determined by linguistically produced intersubjectivity. Systemic problems always have repercussions at the level of action, and it is at this level where communication between social actors occurs that solutions are facilitated or impeded.

14 Weber's concern with Occidental rationalism is also exemplified in the continuous use of the phrase, 'only in the Occident', in *Economy and Society* (see, e.g., 1978a, p.883).

15 Weber's (1976a, p.78) understanding of rationality as 'an historical concept' highlights the fact that he has discarded the long-established Western idea that rationality is inherent in human nature and is unitary in structure.

16 See Turner 1983, p.512; Habermas 1984a, pp.178-85.

17 See Marcuse 1971, pp.143, 149; Clarke 1982, pp.220-29; Brown 1976, pp.205-9.

18 In a similar vein, Weber states that: 'a product of modern European civilization, studying any problem of universal history, is bound to ask himself to what combination of circumstances the fact should be attributed that in Western civilization, and in Western civilization only, cultural phenomena have appeared which (as we like to think) lie in a line of development having universal significance and value' (1976a, p.13).

19 However, Kalberg's (1980, p.1148) interpretation of Weber is such that the fourfold typology of social action refers to what he calls 'universal capacities of *Homo sapiens*'. On Kalberg's reading, the types of social action are located outside history as 'anthropological traits of man'. See also Kalberg 1994, pp.23-49.

20 See Turner and Factor 1994, pp.39-40.

21 Parsons (1949, pp.647-9) also criticizes Weber's relegation of affectual action to a residual category.

22 In this context, Weber (1970, pp.119-22) speaks of the 'ethic of ultimate ends'. Conforming to 'ultimate ends' is equivalent to conforming to demands and rules. 'Ultimate ends' are not traits of the individual personality.

23 Parsons (1949, pp.640-49) attempts to dissolve Weber's distinction between *zweckrational* and *wertrational* action. These types of action, according to Parsons, represent two different criteria of evaluation: the 'norm of efficiency' and 'ultimate value standards'. Parsons' appropriation of Weber must, of course, be understood in terms of the predominance of the normative orientation in his work.

24 The difference between *zweckrational* and *wertrational* action is not always fully understood. 'Ends' and 'values' are often confused. Andreski (1984, p.35), for example, argues that the distinction between means-end rational action and value-rational action is vacuous, because Weber does not indicate the difference between a purpose/goal and a value. In like manner, Runciman states that the distinction between *zweckrational* and *wertrational* action is superfluous, since it can 'be expressed in terms of the traditional distinction between means and ends' (1972, p.14). See also Benhabib 1981, pp.365-6.

25 Or as Portis adroitly puts it in his interpretation of Weber: 'Empirical social knowledge can be nothing more than the knowledge of the extent to which social reality does not conform to the intellectual constructions with which we approach it' (1986, p.64). See also Rasmussen 1973, pp.29-34; Turner and Factor 1994, p.43.

26 Cf. Sewart 1978, pp.335-55; Cohen 1972, p.69; Rasmussen 1973, pp.29, 37-8; Wilson 1976, pp.302-3.

27 Levine (1981, p.11) speaks of 'objectified' rather than 'objective' rationality, because the distinction between 'subjective' and 'objective' rationality is not always well-defined by Weber.

28 Levine's delineation of the forms of 'objectified' rationality in Weber's *oeuvre* corresponds rather closely to Kalberg's interpretation. Kalberg (1980, pp.1145-79) mentiones practical, substantive, formal and conceptual types of rationality. In like manner, Sadri (1983, pp.616-33) refers to practical, substantive, formal and theoretical forms of rationality. Mueller (1979, pp.149-71) speaks of three classes of rationality: purposive, normative and formal. See also Bologh 1984, pp.179-86.

29 Although Weber differentiates various types of rationality, he contends that 'ultimately they belong inseparately together' (1970, p.293; see also 1978a, p.30).

30 See Habermas 1984a, pp.85-8, 279-86.

31 On this score, Schluchter also observes that the absolute individualism expounded by Ascetic Protestantism 'does not even permit a "community of the church based on love". Rather, it completely eradicates all elements of brotherly love which had been part of the Christian ethic from its very beginning' (1981, p.171).

32 Similarly, Weber mentions 'consensus' in an earlier article. 'Consensus' refers to 'that situation when an action oriented towards expectations about the behavior of others has an empirically realistic chance of seeing these expectations fulfilled because of the objective possibility that these others will, in reality, treat those expectations as meaningfully "valid" for their behavior, despite the absence of an explicit agreement' (1981a, p.168).

33 Cf. Hirst 1976a, pp.69-70; Benhabib 1981, p.363; Levine and Levine 1975, pp.165-7.

34 Similarly, Apel observes that any thinker located within the tradition of the modern philosophy of consciousness since Descartes, that is, anyone expounding 'methodical solipsism'—'assumes that he can and must secure a primal understanding of his performative *I think* without presupposing in principle ... *language,* and thereby the existence of other people with whom he is *a priori* united in a communication-community' (1979, p.330; emphasis in original). Cf. also Apel 1980, pp.136-79.

35 See Benhabib 1981, p.369; Sewart 1978, p.356; Löwith 1982, p.57.

36 Cf. Mayrl 1985, p.112; Murvar 1985, p.6; Bendix 1984, p.19; Prager 1981, p.931.

37 See also Schluchter 1981, pp.57-8.

38 Given Weber's rather ambiguous attitude toward a metaphysical view of freedom, he nonetheless concedes that: 'we are ... completely free of the prejudice which asserts that reflections on culture which go beyond the analysis of empirical data in order to interpret the world metaphysically can, because of their metaphysical character fulfil no useful cognitive tasks' (1949, p.59).

39 Cf. Levine and Levine 1975, pp.176-7; Löwith 1982, pp.40-52; Sahay 1972, pp.20-23; Hearn 1985, pp.74-94.

40　In this respect, Gerth and Mills subject Weber to a gross misunderstanding when they claim that 'the quest for freedom is identified with irrational sentiment and privacy' (1970, p.73). See also Hekman 1979, pp.68-9.

41　See Zaret 1980, pp.1183-88; Sewart 1978, pp.334-6; Turner and Factor 1981, pp.5-28; Hekman 1979, pp.67-76.

42　Weber also describes the category of 'objective possibility' as '"an imaginary" experiment which consists in thinking away certain elements of a chain of motivation and working out the course of action which would then probably ensue, thus arriving at a causal judgment' (1978a, p.10).

43　Lukács also utilizes a category of 'objective possibility'. In respect of class consciousness, he declares that: 'the relation with concrete totality and the dialectical determinants arising from it transcend pure description and yield the category of objective possibility. By relating consciousness to the whole of society it becomes possible to infer the thoughts and feelings which men would have in a particular situation if they were *able* to assess both it and the interests arising from it in their impact on immediate action and on the whole structure of society' (1974, p.51; emphasis in original). However, there is a major difference in Lukács' and Weber's approach to 'objective possibility'. That is to say, 'objective possibility' is transformed into 'objective necessity' in Lukács' work. Lukács is concerned with the question of how 'it is actually possible to make the objective possibility of class consciousness into a reality' (1974, p.79). It is the Communist Party that provides 'empirical proof' of a very definite tendency in the direction of this 'objective possibility'. The Party transforms the 'objective possibility' of class consciousness into a 'necessity'. Moreover, the category of 'objective possibility' acquires a normative dimension. The 'objective possibility' of class consciousness is simultaneously the 'objective necessity' for the evolution of society towards such a state of class consciousness.

44　Weber's definition of sociology as 'a science concerning itself with the *interpretive understanding* of social action and thereby with a *causal explanation* of its course and consequences' (1978a, p.4), also attests to the fact that 'meaning' and 'causality' are complementary concepts.

45　Cf. Barker 1980, pp.240-42; Levine and Levine 1975, pp.176-83; Udéhn 1981, pp.132-4; Hirst 1976a, pp.76-7; Bologh 1990, pp.123-4; Eisen 1978, pp.58-9.

46　See also Hearn 1985, pp.165-204.

47　Granted, both the manufacturer and the wage-labourer are subject to objective constraints in modern capitalist society. The vital point, though, is that modern capitalism enables the manufacturer to attain his goal, namely, his subjective interest in profit. However, the fact that the worker is forced to sell his labour-power in order to simply survive cannot, in reality, be perceived as the worker's true subjective interest. This point will be elaborated upon in the fourth chapter.

3 Power and domination

This chapter focuses on key ideal-typical concepts crucial to Weber's study of social stratification. These include: power, resistance, domination and discipline. Interestingly enough, power and domination have been commented on extensively in the secondary literature, whereas resistance and discipline have not been closely scrutinized by many interpreters. The first section of the present chapter concentrates on Weber's voluntarist notion of power, and the fact that Weber's understanding of social stratification in terms of the existence of multiple and diverse bases for the exercize of power, has been misappropriated in much of American sociology. I, further, contend that although Weber gives an irreducible role to resistance in the power relationship, its inclusion is strictly unwarranted. In the second section I consider Weber's replacement of what he regards as the 'sociologically amorphous' concept of power by the 'more precise' concept of domination. In the third section Weber's contention that the exercize of domination is contingent upon discipline is assessed. In the final section of the chapter I examine some important implications that can be drawn from Weber's sociology of domination.

3.1 Power and resistance

Weber had the most heightened sense of the reality of power. He states that the social drive towards power 'is among the most fundamental and universal components of the actual course of interpersonal behavior' (1978a, p.601). Power is central to Weber's treatment of social stratification. According to Weber, '"classes", "status groups", and "parties" are phenomena of the distribution of power within a community' (1978a, p.927). Power is not an independent quality, it is an attribute of economic, social and political relations. Apprehending social stratification as a matter of power is another way of conceptualizing the distribution of economic, social and political resources. Power extends from market relations to the position of the salon to the relations between political entities.

How does Weber perceive power? Power and domination are introduced among the fundamental concepts of sociology (see Weber 1978a, pp.53-4, 926). The definitions of power (*Macht*) and domination (*Herrschaft*) occur after a discussion of social relationships which is prefaced by a discussion of social action. Weber defines power in the earlier essay, 'Class, Status, Party', as:

> ...the chance of a man or a number of men to realize their own will in a social action even against the resistance of others who are participating in the action. (1978a, p.926)

In a later discussion of the fundamental concepts of sociology, Weber defines power as:

> ...the probability that one actor within a social relationship will be in a position to carry out his own will despite resistance, regardless of the basis on which this probability rests. (1978a, p.53)[1]

Essentially, Weber defines power as the probability of forcing one's will on the behaviour of others. As Habermas (1977, pp.3-4) points out, Weber takes the teleological model of action as his starting point.[2] The rational actor chooses the most appropriate means to realize the goal that he has set for himself. To the extent that the probability of attaining his goal depends on the behaviour of another subject, the rational actor must have available the means to bring about the desired behaviour. Weber calls this control over the means to influence or determine the will of another power. Of particular relevance also to the underpinning of power in the teleological model of action, is Weber's emphasis on power as an associative relationship, that is, the most rational type of a social relationship.[3] Power is conceptualized as an asymmetrical relationship. One concentrates on the differential capacities of actors to enforce their will.[4]

Yet another salient feature of Weber's definition of the ideal-type of power is the element of 'probability'.[5] Weber is saying that it is 'probable' that an actor will be able to impose his will, not that it will 'necessarily' follow. The rational actor's ability to execute his will is conditional rather than an established fact. In short, Weber's motive for defining power in non-deterministic terms is to accentuate the relative logical indeterminancy of the link between intention and outcome. The fatefulness of human intention (i.e., 'the paradox of unintended consequences') can never be ignored.

Some important implications can be drawn from Weber's understanding of the nature of power. In the first place, Weber adopts a voluntarist notion of power. Power is equivalent to human agency. It is concerned with the subjective elements of purpose, willing and intention. When an actor or a number of actors attempt to carry out their will, they are trying to actualize their own interests.[6]

'Interest' in this context is closely related to what Giddens (1979b, pp.188-90) calls 'wants'. It is purely subjective because it refers to an actor's perception of his interests in a particular situation.

Contrary to Weber's rendition of power, I would argue that subjective interests can only be understood against the backdrop of objective constraints.[7] The capitalist entrepreneur's ability to enforce his will on the worker, for instance, is conditioned by the nature of modern capitalism. In point of fact, the entrepreneur is already in a structural power position. The profit motive is already firmly established in the modern capitalist market-economy. Put another way, the capitalist system enables the entrepreneur to attain his goal, profit. Therefore, the probability that the capitalist's subjective interest in profit will be misunderstood by him is not very high. Indeed, power can to a certain extent be conceptualized as a 'capacity' (i.e., 'power to') from the vantage point of a power wielder like the capitalist entrepreneur, since the capitalist system 'facilitates' him to attain his goal, profit. Power is perceived 'from above'. However, the wage-labourer who is subject to the capitalist's imposition of will, experiences subjection to an alien will as structural determination. When viewed 'from below', power is experienced as subjection to objective constraints. What is more, the fact that wage-labourers' interests, unlike capitalists' interests, are not well-established in modern capitalist society, makes it much more difficult to pinpoint workers' interests on an objective and subjective level.[8]

Another important implication of Weber's ideal-typical concept of power has to do with the stipulation that power is the probability to realize one's will, 'regardless of the basis on which this probability rests' (1978a, p.53). This statement attests to the existence of multiple and diverse bases for the exercize of power. Weber goes on to say that:

> All conceivable qualities of a person and all conceivable combinations of circumstances may put him in a position to impose his will in a given situation. (1978a, p.53)

The probability of enforcing one's will depends on the different types of resources one possesses. Weber, for example, mentions 'political power' (e.g., 1978a, pp.946, 987, 1261, 1357), 'social power' (e.g., 1978a, p.989), 'military power' (e.g., 1978a, pp.1261, 1266, 1280), 'financial power' (e.g., 1978a, pp.946, 1280) and so on. Moreover, when Weber purports that '"classes", "status groups", and "parties" are phenomena of the distribution of power within a community' (1978a, p.927), he is stressing how the possession of various resources enables one actor to exert power over another.[9] The imposition of one's will over others draws upon resources not available to subordinate actors.

One further relevant issue which I think bears mentioning here is that Weber's understanding of social stratification in terms of the existence of multiple and diverse bases for the exercize of power, has been misconstrued in much of the American literature on social stratification. Many American sociologists in the course of developing their own theories of social stratification, looked to Weber to justify their position.[10] The misappropriation of Weber by many American theorists of social stratification is characterized by a shift from the view that classes, status groups and parties are bases of the aggregation of power to the three-dimensional theory of social stratification consisting of class, status and power. Although this particular American theory of social stratification is regarded as three-dimensional, the social dimension (i.e., status stratification) is usually accorded primacy. The other significant point is that the concept of power becomes a mere internal dimension of social stratification, relegated to a place next to class and status. 'Power' is deemed to be synonymous with 'party'. That is to say, 'power' is confined to the 'political' dimension. But 'party' and 'power', as should be clear from the mere words themselves, do not signify the same thing. It transpires that it is not at all obvious how Weber's differentiation between classes, status groups and parties as phenomena of the distribution of power came to be transposed into class, status and power.[11]

It is my contention that Talcott Parsons laid the theoretical foundation for the misappropriation of Weber's understanding of classes, status groups and parties as phenomena of the distribution of power within much of the American sociology of social stratification. In 1940 Parsons published an essay entitled: 'An Analytical Approach to the Theory of Social Stratification' (1954a, pp.69-88). In 1953 he published a revised version of the 1940 essay. The title of the 1953 essay is: 'A Revised Analytical Approach to the Theory of Social Stratification' (1954b, pp.386-439).[12]

The 1953 essay begins with the general point that 'social stratification is a generalized aspect of the structure of all social systems...' (1954b, p.386). Parsons continues that:

> ...it is a condition of the stability of social systems that there should be an integration of the value-standards of the component units to constitute a 'common value-system'. (1954b, p.388)

Moreover, stratification in its valuational aspect amounts to 'the ranking of units in a social system in accordance with the standards of the common value system' (1954b, p.386). Hence, the fundamental aspects of a stratification system, in Parsons' view, hinge on the interplay between common values and ranking. It is important to emphasize here that what actors in a social system evaluate relative to one another is not the whole actor as a unit, but rather specific properties of actors.[13] The three properties which serve as criteria of evaluation are: 'qualities', 'performances' and 'possessions' (see Parsons 1954a, pp.389-90). 'Qualities' are properties ascribed to the actor as such, 'performances' refer to the things an actor does in contradistinction to what he is, and 'possessions' are situational, transferable objects.

Concerning the problem of deciding which of the three possible bases of ranking is the fundamental factor underlying evaluation in any particular society, the answer, according to Parsons, lies in the actors' shared values in a social system. However, Parsons goes on to claim that the complementarity of social ranking and the value system is possible only in a fully integrated social system. Since such a system does not exist, he felt obliged to reformulate this theorem somewhat more realistically by distinguishing between 'the normatively defined "ideal" ranking order' and 'the actual state of affairs' (1954b, p.391). The discrepancy between these two aspects is accounted for by the phenomenon of power.

Interestingly enough, Parsons in this instance defines power in a way that closely resembles Weber's conception. Power is 'the realistic capacity of a system unit to actualize its "interests"...' (1954b, p.391).[14] To be more precise, power arises from three sets of factors: the valuation of a system unit according to the standards of the common value system, the feasibility of enforcing those standards without the use of sanctions, and the control of possessions. Parsons' argument that power arises from the control of possessions, normative valuation and the enforcement of a standard, brings to mind Weber's conception of classes, status groups and parties as phenomena of the distribution of power.

The difficulty, though, is that Parsons quickly alters his line of reasoning. He contends that two factors of power, namely the control of possessions and the enforcement of a standard, concern deviations from the assumption of the equilibrium model of the social system. Certainly, these two factors of power are very important from an 'empirical' standpoint, but they do not entail any basic modification of the equilibrium model. This being so, Parsons declares that 'analysis should focus on the common value-pattern aspect' (1954b, p.393). Social ranking in the social system should now take place solely against the backcloth of a common value system.

In this light, it is not surprising to find Parsons later reformulating his notion of power by equating power and authority. This identification of power and authority is presented in Parsons' essay entitled: 'On the Concept of Political Power' (1967, pp.240-65). He affirms that power:

...is generalized capacity to secure the performance of binding obligations by units in a system of collective organization when the obligations are legitimized with reference to their bearing on collective goals... (1967, p.244)

Power no longer serves partisan goals. Parsons goes so far as to say that 'the threat of coercive measures, or of compulsion, without legitimation or justification, should not properly be called the use of power at all...' (1967, p.254).

I would argue, then, that the emergence of two fundamental traits of the American misappropriation of Weber's rendering of social stratification can be detected in Parsons' writings on social stratification. Firstly, Parsons highlights the importance of social ranking in terms of a common value system. The institutionalization of relations of inequality of status 'constitutes an essential aspect in the solution of the problem of order in social systems through the legitimation of essential inequalities...' (Parsons 1977, p.327). Secondly, Parsons' study of social stratification testifies to the beginning of a shift away from Weber's idea relating to classes, status groups and parties as bases of the aggregation of power towards authority in the sense of power restricted exclusively to the political dimension.

One final important ramification that can be teased out of Weber's definition of power bears on the significance of resistance. Weber says that power is the chance to realize one's will 'even against the resistance of others' (1978a, p.926). The inference is that resistance need not necessarily be part of every power relationship.[15] Weber's use of the term 'even' does not mean, though, that the presence or absence of resistance is irrelevant for an understanding of differential capacities in a power relation. Weber later defines power as the probability of enforcing one's will 'despite resistance' (1978a, p.53). The use of the term 'despite' resistance rather than 'even against' resistance indicates, as Barbalet pointedly remarks:

> ...not merely that resistance may or may not be empirically present, but provides a further crucial dimension to the argument, namely, that (in the presence of resistance) power only exists when the resistance of others is overcome. (1985a, p.534)

In effect, Weber's later definition of power implies that power is not just the carrying out of one's will in the presence or absence of resistance, but the carrying out of one's will 'in spite of' resistance. The crucial point for Weber is 'not' that resistance is a necessary precondition for the existence of all power relations, but that the subjugation of resistance, if present, is an essential feature of these relations.[16] In view of Weber's insistence on the significance of resistance for an understanding of any power situation, it is clear that 'power' and 'resistance' are what Barbalet regards as *distinct but interdependent aspects* of ... the power relation' (1985a, p.535; emphasis added). 'Resistance' constitutes the irreducible counterpart of 'power' in the power relationship. Quite simply, 'power' and 'resistance' are complementary concepts.

The contemporary French philosopher, Michel Foucault, has developed an understanding of the irreducible role of resistance in the analysis of power relations which is somewhat similar to Weber's view. Foucault maintains that:

> Every power relationship implies, at least *in potentia*, a strategy of struggle, in which the two forces are not superimposed, do not lose their *specific* nature, or do not finally become confused. (1982, p.794, emphasis added; see also 1977a, pp.218-33)

Resistance is the 'irreducible opposite' of power in the power relation (Foucault 1981a, p.96). There is no power without the possibility of resistance/revolt. If some individuals can completely determine others' conduct, those subject to absolute subordination are, according to Foucault, not human agents at all. Rather, 'without the possibility of recalcitrance, power would be equivalent to a *physical determination*' (1982, p.790, emphasis added; see also 1981b, pp.5-9; 1981c, p.253). Foucault perceives revolt/opposition against power as 'freedom's refusal to submit' (1982, p.790). Resistance corroborates the fact that power is exercized over individuals as 'free agents' rather than 'inanimate objects'. Besides, 'free agents' must exist for power to be wielded at all. For Foucault, then, power relations comprise 'an above' and 'a below' (1980, p.201). Power and resistance are two forms of potential influence in a power relation.[17]

Given Foucault's espousal of the 'specific nature' (1982, p.792) of both 'power' and 'resistance', the crux of the problem is that his writings also support the contrary view, that is, the constitution of resistance by power itself. Foucault declares that:

> Where there is power, there is resistance, and yet, or rather consequently, *this resistance is never in a position of exteriority in relation to power ...* one is always 'inside' power, there is no 'escaping' it, there is no absolute outside where it is concerned... (1981a, p.95, emphasis added; see also 1977b, p.160)

Foucault is now arguing that resistance has no independent foundation. It is no longer power's irreducible counterpart. To the contrary, resistance is now coextensive with power. Power is '"always already there"...' (Foucault 1980, p.141). Power 'produces' resistance. One is never 'outside' power. Resistance 'from below' is constituted as resistance by the very effect of power. It is ensnared by power. Seen in this light, it is obvious that Foucault's inclusion of resistance in the power relation is a strictly gratuitous assertion. At this point in the discussion, it is only necessary to indicate that although Weber gives an irreducible role to resistance in the power relationship, its inclusion is likewise a strictly unwarranted assertion. Resistance 'from below' has no independent, sociological reality in such a relationship.

One final issue regarding the inclusion of resistance in Weber's definition of power must be broached. Some interpreters within the Weberian tradition allege that power is discernible only when resistance is overcome. This leads to an overemphasis on overt conflict.[18] In their endeavour to develop an operational concept of power, Pluralists, for example, concentrate on decision-making procedures. Decisions involve observable behaviour. More to the point, these decisions involve 'overt', that is, observable conflict. Visible conflict is built into the Pluralist idea of power. In this regard, Polsby affirms that who prevails in decision-making:

> ...seems the best way to determine which individuals and groups have 'more' power in social life, because *direct conflict between actors* presents a situation

most closely approximating an experimental test of their capacities to affect outcomes. (1980, p.4; emphasis added)

Therefore, the power of A over B is determined by the amount of opposition by B which can potentially be crushed by A.[19] The end-result of the Pluralist line of reasoning is that a power situation cannot be identified where there is no visible conflict.

But Weber's crucial point is that resistance can take many diverse forms. It is not confined to manifest conflict. As a matter of fact, Weber speaks of state agencies using their legitimate power 'against internal resistance in both *war* and *peace*' (1949, p.46; emphasis added). What is more, conflict itself cannot be simply equated with overt conflict. Weber writes that:

A social relationship will be referred to as 'conflict' insofar as action is oriented intentionally to carrying out the actor's own will *against the resistance* of the other party or parties. (1978a, p.38, emphasis added; see also 1981a, p.173)

Resistance is built into Weber's conception of conflict. And since resistance can take different forms, Weber believes that conflict likewise can manifest itself in varied forms. He, for instance, says that 'peace is nothing more than a change in the form of conflict...' (1949, p.27).[20] In this instance, the absence of observable conflict is not symptomatic of complete social harmony. Indeed, I would argue that submission can often be charged with great hostility.

3.2 Domination

Weber's definition of power (*Macht*) paved the way for his definition of domination (*Herrschaft*). For Weber, 'the concept of power is sociologically amorphous' (1978a, p.53). So Weber goes on to recommend its replacement with the 'more precise' concept of domination (1978a, p.53). Domination is a more refined and restricted concept than power because all uses of power do not qualify as domination. As Roth puts it, 'domination transforms amorphous and intermittent social action into persistent association' (1978, p.1xxxix).

The first issue that must be considered is the controversy surrounding the translation of *Herrschaft*.[21] Several authors translate *Herrschaft* as 'authority', 'rule' or use some other similar term. In view of the fact that Parsons' writings, for example, are based upon his treatment of the problem of order in terms of common values, there is a propensity to read this into Weber's analysis of *Herrschaft*. *Herrschaft* is translated by Parsons as 'authority' (1949, p.656) or 'leadership' (1960, p.752). According to Parsons, the translation of *Herrschaft* as 'domination' suggests that a leader has power 'over' his followers, when 'the integration of the collectivity, in the interest of effective functioning ... is the critical factor from Weber's point of view' (1960, p.752).[22] But Weber admonishes against this type of reasoning. He asserts, as already indicated, that the 'functional frame of reference is convenient for purposes of practical illustration and for provisional orientation' (1978a, p.15).[23] Like Parsons, Clegg (1975, p.59) submits that the confusion surrounding the meaning of the concepts, *Macht* and *Herrschaft*, diminishes when *Herrschaft* is translated as 'rule'. Parkin suggests that domination for Weber is simply another way of speaking of 'legitimate authority' (1982, p.75). A positive commitment on the part of the subordinates to the authority they obey is a most important feature of domination.[24] Other interpreters of Weber such as Bendix (1966), Dahrendorf (1959) and Roth and Wittich in their translation of *Economy and Society* (Weber 1978a), alternate between 'authority' and 'domination' in rendering *Herrschaft*. And yet other interpreters translate *Herrschaft* as 'domination'.[25] This thorny problem of translating Weber's concept of *Herrschaft* is solved, when the fact that Weber found it necessary to speak of *legitime Herrschaft* as a special case of *Herrschaft* is taken into account. The use of *legitime Herrschaft* bears out the fact that *Herrschaft per se* cannot be used interchangeably with 'authority'. In sum, then, Weber's concept of 'power' (*Macht*) covers a wider framework than 'domination' (*Herrschaft*) which, in turn, is a broader term than 'authority' (*legitime Herrschaft*).[26]

How does Weber, then, perceive the ideal-typical concept of domination? In the earlier Part II of *Economy and Society*, Weber makes clear that domination constitutes 'a special case of power' (1978a, p.941; see also pp.942-55).[27] Domination in the quite general sense of power can emerge in the most diverse forms. It can:

>...emerge from the social relations in a drawing room as well as in the market, from the rostrum of a lecture-hall as well as from the command post of a regiment, from an erotic or charitable relationship as well as from scholarly discussion or athletics. (Weber 1978a, p.943)

Such a broad definition, however, is scientifically useless. Therefore, Weber goes on to suggest that there are two major contrasting ideal-types of domination: domination by virtue of a constellation of interests and domination by virtue of authority. The purest case of the former is what Weber calls 'monopolistic domination in the market' (1978a, p.943). The purest case of the latter is 'patriarchal, magisterial, or princely power' (ibid.).[28] Weber continues that the first ideal-type of domination in its purest form, is grounded in influence derived solely from 'the possession of goods or marketable skills' (ibid.). The second ideal-type in its purest form, originates from an 'alleged absolute duty to obey, regardless of personal motives or interests' (ibid.). Weber (1978a, p.946), indeed, suggests that because of the very absence of rules, domination which arises in the market or as a result of some other association of interests, may be regarded as much more oppressive than an authority in which the duties of obedience are clearly established.

When Weber makes the distinction between two main ideal-types of domination (i.e., the special cases of power), he is pointing to the existence of different resources that can be drawn upon in the exercize of domination: possession (in the main, of goods and marketable skills) and authority. In contradistinction to his voluntarist conception of power, Weber is not in this instance expounding a voluntarist notion of domination. Rather, he is pointing to the significance of prime resources in society. These resources cannot simply be understood in terms of social actors having goods, marketable skills, authority and so on. To the contrary, the pre-existing social structure (e.g., the modern capitalist market-economy, the feudal estate order) dictates what resources are at the disposal of different categories of social actors (e.g., capitalists and wage-labourers, knights and mediaeval peasants).[29] Seen in this light, the dominating actors (individual or collective) in a particular society can be conceptualized as those who stand in a favourable relationship to the prime resources of that society (e.g., private property in the modern capitalist market-economy, social honour in the feudal estate order). The dominating actors are already in a structural power situation which, then, enables them to dominate others less favourably placed in relation to society's prime resources.

In the last resort, however, the borderline between the two ideal-types of domination is not well-defined by Weber. He argues that 'any type of domination by virtue of constellation of interests may, however, be transformed gradually into domination by authority' (1978a, p.943). This is especially relevant in the case of domination originally based on some kind of monopoly. Weber goes on to exclude domination arising from the aggregation of interests from his typology of domination. He, then, uses the term domination only in the sense of 'authoritarian power of command':

> To be more specific, *domination* will thus mean the situation in which the manifested will (*command*) of the *ruler* or rulers is meant to influence the conduct of one or more others (*the ruled*) and actually does influence it in such a way that their conduct to a socially relevant degree occurs as if the ruled had made the content of the command the maxim of their conduct for its own sake. Looked upon from the other end, this situation will be called *obedience*. (1978a, p.946; emphasis in original)

According to Weber, this is the only 'usable concept of domination' (1978a, p.948). The heart of this definition lies in its capacity to make the ruled internalize the will of the ruler as though it were their own. Or as Luhmann succinctly puts it, 'a person who exercises domination has the opportunity to make his ends the ends of others' (1982, p.23). Later in the conceptual exposition of *Economy and Society*, Weber defines domination as 'the probability that a command with a given specific content will be obeyed by a given group of persons' (1978a, p.53; see also p.212). Weber in this instance is stating that it is 'probable' that a ruler

80

will be able to enforce his commands, not that it will necessarily follow. To anticipate a later discussion, the probability of commands being obeyed is very much dependent on the nature of the discipline to which the ruled are subject.

After having defined domination in terms of 'authoritarian power of command' (i.e., 'legitimate domination'), Weber goes on to present a typology of *legitime Herrschaft* (see 1978a, pp.212-301, 954; 1970, pp.295-8).[30] The three ideal-types of legitimate domination/authority are: legal-rational domination, traditional domination and charismatic domination. These ideal-types depend on the previous classification of the corresponding ideal-types of social action, which in turn are predicated on the presence or absence of purposive rationality. Purposive-rational action oriented towards means and ends being rationally taken into account and assessed, grounds legal-rational domination which finds its purest expression in modern bureaucracy.[31] Traditional action referring to behaviour determined by ingrained habituation, underpins traditional domination which finds its typical expression in patriarchalism and patrimonialism. Affectual action involving behaviour determined by the actor's specific aggregation of affects, grounds charismatic domination which finds its typical expression in a charismatic structure of domination. The charismatic structure of domination is constituted by the personal retainers or disciples of the charismatic ruler.

As regards value-rational action, certain interpreters maintain that a corresponding type of legitimate domination is missing in Weber's typology. Willer (1967, p.235) suggests that value-rational action dealing with activity guided by a conscious belief in the value for its own sake, underlies 'ideological authority'. Similarly, Spencer (1970, pp.123-34) introduces the concept of 'value-rational authority' to fill the apparent Weberian gap.

Of particular relevance in this context is Weber's stipulation that legal-rational authority is dependent upon the acceptance of the idea that:

> ...any given legal norm may be established by *agreement* or by *imposition*, on grounds of *expediency* or *value-rationality* or both, with a claim to obedience at least on the part of the members of the organization. (1978a, p.217, emphasis added; see also pp.36, 218; 1970, p.294)

It is Weber's contention that any given legal norm can be considered legitimate by virtue of mutual agreement among the relevant parties, or by virtue of promulgation by an authority which is regarded as legitimate. Furthermore, the relevant legal norm can be legitimized in instrumental or value-rational terms.

Weber's point that any legal norm 'may be established by agreement' raises a fundamental question. Is Weber claiming here that individuals can come together and create a shared system of legal norms by dint of mutual consensus? But such a standpoint would be diametrically opposed to Weber's idea of 'the social' as merely the interplay of self-seeking interests among impeccably rational actors. Within the Weberian action framework an orientation towards 'others' is regarded as necessary by the rational actor only as a 'means' for the attainment of his own goals. Moreover, I would argue that the notion of a shared system of legal norms is opposed to Weber's epistemological standpoint concerning the incessant struggles between different values. To reiterate, a collective value-system achieved by way of a rationally arrived-at public consensus is, on Weber's reading, an impossibility. Given both Weber's rendition of social action and interminable value-conflict, he is unable, for instance, to conceptualize a co-operative, democratic society in which social agents could collectively reach a rational consensus. Such a society is deemed *a priori* impossible.[32]

Another pertinent point is Weber's statement that:

> Today the most common form of legitimacy is the belief in legality, the compliance with enactments which are *formally* correct and which have been made in the accustomed manner. In this respect, the distinction between an order derived from voluntary agreement and one which has been imposed is only relative. For so far as the agreement underlying the order is not unanimous, as in the past has often been held necessary for complete legitimacy, the order is actually imposed upon the minority... (1978a, p.37; emphasis in original)

Quite simply, Weber acknowledges here that belief in the legality of a procedure produces legitimacy in modern society. Legalism is the basis on which a claim to obedience is made. Weber envisages a purely expediently statuted order which is deemed legitimate simply by reason of positive statutes being decreed by some agency accepted as legitimate. More particularly, Weber sees laws being authorized 'from above' through what Habermas aptly calls 'the imposition of a powerful will' (1984a, p.266), that is, through enforcement by a legitimately valid ruler.[33] Or as Weber puts it, 'an order is always "imposed" to the extent that it does not originate from a voluntary personal agreement of all the individuals concerned' (1978a, p.51). But even when a majority of individuals acquiesce in a certain social order, this order is still imposed on the minority. This minority has no alternative but to capitulate.

With regard to Weber's other major point, namely, that legal-rational authority is dependent upon the idea 'that any given legal norm may be established ... on grounds of expediency or value-rationality or both' (1978a, p.217), it is important to remember Weber's observation that value-rational action may have 'various different relations' (1978a, p.26) to means-end rational action. On this score too, Barker's (1980, pp.224-45) and Albrow's (1972, pp.483-7) claim that Weber was logically constrained to exclude value-rationality from his ideal-types of legitimate domination because value-rationality entails acting freely, must be examined. Granted, it is Weber's view that one can be regarded as a free, autonomous individual, only when one's actions are rationally consistent with ultimate values. Value-orientations, for instance, are at the very core of the heroic personality.[34] However, as previously indicated, value-rational action itself may require instrumentally rational action for the actualization of values. An heroic personality like the charismatic leader in the German nation-state, uses the electoral masses as a means for the imposition of his values. Contrary to Barker's and Albrow's claim, then, commanding others may be the precondition that facilitates the free individual to commit himself to certain ultimate values. In light of the general impetus of the discussion so far, it is valid to argue that Weber was logically bound to ground legal-rational domination in both purposive- and value-rationality.[35]

Taking account of the fact that legal-rational domination can be rooted in purposive- or value-rationality or both, Weber nonetheless recognizes that the process of rationalization is proceeding 'in favor of a morally sceptical type of rationality, at the expense of any belief in absolute values' (1978a, p.30). Purposive-rationality is historically advancing at the expense of value-rationality. This means, of course, that legal-rational domination is no longer dependent upon the idea that any given legal norm may be grounded in value-rationality. Of particular relevance is that 'the purest type of legitimacy based on value-rationality is *natural law*' (Weber 1978a, p.37; emphasis in original). Because of the inexorable onslaught of purposive-rationality, natural law is, on Weber's interpretation, irrelevant in modern capitalist society. Weber also points out that the natural law doctrine was destroyed by what he calls: 'the evolutionary dogmatism of Marxism', 'the Comtean evolutionary scheme', 'historicist theories of organic growth', and '*Realpolitik*' (1978a, p.874). In fine, then, Weber is historically bound to exclude value-rationality as an adequate foundation for legal-rational domination in modern society.

3.3 Discipline

Weber first introduces the concept of discipline in the chapter on 'Charisma and Its Transformation' in the earlier Part II of *Economy and Society* (1978a, pp.1148-57). In the later Part I of *Economy and Society*, discipline is introduced immediately after the definition of domination.[36] Weber declares that:

> 'Discipline' is the probability that by virtue of habituation a command will receive *prompt and automatic obedience in stereotyped forms*, on the part of a given group of persons. (1978a, p.53, emphasis added; see also p.1149)

Discipline is the *sine qua non* of domination. That is to say, domination needs discipline—because the probability that a certain command will be obeyed is contingent upon 'prompt and automatic obedience' on behalf of a given group of persons.

It is obvious that obedience is a key concept in Weber's rendering of domination and discipline. Weber avers that:

83

'Obedience' will be taken to mean that the action of the person obeying follows in essentials such a course that *the content of the command may be taken to have become the basis of action for its own sake.* Furthermore, the fact that it is so taken is referable only to the formal obligation, without regard to the actor's own attitude to the value or lack of value of the content of the command as such. (1978a, p.215; emphasis added)

To obey is to become the instrument of another's will. To obey is to be treated merely as a means. When an individual obeys, he relinquishes the capacity to act on his own motives and intentions. The disciplined individual, on Weber's reading, behaves rather than acts, because his conduct is devoid of subjective meaning. That is, his conduct does not involve purposeful action whereby means and ends are rationally taken into account and appraized. The disciplined individual internalizes the ends of the commanding individual. He 'is unswervingly and exclusively set for carrying out the command' (Weber 1978a, p.1149). The conduct of the disciplined individual is essentially irrational, habitual, unreflecting and unresisting. Within a Weberian framework it is only the individual equipped with authoritarian power of command who acts. The precondition of social action is the imposition of one's will on disciplined others.

In light of the aforesaid, it might appear that the disciplined individual is solely 'conditioned to obedience...' (Weber 1970, p.80). However, Weber's definition of discipline mentions that it is the probability that, by reason of habituation, a command will receive 'prompt and automatic obedience' (1978a, p.53). It does not of necessity follow that a command will be obeyed. Obedience is not, in fact, inevitable. The inference is that although we live in a disciplinary society, individuals are never totally programmed to submit to orders.

Another issue of paramount importance concerns Weber's distinction between the nature of discipline under traditional and legal-rational domination. Regarding the nature of discipline in feudal society in the West where traditional relations of domination prevailed, Weber writes that:

The discipline of the manor of the Middle Ages and the modern area was considerably less strict because it was *traditionally stereotyped,* and therefore it somewhat limited the lord's power. (1978a, p.1156; emphasis added)

Custom and tradition restricted the lord's capacity to compel the serf, for example, to submit to his commands. In a somewhat similar vein, Tocqueville remarks that in a traditional society 'military discipline is nothing but an enhancement of social servitude' (1954, p.295).

In modern society discipline is, according to Weber, rational. Discipline relies upon the obedience of a plurality of individuals being 'rationally uniform' (1978a, p.1149). For instance, 'organizational discipline in the factory has a completely rational basis' (Weber 1978a, p.1156). Mass discipline is decisive if a command is to be successfully executed. Moreover, discipline is 'impersonal' (Weber 1978a, p.1149). The disciplined individual is trained 'exclusively for submission under the disciplinary code' (ibid.). The fact that the obligation to obey is justified by reference to a 'disciplinary code', corroborates the notably close relation between legal-rational domination and rational discipline. In the case of legal-rational domination, legal norms regulate the relationship of command and submission. The reason for the disciplined individual's capitulation to a command is not, as in the case of charismatic authority, the extraordinary quality of the person issuing the command. Weber purports that:

> Discipline puts the drill for the sake of habitual, routinized skill in place of heroic ecstasy, loyalty, spirited enthusiasm for a leader and personal devotion to him, the cult of honor, or the cultivation of personal fitness as an art. (1978a, p.1149)

Bureaucracy represents the 'most rational offspring' (Weber 1978a, p.1149) of discipline in modern society.

Of primary significance also is Weber's understanding of the historical origins of the disciplined individual in modern society. Weber concentrates on 'internal discipline' (1978a, p.1149). In addition to cultural and societal rationalization, Weber analyzes the process of rationalization at the level of the personality system. In other words, he studies the origins of the methodical conduct of life which is an essential feature of the modern capitalist market-economy and the modern nation-state.

The emergence of a methodically disciplined life points to a major transformation in the individual psyche. An internal process of regulation occurs. This internal process of regulation was brought about in the Occident by Christian asceticism, that is, first of all by monastic asceticism and later by Protestant asceticism. According to Weber, monastic and Protestant asceticism:

> ...converge in the *method of exercise* (this is finally the meaning of the word 'asceticism')—a stringent use of time, work, and silence as a means of suppressing instinctual urges. (1978c, p.1121, emphasis added; see also 1976a, pp.118-28, 155-83; 1978a, pp.1168-70; 1981b, pp.352-69)

Christian asceticism originated a systematic method of rational conduct with the purpose of subjecting the individual 'to the supremacy of a purposeful will, to bring his actions under constant self-control with a careful consideration of their ethical consequences' (Weber 1976a, p.119). The aim is complete control over the self and natural drives, since these prevent union with God. Weber argues that in the Middle Ages the monk was the first human being who lived rationally, who worked methodically and, hence by rational means, aimed to attain a goal, namely, the future life.[37] The later emergence of rational Protestant asceticism differs, on Weber's reading, from monastic asceticism in three ways: it rejects all irrational, ascetic practices,[38] contemplation is renounced and, finally, the exercize of asceticism is guided towards an inner-worldly conduct of life in the family and in one's occupation (Weber 1978c, p.1122).

Another important ramification of the emergence of Protestant asceticism during the Reformation, on Weber's account, lies in the fact that it was no longer only the monk who lived methodically. Rather, 'every Christian had to be a monk all his life' (Weber 1976a, p.121)—because 'asceticism was carried out of monastic cells into everyday life...' (Weber 1976a, p.181; see also pp.155-83). Put more precisely, the exercize of asceticism in everyday life takes the form of rational labour in a calling. The diligence and method with which the individual pursues his calling provides proof of his state of grace. Continuous, systematic labour in a worldly calling is an exercize in ascetic virtue. If the accumulation of wealth is, for example, the end-product of this practice of methodical self-control in a calling, it is a sign of God's blessing. For Weber, then, the end-result of the psychic self-disciplining of the individual brought about in the Occident through Christian asceticism—was that 'the moral conduct of the average man was thus deprived of its planless and unsystematic character and subjected to a consistent method for conduct as a whole' (1976a, p.117).[39]

This internal process of regulation was in conformity with the emergence of modern rational capitalism. Psychic self-disciplining in the form of religious asceticism, for instance, provided the capitalist entrepreneur with 'sober, conscientious, and unusually industrious workmen' (Weber 1976a, p.177). In this context, the probability that the entrepreneur's commands would be obeyed by the disciplined labourers in the modern capitalist factory was high. Moreover, Weber argues that the process of psychic self-disciplining plays an important role in the charismatic leader's efforts to tame the electoral masses into submission in a modern democracy.

As a matter of fact, Weber can be seen as the forerunner of Foucault's conception of modern 'disciplinary society'.[40] It is Foucault's contention that modern man lives in a society of disciplined surveillance. Foucault takes Bentham's Panopticon as the symbol of the general form of power in modern society, that is, 'disciplinary power' (see Foucault 1979, 1980, 1981a).[41] He purports that Panoptism 'was a technological invention in the order of power, comparable with the steam engine in the order of production' (1980, p.71). Beginning at the end of the eighteenth century, modern power developed only slowly in local, piecemeal fashion in what Foucault calls 'disciplinary institutions' (e.g., prisons, hospitals and schools). In the nineteenth century closed disciplinary institutions perfected a variety of methods and devices for the fabrication and subjugation of individuals as epistemic objects and as targets of power. These devices included the keeping of files and the utilization of capillary agents like social scientists and technocrats for the collection of detailed knowledge about every individual. The authorities within the prison system, for instance, aimed at the reshaping of deviants as functional and docile bodies to be reinserted into the social machine (i.e., society). Disciplinary power, on Foucault's interpretation, replaces violence and force with the more subtle constraint of continuous visibility. This form of power is less barbarous in its investment of the body. Disciplinary power is a machine, the function of which is that of the anonymous and continuous exercize of power. In accordance with Weber, Foucault sums up the vital importance of discipline in modern society when he says that:

> *The deliberate attitude of modernity is tied to an indispensable asceticism.* To be modern is not to accept oneself as one is in the flux of the passing moments; it is to take oneself as object of a complex and difficult elaboration... (1984, p.41; emphasis added)

3.4 Domination and discipline: implications

In the light of my examination of Weber's concepts of domination and discipline in the preceding two sections, some important implications can be unravelled. To begin with, Weber is often criticized for being solely concerned with legitimate domination at the expense of the hard realities of violence, coercion, force and so on. For example, Hirst's reading of Weber is such that 'domination, to be social, must rest upon subjectively meaningful conditions of compliance and not external brute force which merely compels certain behaviours' (1976a, p.81). In a similar vein, Beetham (1974, p.259) declares that Weber's political writings are concerned with power, struggle and conflict, whereas Weber concentrates on the concept of legitimacy in his sociology of domination contained in *Economy and Society*. The category of order, it is argued, is primordial in the sociology of domination.[42]

Bearing in mind these criticisms, it is of overriding importance to stress the ideal-typical nature of Weber's concepts of domination (*Herrschaft*) and legitimate domination (*legitime Herrschaft*). It is incorrect to interpret Weber's ideal-types in empirical terms. It will be recalled that an ideal-type is a synthetic construct which aims not to reproduce reality but rather mental constructs. The expression mental construct is exceedingly important because the ideal-type relates to a thought or idea, in principle, embodied in reality. The ideal-type is a one-sided viewpoint which clarifies the aspects of reality with which it can be compared. With respect to the ideal-types of legitimate domination, Weber proclaims that 'the sociological character of domination will differ according to the basic differences in the major modes of legitimation' (1978a, p.947). Weber is stating that the ideal-types of legitimate domination are differentiated on those grounds upon which are based the claims to obedience advanced by the ruler. The cogency of the claims to legitimacy made by the ruler may be based on rational grounds, traditional grounds or charismatic grounds (see Weber 1978a, pp.215-6, 954).

Since the crucial factor for establishing the validity of any relationship of legitimate domination is the variety of claims put forward by the ruler, it follows that the motivations for obedience on the part of the ruled simply emulate the claims to legitimacy proffered by the ruler. On this score, a basic aspect of a stable relationship of authority is the belief of the ruled in the legitimacy of the rule of the ruler. The merely external fact of a command being obeyed is not, in Weber's view, adequate to indicate the existence of a relationship of authority (1978a, p.946). Quite the contrary. Every system of legitimate domination 'attempts to establish and to cultivate the belief in its legitimacy' (Weber 1978a, p.213). In short, then, Weber constructs the ideal-types of legitimate domination in such a fashion that the basis of legal-rational, traditional and charismatic domination and, concomitantly, of every kind of willingness to obey—'is a belief, a *belief* by virtue of which persons exercising authority are lent prestige' (Weber 1978a, p.263; emphasis in original).

Besides the importance of a belief in legitimacy, another related point is that those who draw upon economic, social and political resources in the course of issuing commands, have the greatest need to justify their procurement and possession of these resources. In this connection, Weber declares that:

> For a domination, this kind of justification of its legitimacy is much more than a matter of theoretical or philosophical speculation; it rather constitutes the basis of very real differences in the empirical structure of domination. The reason for this fact lies in the generally observable need of any power, or even of any advantage of life, to justify itself. (1978a, p.953)

The individuals and groups who stand in a favourable relationship to the prime resources of a given society, feel a need to regard their secured advantages as well-earned, as legitimate.[43] In other words, those who command have a craving for legitimacy. Weber also underlines the dire consequences that follow (i.e., from a ruler's standpoint), once the ruled no longer accept as legitimate the claims to obedience advanced by the rulers. In such a situation, 'that very myth of the highly privileged about everyone having desired his particular lot has often become one of the most passionately hated objects of attack...' (Weber 1978a, p.953). Interpreted in this light, the principles of legitimation have, indeed, very real consequences for the maintenance of any prevailing structure of domination.[44]

Weber goes so far as to say that a system of domination may be so completely safeguarded both by the 'community of interests' between the leader and his administrative staff, and by the helplessness of the subordinates, that 'it can afford to drop even the pretense of a claim to legitimacy' (1978a, p.214).[45] In such circumstances, the ruled have been totally conditioned to subservience.

Although the belief in legitimacy is incorporated into the ideal-types of legitimate domination, Weber acknowledges that in reality subordinates may yield to the imposition of orders for many different reasons. He stipulates that:

> In a concrete case the performance of the command may have been motivated by the ruled's own conviction of its propriety, or by his sense of duty, or by fear, or by 'dull' custom, or by a desire to obtain some benefit for himself. (1978a, pp.946-7; see also pp.38, 214, 312, 314-15, 1378; 1970, p.79)

Weber's apprehension of the ideal-types of legitimate domination does not mean that all the subordinates who in 'a concrete case' succumb to commands, are impelled by a belief in their validity. Rather, the motives for obedience in a relationship of legitimate domination can include: physical force, ingrained habituation, rational calculation of advantages, fear, a sense of duty and so forth.[46] Even though these empirical factors, on Weber's interpretation, 'are not decisive for the classification of types of domination' (1978a, p.214), they nonetheless constitute 'sociologically relevant behavior' (1978a, p.4). For the deviation of any concrete case from a relevant ideal-type warrants sociological investigation.

In this respect, the fact that Weber entitles the earlier Part II of *Economy and Society*, 'The Economy and the Arena of Normative and *De facto* Powers', is especially relevant (1978a, pp.311-1372). '*De facto* powers' are precisely powers that are not 'legitimate', but are simply 'the way things are'.[47] The divergence of these '*de facto* powers' from the ideal-types of legitimate domination necessitates sociological exploration. Hence, Weber's concern with conflict, violence, physical force, unreflective habituation, fear and the like as motives for obedience. Indeed, subordinates obeying a ruler may not in many cases be aware of their reasons for complying with his commands. 'In such cases,' according to Weber, 'the sociologist must attempt to formulate the typical basis of validity' (1978a, p.38).

Weber also points out that a relationship regarded as legitimate may originally have been founded on coercion. He writes that:

> ...it is very common for minorities, by force or by the use of more ruthless and far-sighted methods, to impose an order which in the course of time comes to be regarded as legitimate by those who originally resisted it. (1978a, p.37)

Moreover, the fact that a relationship of legitimate domination may have originated in coercion bears out the precarious nature of this type of domination. Belief in the legitimacy of commands on the part of those who obey can, as Burger (1985, p.17) contends, signify an accommodation to an order over which they have little control.

Weber further amplifies the perilous nature of the belief in legitimacy when he refers to the insoluble and incessant conflict between the formal and substantive rationality of the law underlying the three ideal-types of legitimate domination (see Weber 1978a, pp.809-38, 865-900).[48] Within each structure of legitimate domination a struggle between formal and substantive principles of justice and between the individuals and groups committed to them, goes on interminably.

Under the system of legal-rational domination laws are regarded as legitimate if they have been enacted by the proper authorities on the basis of procedures which have the sanction of law (see Weber 1978a, pp.217-26). Legal-rational domination, it is true, is sustained by a belief in formal legality, but ideas of equity and justice intervene frequently to modify this formalism. And by the same token, formal procedures modify equity and justice (cf. Weber 1978a, pp.880-900). In the modern capitalist market-economy, for instance, the class demands of the working class grounded in such ethical postulates as justice and human dignity are utterly opposed to formal principles of justice advocated by legal experts, bureaucratic officials and so forth.

Similarly, under the system of traditional domination (e.g., Western feudalism) the ruler's exercize of authority is fixed by immemorial custom (see Weber 1978a, pp.226-41). This leads to the establishment of traditional law with objective norms. The interest of the ruler and the subjects, however, remains focused on the content of the norms. Their basic orientation is substantive, not formal. Yet, there is room for considerable conflict within this basic orientation, depending on whether a ruler is prone towards an arbitrary exercize of his will, or tends more towards a stereotyped form of traditional order. Essentially, Weber observes that 'the exercise of power is oriented towards the consideration of how far master and staff can go in view of the subjects' traditional compliance without arousing their resistance' (1978a, p.227). If the ruler, then, is predisposed towards an arbitrary exercize of his will, he attempts to minimize traditional limitations in favour of his discretionary powers. In such circumstances the ruler may have to deal with calls for substantive justice on behalf of his subjects, who can claim that their customary rights are being infringed upon. If, on the other hand, the rulership tends towards strictly upholding the traditional order, this will favour the formal traditional limitations embodied in immemorial custom.

Finally, under the system of charismatic domination the ruler's exercize of authority is sustained by his disciples' belief in his magical or heroic powers (cf. Weber 1978a, pp.241-5). In contradistinction to legal and traditional domination based on enacted and traditional law respectively, charismatic domination, according to Weber, is grounded in revealed law. Although the legitimation of the leader's rule derives from revealed law, this is not tantamount to unlimited discretion. On the contrary, the charismatic ruler's followers time and again demand proof of his power through the performance of miracles or heroic deeds (i.e., substantive rationality). If the charismatic leader does not offer sufficient proof of his charismatic qualities, he may arouse the ire of his followers.

In the context of this discussion of the ideal-typical nature of Weber's concepts of legitimate domination, it is also important to remember that these three concepts are 'general', sociological ideal-types. Or as Bendix reasons, they 'refer to archetypes of human experience' (1966, p.389). With reference to the construction of the three ideal-types of legitimate domination, Weber affirms that:

> Its usefulness is derived from the fact that in a given case it is possible to distinguish what aspects of a given organized group can legitimately be identified as falling under or approximating one or another of these categories. (1978a, pp.263-4)

The fact that Weber elaborates his typology of the three ideal-types in the reverse order (i.e., legal-rational, traditional and charismatic), also confirms their 'general', sociological rather than 'individual', historical nature (1978a, pp.217-45). Moreover, Weber proclaims that 'the three basic types of domination cannot be placed into a simple evolutionary line: they in fact *appear together in the most diverse combinations*' (1978a, p.1133; emphasis added).[49] Let me hasten to add that Weber was not devising universal, analytical concepts to explicate all of social reality. The point especially pertinent here is that the ideal-types of legitimate domination reduce but do not eliminate context-dependency. 'General', sociological ideal-types gather data from as many historical periods and societies as possible. It is only in this sense that they are more abstract than 'individual', historical ideal-types.

In addition to the ideal-typical nature of the concepts of legitimate domination, another major implication relates to the ruler-centric component. The crucial issue is that Weber defines the ideal-types of legitimate domination in such a manner that he starts from the standpoint of the kind of legitimacy to which rulers appeal. Weber contends that:

> For our limited purposes, we shall emphasize those basic types of domination which result when we search for the ultimate grounds of the *validity* of domination, in other words, when we inquire into those grounds upon which there are based the claims of obedience made by the master against the 'officials' and of both against the ruled. (1978a, p.953, emphasis in original; see also p.214)

In effect, when characterizing the validity of a structure of domination, Weber concentrates on the bases of claims to legitimacy on the part of rulers at the expense of the 'bases of compliance' on the part of the ruled. To be sure, the 'belief in legitimacy' on the part of subordinates is built into Weber's ideal-types of legitimate domination. But as Merquior astutely observes, 'belief just mirrors on the side of the ruled, the ruler's claim to legitimacy' (1980, p.133; emphasis removed). Even when Weber lists other motives for obedience 'in a concrete case' (1978a, p.946), he still does not concern himself with how compliance on behalf of subordinates is actually accomplished.[50] Rather, Weber apprehends obedience in ruler-centric terms. Weber's sociology of domination is what Therborn correctly calls 'a sociology "from above"' (1980a, p.300). The heart of the matter concerns what form and to what extent obedience can be marshalled by those in command.

Furthermore, the validity of the particular claims to legitimacy 'helps to determine *the choice of means* of its exercise' (Weber 1978a, p.214; emphasis added). In this regard, Barbalet (1986a, p.13) underlines the fact that for Weber the validity of the claim to legitimacy is more important for providing the means to administer rule than it is to gain support from the ruled for the ruler and his staff. Indeed, Weber himself declares that 'we are primarily interested in "domination" in so far as it is combined with "administration"' (1978a, p.948).

When Weber mentions the relevance of the consent of the ruled at all for the maintenance of a relationship of legitimate domination, it is in a rather cynical way. Weber purports that:

> After all, a certain minimum of consent on the part of the ruled, at least of the socially important strata, is a precondition of the durability of every, even the best organized domination. (1978a, pp.1407-08)

In other words, Weber simply conceptualizes subordinates from a position of control. Acquiescence in the ruler's enforcement of orders on the part of the ruled, bestows a veneer of legitimacy on the relationship of domination.

Because Weber in a few instances refers to a relationship of legitimate domination as a 'meaningful interrelationship', Thomas (1984, p.239) maintains that Weber's understanding of domination is not, after all, distinguished by a ruler-centric bias. Weber himself writes that:

> *Herrschaft* (domination) does not mean that a superior elementary force asserts itself in one way or another; it refers to a *meaningful interrelationship* between those giving orders and those obeying, to the effect that the expectations towards which action is oriented on both sides can be reckoned upon... (1978a, p.1378, emphasis added; see also 1981a, p.168)

Given this statement, it is important to recall that the defining principle of a social relationship for Weber is that there must, at least, be a minimum of mutual orientation of each individual to that of other individuals. However, there need not be reciprocity or solidarity. Viewed in this light, the ruler and ruled in a relationship of legitimate domination are mutually oriented to each other. More pointedly, the ruler perceives his claim to legitimacy as 'meaningful'. And since the belief in legitimacy on the part of the ruled mirrors the ruler's claim for obedience (in the ideal case), it is of necessity also deemed 'meaningful'. In short, then, the rendering of a relationship of legitimate domination as 'meaningful', implies that there must at least be a minimum of mutual orientation of the activity of rulers and subordinate subjects.

The ruler-centric bias inherent in the ideal-types of legitimate domination is not peculiar to Weber alone. In fact, this predisposition to consider domination from a ruler's perspective has a long history in Western political thought. It is what

Foucault refers to as the 'juridical view of power'. The model of power prescribed by the juridico-philosophical thought of the sixteenth and seventeenth centuries, in Foucault's view, reduced the problem of power to that of sovereignity. In Western societies since mediaeval times, it is royal power that has provided the point of reference around which legal thought has been elaborated. 'Right in the West is the king's right' (Foucault 1980, p.94). When Foucault says that 'sovereignity' is the central problem of right in Western societies, what he at bottom means is that the function of the discourse and technique of right has been to conceal the domination intrinsic to power by regarding the latter as the legitimate rights of sovereignity and the legal obligation to obey it.

However, Foucault declares that right should not be viewed in terms of legitimacy, but in terms of the methods of subjugation that it instigates. Accordingly, Foucault's aim is to invert the discourse of right, 'to give due weight, that is, to the fact of domination, to expose both its latent nature and its brutality' (1980, p.95). In a word, Foucault expounds a 'microphysics of power' (what he also calls 'disciplinary power') to compensate for the ruler-centric bias embedded in the Western political tradition. He engages in an 'ascending' rather than a 'descending' analysis of power. Foucault argues that 'power comes from below, that is, there is no binary and all-encompassing opposition between rulers and ruled at the root of power relations...' (1981a, p.94). Foucault's two later books, *Discipline and Punish* (1979) and *The History of Sexuality* (Vol.I) (1981a), deal with local forms of power where it touches the very bodies of individuals. Modern power is 'capillary', it is at work in the lowest extremities of the social body in everyday social practices. Everyday life is pervaded by countless 'technologies of power' that rely on science, knowledge and discourses.

Granted, Weber also accentuates the central role of discipline in modern society. Unlike Foucault, though, Weber merely evaluates the role of discipline from a ruler's perspective, that is, from a position of control and advantage. He does not appraize discipline from the point of view of subordinate subjects, that is, from a position of a lack of control and disadvantage.

Although Foucault elucidates the decisive importance of disciplinary power for an understanding of the nature of power in modern society, this does not entail the total neglect of the well-established juridical view of power, as exemplified in Weber's sociology of domination. To the contrary, Foucault, like Weber, contends that 'sovereignity and disciplinary mechanisms are two absolutely integral constituents of the general mechanism of power in our society' (1980, p.108). 'Sovereignity' and 'discipline' complement each other. In fact, Foucault (1980, p.105) alleges that the notion of 'Right' has an ideological function in modern society, because it conceals the operation of disciplinary mechanisms and, hence, contributes to the further development of these mechanisms.

Finally, the place of resistance in Weber's sociology of domination must be broached. Taking account of the fact that domination 'constitutes a special case of power...' (Weber 1978a, p.941), it might be reasonably assumed that domination and resistance comprise two separate but interrelated phenomena within a relationship of legitimate domination/authority. However, it was stated earlier that Weber's inclusion of resistance in the power relationship is strictly unwarranted. Weber's inability to conceptualize resistance is built into the ideal-type of legal-rational domination.

To begin with, legal-rational domination is grounded in *zweckrational* action. It will be recalled that Weber's definition of *zweckrational* action is such that most individuals in modern society do not rationally assess means and ends; they do not act on their own motives. In view of the fact that the banal, irrational world of ordinary individuals is primarily governed by emotion and habit, it constitutes a social space where purposive-rational action has little significance. The other related point is that control is built into *zweckrational* action. Rational control of others (i.e., behaving individuals) is the most efficient tool at the disposal of the impeccably rational actor in his attempt to achieve his own egoistic goals. Interpreted in this light, it is obvious that a notion of resistance is written out of means-end rational action underpinning legal-rational domination. To act rationally is to control others. It is not possible to conceptualize individuals/groups countering the control of others within this Weberian action framework.

Another fundamental reason, I would suggest, for Weber's inability to integrate a concept of resistance into a relationship of legal-rational domination, lies in the fact that domination and discipline are distinct but interrelated aspects of such a relationship. In such a relationship subordinate subjects are conditioned to submission. To obey is to engage in reactive behaviour rather than act. Weber writes that discipline 'includes the habituation characteristic of *uncritical and unresisting mass obedience*' (1978a, p.53; emphasis added). In this regard, Hirst observes that the fact of obedience places the disciplined individual 'below the level of sociological recognition except as a means of action' (1976a, p.87). The ruled are sociologically relevant only to the extent that they can be wielded as tools by an acting individual like the ruler in the course of carrying out his commands. Quite simply, resistance 'from below' has no independent, sociological reality in a relationship of legal-rational domination, because such a relationship is very much viewed by Weber from the vantage point of sustaining it.[51]

The fact that the concept of resistance has no independent, sociological reality in a relationship of legal-rational domination, is also inextricably intertwined with Weber's rendition of value-freedom. Through the utilization of one's reason, it is possible to make logical deductions and establish empirical truths. Normative truths, however, cannot be rationally underpinned. Values, according to Weber, can only be posited subjectively. Objective reason is dismissed in the sphere of values. A critical judgement involving a normative evaluation of values is denied the status of scientific knowledge. In the context of Weber's sociology of domination, one cannot speak of a ruler making illegitimate or unjust demands on subordinate subjects. For, as Factor and Turner (1979, pp.329-30) correctly point out, Weber does not recognize the existence of any overarching rational principles of political morality that would support an allegation of the ruler's illegitimate or unjust demands.[52] Weber in the course of delineating his ideal-type of legal-rational domination, constructs a logical rather than a moral utopia. The normative correctness of this ideal-type is irrelevant. Weber is simply concerned with the legal-rational nature of legitimacy abstracted from its normative foundations.

Similarly, in the case of subordinate subjects in a relationship of legal-rational domination, no supervening, rational norms are available to them within a Weberian framework to justify resistance/opposition to the ruler's commands. Indeed, Weber's work reveals a profound anti-utopian scepticism in the sense that he is logically bound to exclude any possibility of transcending or going beyond the prevailing social order. In view of the scientific status of sociology, the sociologist cannot derive an ought from the empirical world. He concentrates solely on 'what is'.

But the pivotal point from an utopian vantage point is that the possibility of resisting/ opposing a ruler's commands in a certain social order is tenable, only if some preferable form of society can at least be envisaged. It must be feasible for the ruled to be guided by alternative normative claims/standards of legitimacy such as: inalienable human rights, equity and social justice. Or to use Parkin's (1972, pp.97-102) terminology, the development of a 'radical value system' is indispensable. This is a moral framework which fosters oppositional thinking. Normative claims/radical values have a practical function to the extent that they provide orientations from which the existing social order can be critically evaluated and opposed 'from below'. It is my contention, then, that resistance 'from below' (if it occurs at all) is equivalent to blind spontaneity, if rationally validated normative claims or alternative social images cannot be called forth. Or as Habermas pointedly remarks:

> People do not fight *for* abstractions, but *with* images. Banners, symbols and images, rhetorical speech, allegorical speech, utopia-inspired speech, in which concrete goals are conjured up before people's eyes, are indeed necessary constituents of movements which have any effect on history at all. Everything else, by comparison, is re-working and stasis. (1986a, p.146; emphasis in original)[53]

In accordance with Weber's treatment, I would contend that the concept of resistance has likewise no independent, sociological reality in Foucault's analysis of power relations. Foucault's abhorrence of disciplinary power in modern society is continually underscored by the use of phrases such as: 'the disciplinary society', 'the carceral archipelago', 'subjugation', 'domination', 'struggle' and so on. Foucault, for example, argues that theory 'involves *a struggle against the establishment* to force power and authority into the open and impair them where they are most visible and insidious' (1973, p.104; emphasis added). The difficulty, though, is that Foucault is unable to account for the normative, political judgements which he constantly makes. He (1980), for instance, rejects humanistic ideals like: commitment to the principles of human autonomy, human dignity and human rights. In other words, Foucault wants to simply concentrate on the way power actually operates in modern society. He gives a rich, empirical account of modern power practices.

In like manner, Foucault encourages resistance in concrete situations. He directs his attention to 'what enables people there, *on the spot*, to resist the Gulag...' (1980, p.136; emphasis added). But since Foucault rejects any normative framework, he ends up in the paradoxical situation of being unable to justify opposition 'on the spot' against disciplinary power. There must be some reason to validate resistance 'from below'. If subordinates revolt against disciplinary mechanisms in modern society, they must have some preferable form of social life in mind. Otherwise, opposition 'from below' is symptomatic of nothing more than blind activism. In fact, it does seem that Foucault, after all, recognizes the decisive importance of grounding resistance in some normative claims, because he continues to make tacit use of humanist principles. He concedes in the article, 'Is it Useless to Revolt?', that 'against power it is always necessary to oppose unbreakable law and unabridgeable rights' (1981b, p.8; see also 1974, p.161).

So far, I have argued that the concept of resistance has no independent, sociological reality in Weber's ideal-type of legal-rational domination.[54] But this is not to say that Weber does not speak of resistance at all in this context. When Weber mentions resistance, he does not consider it in relation to the experience of the ruled. Rather, resistance is viewed from the standpoint of legality and administrative control. Concerning the 1918 revolution in Germany, for example, Weber writes that:

> ...*systematic habituation to illegal behavior*, undermined the amenability to discipline both in the army and in industry and thus prepared the way for the overthrow of the older authority. (1978a, p.265; emphasis added)

From Weber's ruler-centric perspective, the cause of the 1918 German revolution resides in the fact that recalcitrant individuals in the army and industry were no longer sufficiently disciplined for carrying out their superiors' commands.[55] Within a Weberian framework it is *a priori* impossible to view the 1918 revolution from a revolutionary vantage point. The revolution might be deemed legitimate from such a position, because the dominated individuals could possibly be fighting for basic human rights, equity, social justice and so forth. The revolutionaries could be applying different standards of legitimacy, that is, they could be arguing for the legitimacy of resistance 'from below'. The fundamental question, then, would be: Why do the ruled not revolt?[56]

This chapter has explored key ideal-typical concepts central to Weber's study of social stratification. Because the ideal-types of legitimate domination/authority are considered by Weber as 'more precise' concepts than the ideal-typical concept of power, they will be commented on most frequently in the following three chapters. In his study of the nature of social stratification in the modern capitalist market-economy, the feudal estate order and the German nation-state, Weber comments extensively on relations of legitimate domination. However, I will also continue to employ the terminology of power in the most general sense, since it is simply unavoidable in a study of Weber's understanding of structural inequalities. Classes, status groups and parties are, after all, regarded by Weber as phenomena of the distribution of power. Weber's contention that disciplined, docile individuals are a prerequisite for the exercize of legitimate domination, will also be emphasized in the following chapters. Moreover, the ideal-typical nature of the different forms of legitimate domination identified by Weber will be underlined. Weber's ruler-centric pattern of thinking will be another principal theme pervading the discussion in the remainder of the book. It is exceedingly important to bear in mind that Weber continually evaluates relations of domination 'from above', that is, from a vantage point of control. Finally, the fact that resistance/opposition 'from below' has no theoretical foundation in a relationship of legal-rational domination, is central to my interpretation of Weber's analysis of the distribution of power in the modern capitalist market-economy and the German nation-state.

Notes

1   Weber also defines power as 'the possibility of imposing one's own will upon the behavior of other persons...' (1978a, p.942).

2   Hence, Wallimann et al. reason incorrectly when they claim that Weber's definition of power 'is restricted to wholly human relationships, of a non-*teleological* kind' (1980, p.266; emphasis in original).

3   In this regard, Gerth's and Mills' translation of Weber's earlier definition of power is not strictly correct. Gerth's and Mills' translation is as follows: 'the chance of a man or of a number of men to realize their own will in a *communal action* even against the resistance of others who are participating in the action' (Weber 1970, p.180; emphasis added).

4   See Lukes 1979, pp.636-8; Spencer 1977, pp.514-16.

5   The terms 'chance' (1978a, p.926) and 'possibility' (1978a, p.942) were used by Weber in the earlier definitions of power.

6   The Pluralists have appropriated Weber's voluntarist notion of power. Pluralists, like Dahl, stress the subjective elements of 'purpose' and 'willing'. The 'actual' exercize of power is crucial in the Pluralists'

conception of power. Hence, the obsession with decision-making procedures. The influence of institutional factors on 'observable' acts of power is neglected. See, e.g., Dahl 1961, Keller 1963, Polsby 1980, Rose 1967, Danzger 1964 , pp.707-17; Wolfinger 1960, pp.636-44.

7   Hindess (1982, pp.498-511) expatiates on the fact that the securing of outcomes in social relationships is subject to objective constraints that cannot be reduced to the capabilities of individuals. Cf. also Betts (1986, pp.39-64), Ashcraft (1972, p.157), Dahrendorf (1959, p.166) and Poulantzas (1978, p.147) who all contend that Weber's conception of power is at bottom tied to individuals.

8   See Offe and Wiesenthal 1980, pp.67-115.

9   In a Weberian vein, Etzioni (1961, p.5) also distinguishes between 'remunerative power' (based on control over material resources and rewards), 'normative power' (based on the allocation and manipulation of symbolic rewards and deprivations), and 'coercive power' (based on the application or the threat of application of physical sanctions).

For other similar appropriations of the Weberian conception of power, see Wild 1971, pp.175-6; Wild 1978a, p.4; Ingham 1970, pp.108-11.

10 Polsby, for instance, declares that Weber is 'the most important founding father of modern stratification analysis' (1980, p.118).

11 All of the following studies utilize the three-dimensional theory of social stratification as their frame of reference: Hodges 1964, Heller 1972, Bendix and Lipset 1967, Abrahamson et al. 1976, Archer and Giner 1971, Rossides 1976, Jackson 1968, Runciman 1968, pp.25-61; Kelsall and Kelsall 1974, Owen 1968, Littlejohn 1972, Lane 1982, Encel 1970, pp.27-46; Krauss 1976, pp.304-5; Curtis and Scott 1979. Sociologists like Wesolowski (1979) in Eastern Europe also employ the paradigm of class, status and power.

12 Cf. also Parsons 1977, pp.321-80; Boskoff 1971, pp.289-308; Bourricaud 1981, pp.260-84; Tausky 1965, pp.128-38; Giddens 1968, pp.257-72.

13 In this instance, 'actor' means not only the individual actor but also the collective actor.

14 In the 1940 essay, Parsons likewise alleges that: 'a person possesses power only in so far as his ability to influence others and his ability to achieve or to secure possessions are not institutionally sanctioned' (1954a, p.76). In fact, Parsons refers explicitly to Weber when he says that power 'is *any* capacity for an acting unit in a social system to "get what it wants", as Weber ... said, with or without opposition, in a nexus of social relationships' (1976a, p.99; emphasis in original).

15 Cf. Murphy 1982, pp.180-81; Giddens 1976a, p.112; Doorn 1962-63, p.7.

16 Interestingly enough, the exchange theorist, Blau, also defines power as: 'the ability of persons or groups to impose their will on others *despite resistance* through deterrence either in the form of withholding regularly supplied rewards or in the form of punishment, inasmuch as the former as well as the

latter constitute, in effect, a negative sanction' (1964, p.117; emphasis added). In the light of this definition, however, it would seem that Blau regards resistance as a 'necessary precondition' in any power situation.

17 Other writers also underscore the significance of resistance/opposition in the analysis of power relations. However, the fact that 'power' and 'resistance' are two 'separate' but 'interrelated' phenomena within a power relation is not always fully understood. The insufficiently rigorous terminology exemplifies this. Schermerhorn (1961, pp.71-2) refers to 'counter-vailing power'. Benton (1981, p.181) states that 'it is a condition of possibility of "struggle" that opposition of some form persists'. Giddens (1982, pp.28-45) speaks of a 'dialectic of control'. Touraine's (1977, pp.118-25) reflections on a 'double dialectic of social classes' demonstrate that no social situation can be simple equated with a logic of domination.

18 Ingham (1970, p.109), Giddens (1979a, p.338) and Barbalet (1985a, p.532) also highlight this misappropriation of Weber.

19 Refer to Note 6 on the Pluralists. Other writers like Martin (1977, p.37) and Baldus (1979, p.170) also claim that conflict is incorporated into Weber's definition of power. Dahrendorf, on the other hand, refutes this argument when he affirms that 'Weber has failed to connect his theory of power and authority with the analysis of conflict' (1959, p.194).

20 In like manner, Foucault describes 'peace' as 'a form of war' (1980, p.123).

21 In this respect, it is interesting to consider Hegy's argument concerning the concepts of power in different languages being related to the ideology of the respective societies. Hegy (1974, pp.329-39) concentrates on the French and English rendering of power.

22 It is interesting to note, though, that Parsons in a very early discussion of Weber's three types of authority argues that: 'The basis of the classification lies in the first instance in variation in the nature of the claim to "legitimacy" that is made for the holders of a position of authority, that is of their having a "right" to exercize authority over others and claim obedience as a duty, as distinguished from merely compelling it by *force majeur*. It is this claim which distinguishes "authority" (*legitime Herrschaft*) from *Herrschaft* in general' (1942a, p.65). When this statement is taken into account, it would seem that Parsons in his very early writings did take cognizance of the threat of force, coercion and so on inherent in the more general concept of *Herrschaft*, as distinguished from *legitime Herrschaft*.

23 The pivotal point is that in the study of social collectivities, one can go beyond merely demonstrating functional relationships and uniformities. That is, we can accomplish the subjective understanding of the action of individuals in society.

24 Other interpreters who translate *Herrschaft* as 'authority' include: Bruun 1972, p.287; Spencer 1970, pp.123-34; Murvar 1964, pp.374-84. Gerth entitles a translation of Weber: 'The Three Types of Legitimate Rule' (Weber 1961, pp.4-14). Banton (1972, pp.86-8) commits an egregious error

when he translates *Macht* as 'might' and *Herrschaft* as 'power'. Similarly, Poulantzas (1978, p.104) translates 'power' as *Herrschaft*. His quotation from Weber is, in fact, the definition of 'domination' rather than 'power'. Ferrarotti (1982, p.95) commits the same error. Atkinson (1972, p.78) goes so far as to say that there are two quite distinct types of 'domination' in Weber's oeuvre: 'power' and 'authority'. Andreski (1984, p.96) translates *Herrschaft* as: 'rule', 'power' or 'domination'. Hegy (1974, p.333) argues that Weber differentiates two types of 'authority': *Macht* and *Herrschaft*. And Lane's reading of Weber is such that 'authority' is not a sub-category of 'power'. That is to say, 'a social relation can be a relation of authority and at the same time not a relation of power' (1976, p.223).

25 The interpreters translating *Herrschaft* as 'domination' include: Weights 1978, pp.56-73; Wrong 1979, pp.36-9; Mommsen 1974, pp.72-94; McIntosh 1970, pp.901-11; Schluchter 1981, pp.106-38; Turner 1982, pp.367-91; Cohen 1972, pp.63-86; Lukes 1979, pp.662-5; Luhmann 1982, pp.20-46; Willer 1967, pp.231-9; Freund 1972, pp.218-45; Wallimann et al. 1980, pp.261-75; Cohen et al. 1975, pp.229-41; Merquior 1980.

26 In the remainder of this study 'authority' and 'legitimate domination' will be used interchangeably.

27 Part II encompasses Weber (1978a, pp.311-1469).

28 Weber confuses the situation here when he reverts to the terminology of power, although he is now discussing what he perceives as a special type of 'power', namely, 'domination'. Weber (1978a, p.945) also utilizes the terminology of 'power' in his discussion of 'domination'. He notes 'the clear-cut antithesis between factual power which arises completely out of possession and by way of interest compromises in the market, and, on the other hand, the authoritarian power of a patriarch or monarch with its appeal to the duty of obedience as such'. On the following page (1978a, p.946), Weber returns to the term 'domination'.

29 See also Betts 1986, pp.39-64.

30 Cf. Matheson 1987, pp.199-215; Parsons 1949, pp.658-9.

31 Weber tends to use 'rationality', 'legality' and 'bureaucracy' interchangeably. He acknowledges that 'the purest type of exercise of legal authority is that which employs a bureaucratic administrative staff' (1978a, p.220). The pivotal point, though, is that 'legal authority can be exercised in a wide variety of different forms...' (Weber 1978a, p.219).

32 In this connection, Thomas reasons that Weber's argument for the limited application of radically democratic principles is '*not* analytically derived from an *a priori* conception', but is empirically grounded (1984, p.229; emphasis in original). Radical democracy, that is, direct/immediate democracy rests, according to Weber, on two fundamental principles: 'the assumption that everybody is equally qualified to conduct the public affairs' and that 'the scope of power of command is kept at a minimum' (1978a, p.948; see also pp.949-52, 289-90). However, the bases for the application

of these radical democratic principles have been eroded in modern society, because of growing population, increased technical complexity and legal-rational domination (Weber 1978a, pp.951-2, 291-2). Hence, it is true that Weber's contention pertaining to the limited possibilities for the application of democratic principles in modern society, is the outcome of empirical analysis. But the fact that Weber's theoretical framework, in any case, rules out the possibility of a democratic society also remains valid.

33   Cf. Mommsen 1984, pp.449-52; Graber 1985, p.94; Habermas 1984a, pp.254-70.

34   Weber (1978a, pp.36-7) also refers in Section 7 of the first chapter of *Economy and Society* to a possible fourth type of legitimation involving the affirmation of an absolute value.

35   In this regard, it is also important to note that both Spencer (1970, pp.123-34) and Barker (1980, pp.224-45) are incorrect to assume that action rooted in value-rationality, must necessarily gravitate in a democratic direction. Values cannot simply be equated with democratic ones. Admittedly, there was a clear relation between direct/immediate democracy and the value-rational commitment of the Protestant sects in the earlier phases of modern capitalism (see Weber 1970, pp.302-22). But as Thomas discerns, this was an historical rather than a logical relation (1984, p.231; see also pp.216-40).

36   Wilson (1976, p.304) remarks that discipline was 'central to Weber's writing and to his life...'.

37   See also Collins 1986b, pp.52-8.

38   Weber, however, notes that these irrational, ascetic practices had also been rejected by certain very important Catholic orders like the rules of St. Benedict, the monks of Cluny, the Cistercians and the Jesuits (1976a, p.118; 1978c, p.1122).

39   In a somewhat similar vein, Elias (1978, 1982, esp., pp.229-333) writes about 'the civilizing process' that occurred in the course of the transition from the warlike society of feudal Europe to the more peaceful society of later centuries. This process involves a specific change in human conduct and sentiment. Simply put, 'the civilizing process', according to Elias, concerns 'a transformation of the whole drive and affect economy in the direction of a more continuous, stable and even regulation of drives and affects in all areas of conduct...' (1982, p.240). An increasingly differentiated regulation of impulses is brought about (what Weber apprehends as psychic self-disciplining). Elias also highlights the close connection between the monopolization of physical violence by a political center (e.g., the absolutist state and the modern state) and the control of drives and affects in every 'civilized' individual (i.e., 'disciplined' individual). The monopolization of physical violence forces 'unarmed' individuals to limit their own violence, that is, it compels them to exercize a greater or lesser degree of self-control.

40   Cf. O'Neill 1986, pp.42-60; Turner 1982, pp.383-6.

41   Of course, Foucault's terminology differs from that of Weber. 'Domination' and 'discipline' are complementary concepts within the Weberian schema.

42   Several other interpreters also allege that Weber's concept of domination concentrates on legitimacy at the expense of coercion, force and so forth: Spencer 1970, p.133; Spencer 1977, p.517; Factor and Turner 1979, pp.329-30; Blau 1963, pp.306-7; Mommsen 1974, pp.83-7; Parkin 1982, pp.74-80; Therborn 1980a, pp.296-304.

43   On this score, it is worthwhile noting Abercrombie's and Turner's (1982, pp.396-414) and Mann's (1982, pp.373-95) point that only those who actually have a share in the power of a particular society, need to develop a consistent set of justificatory beliefs.

44   In this respect, it is worthwhile noting Sharp's point that 'obedience is at the heart of political power' (1973, p.16; see also pp.17-32). Cf. also Kronman 1983, pp.40-43.

45   There is a telling parallel between this situation of the complete and utter helplessness of the dominated and Gramsci's notion of 'hegemony'. For 'hegemony' presupposes the existence of something which is truly total. Gramsci's notion of 'hegemony' deeply penetrating the consciousness of a society, constitutes the limits of what is possible for most social actors under its influence (see Gramsci 1971).

46   The following authors stress the coercive aspects of Weber's concept of domination: McIntosh 1970, pp.901-11; Turner 1982, pp.367-91; Lukes 1979, pp.662-5; Cohen et al. 1975, pp.229-41; Wallimann et al. 1980, pp.264-75; Thomas 1984, pp.216-40; Bendix 1966.

47   See Collins 1986a, p.127; Roth 1978, p.1xv.

48   Cf. Schluchter 1981, pp.106-26.

49   However, legal-rational domination is peculiar to modern society in the West. This form of domination is, in the main, grounded in purposive-rational action.

50   Cf. also Hirst 1976a, pp.83-8; Parkin 1982, pp.74-80; Luhmann 1982, pp.29-36; Giddens 1982, pp.33-8; Merquior 1980, pp.130-36; Barbalet 1986a, pp.12-19; Therborn 1980a:300-2.

51   Although contemporary elitists, especially so-called left-wing elitists like C. Wright Mills, would not consciously support Weber's ruler-centric bias, the irony is that elitists on the whole are obsessed with the 'governing elite' at the expense of the ruled. The classic, elitist paradigm treats the concentration of political power in the hands of a small, cohesive elite group. It juxtaposes an all-powerful, active elite to an amorphous, inert mass. The implication is that the passive mass is shorn of any capacity to resist the all-powerful elite. See, e.g., Domhoff 1967, Domhoff 1979, Hunter 1959, Mills 1959, Aaronovitch 1979, Miliband 1973. It is, however, important to mention that Field and Higley (1980) are an exceptional case. They set out to 'restate the elitist paradigm' by, firstly, characterizing elites

as always needing the support of non-elites and, secondly, by representing elites as constrained by the requests which of necessity they must make for non-elite support (1980, p.19).

52   See also Midgley 1983, p.49.

53   See also Giddens (1981b, p.116) on the notion of 'revolutionary consciousness'.

54   In the course of the discussion of Weber's views on peasant rebellion in the feudal estate order in Chapter V.6, I will refer to Weber's brief commentary on the kind of resistance usually found in a relationship of traditional domination.

55   Interestingly enough, Weber planned to write a chapter 'on the theory of revolutions' (1978a, p.266).

56   See, e.g., Moore 1978, pp.459-505; Schwarz 1964, pp.126-34.

4 Class

In the present chapter I explore Weber's thesis that classes are phenomena of the distribution of economic power within the modern capitalist market-economy. In the first section of the chapter I focus attention on the 'historical individual', modern rational capitalism. In the second section I will assess Weber's thesis that 'property' and 'lack of property' constitute the most important bases for the formation of classes in the modern capitalist market-economy. In this particular section I also dispute the claim made by many interpreters of Weber, namely, the fact that Weber develops a wholly individualist idea of class at the expense of a structural explanation. Furthermore, Weber's argument that the modern nation-state tailored to bureaucratic administration facilitates 'monopolistic domination in the market', is examined. The third section of the chapter concentrates on Weber's understanding of the modern capitalist factory as a disciplinary institution. In the final section I contend that Weber's analysis of modern rational capitalism is rather partisan. His principal concern is the preservation of bourgeois freedom. In this final section I also consider Weber's views on the problematic nature of class action.

4.1 The modern capitalist market-economy

Weber states that modern capitalism 'is a specific product of modern European man' (1994, p.89). It is 'the most fateful force in our modern life' (Weber 1976a, p.17). It is the inescapable condition of our contemporary situation. More pointedly, Weber stipulates that:

> The most general presupposition for the existence of this present-day capitalism is that of rational capital accounting as the norm for all large industrial undertakings which are concerned with provision for everyday wants. (1981b, p.276; see also pp.223-9, 275-8; 1976a, pp.17-25; 1978a,

Rational capital accounting is a form of monetary calculation peculiar to rational economic profit-making. In other words, rational capital accounting pertains to 'activity which is oriented to opportunities for seeking new powers of control over goods on a single occasion, repeatedly, or continuously' (Weber 1978a, p.90; see also 1976a, pp.17-19). The most important word in Weber's definition of profit-making activity is the procurement of additional 'powers of control' which will add to the total economic value (i.e., the net worth) of the modern capitalist enterprise.[2]

This key feature of rational profit-making is accentuated in Weber's definition of rational capital accounting as:

> ...the valuation and verification of opportunities for profit and of the success of profit-making activity by means of a valuation of the total assets (goods and money) at the beginning of a profit-making venture, and the comparison of this with a similar valuation of the assets still present and newly acquired at the end of the process; in the case of a profit-making organization operating continuously, the same is done for an accounting period. (1978a, p.91; see also pp.154-5)

The highest possible degree of calculability of profits and losses is the basis for efficient capital accounting in the modern capitalist enterprise. From the technical point of view, capital accounting, according to Weber, reaches a maximum level of efficiency with double-entry bookkeeping (1978a, pp.92-3; 1981b, p.275). Seen in this light, a modern profit-making enterprise is deemed successful only if the total value of the assets owned by the enterprise is greater at the end of the relevant accounting period than it was at the commencement of this period.[3]

Bearing in mind that rational capital accounting is the most fundamental condition for the existence of modern capitalism, Weber (1981b, pp.276-8) goes on to mention several other factors indispensable for obtaining the maximum of formal rationality of capital accounting in the modern industrial enterprise. These include: appropriation of all physical means of production, freedom of the market, rational technology, calculable law, free labour and the commercialization of economic life. All of these other factors which are essential for the operation of rational capital accounting procedures in the modern industrial enterprise, are also considered by Weber as basic preconditions of modern rational capitalism. When Weber underlines the importance of private ownership of the means of production, the sale of labour power and the role of rational technology in the development of modern rational capitalism, he moves closer to Marx. However, Weber deviates from Marx when he accentuates the importance of freedom of the market and calculable law.

With reference to free labour as a prerequisite for the maximization of the formal rationality of capital accounting, Weber stipulates that workers under 'the compulsion of poverty' (1981b, p.167) are compelled to sell their labour-power to capitalist entrepreneurs on the market. Contrary to Marx, though, Weber contends that the calculability of free labour is merely one factor tending to maximize rational capital accounting within the modern industrial enterprise.[4] A formally free labour force enables the capitalist entrepreneur to select workers solely on grounds of technical efficiency. Moreover, free labour creates a mobile labour force ready to respond to the demands of the capitalist market (see Weber 1978a, pp.128-9, 162). And, further, the advantage of free labour is that 'this system involves the transferral, in addition to the responsibility for reproduction (in the family), of part of the worries about selection according to aptitude to the workers themselves' (Weber 1978a, p.151). Unfree labour (e.g., slaves, serfs), on the other hand, is not amenable to rational capital accounting procedures, because the owner has to accommodate his production plans to the aptitudes and skills of the unfree workers already at his disposal (see Weber 1978a, pp162-3; 1981b, pp.128-9; 1983a, pp.43-51).

With regard to the expropriation of the worker from the means of production as a necessary condition for the maximization of the formal rationality of capital accounting, Weber maintains that it is generally feasible to attain a higher degree of economic rationality (i.e., quantitative calculation), 'if the management has extensive control over the selection and the modes of use of workers...' (1978a, p.137). But in contrast to Marx's position, the expropriation of the worker from the means of production is not, on Weber's reading, peculiar to the modern industrial enterprise. Quite the contrary:

> This all-important economic fact: the 'separation' of the worker from the material means of production, distribution, administration, academic research, and finance in general is the common basis of the modern state, in its political, cultural and military sphere, and of the private capitalist economy. In both cases the disposition over these means is in the hands of that power whom the bureaucratic apparatus (of judges, officials, officers, supervisors, clerks and non-commissioned officers) directly obeys or to whom it is available in case of need. This apparatus is nowadays equally typical of all those organizations, its existence and function are inseparably cause and effect of this concentration of the means of operation—in fact, the apparatus is its very form. (Weber 1978a, p.1394)

Essentially, Weber is saying that the separation of the worker from the means of production is typical of all the major bureaucratic structures in modern society. And in view of the fact that a hierarchy of control/subordination is constitutive of any bureaucratic apparatus, a process of expropriation may occur.

As regards Weber's notion that the formal rationality of capital accounting is maximized by a 'complete calculability of the technical conditions of the production process, that is, a mechanically rational technology...' (1978a, p.162)—it is first of all necessary to mention that although Weber discusses technology in some detail in *General Economic History* (1981b, pp.115-35, 162-77, 199-201, 302-14), he states that 'it is quite out of the question ... to develop even the most modest outline of a theory of the evolution of the technology and economics of tools and machinery' (1978a, p.121). Weber simply gives a few insignificant definitions of 'tools', 'apparatus' and 'machines'.[5] Technological progress is not for Weber, as Schmidt (1976, p.67) notes, an exogenous social phenomenon. Rather, it is inextricably intertwined with the development of modern rational capitalism. On this score, Weber affirms that the rationality of Western capitalism is:

> ...today essentially dependent on the calculability of the most important technical factors. But this means fundamentally that it is dependent on the peculiarities of modern science, especially the natural sciences based on mathematics and exact and rational experiment. On the other hand, the development of these sciences and of the technique resting upon them now receives important stimulation from these capitalistic interests in its practical economic applications. (1976a, p.24; see also 1971a, pp.104-16; 1978a, p.67; 1978c, p.1128)

Science and technology are relevant for capitalist interests only to the extent that they contribute to increased productivity and, hence, profitability. Weber (1981b, p.311), for instance, observes that most important inventions during the early period of industrial capitalism were propelled by the goal of cheapening production. The key economic feature of mechanization is that it is only possible with mass production. Moreover, production on a massive scale is not feasible without a high degree of predictability that a mass market will be available for the products, as exemplified in the capitalist market.

In respect of freedom of the market allowing for the maximum formal rationality of capital accounting, it is first of all necessary to consider Weber's understanding of the 'market situation'. According to Weber, 'the "market situation" for any object of exchange' means 'all the opportunities of exchanging it for money which are known to the participants in exchange relationships and aid their orientation in the competitive price struggle' (1978a, p.82; see also pp.109, 113, 635, 640). Haggling over prices pervades a market-economy. Moreover, co-operation in this type of economy means nothing more than the interplay of self-seeking interests in the exchange process.

Regarding market freedom, it has to do with the degree of autonomy which the parties involved in market relationships have in price struggles and competition (Weber 1978a, p.82). That is to say, market freedom, on Weber's interpretation, implies 'complete appropriation of all material means of production by owners and the complete absence of all formal appropriation of opportunities for profit in the market...' (1978a, p.161; see also pp.112-13). Market freedom in modern rational capitalism entails the expropriation of the workers from the means of production and the absence of monopolies, either of the 'imposed and economically irrational' (i.e., orientation away from the market) type, or the 'voluntary and economically rational' (i.e., market oriented) type (Weber 1978a, p.108). Weber dubs certain regulations upon the market as 'economically irrational'—when the groups dominating the market (e.g., estates in the feudal social order) are not interested in maximizing the opportunities of participants in the market for either profit or the mere satisfaction of needs. In this sense, regulation of the market may be determined by adherence to tradition, by convention or by law (see Weber 1978a, pp.82-5, 351). Conversely, Weber designates certain limitations upon the market as 'economically rational'—when the groups dominating the market promote 'the orientation of the economic activity of strata interested in purchase and sale of goods on the market to the market situations' (Weber 1978a, p.84). 'Economically rational' market regulation is fostered by highly developed profit-making interests like capitalist entrepreneurs. Such interests, in Weber's view, often increase their own control over goods in the market to the point of establishing monopolies through the price regulation of opportunities for purchase and sale of goods, the regulation of transport facilities, a monopoly on the production of certain goods, and the extension of credit and financing. When market freedom is limited by either economically rational/irrational means, it hinders the development of one of the major conditions making possible a maximum degree of formal rationality of capital accounting in the modern industrial enterprise.[6]

With reference to calculable law as one of the principal conditions requisite for obtaining a maximum of formal rationality of capital accounting in the modern profit-making enterprise, it is essential to inquire into the nature of modern rational law. In contradistinction to traditional and revealed (charismatic) law, modern, formally rational law develops a logically consistent set of autonomous, general, abstract rules which are administered by means of formal procedures. These procedures guarantee that the relevant rules are heeded in all cases.[7] The ideal-type of modern rational law is predicated, according to Weber, on the following five postulates:

> ...first, that every concrete legal decision be the 'application' of any abstract legal proposition to a concrete 'fact situation'; second, that it must be possible in every concrete case to derive the decision from abstract legal propositions by means of legal logic; third, that the law must actually or virtually constitute a 'gapless' system of legal propositions, or must, at least, be treated as if it were such a gapless system; fourth, that whatever cannot be 'construed' rationally in legal terms is also legally irrelevant; and fifth, that every social action of human beings must always be visualized as either an 'application' or 'execution' of legal propositions or as an 'infringement' thereof, since the 'gaplessness' of the legal system must result in a gapless 'legal ordering' of all social conduct. (Weber 1978a, pp.657-8)

This ideal-type of modern rational law may be called 'legalism' because it involves an autonomous body of legal rules as the main source of normative order in modern society. These rules are followed because they are believed to be rationally enacted. In short, this set of legal rules 'enables the legal system to operate like a technically rational machine' (Weber 1978a, p.811).

In the context of the modern profit-making enterprise, modern rational law allows for a maximum of formal rationality of capital accounting, since it guarantees predictability, stability and freedom from arbitrary interference.[8] In this respect, Weber purports that:

> To those who had interests in the commodity market, the rationalization and systematization of the law in general and ... the increasing calculability of the functioning of the legal process in particular, constituted one of the most important conditions for the existence of economic enterprise intended to function with stability and, especially, of capitalist enterprise, which cannot do without legal security. (1978a, p.883)

Modern rational law facilitates legal security in the modern capitalist market-economy by ensuring that contracts between private parties will be executed in accordance with a stable set of legal rules (see Weber 1978a, pp.666-70). Moreover, by contributing to the predictability of performance among contractual partners, modern rational law furthers the development of exchange relationships in the modern capitalist market. Finally, this type of law is instrumental in the maximization of the formal rationality of capital accounting by developing certain legal techniques such as the law of 'agency' and 'free negotiability'. Weber writes that:

> Every rational business organization needs the possibility of acquiring contractual rights and of assuming obligations through temporary or permanent agents. Advanced trade, moreover, needs not only the possibility of transferring legal claims but also and quite particularly, a method by which transfers can be made legally secure and which eliminates the need of constantly testing the title of the transfer. (1978a, pp.681-2)

The utilization of agents by the modern profit-making enterprise and the freedom to transfer legal claims in accordance with fixed legal rules are, in Weber's view, essential for a modern capitalist market-economy (1978a, p.682). Without such legal techniques profit-making can only be rationalized to a limited degree.[9]

Taking account of the various factors necessary for the maximization of the formal rationality of capital accounting, it is rather apparent that, on Weber's reading, modern capitalism denotes what Käsler adroitly calls one of those 'component phenomena in a general historical development of the rationalization of life' (1988, p.172; emphasis in original).[10] Modern capitalism understood in terms of rational capital accounting represents one of the keystones in the all-encompassing rationalization of modern life.[11]

It is necessary at this point to examine the type of 'economic action' corresponding to 'the structure of that peculiar "system" which has been thrust upon the population by the organisation of large-scale industrial production...' (Weber 1971a, p.154; see also 1978a, p.929; 1978c, p.1128; 1994, p.90). For the 'rational capitalist *system*' (Weber 1978a, p.1102; emphasis in original), in so far as it exists historically, can only be reproduced through human agency. More to the point, 'economic action' is perceived by Weber as a special case of 'economically oriented action'. The economic order, in Weber's view, is comprised of the totality of 'economically oriented action', that is, it 'includes all primarily non-economic action and all non-peaceful action which is influenced by economic considerations' (1978a, p.64).

'Economic action', on the other hand, is constitutive of a partial domain of the economic order.[12] Weber defines 'economic action' as:

> ...any peaceful exercise of an actor's control over resources which is in its main impulse oriented towards economic ends. 'Rational economic action' requires instrumental rationality in this orientation, that is, deliberate planning. (1978a, p.63; see also p.339)

And by the same token, an action has an 'economic end' in so far as 'according to its subjective meaning, it is concerned with the satisfaction of a desire for "utilities"' (Weber 1978a, p.63).[13] In accordance with Weber's general definition of means-end rational action, 'rational economic action' is understood in terms of its subjective meaning. 'Rational economic action' is deemed meaningful in so far as it concerns the rational actor's purposeful orientation to the end of the satisfaction of a desire for utilities. It is this alone which makes economic phenomena accessible to rational understanding.

The most important type of 'rational economic action' is profit-making (i.e., capitalist economic action) which Weber defines as:

> ...one which rests on the expectation of profit by the utilization of opportunities for exchange, that is on (formally) peaceful chances of profit ... Where capitalistic acquisition is rationally pursued, the corresponding action is adjusted to calculations in terms of capital. (1976a, pp.17-18; see also 1978a, p.340)

In effect, the modern capitalist market-economy, in so far as it exists historically, can only be reproduced by virtue of capitalist economic action. Or as Cohen pertinently puts it, 'only the capitalist entrepreneur can set the modern industrial enterprise in motion as a means to pursue particular ends' (1981, p.xlix). However, I have already suggested that Weber's more general attempt to link social action and social collectivities/social structures remains problematic in the context of modern society. For very few individuals, in fact, act within a Weberian framework. Similarly, I would suggest that in the case of the connection between the 'rational capitalist *system*' and capitalist economic action, it is only capitalist entrepreneurs who act in a purposive-rational manner and, thereby, contribute directly to the reproduction of the capitalist system. Workers, on the other hand, merely engage in reactive behaviour. They do not act on their own motives. They contribute to the reproduction of the capitalist system in the course of being used as a means of rational profit-making activity.

4.2 'Property' and 'lack of property'

Weber's ideal-typical concept of class can only be examined against the backdrop of the all-embracing 'rational capitalist *system*'. Weber considers 'property'/'lack of property' as the most important bases for the formation of classes in the modern capitalist market-economy. He declares that:

> The mode of distribution gives to the propertied a monopoly on the possibility of transferring property from the sphere of use as 'wealth' to the sphere of 'capital', that is, it gives them the entrepreneurial function and all chances to share directly or indirectly in returns on capital. *All this holds true within the area in which pure market conditions prevail. 'Property' and 'lack of property' are, therefore, the basic categories of all class situations.* (1978a, p.927, emphasis added; see also p.699; 1958, p.39; 1970, p.301)[14]

Property/ownership involves diverse powers of control and disposal. That is to say, the individual is in a situation whereby he is able to make use of objects at his own convenience. The modern capitalist market-economy 'consists in a complete network of exchange contracts, that is, in deliberate planned acquisitions of powers of control and disposal' (Weber 1978a, p.67; see also p.312). The economic actor (e.g., the capitalist entrepreneur) rationally takes into account and evaluates the possibility of procuring new powers of control and disposal over the material means of production, capital goods and the like.

Of particular relevance is that Weber's concept of 'powers of control and disposal' (*Verfügungsgewalt*) is, as Parsons indicates, of legal origin (see Weber 1978a, p.206, note 5). Indeed, the types of property found in the modern capitalist market-economy involve legitimately guaranteed powers of control and disposal. Weber writes that:

> The normal intention in an act of exchange is to acquire certain subjective 'rights', i.e., in sociological terms, the probability of support of one's power of disposition by the coercive apparatus of the state. Economic goods today are normally at the same time *legitimately acquired rights*; they are the very building material for the universe of the economic order. (1978a, p.329, emphasis in original; see also pp.72, 333-7; 1981b,

111

pp.338-51)

The significance of Weber's understanding of property in the modern capitalist market-economy in terms of legitimately sanctioned powers of control and disposal, testifies to the fact that a clear distinction must be made between 'possession' and 'ownership'. 'Possession', as Kronman (1983, p.141) and Curtis (1968, p.95) point out, merely requires physical control over objects. It simply involves the ability to seize concrete material things. 'Ownership', on the other hand, necessitates that the possessed objects be designated as the legitimate possession of the owner. Furthermore, others must believe in the legitimacy of the owner's right to the possession of the relevant object. Ownership in the modern capitalist market-economy relates to legally sanctioned claims.[15] The legal assurance of powers of control and disposal is, according to Weber, 'today empirically an indispensable basis for economic activity with the *material* means of production' (1978a, p.72; emphasis in original).[16] In other words, the legitimacy of powers of control and disposal over any object in the modern capitalist market-economy is contingent upon the development of a logically consistent set of autonomous, general, abstract, legal rules which are administered by means of formal procedures (i.e., legalism).[17]

Weber's rendering of property in terms of 'powers of control and disposal' can also be viewed from the standpoint of 'appropriation'. 'Appropriation' concerns the monopolization of advantages in a closed social relationship. Weber calls 'appropriated advantages' "'rights'" (1978a, p.44). These 'rights', in turn, will be safeguarded from individuals outside the closed social relationship, either through tradition or through modern rational law. Weber designates 'appropriated rights' enjoyed through inheritance or by hereditary groups of a communal or associative nature as 'the "property" of the individual or of groups in question' (1978a, p.44). Conversely, these 'appropriated rights' are dubbed "'free" property' to the extent that they are alienable. In the context of Weber's interest in the modern capitalist market-economy, he classifies the various 'economic advantages' which may be appropriated:[18]

> Objects of appropriation may be: the opportunities of disposing of and obtaining a return from human labor services; the material means of production; and the opportunities for profit from managerial functions. (1978a, p.126)

Regarding appropriation of the material means of production, Weber says that they may be appropriated by workers individually or collectively as an organization. The other possibility is appropriation by owners or by regulating groups consisting of third parties. It is legally ratified appropriation of the material means of production by owners that is of paramount importance in the modern capitalist market-economy.[19] An owner may appropriate land, subterranean wealth, sources of power, work premises, labour equipment (e.g.,

112

tools, machinery) and raw materials. Of particular relevance also is Weber's reference to 'ownership or non-ownership of material goods' (1958, p.39; see also 1978a, pp.302, 312, 342, 928).[20] Indeed, Weber concedes that 'material goods have gained an increasing and finally an inexorable power over the lives of men as at no previous period in history' (1976a, p.181). It is legally guaranteed powers of control and disposal over 'capital goods', that is goods 'administered on the basis of capital accounting' (Weber 1978a, p.94), that are decisive in the modern capitalist market-economy.

In respect of human labour services being treated as objects of appropriation, Weber purports that:

> The concept of powers of control and disposal will here be taken to include the possibility of control over the actor's own labor power, whether this is in some way enforced or merely exists in fact. That this is not to be taken for granted is shown by its absence in the case of slaves. (1978a, p.68; see also p.928)

Weber is referring here to 'free' labour. Only the individual has legally sanctioned powers of control and disposal over his labour-power (i.e., his capacity to labour). An individual's labour-power can only be 'owned' by him.[21] 'Free' labour is an integral feature of modern rational capitalism. 'Unfree' labour (e.g., slaves, serfs), on the other hand, means that 'the right of utilization of labor services is appropriated to an "owner" of the worker...' (Weber 1978a, p.126). In contrast to the modern capitalist market-economy (where persons can only 'own' material things, but not other persons), the 'ownership' of one human being by another was a legitimate form of ownership in the case of slavery in Antiquity. The fact that slaves were perceived as the 'property' of other human beings, namely slave-owners, meant that slaves were categorized as 'material things' rather than 'persons'. Hence, slaves were 'subject to the unlimited exploitation of their labour-power by their master' (Weber 1971b, p.265). The modern concept of 'property', on the other hand, limits the designation 'material things' to non-human things.[22]

Even though the individual has legally guaranteed powers of control and disposal over his own labour-power in the modern capitalist market-economy, he can 'sell' its 'use' to another individual for a fixed period of time.[23] The wage-labourer sells his labour-power to the owner of the material means of production for an agreed-on period of time. During this period, the wage-labourer is, as Weber points out, 'oriented to the instructions of a managerial agency' (1978a, p.114). Or as Marx puts it, the worker during this period of sale has no 'power of disposition over living labour capacity' (1973, p.359). The capitalist through the labour contract legally appropriates the productive capacity of the wage-labourer (e.g., specific skill) for a limited period of time. The wage-labourer *divests* himself of labour as the force productive of wealth; capital appropriates it, as such' (Marx 1973, p.307; emphasis in original).

113

Of greatest importance is that although the labour contract entered into by the capitalist and the wage-labourer is formally 'free' on both sides, the salient point is that the wage-labourer is in reality constrained to offer his formally 'free' labour-power for sale on the labour market. In contrast to what Kronman (1983, p.145) terms the 'positive' understanding of 'free' labour (i.e., the worker's powers of control and disposal over his labour-power), the 'negative' notion refers, firstly, to the fact that workers have been expropriated from the material means of production. Secondly, there is what Weber calls the 'complete absence of appropriation of jobs and of opportunities for earning by workers' (1978a, p.162). Thirdly, the capitalist's legally secured powers of control and disposal over the 'products' created by the utilization of the workers' labour-power are permanent. Quite simply, the workers 'lack property'. They have been expropriated from their means of subsistence.[24] Therefore, in order to simply survive, the 'free' workers are, as Marx pointedly remarks, 'hurled onto the labour-market as free, unprotected and rightless proletarians' (1976b, p.876). Workers are not 'free' to remove themselves from the labour-market.

Taking account of the negative understanding of 'free' labour, it is not, in my view, tenable to treat legally authorized powers of control and disposal over labour-power as a form of 'property'. Rather, within a Weberian framework labour-power (e.g., a specific skill) can also be regarded as a 'service'. That is to say, it is one of those 'utilities derived from a human source, so far as this source consists in active conduct...' (Weber 1978a, p.68; see also p.928).[25]

With reference, finally, to legally secured powers of control and disposal over managerial functions, Weber affirms that:

> In cases where managerial functions are, from a formal point of view, wholly appropriated, the appropriation of the means of production or of the credit necessary for securing control over them is in practice, in a capitalistic form of organization, identical with appropriation of control of management by the owners of the means of production. *Owners can, in such cases, exercise their control by personally managing the business or by the appointment of the actual managers.* (1978a, p.136, emphasis added; see also p.139)

Weber is underlining the complementarity of appropriation of managerial functions (management) and appropriation of the means of production (ownership) in the modern capitalist market-economy. The capitalist who has legally authorized powers of control and disposal over the means of production, either 'manages' the business enterprise himself or 'appoints' a manager. The legal owner of the means of production has the ultimate control over the way in which managerial functions may be carried out.[26]

Although Weber speaks of legally guaranteed powers of control and disposal over the means of production, labour-power and managerial functions (i.e., legally acquired rights) in the modern capitalist market-economy, this market-economy is not, as Giddens points out, 'a normatively defined system of authority in which the distribution of power is, as such, sanctioned as legitimate' (1981b, p.102; emphasis removed). To the contrary, legally secured rights uphold inequalities based on already given economic conditions (e.g., the unequal distribution of powers of control and disposal over the material means of production). Legally procured rights, like the contractual rights of the capitalist and wage-labourer in a market exchange, simply define the general conditions governing contractual economic relationships, rather than intervening directly in the functioning of 'free' economic exchange. Accordingly, Weber writes that "'legal empowerment rules'" do 'no more than *create the framework for valid agreements* which, under conditions of formal freedom, are officially available to all' (1978a, p.730; emphasis added). In the case of traditionally secured private rights and privileges of status groups in Antiquity and feudal Europe, on the other hand, the distribution of power as such is legitimized on the basis of socially constructed norms.[27]

Besides Weber's delineation of diverse forms of property, he further argues that:

> Those who have no property but offer services are differentiated just as much according to their kinds of services as according to the way in which they make use of these services, in a continuous or discontinuous relation to a recipient. (1978a, p.928)

Weber is referring here to the second major dimension of inequality in the distribution of economic power in the modern capitalist market-economy, namely, that pertaining to the possession of marketable skills. Given the diverse forms of property and marketable skills, Weber declares that 'in principle, the various controls over consumer goods, means the production, assets, resources and skills each constitute a *particular* class situation' (1978, p.302; emphasis in original).[28] The end-result of such a pattern of thinking, however, would be an infinite number of class situations.[29] So Weber tightens up his enumeration of class categories. He develops a set of class categories differentiated on two major counts: one premised upon the kind of property that is usable for returns in the market and the kind of services that can be offered in the market, the other dependent upon the chances for mobility between class situations.

On the basis of the distinction between property and services in the market, Weber goes on to discriminate between 'property classes' and 'commercial classes' (1978a, pp.303-4). The property and commercial classes are subject to further differentiation on the basis of privilege, that is, positively privileged and negatively privileged property and commercial classes are delineated. Positively privileged property classes (i.e., owners of property) receive income from property rents (e.g., land, mines and so on) and securities. Negatively privileged property classes (i.e., the propertyless) include: slaves, the declassed, debtors and the poor. Positively privileged commercial classes have a monopoly on the management of business enterprises. These classes, furthermore, protect business interests by influencing economic policy to the advantage of business. Negatively privileged commercial classes are usually labourers. They are made up of the skilled, semi-skilled and unskilled (see Weber 1971a, p.115).[30] Weber includes the diverse groups labelled the 'middle classes' between the various positively and negatively privileged classes.

The inclusion of the 'middle classes' in the set of class categories is notable— because it enables Weber to analyze what is more appropriately called the rise of the 'new middle class' of salaried possessors of marketable skills distinct from both capitalist entrepreneurs and wage labourers during the first decades of the twentieth century in Europe. Weber (1978, p.304), for instance, includes 'public and private officials' in the 'middle classes' located between the positively privileged and negatively privileged commercial classes. As a matter of fact, Weber concedes that 'private salaried employees grow statistically faster than the workers' (1978a, p.1394).

'Social classes' constitute Weber's other major category. The emergence of a social class is contingent upon possibilities for mobility between class situations. Weber states that 'a "*social* class" makes up the totality of those class situations within which individual and generational mobility is easy and typical' (1978a, p.302; emphasis in original). He is referring to a notion of class grounded in mobility chances. An individual's life chances depend upon the range and rate at which he passes through a number of class situations. Weber identifies a few major social classes: the working class, the petty bourgeoisie, the propertyless intelligentsia, and various specialists and classes in a privileged position because of the ownership of property and access to education.

In the final analysis, the primary significance of Weber's typology of classes would appear to be the fact that it highlights the tendency towards differentiation within the various classes. In his lecture on 'Socialism', Weber declares that 'the development of the general system of stratification is very far from going in an obviously proletarian direction' (1978b, p.261). Quite the contrary. The general tendency seemed to indicate an increasing differentiation within the working class.[31] Although Weber's typology of classes may point to increasing differentiation, there are nonetheless major problems associated with this typology.

In the first place, the boundaries between the 'property classes', 'commercial classes' and 'social classes' are not well-defined at all. Weber, for instance, identifies the 'commercial classes' as a distinct grouping. However, a sub-group within the positively privileged commercial classes, namely the entrepreneurs, are also included among the middle classes located between the positively privileged and negatively privileged property classes. In like manner, professionals with qualifications in demand or a privileged education and workers with monopolistic qualifications and skills, are found among both the positively privileged commercial classes and the middle classes located between the positively privileged and negatively privileged commercial classes. Furthermore, entrepreneurs like shipowners are numbered among the positively privileged property classes and the positively privileged commercial classes. And it seems incongruous to incorporate proletarians with negative privileges alongside entrepreneurs with mainly positive privileges in the middle classes located between the positively privileged and negatively privileged property classes. Similarly, it appears absurd to number such diverse groupings as liberal professionals (e.g., lawyers, physicians) and highly skilled workers in the same positively privileged commercial class. In a word, Weber's typology of classes evokes a model of society made up of countless class divisions.[32] There are no solid class boundaries identifying distinct classes. What is more, it seems that Weber makes little use of the class typology in his empirical writings.[33] In the last resort, it is the fundamental 'property'/'lack of property' (capital/wage-labour) dualism adumbrated earlier that Weber employs most often. Furthermore, as we shall see, the significance of the 'new middle class' is obvious in both Weber's examination of the private officials administering the modern capitalist factory and the public officials administering the modern bureaucratic nation-state.

The fact that Weber regards 'property'/'lack of property' and the possession of marketable skills as the key objective criteria in the formation of classes in the modern capitalist market-economy has, thus far, been underlined. However, Weber also introduces subjective criteria. In the case of the category of 'property', he contends that ownership of various material objects (e.g., dwellings, workshops, mines, disposition over mobile instruments of production, various capital goods) differentiates the class situation of the propertied, 'just as does the "meaning" which they can give to the use of property, especially to property which has money equivalence' (Weber 1978a, p.928). It is worthwhile recalling at this point that *zweckrational* action is rendered meaningful in so far as the actor rationally takes into account and weighs means and ends. Propertied groups like capitalists give 'meaning' to their utilization of legally secured powers of control and disposal over the means of production, capital goods and so forth to the extent that they engage in rational profit-making activity. Capitalists rationally calculate the most efficient means to make a profit.

It is my contention that in respect of a propertyless group like wage-labourers, who offer labour-power as a service on the capitalist market, the instrumental notion of meaning is not applicable. The worker is unable to rationally calculate and assess means and ends. The worker is not allowed to decide on the way he will employ his service, labour-power, once it is purchased by the capitalist on the market. The worker's economic 'ends' are specified 'for' him by the capitalist and not 'by' himself. Seen in this light, subjective meaning is within a Weberian framework not important in the treatment of wage-labourers as a class. The constitution of workers as a class is independent of the subjective meaning which individual workers may confer on the 'rational capitalist *system*'.[34]

In respect of Weber's typology of classes, another fundamental problem, as

Cox indicates, is that the typology 'seems to be made to range over different social systems in a unsystematic way, with illustrations derived practically at convenience' (1950, p.227). Firstly, the inclusion of 'slave-owners' among the positively privileged property classes and of 'slaves' among the negatively privileged property classes is confusing. Weber had previously stated that:

> Those men whose fate is not determined by the chance of using goods or services for themselves on the market, e.g., slaves, are not, however, a class in the technical sense of the term. They are, rather, a status group. (1978a, p.928)

'Slaves' are a negatively privileged status group (i.e., devoid of any political rights), whereas 'slave-owners' are a positively privileged status group (i.e., possessing political rights sanctioned by custom or law). Moreover, the fact that slavery involves the 'possession' of one human being (the slave) by another (the slave-owner) as a legitimate form of ownership, is diametrically opposed to the notion of a class of formally 'free' workers, one of the key factors requisite for the emergence of modern rational capitalism. In this same connection, Weber declares that:

> We can learn little or nothing for our contemporary social problems from ancient history. A modern proletarian and a Roman slave would be as unable to understand one another as a European and a Chinese. *Our problems are of a completely different character.* (1971b, p.256; emphasis added)

The fact that Weber appears to apply his typology of classes to different historical periods in an unsystematic manner is also evident—when he employs the term 'class struggle' to refer to the conflict between creditors and debtors in Antiquity, and to the antagonism between landlords and serfs/tenants in the Middle Ages (see Weber 1978a, pp.303, 305, 928-31, 953-4, 1340-9; 1976a, p.23; 1970, p.301).[35] It seems as if Weber recognizes 'classes' outside of the modern capitalist market-economy. Weber, for example, incorporates the *proletarii* of Antiquity among the negatively privileged property classes (1978a, p.303). But Weber also maintains that:

> The element which differentiates the grain policies of ancient from modern states is essentially the contrast between the modern proletariat and the so-called ancient proletariat. The latter was a consumer proletariat, a mass of impoverished petty bourgeois, rather than, as today, a working class engaged in production. *The modern proletariat as a class did not exist in Antiquity.* (1976b, pp.41-2, emphasis added; see also 1976a, p.23; 1978a, pp.299, 930)

The modern proletariat, characterized by their legally secured powers of control and disposal over their labour-power, which they are nevertheless bound to offer for sale to capital on the modern labour market, are unknown in the ancient world.[36] Or as Weber puts it, 'the labor market (in the modern sense of the term) did not yet determine the class situation of the masses' (1978a, p.352; see also p.931). Similarly, the concept of 'the bourgeoisie' has not existed 'outside the modern Occident' (Weber 1976a, p.23; see also 1981b, p.337).[37]

Another point especially pertinent to the present discussion is, as Jones (1975, pp.739-40) stresses, Weber's observation that the 'ancient proletariat' exist only by reason of 'political rights'. In Antiquity, on Weber's reading, 'the *civis proletarius,* the "descendant"—namely, of a full citizen—was the typical *déclassé*' (1978a, p.1341; see also p.1340). In effect, the 'ancient proletariat' were constituted as a 'status group'. What Weber, on the other hand, calls 'the two "capitalist" classes, the bourgeoisie and, especially, the working class' (1978a, p.1196)—are constituted, in the first instance, by virtue of the unequal distribution of legally sanctioned powers of control and disposal over the means of production, capital goods and the like in the modern capitalist market-economy. That is, 'the factor that creates "class" is unambiguously economic interest, and indeed, only those interests involved in the existence of the market' (Weber 1978a, p.928). In contrast to the 'politically' secured rights of the 'ancient proletariat', the 'legally' sanctioned rights of 'the two "capitalist" classes' in the modern market-economy merely uphold inequalities based on already given economic conditions.[38]

In light of the preceding discussion of Weber's incorporation of slave-owners into the positively privileged property classes and of slaves and the 'ancient proletariat' into the negatively privileged property classes, it is reasonable to assume that 'the two "capitalist" classes' (the bourgeoisie and the modern proletariat) represent 'individual' ideal-types. In other words, the constellation of elements constituting 'the bourgeoisie in the modern sense of the word' (Weber 1981b, p.337) and the modern proletariat is restricted to the modern capitalist market-economy.

Given that Weber identifies the bourgeoisie and the wage-labourers as 'the two "capitalist" classes', it is now mandatory to examine in more detail these classes as phenomenon of the distribution of economic power within the modern market-economy. Weber asserts that 'an instance of "class position"' is 'those persons who were economically privileged in the formally "free" competitive struggle of the market by virtue of their position as property owners' (1978a, p.699; see also pp.639, 930). Domination owing to a constellation of interests prevails in the modern capitalist market. What distinguishes this form of domination is that it does not express itself through commands; it has not been transformed into a formally regulated relationship of authority between entrepreneur and wage-labourer. Weber (1978a, pp.943-4) argues that capitalist interests such as credit banks exercize a 'dominating' influence in the market simply on account of their monopolistic position. It is not necessary for credit banks to wield authority in the sense of demanding submission on the part of debtors. These credit banks (and, more generally, all capitalist interests) are already in a structural power situation.[39] This is tantamount to saying that the 'structure of interests' (Weber 1978a, p.83) is such that it *permits* it only to this particular class of economic actors to conduct their operations in accordance with the "interest" criterion' (Weber 1978a, p.98; emphasis added).

The capitalist's interest in rational profit-making activity is not merely subjective. This interest is not simply dependent upon the fact that the capitalist is aware of it. Rather, this interest in profit is objectively prescribed by structural conditions. The capitalist's interest in rational profit-making is already firmly established in the 'rational capitalist *system*'. In this regard, Weber purports that:

> The capitalist economy of the present day is an immense cosmos into which the individual is born, and which presents itself to him, at least as an individual, as an unalterable order of things in which he must live. *It forces the individual, in so far as he is involved in the system of market relationships, to conform to capitalistic rules of action.* The manufacturer who in the long run acts counter to these norms, will ... be eliminated from the economic scene ... Thus *the capitalism of to-day, which has come to dominate economic life, educates and selects the economic subjects which it needs, through a process of economic survival of the fittest.* (1976a, pp.54-5; emphasis added)

The capitalist's survival is contingent upon his capacity 'to conform to capitalistic rules of action'. His 'true' interest involves engaging in rational profit-making activity 'by the utilization of opportunities for exchange, that is on (formally) peaceful chances of profit' (Weber 1976a, p.17). The capitalist's class situation is such that he can take advantage of the 'mode of distribution' to transfer 'property from the sphere of use as "wealth" to the sphere of "capital"...' (Weber 1978a, p.927). Hence, the capitalist can increase his monopoly of legally secured powers of control and disposal over the means of production, capital goods and so on.

Of primary importance also is that capitalists' 'monopolistic domination in the market' further improves their 'life-chances'. Weber states that:

> ...the kind of chance in the *market* is the decisive moment which presents a common condition for the individual's fate. Class situation is, in this sense, ultimately market situation. The effect of naked possession *per se* ... is only a fore-runner of real 'class' formation. (1978a, p.928; emphasis in original)

It is the utilization of the powers conferred by property ownership and control over marketable resources in the modern capitalist market that is crucial for the determination of one's life-chances (e.g., access to education). It goes without saying, then, that capitalist entrepreneurs, middle class groups like public and private officials and wage-labourers have differential life-chances.

The end-result of capitalists' 'monopolistic domination in the market' is such that they are 'in a position to influence the market situation in such a way as actually to abolish the market freedom of others' (Weber 1978a, p.83; see also pp.84-5). It is the 'market freedom' of workers that is, in the main, abrogated by entrepreneurs in the modern capitalist market-economy. Weber avers that:

> The formal right of the worker to enter into any contract whatsoever with any employer whatsoever does not in practice represent for the employment seeker even the slightest freedom in the determination of his own conditions of work, and it does not guarantee him any influence on this process. It rather means, at least primarily, that *the more powerful party in the market*, i.e., normally the employer, has the possibility to set the terms to offer the job 'take it or leave', and, given the normally more pressing economic need of the worker, to impose his terms upon him. *The result of contractual freedom, then, is in the first place the opening of the opportunity to use, by the clever utilization of property ownership in the market, these resources without legal restraints as a means for the achievement of power over others.* (1978a, pp.729-30, emphasis added; see also p.110)

In effect, there are no symmetrical exchanges in the modern capitalist market-economy. The worker is subject to structural compulsion. An objective inequality of conditions prevails between the capitalist and the wage-labourer. The capitalist is not constrained to purchase the worker's labour-power continuously on the market. He is 'free' to buy it only when it contributes to profitability. Otherwise, the worker is deemed superfluous. Because the worker has been expropriated from his means of subsistence, he is not 'free' to withhold the sale of his labour-power. As Marx sarcastically puts it, the worker 'is compelled to sell himself of his own free will' (1976b, p.932). The class situation of the worker is such that he is forced to sell his labour-power continually in order to merely survive. Put another way, the worker's 'interest', as dictated by objective conditions, is such that he must adapt himself to the 'capitalistic rules of action'.[40] The alternative is to 'be thrown into the streets without a job' (Weber 1976a, p.55). The structural constraints to which workers are subject in the modern capitalist market-economy, are powerfully evoked in Weber's statement that the compulsive sale of their labour-power is 'the *fate* of the entire working class' (1978a, p.110; emphasis added).[41]

The fact that not only workers but also capitalists must 'conform to capitalistic rules of action', testifies also to the growing anonymity and impersonality of the exercize of economic power in the modern capitalist market. On this score, Weber writes that:

> The growing impersonality of the economy on the basis of association in the market place follows its own rules, disobedience to which entails economic failure and, in the long run, economic ruin. (1978a, p.585; see

also pp.600, 635-640, 731, 975, 1186-87; 1979, pp.190-1)

Weber goes so far as to say that 'victorious capitalism ... rests on mechanical foundations...' (1976a, pp.181-2). In contrast to the feudal estate order in which it is necessary to act differently towards persons of different status, the modern capitalist market-economy involves a mode of activity devoid of concern for persons. This market-economy, according to Weber, is distinguished by 'the universal domination of the "class situation"' (1978a, p.975). Personal relationships of domination are replaced by the impersonal dominance of class interests. Weber affirms that 'as personal relationships are replaced by the dominance of class, so personal hatred is replaced with natural inevitability by the phenomenon of "objective hatred"—the hatred of one class for another' (cited in Beetham 1974, p.219). It is no longer a question of individual persons as such confronting one another in the modern capitalist market, but of individuals as 'types' of their respective classes. The impersonal nature of the domination of capitalist interests implies, on Weber's reading, that the capital-labour relationship cannot be ethically regulated. What is more, the growing anonymity of domination by virtue of a constellation of capitalist interests leads to domination becoming more opaque and inaccessible.[42] In his study of the change from a feudal estate order to a modern, capitalist, agricultural market-economy in East Elbe, Weber speaks of the agricultural entrepreneur's commercial exploitation of agricultural labourers 'which, arising almost unnoticed, was actually much harder to evade...' (1979, p.190).[43]

In light of the aforesaid, it might appear that Weber is advocating a wholly structuralist perspective. On this account, capitalists and wage-labourers are the mere effects of the 'rational capitalist *system*'. It will be recalled, however, that within a Weberian action framework the capitalist system, in so far as it exists historically, can only be reproduced by virtue of rational profit-making activity. In this sense, the modern capitalist market-economy is a modality of capitalist economic action. The 'rational capitalist *system*' and capitalist economic action are reciprocally conditioned by each other. However, I would argue that workers do confront the 'rational capitalist *system*' in a more all-pervasive way as a series of objective constraints to which they have no kind of meaningful relationship. Workers are merely wielded as tools in the course of rational profit-making activity. They are subject to what Weber calls a '"masterless slavery"' (1978a, p.1186). Even so, it might be reasonably assumed that all workers orient themselves to the 'rational capitalist *system*', even if it involves nothing more than unthinking acquiescence in the present state of affairs.

Thus far, Weber's argument that domination by virtue of a constellation of interests is characteristic of the modern capitalist market-economy, has been highlighted. Regarding 'property'/'lack of property', however, Weber contends that 'it does not matter whether these categories become effective in the competitive struggles of the consumers or of the producers' (1978a, p.927). It is apparent, then, that Weber is not only interested in the 'dominating' influence exercized by capitalist interests over workers but also over consumers in the market. In this connection, Weber stipulates that:

> For purposes of economic theory, it is the marginal *consumer* who determines the direction of production. In actual fact, given the actual distribution of power, this is only true in a limited sense for the modern situation. To a large degree, even though the consumer has to be in a position to buy, his wants are 'awakened' and 'directed' by the entrepreneur. (1978a, p.92, emphasis in original; see also pp.99-100, 108)

Owing to the fact that capitalists are already in a structural power position, they can invest in aggressive advertizing campaigns and, hence, generate new consumption wants, whilst simultaneously allowing others to become insignificant. In other words, capitalists act as the 'hidden persuaders' creating the consumption wants requisite for the sale of their capital goods in the modern capitalist market. Consumers, on the other hand, lack the resources to resist the power of capital (e.g., overpriced goods).[44] On this score, Weber writes that:

> ...judging by experience, *consumers as a type have only a limited capacity for organisation.* People who have a specific interest in making money can easily be brought together once they are shown that combining in this way will help them to realise a profit or to guarantee profitability ... On the other hand, it is extraordinarily difficult to persuade people to join together when they have nothing more in common with each other than a desire or intention to buy something or to provide for their needs, since *the whole situation of the consumer stands in the way of socialisation.* (1978b, p.255; emphasis added)

Although Weber underlines the 'dominating' influence of capitalist interests over consumers in the modern market-economy, he did not, in my view, fully appreciate the fundamental significance of the consumption ethic for the continuous development of modern capitalism.[45] Weber's (1976a, p.172) treatment of capitalism is more relevant to the rise of modern market-oriented capitalism, when the ascetic prohibition of immediate consumption was essential in the interests of capital accumulation. It was still imperative at this early stage to accumulate through continual investment in the productive apparatus.[46] However, what Wiley (1983, p.36) appropriately calls the 'saving ethic' is no longer socially relevant to advanced capitalism characterized by mass production. To the contrary, a hedonistic consumption ethic underpins mass production in the contemporary phase of modern rational capitalism. An unappeasable desire for consumer goods is the *sine qua non* for capital accumulation in advanced capitalism.[47]

In view of the objective inequality of conditions prevailing between capitalists and wage-labourers/consumers in the modern capitalist market-economy, conflict is inevitable. Indeed, Weber affirms that 'the battle of man against man on the market is an essential condition for the existence of rational money-accounting...' (1978a, p.93).[48] The struggle between capitalists and workers/consumers manifests itself in conflict over prices (Weber 1978a, p.82). Money is primarily a weapon in this struggle between capitalists and workers/consumers. Prices, on the other hand, are expressions of the struggle. That is, 'they are instruments of calculation only as estimated quantifications of relative chances in this struggle of interests' (Weber 1978a, p.108).[49]

In point of fact, the price of labour is, according to Weber (1978a, pp.930-1), the major issue in price struggles in the modern capitalist market-economy. The dominant exchange relationship is that between capitalists and wage-labourers in the labour market.[50] Contrary to Weber, though, the purchase of labour-power is not as simple as buying capital goods in the commodity market. Labour-power is 'living' labour. It is a resource which inheres in the person of the worker, whereas all capital goods (e.g., consumer goods) are distinct from the individuals/classes competing for them.[51] The worker is the 'carrier' of labour-power. Regarding the price offered to wage-labourers for the sale of their labour-power, the capitalists are already structurally in a superior bargaining position. That is, owing to their legally secured powers of control and disposal over the means of production, capital goods and the like, capitalists can dictate the price of labour to the workers (see Weber 1978a, pp.138, 943). In view of the fact that propertyless workers' incomes are derived solely from wages, they are structurally bound to accept the price offered for the sale of their labour-power (e.g., specific skill) by the capitalist. In short, workers' incomes are ultimately dependent upon the power of private property in the labour market.

Of pivotal importance also is Weber's statement that:

One must ... distinguish between 'propertied classes' and primarily market-determined 'income classes'. Present-day society is predominantly stratified in classes, and to an especially high degree in income classes. (1970, p.301)

Granted, modern rational capitalism is primarily stratified in 'income classes', the major sources of income being wages and salaries. Income derived from ownership of the means of production (e.g., profit), on the other hand, is monopolized by a relatively small group (see Weber 1978a, pp.202-6). It should be emphasized, though, that the income obtained by wage-labourers and private and public salaried employees in return for the sale of their respective skills, is ultimately premised upon capitalists' legally secured powers of control and disposal over the means of production. What is more, income differentials are related to the differential capacities of different categories of these workers and salaried employees to oppose capitalists' 'monopolistic domination in the market'.[52]

It should, further, be noted that Weber perceives any conflict over prices in the modern capitalist market-economy as essentially 'peaceful' and 'regulated'. For Weber, 'a peaceful conflict' entails 'competition' 'insofar as it consists in a formally peaceful attempt to attain control over opportunities and advantages which are also desired by others' (1978a, p.38). A 'competitive process', in turn, is '"regulated" competition to the extent that its ends and means are oriented to an order' (ibid.).[53] In effect, Weber is espousing the liberal principle of 'free competition'.[54] Only where there is 'a genuine competitive process' (i.e., regulation) does 'conflict' exist (Weber 1978a, p.39). The survival of the modern capitalist market-economy is, on Weber's interpretation, conditional upon the continuation of this regulated conflict.[55]

Weber's espousal of the liberal principle of 'free competition' is certainly not applicable in the case of conflict concerning the price of labour-power. As Barbalet indicates, 'any resource allocated by competitive rivalry is necessarily distinct from those in competition for it' (1982, p.490). But given that the worker himself is the 'carrier' of labour-power, it cannot be apportioned through the competitive process. In the struggle between capitalists and wage-labourers over the price of labour-power, the worker himself is the very resource involved.

Of particular relevance in the present discussion also is that the modern state tailored to bureaucratic administration, facilitates the domination of capitalist interests in the market. It has already been shown that modern rational law guarantees the predictability, stability and freedom from arbitrary interference requisite for the effective functioning of the modern capitalist market-economy. But the legal security afforded by modern rational law is, in the last resort, predicated upon the modern state, that is, upon the political organization that successfully claims a legitimate monopoly of physical force within a given territory (Weber 1978a, p.56). Weber avers that:

> ...certainly the modern economic order under modern conditions could not continue if its control of resources were not upheld by the legal compulsion of the state; that is, if its formally 'legal' rights were not upheld by the threat of force. (1978a, p.65; see also 1949, p.46; 1981a, p.172)

This statement highlights the fact that Weber sees the modern state, in ideal-typical terms, as concerned mainly to uphold/guarantee the pre-existing mode of distribution of economic resources, rather than intervening directly in the functioning of the formally autonomous exchange process in the modern capitalist market. Weber is, in fact, thinking of 'the pure *laissez-faire* state which would leave the economic activity of individual households and enterprises entirely free and confine its regulation to the formal function of settling disputes connected with the fulfillment of free contractual obligations' (1978a, p.75). It is the *laissez-faire* state, for instance, which ultimately guarantees that the labour contract entered into autonomously by the capitalist entrepreneur and the wage-labourer in the market, will be executed in accordance with the relevant set of legal rules.

That said, Weber has to concede that a notion of the modern state concerned primarily with securing the market by means of judicial and fiscal policy, is not 'empirically' feasible.[56] That is to say:

The dividing line between 'regulation of economic activity' and mere 'enforcement of a formal order' is vague. For, naturally, the type of 'formal' order not only may, but must, in some way also exert a material influence on action; in some cases, a fundamental influence ... Indeed, a really strict limitation to purely formal rules is possible only in theory. (Weber 1978a, p.75)

Seen in this light, one can envisage the modern state in the 'concrete' situation exerting quite considerable 'material influence' on the distribution of legally sanctioned powers of control and disposal over the means of production, capital goods and so on in favour of capitalist interests in the modern market-economy.[57]

In light of the foregoing, it is important to bear in mind that there is nonetheless a contradiction built into the intervention of the modern state in the functioning of the modern capitalist market-economy. The kernel of the problem as Poggi (1978, p.95) reasons, is that although the modern state as a 'compulsory organization' (Weber 1978a, p.56) claims to be the repository of the most drastic means of exercizing physical force, it actually acts in the capacity of a guarantor for power relations that arise outside of it, and that it does not control. This is tantamount to saying that the modern state secures relations of domination which derive from private control over capital. Given private capital's 'monopolistic domination in the market', the modern state is, further, structurally bound to pay particular attention to the interests of capital. If capital depends upon the modern state to uphold its legally secured powers of control and disposal over the means of production, capital goods and the like, the modern state, by the same token, cannot ignore capital's structural power situation.

In addition to the treatment of the modern state as an agent intervening in the functioning of the modern capitalist market-economy, Weber also expresses another view in which this market-economy itself is subordinated to the political interests of the German national state. In this context, he understands himself as an '"economic nationalist"' (cited in Weber 1988, p.218).[58] In his inaugural lecture at Freiburg in 1895, Weber declares that:

The science of political economy is a *political* science. It is a servant of politics, not the day-to-day politics of the individuals and classes who happen to be ruling at a particular time, but the lasting power-political interests of the nation. And for us the *national state* is ... the temporal power-organization of the nation, and in this national state the ultimate standard of value for economic policy is 'reason of state'. (1980, p.438; emphasis in original)

Weber is arguing in this instance that the 'power-political interests' of the nation-state represent the yardstick against which the functioning of the modern capitalist market-economy should be evaluated. The role of this market-economy is now to promote the 'power-political interests' of the German nation-state.

In his study of the emergence of a modern, capitalist, agricultural market-economy from a feudal structure of domination in East Elbe, for instance, Weber viewed developments 'from the standpoint of Germanism' (1980, p.435). That is, he was principally concerned with the influx of Polish agricultural labourers into the East to replace the German workers who were migrating to the cities in the West. Although this inflow of Polish labourers was contributing to the emergence of a dynamic, modern, capitalist, agricultural market-economy, the key issue, according to Weber, was that 'the German character of the East ... *should* be protected, and that the economic policy of the state *should* also enter into the lists in its defence' (1980, p.436, emphasis in original; see also 1979, pp.177-205).[59] In the case of the rise of a modern, capitalist, agricultural market-economy in East Elbe, then, a conflict arose between the economic interests of capital and the 'power-political interests' of the German nation-state.[60]

Weber also points to the international character of modern rational capitalism. He makes the general observation that the existence of the various European nation-states contributed to the development of capitalism in the West. It was the perpetual struggle between different nation-states which played a major role in the rise of present-day capitalism. Weber declares that:

This competitive struggle created the largest opportunities for modern western capitalism. The separate states had to compete for mobile capital, which dictated to them the conditions under which it would assist them to power. Out of this alliance of the state with capital, dictated by necessity, arose the national citizen class, the bourgeoisie in the modern sense of the word. Hence it is the closed national state which afforded to capitalism its chance for development—and *as long as the national state does not give place to a world empire capitalism will also endure.* (1981b, p.337; emphasis added)

The various European nation-states engaged in a relentless conflict for political power, 'needed ever more capital for political reasons and because of the expanding money economy' (Weber 1978a, p.353). In the course of trying to expand its domination in the international political arena, a nation-state like Germany was very much dependent, for example, upon the investment of capital in the production of raw materials.

Weber, further, contends that 'every expansion of a country's power sphere increases the profit potential of the respective capitalist interests' (1978a, p.346). In the course of a discussion of the economic foundations of imperialism, he observes that the workers in creditor nations are of a strongly pacifist mind. They are not interested in forcibly participating in the exploitation of foreign colonial territories. This is the obvious outcome of the workers' 'immediate' class situation—where 'class antagonisms that are conditioned through the market situations are usually most bitter between those who actually and directly participate as opponents in price wars' (Weber 1978a, p.931; see also 1978b, pp.260-61). It is the manufacturers and business executives who are the 'direct' opponents of workers in wage conflicts within the domestic market-economy. The individuals interested in expropriating tribute from overseas colonial territories are, according to Weber, those who belong to the 'opponent class', like the capitalist entrepreneurs (1978a, p.920). Any successful imperialist policy strengthens 'the domestic prestige and therewith the power and influence of those classes, status groups, and parties under whose leadership the success has been attained' (Weber 1978a, p.920). Weber is once again calling attention to the international character of modern rational capitalism.[61]

This international dimension is also highlighted by Weber when he refers to the relationship holding between the domination of the workers in the creditor nations and the domination of overseas debtor territories. Although the investment of capital in the production of raw materials creates jobs and income opportunities for the masses of the creditor nation, the masses are nonetheless dominated. The reason for this lies in the fact that the means of war are, on Weber's reading, raised by levies 'which the ruling strata, by virtue of their social and political power, usually know how to transfer to the masses' (1978a, p.921). These means of war are, in turn, employed by members of the 'opponent class' to dominate overseas debtor territories.[62]

In sum, then, the discussion in this section has unravelled the implications inherent in Weber's conception of 'property'/'lack of property' as the most important bases for the formation of classes in the modern capitalist market-economy. Weber's key argument is that 'property' and 'lack of property' structure class relations through the medium of the modern capitalist market.[63]

4.3 The modern capitalist factory

Although Weber argues that 'property' and 'lack of property' structure class relations through the medium of the modern capitalist market, this is not to say that Weber ignores the relationship holding between the capitalist entrepreneur and the wage-labourer in the modern factory. Weber concedes that the '"class situation" also comprises ... *the necessity of complying with the discipline of a capitalist proprietor's workshop*' (1970, p.301, emphasis added; see also 1978a, p.930).[64] For Weber, the modern factory 'is a category of the capitalistic economy' (1978a, p.135). Moreover, this particular type of factory is a 'structure of dominancy' (Weber 1978a, p.942). The maximum of formal rationality in capital accounting oriented to profitability can be attained in the modern capitalist factory, on Weber's reading, 'only where the workers are subjected to domination by entrepreneurs...' (1978a, p.138; see also pp.108, 117).

Unlike domination by dint of a constellation of interests in the market-situation, domination in the factory is transformed into a formally regulated relationship of authority. To be more precise, it is a particular type of 'legitimate domination' ('authority'), namely legal-rational domination, which prevails in the modern capitalist factory. Furthermore, the probability that the capitalist entrepreneur's commands will be obeyed, is contingent upon 'prompt and automatic obedience' (Weber 1978a, p.53) on the part of a given group of workers. In effect, rational mass discipline is for Weber the *sine qua non* of legal-rational domination in the modern capitalist factory.

Bearing in mind Weber's notion of the modern capitalist factory as a disciplinary institution, he continues that:

...the concept of 'factory' will ... be limited to organized workshops where the material means of production are fully appropriated by an owner, but the workers are not; where there is internal specialization of functions, and where mechanical power and machines which must be 'tended' are used. (1978a, p.136; see also pp.117, 135; 1978b, pp.252; 1981b, pp.169, 302; 1971a, pp.103-55)

These three components defining the modern capitalist factory are all conducive to the creation of a disciplined workforce ready to obey the capitalist entrepreneur.[65]

In the first place, the capitalist's legally secured powers of control and disposal over the means of production means, as already shown, that the workers have been expropriated from their means of subsistence. Therefore, the fact that 'free' workers are bound to sell their labour-power in order to simply survive, creates the most favourable conditions for workers' submission. In this respect, Weber proclaims that:

...willingness to work on the part of factory labor has been primarily determined by a combination of the transfer of responsibility for maintenance to the workers personally and the corresponding powerful indirect compulsion to work, as symbolized in the English workhouse system... (1978a, p.153; see also p.151; 1981b, p.129)

Workers' willingness to comply with the capitalist's commands is explained in terms of objective economic circumstances. The docility of workers can signify an accommodation to structural conditions over which they have little control.[66] This, in turn, implies, I would suggest, that workers' capitulation in the modern factory is 'in reality' not necessarily normative; it does not of necessity entail a belief in the legality of the capitalist's orders.

Regarding technical specialization and the application of mechanical sources of power, Weber speaks of the modern capitalist factory in terms of:

...its official hierarchy, its discipline, its chaining of worker to machine, its agglomeration and yet at the same time (compared, say, with the spinning rooms of the past) its isolation of workers; its huge calculating machinery, stretching right down to the simplest manipulation of the worker... (1971a, p.155; see also p.112; 1978a, pp.1402, 1156; 1978b, p.252; 1981b, p.174)[67]

Modern factory production concerns the rationalization/disciplining of human labour in relation to the technical apparatus. Technical control is built into the physical structure of the labour process. The workers are integrated into the technical apparatus as its living appendages. The operations carried out by the workers in the modern capitalist factory simply entail the proper responses to the requirements of the machinery. It is the technical apparatus which paces and controls the workers.[68] Quite simply, Weber is saying that the workers are forged into a force of capitalist production. That is, 'the optimum profitability of the individual worker is calculated like that of any material means of production' (Weber 1978a, p.1156).

Of decisive importance also is that the logic of capital accumulation is such that technical change is inevitable. Weber explains that:

The mode of composition of an industry's capital, and that means decomposition of the elements of its production costs, manifests itself chiefly in the direction in which its propensity for labour-saving is moving. (1971a, p.108)

The installation of any new technically improved machine by capital to reduce labour costs signifies that certain hitherto indispensable qualities in the workers become obsolete, whilst the development of certain other qualities becomes essential. This is tantamount to saying that the modern capitalist factory 'produces' the workers with the special qualities requisite for the performance of certain specified technical functions at a particular time. Expressed another way, the impersonal system of technical control intrinsic to the modern capitalist factory completely dictates the occupational 'fate' of the worker. In this regard, Weber writes that:

...it is the 'technical' peculiarity of the production process, especially of the machines, which *directly* determines in the workers all the qualities the individual industry needs, and their potential career as well. (1971a, p.112; emphasis in original)

The title of the report that Weber wrote for the *Verein für Sozialpolitik* in 1907-1908 on the research strategy to be employed for the study of the

130

occupational careers of workers in large industries, also conveys the fact that workers were subject to objective technical constraints over which they had little control. The relevant title is: 'Methodological Introduction for the Survey of the Society for Social Policy concerning *Selection* and *Adaptation* (Choice and Course of Occupations) for the Workers of Major Industrial Enterprises' (1971a, p.103; emphasis added). The phrase, 'selection and adaptation', was not part of the original title chosen by the *Verein für Sozialpolitik*. Weber added this phrase when he took over the direction of the survey.[69]

In light of the foregoing, it is important to underline the fact that Weber does not, however, analyze the connection between science/rational technology and the domination exercized by capital in any detail. He is more concerned with science/technology in the context of the relentless march of rationalization in all orders of society, including the modern capitalist factory. Accordingly, Weber says that 'the practical and not merely incidental but, rather, methodical inclusion of rational science in the service of the economy is one of the keystones in the development of regulation of life in general' (1978c, p.1129).[70]

Although the worker has simply become an appendage of the technical apparatus in the modern capitalist factory, Weber does acknowledge that the process of the insertion of workers into this apparatus encountered resistance such as that of traditionalism. He avers that:

> A man does not 'by nature' wish to earn more and more money, but simply to live as he is accustomed to live and to earn as much as is necessary for that purpose. Wherever modern capitalism has begun its work of increasing the productivity of human labour by increasing its intensity, it has encountered *the immensely stubborn resistance of this leading trait of pre-capitalist labour*. And to-day it encounters it the more, the more backward (from a capitalist point of view) the labouring forces are with which it has to deal. (1976a, p.60, emphasis added; see also pp.59-63; 1978a, pp.127-9, 240; 1981b, pp.175, 355)[71]

The resistance of the Russian peasantry against intensified capitalist development led to, for example, an increase in '"archaic" *agrarian* communism'(Weber 1995, p.92, emphasis in original; see also pp.93-101).

Weber, in my view, appraizes the resistance of pre-capitalist labour 'from above', that is, from a position of advantage and control. Where traditional motivations to work exist, it is exceedingly difficult from the standpoint of a capitalist to 'manage' labour on a rational basis and, hence, increase productivity.[72] In the case of appropriated workers like slaves and serfs, any attempt by the owner to exact performance from them beyond the traditional limits could endanger the traditional basis of the owner's authority. True, a traditional, patriarchal relationship to a feudal lord, for instance, could sustain a high level of affectual incentive to work (see Weber 1978a, p.151). But the vital point is that:

> *The bourgeoisie depends economically on work which is continuous and rational* (or at least empirically rationalized); *such work* contrasts with the seasonal character of agricultural work that is exposed to unusual and unknown natural forces, it *makes the connection between means and ends, success and failure relatively transparent.* (Weber 1978a, p.1178; emphasis added)

In the course of the transition to modern rational capitalism, then, it was crucial for capitalist interests to overcome customary ideas concerning labour effort.[73]

Weber contends, as previously mentioned, that psychic self-regulation in the form of Protestant asceticism played a major role in the fabrication of disciplined, industrious workers ready to respond to the commands of the capitalist entrepreneur in the modern factory.[74] For 'capitalism at the time of its development needed labourers who were available for economic exploitation for conscience' sake' (Weber 1976a, p.282). The Calvinist notion of the calling was such that the diligence and method with which the individual worker laboured in the factory, provided proof of his state of grace. The Calvinist ethic propelled workers into the modern capitalist factory with a compulsive sense of duty and obligation.[75] Weber argues that 'the continuous and unobtrusive ethical discipline' (1970, p.320) of the Protestant sects played a crucial role in the production of assiduous labourers during the rise of modern rational capitalism (see Weber 1970, pp.302-22; 1976a, pp.144-54). He goes so far as to say that 'such a powerful, unconsciously refined organization for the production of capitalistic individuals has never existed in any other church or religion...' (1981b, p.368).

In this same connection, Weber states that efforts on the part of capitalist employers (who were, of course, primarily men) to improve the performance of women workers, especially unmarried ones, was exceedingly difficult. The kernel of the problem was that traditional attitudes toward labour persisted. Increases of piece-rates, for example, were 'without avail against *the stone wall of habit*' (Weber 1976a, p.62; emphasis added). However, Weber continues that those working girls with a religious background, particularly a Pietistic background, performed very well in the modern capitalist factory. Indeed, 'statistical investigation confirms it, that by far the best chances of economic education are found among this group' (Weber 1976a, pp.62-3).

If the treatment of labour as a calling became characteristic of the wage-labourer in the factory during the emergence of modern rational capitalism, a corresponding attitude towards rational profit-making distinguished the entrepreneur. Weber affirms that:

> From their religious life ... there emerged a 'habitus' among individuals which prepared them in specific ways to live up to the specific demands of

early modern capitalism. Schematically expressed, an entrepreneur with an untarnished conscience stepped into the place of the one whose desire for gain was at most tolerated by God ... *This entrepreneur was filled with the conviction that Providence had shown him the road to profit not without particular intention.* (1978a, p.1124, emphasis added; see also 1976a, p.172; 1981b, p.367)[76]

Rational profit-making activity received religious justification. Protestant asceticism, in Weber's view, freed the acquisition of goods from the restraint imposed by traditional Christian ethics. And the Calvinist idea of the calling, by the same token, legitimized the capitalist's 'ruthless exploitation' of wage-labourers (Weber 1981b, p.367).

Even though Weber maintains that the Calvinist notion of the calling was the organizing creed in the creation of disciplined workers and efficient entrepreneurs in the course of the rise of modern rational capitalism, he also concedes that 'the religious root of the modern economic outlook is dead; and the concept of a "calling" is a relic in the world of today' (1983b, p.158; see also 1976a, pp.72, 176, 181-2; 1978c, p.1125). Modern capitalism is 'able to force people to labour without transcendental sanctions' (Weber 1976a, p.282). The moral order of present-day capitalism inheres in the imposition of a Calvinist mode of activity without the assistance of the Calvinist religious ethic.[77] In fact, Weber alleges that the role of the Protestant sects in the fabrication of disciplined, industrious workers 'is gradually being taken away from them by purely secular organizations' (1978c, p.1117; see also 1978a, p.150). Protestant asceticism is replaced by the profane scientific disciplines of the factory such as Taylorism and Fordism. Taylorism, for example, points to the emergence of a new mode of exerting control over the workers in the modern capitalist factory, that is, by means of 'scientific management'. Taylorism bears principally on the optimization of the calculable performance of labour by defining and fixing effort levels.[78]

In view of the fact that a disciplined workforce is the prerequisite for the effective enforcement of the entrepreneur's legal-rational authority, Weber states that one variant of the legal-rational domination/authority predominates in the modern capitalist factory, that is, bureaucratic organization. The primary characteristics of Weber's 'individual' ideal-type of modern bureaucracy include: the principle of official jurisdictional areas which are generally controlled by rules, the principle of office hierarchy, the management of the modern office is based on written documents ('the files'), the office entails training in a field of specialization, the office also demands the full working capacity of the official and, finally, the management of the office is in accordance with general rules (see Weber 1978a, pp.221-6, 956-8). From a purely technical standpoint, Weber purports that the strictly bureaucratic type of administrative organization, namely, the monocratic type is:

...capable of attaining the highest degree of efficiency and is in this sense *formally the most rational known means of exercising authority over human beings.* It is superior to any other form in precision, in stability, in the stringency of its discipline, and in its reliability. It thus makes possible a particularly high degree of calculability of results for those acting in relation to it. It is finally superior both in intensive efficiency and in the scope of its operations, and is formally capable of application to all kinds of administrative tasks. (1978a, p.223, emphasis added; see also p.975)

In the context of the modern factory, the bureaucratic form of organization is the most rational means of controlling wage-labourers. For Weber, the bureaucracy staffed by private officials is the most efficient instrument available to the entrepreneur to exercise his legally secured powers of control and disposal over managerial functions. The entrepreneur's right to enforce orders is sanctioned by adherence to fixed rules, that is, rules based on procedures which have the sanction of law. Put another way, the "'objective" discharge of business primarily means a discharge of business according to *calculable* rules and "without regard for persons'" (Weber 1978a, p.975; emphasis in original).[79] This "'objective" discharge of business' also includes disciplined workers submitting to the entrepreneur's legally authorized commands. In other words, the obedient workers are merely viewed as reflexes of the capitalist's will.

I would argue that docile workers are within the Weberian action schema inaccessible to sociological analysis except as a means of rational profit-making activity. Workers are not rational economic agents acting on their own motives. They are not free to choose means and ends. The capitalist entrepreneur is the only 'real' subject of rational economic action. Stated otherwise, the fact that the modern capitalist factory is a model of strict bureaucratic organization enhances the subjective freedom of the capitalist, whilst simultaneously curtailing it for the workers. Modern bureaucracy as a 'precision instrument' (Weber 1978a, p.990) *par excellence,* enables the entrepreneur to employ the worker more efficiently as a tool for securing the goal of profitability and, hence, his own subjective freedom.

In contrast to Weber's apprehension of the relationship between 'the two "capitalist" classes' (1978a, p.1196) in the modern factory in terms of relations of domination (i.e., command-obedience relations), Marx treats this relationship in terms of relations of production. Hence, Marx's primary concern with economic exploitation. Weber does not extend his analysis of the modern capitalist factory into what Marx (1976b, p.279) calls 'the hidden abode of production'. In other words, Marx understands the modern capitalist factory as a 'structure of exploitation', whereas Weber views it as a 'structure of dominancy'.[80]

Pertinent to the issue at hand here also is that although Weber describes the bureaucratic organization of the modern factory as an 'animated machine' (1978a, p.1402) conducive to impersonal domination, he nevertheless insists that this type of factory does not become totally bureaucratized and dehumanized. That is to say:

> There is no question but that the 'position' of the capitalist entrepreneur is as definitely appropriated as is that of a monarch. Thus *at the top of a bureaucratic organization, there is necessarily an element which is at least not purely bureaucratic.* The category of bureaucracy is one applying only to the exercise of control by means of a particular kind of administrative staff. (Weber 1978a, p.222; emphasis added)

Thus, it is not only the docile wage-labourers who capitulate to the capitalist entrepreneur's orders. Indeed, bureaucratic officials are themselves the administrative means of imposing the entrepreneur's will in the modern factory. The bureaucratic staff (i.e., private officialdom of white collar employees) is the administrative tool in the hands of the entrepreneur to gain the subservience of the workers. As in the case of workers, 'the discipline of officialdom' concerns 'its habit of painstaking obedience within its wonted sphere of action' (Weber 1978a, p.988).

Seen in this light, it is only the capitalist entrepreneur who is immune to bureaucratic domination in the modern factory. For Weber, the capitalist entrepreneur, as opposed to the worker and the professional bureaucrat, is the one personality capable of exercizing individual responsibility and acting on his own motives. The capitalist entrepreneur is the one self-assertive personality in the administered, dehumanized world that is the modern factory. Indeed, the fact that the dominant will of the capitalist operative at the top of the bureaucratic enterprise 'is at least not purely bureaucratic', exemplifies Weber's key interest in a will-centred notion of personality (i.e., voluntarism) as the counter-force to the onset of bureaucratization. This obsession with the dominant will also attests to Weber's intense elitism. A modern factory without a capitalist entrepreneur in control is inconceivable to Weber. All in all, then, Weber places the capitalist entrepreneur's 'will to power' above the 'objectified authority' of the bureaucracy.[81]

That said, Weber recognizes the independent power base of the officials staffing the bureaucracy. He declares that 'bureaucratic administration means fundamentally domination through knowledge' (1978a, p.225). More to the point, the power of all bureaucrats rests on two kinds of knowledge: 'technical knowledge' procured through specialized training, and 'official information' which is available only through administrative channels (see Weber 1978a, pp.1417-18).[82] In this sense, the capitalist's ability to exert 'control by means of a particular kind of administrative staff' in the modern factory, is restricted to the extent that he is 'in reality' dependent upon the functioning of the bureaucratic machine to attain his goal, profit. Given his reliance upon the independent power base of private officialdom, the capitalist is not, thereby, free to act solely on his own motives. The 'dictatorship of the official' (Weber 1978b, p.260) limits individually differentiated activity on the part of the capitalist entrepreneur himself.

At this point in the discussion, it is once again important to reiterate the ideal-typical nature of Weber's concept of modern bureaucracy. For bureaucratic administration may not in the 'concrete' situation be 'the most rational known means of exercising authority over human beings'. Since the functioning of a bureaucracy relies upon the coordination of all the specific activities assigned to the different members of the organization, increased 'inter-dependence' is, as Giddens (1982, p.36) observes, the result. Hence, disruption at any level of the bureaucratic hierarchy can affect its overall functioning. Viewed in this light, the process of production in the modern capitalist factory (as opposed to, for instance, the putting-out system) is much more susceptible to disruption by strategically placed groups of workers. Workers may oppose the capitalist's legally sanctioned authority and control through individual or collective acts of sabotage, slowdowns, the threat or actual withdrawal of labour and the like.[83]

Interestingly enough, Weber himself also conceded that the smooth functioning of bureaucratic administration could be obstructed in the 'concrete' situation. At the convention of the *Verein für Sozialpolitik* in 1909, the subject of discussion was whether, from the standpoint of social policy, municipal ownership of public utilities and transportation was more desirable than private ownership. Weber (1954, p.95-9) argued that if state and municipal officials procured more authority over the workers, they would soon treat them in the same manner as capitalist entrepreneurs. He, further, observed that labour relations were particularly bad in state-owned mines. Assessing these poor labour relations from the vantage point of a public official, Weber writes that:

> If I were in such a position I would also find it impossible in the long run to prevent such conditions arising; if I had *the daily friction with workers*, either individually or in organizations, so that I could feel my temper rising at *the eternal interference with my carefully worked-out plans* and wished I could send all these people to the devil; for I would be underestimating myself as a true bureaucrat if I did not claim to know, much better than these blockheads, what was good for them. In such *quarrels* the minds of the public officials, who rightly enough consider themselves to be far more intelligent than their workers, will work on the lines that I have just described. However capable and farsighted these gentlemen may be, they become brittle in *the daily clash of interests*; I would also become brittle and draw the same conclusions as I have imputed to them. (1954, p.98; emphasis added)

This description of the 'daily clash of interests' between public officialdom and wage-labourers in state-owned mines, represents a striking deviation from Weber's 'individual' ideal-type of modern bureaucracy. The fact that bureaucratic administration may not be 'the most rational known means of exercising authority over human beings', is implicit in Weber's depiction of the poor labour relations in mines owned by the state. The workers had not been tamed into complete submission. They were not merely reflexes of the public official's 'carefully worked-out plans'.

The salient point, though, is that Weber views workers' opposition from the standpoint of an official, that is, from a position of administrative control. He does not consider resistance in relation to the experience of the workers. It is my contention that Weber cannot, in any case, conceptually elaborate workers' resistance to bureaucratic domination in a systematic fashion—because workers within the action schema are excluded from the sociological domain except as a means of rational profit-making activity.[84]

4.4 Critique and class action

In this final section, it is necessary to consider whether Weber offers any critical analysis at all of modern rational capitalism. Moreover, it is essential to ascertain whether Weber identifies distinct modes of class action.

In respect of Weber engaging in a critical treatment of modern rational capitalism, it is interesting to point out that he acknowledges that:

> The fact that the maximum of *formal* rationality in capital accounting is possible only where the workers are subjected to domination by entrepreneurs, is a further specific element of *substantive* irrationality in the modern economic order. (1978a, p.138; emphasis in original)

At bottom, Weber is stating that rational profit-making activity is opposed to the satisfaction of human needs. Capital goods are produced to satisfy 'effective demand' and, therefore, production decisions are determined 'by the structure of marginal utilities in the income groups which have both the inclination and the resources to purchase a given utility' (Weber 1978a, p.108; see also p.340). The laws of supply and demand rather than the satisfaction of human wants predetermine the quantity and quality of the goods made available on the market. In other words, rational profit-making activity 'does not reveal anything about *the actual distribution of goods*' (Weber 1978a, p.108; emphasis added). There is no necessary relationship between rational profit-making and the equitable distribution of goods and income in the modern capitalist market-economy.

But, then, Weber also says that:

> ...if the standard used is that of the provision of a certain minimum of subsistence for the maximum size of population, the experience of the last few decades would seem to show that formal and substantive rationality coincide to a relatively high degree. (1978a, pp.108-9)

Despite the fact that formal rationality gives us no indication as to what 'real want satisfaction' (Weber 1978a, p.109) involves, rational profit-making nonetheless has met the ethical requirement for an improvement in the economic conditions of the propertyless masses. Indeed, Weber goes so far as to say that:

> Increasingly the material fate of the masses depends upon the continuous and correct functioning of the ever more bureaucratic organizations of private capitalism, and the idea of eliminating them becomes more and more utopian. (1978a, p.988)

The substance of Weber's thinking is such, then, that the ethical demand for social justice is contingent upon the bureaucratic organization of modern market-oriented capitalism. What is darkly ironic is the fact that the 'material fate' of the workers is predicated upon capital's employment of them as tools in the course of rational profit-making activity.

Given the Weberian principle of value-freedom one is, however, logically debarred from appraizing the normative validity of capital's utilization of workers as instruments. Ethically neutral social science is solely concerned with the attainment of 'empirical' knowledge. It concentrates wholly on 'what is'. In respect of the fate of wage-labourers in the modern factory, Weber avers that:

> The issue is *not* how social conditions in industry are to be 'assessed' or, in particular, whether the situation in which self-contained industry places the workers today is satisfactory or not ... No; it is exclusively a matter of the unbiased, objective statement of facts and the ascertainment of their causes in industrial conditions and the individual character of its workers ... The whole problem at issue ... is, socio-politically speaking, a totally neutral one by its very nature. (1971a, pp.104-5; emphasis in original)

An ethical evaluation of the workers' socio-economic conditions in the modern factory is, on Weber's reading, an extra-scientific question, answerable only from the vantage point of a particular value-commitment.[85] It is logically impossible for Weber to judge capital's use of wage-labour as unjust or exploitative—since he does not, in the first place, recognize the existence of any rationally validated principles of morality that could corroborate such allegations.

Of paramount importance also is Weber's (1978b, pp.251-62) assessment of socialism as a possible alternative to modern rational capitalism. Weber principally expands upon one ideal-type of socialism, that is, state-socialism. For Weber, state-socialism is concerned with the penetration of the economy by the modern bureaucratic state. 'It is based on collaboration between the combined entrepreneurs in a particular branch of the economy and state officials, either military or civilian' (Weber 1978b, p.254). In this sense, Weber maintains that the socialization of the economy means the continuation of subjection to bureaucratic domination.[86] Indeed, it is Weber's contention that:

> ...the structure of that peculiar 'system' which has been thrust upon the

population by the organisation of large-scale industrial production transcends even the scope of the question of 'capitalist' or 'socialist' organisation of production in its significance for their fate, because the existence of this 'equipment' *as such is independent* of this alternative. (1971a, p.154-5; emphasis in original)

Modern rational capitalism and modern state-socialism represent component phenomena in the all-encompassing bureaucratization of modern society.[87]

In point of fact, Weber alleges that state control of the economy would extend and accelerate the bureaucratization already taking place in capitalist organizations like the modern factory.[88] The kernel of the problem, in Weber's view, is that the two key values intrinsic to socialism (as he understands it), the satisfaction of human needs and freedom from domination, are contradictory. State-socialism would entail rational planning of production oriented to the most efficient satisfaction of human wants, instead of private profit. But it transpires that the satisfaction of human wants (substantive rationality) necessitates increased centralized planning by the modern bureaucratic state (formal rationality). Accordingly, Weber states that:

It would be a question whether in a socialistic system it would be possible to provide conditions for carrying out as stringent a bureaucratic organization as has been possible in a capitalist order. *For socialism would, in fact, require a still higher degree of formal bureaucratization than capitalism.* (1978a, pp.224-5, emphasis added; see also pp.139, 972-3; 1949, p.47)

For Weber, then, the rise of state-socialism would mean the replacement of a dynamic capitalist society by a static socialist one.

Although Weber also underscored the inexorable onslaught of bureaucratization in modern rational capitalism, he nevertheless claimed that the class of capitalist entrepreneurs would act as a counter-force to this onslaught. No such oppositional force would be found in a state-socialist society. What is more, Weber (1978b, p.255) believed that the tension between the economic bureaucracy of private capitalism and the political bureaucracy of the modern state maintained an element of dynamism in modern society. Hence, the crucial point, on Weber's interpretation, is that 'state bureaucracy would rule *alone* if private capitalism were eliminated' (1978a, p.1402, emphasis in original; see also pp.139, 154; 1978b, p.255).

In the last resort, it is not far-fetched to claim that Weber's treatment of modern rational capitalism is rather partisan. His primary concern is the preservation of bourgeois freedom, that is, a kind of freedom which allows the capitalist to wield workers and private officials as means in the course of rational profit-making activity. This bourgeois bias is built into Weber's analysis of modern capitalism. This bourgeois predisposition, as already adumbrated earlier, is ultimately rooted in the logic of Weber's action framework. Moreover, the fact that Weber is a self-proclaimed member of the bourgeoisie (if a somewhat uncomfortable one) is made quite clear, when he writes that: 'I am a member of the bourgeois classes. I feel myself to be a bourgeois and I have been brought up to share their views and ideals' (1980, p.444). Taking account of Weber's interest in the maintenance of the modern capitalist market-economy to safeguard bourgeois freedom, it could be argued that he is offering quite a positive appraizal of modern capitalism. Certainly, Weber believes that the maintenance of the modern capitalist market-economy is worthwhile to preserve some remnant of bourgeois freedom.

Weber (1980, p.447) did not, on the other hand, regard social justice and the material well-being of the workers as the most important issues.[89] The fact that rational profit-making activity met the ethical demand for an improvement in the economic conditions of the workers was simply an historical contingency. It was an 'unintended consequence' of rational profit-making activity. Even when Weber developed a keen interest in the socio-economic conditions of agricultural workers in the 1890s, this interest was determined by a political motive.[90] Matters of state were paramount in Weber's (1979, pp.177-205) study of the socio-economic conditions of the rural workforce in East Elbe. In the case of industrial workers, Weber likewise asserts that:

> When it acts with solidarity, the industrial proletariat is certainly an immense power in dominating the street. In comparison, however, with entirely irresponsible elements, it is a force at least capable of order and of orderly leadership through its functionaries and hence through rationally thinking politicians. From the point of view of state policy, all that matters is to increase the power of these leaders, in Germany of trade-union leaders, over the passions of the moment. (1970, p.395; see also 1994, p.302)

Matters of state were once again uppermost in Weber's mind, not the solidarity of the proletariat as such. Weber was especially interested in the employment of trade-union leaders to gain working-class support for the national policies of the German state. He (1980, pp.445-8) also favoured the development of progressive social policies to secure the backing of the workers (particularly, the upper strata) for national policies.[91]

In light of the aforesaid, it is worthwhile asking at this point whether Weber envisages workers and capitalists engaging in distinct forms of class action to defend their respective interests? To begin to answer this question, it is first of all imperative to ascertain whether a class within the Weberian schema represents anything more than an aggregate of individuals. Roth's and Wittich's translation of Weber is such that 'a class does not in itself constitute a *group*' (Weber 1978a, p.930; emphasis added). Gerth's and Mills' translation, on the other hand, reads as 'a class does not in itself constitute a *community*' (Weber 1970, p.184;

emphasis added). The latter translation is the more correct because *Gemeinschaft* is usually translated as 'community'. What is more, the former translation fails to sufficiently grasp Weber's understanding of the crucial difference holding between classes and status groups. That is to say, classes are not 'communities', whereas status groups usually are.[92] But Weber certainly believes that '"classes" are *groups of people* who, from the standpoint of specific interests, have the same economic position' (1958, p.39; emphasis added). The members of a class constitute a kind of mass group in so far as they share common economic interests (see Weber 1978a, p.302).[93]

However, if a 'group of people' like capitalist entrepreneurs are to defend their shared economic interests, some form of collective action may be required. The difficulty, though, is that 'the emergence of an association or even of mere social action from a common class situation is by no means a universal phenomenon' (Weber 1978a, p.929). The rational association of class members, according to Weber, *'does not necessarily happen'* (1978a, p.302, emphasis added; see also p.303). Such a rational association is problematical rather than inevitable. Weber is, in effect, accentuating the unpredictable nature of collective action on the part of class members. There is no necessary correlation between the location of class members in the 'rational capitalist *system*' and 'class action'.

The most important polemical target of Weber's comments on the contingent nature of collective action on the part of individuals in the same class situation was:

...that kind of pseudo-scientific operation with the concepts of class and class interests which is so frequent these days and which has found its most classic expression in the statement of a talented author, that the individual may be in error concerning his interests but that the class is infallible about its interests. (1978a, p.930)[94]

Taking account of Weber's key idea that only individuals are real, he vehemently opposed the notion that a 'class' could be a real entity with interests of its own which might differ from what the 'members' of a class regarded as their 'true' interests.

Owing to the problematic nature of 'class action', then, Weber contends that:

The degree in which 'social action' and possibly associations emerge from the mass behavior of the members of a class is linked to *general cultural conditions,* especially to those of an intellectual sort. It is also linked to the extent of the contrasts that have already evolved, and is especially linked to *the transparency of the connections between the causes and the consequences of the class situation.* (1978a, p.929; emphasis added)

The secularization/intellectualization of culture in modern Western society suggests that the modern proletarian no longer finds consolation in religion for the structural constraints to which he is subject in the modern capitalist market-economy. On this score, Weber explains that the modern worker 'is threatened not by demons and natural forces that must be magically checked, but by social conditions that can be rationally understood' (1978a, p.1194; see also 1978a, pp.485-6, 953-4; 1978b, p.283). The working class was able to accept its 'fate' 'as long as the promise of eternal happiness could be held out to it' (Weber 1981b, p.369). But when the working class ceased to find solace for its lot in religion, it was inevitable that the strains and stresses built into modern capitalist society (i.e., class conflict) should intensify. Ironically enough, it was the rationalization/intellectualization of culture promoted by modern capitalism itself that gave birth to scientific socialism.

If the intellectualization of culture makes it easier for workers to rationally apprehend the objective constraints to which they are subject in the modern capitalist market-economy, it obviously follows that a growing consciousness of mutual identity of interests will result in the establishment of class-conscious organizations. Weber (1978a, p.305) mentions four criteria for the success of class-conscious organization. Firstly, he maintains that class-conscious organization has a greater chance of success against the 'direct' economic opponents. For the growing anonymity and impersonality of the exercize of domination in the modern capitalist market-economy makes it extremely difficult to identify those individuals and groups, who have the 'real' 'powers of control and disposal' over the means of production, capital goods and the like. Put another way, the anonymous and impersonal nature of domination by virtue of a constellation of interests in the modern capitalist market, implies that the clarity of the links between 'the causes and consequences of the class situation' are more difficult to disentangle. In the case of industrial workers, this indicates, according to Weber (1978a, p.931; 1978b, pp.260-1), that the setting up of an organization to achieve certain goals will be more successful against the manager in the modern factory, as opposed to the shareholder, who 'really' is the repository of unearned income.

Weber's second precondition for the success of class-conscious organization has to do with large numbers of individuals being concentrated in the same class situation. For instance, substantial numbers of individuals must, in order to survive, sell the use of their labour-power to entrepreneurs for a fixed period of time in the modern capitalist market-economy.

Weber's third precondition for the success of class-conscious organization bears on how easy it is to technically organize the individuals in the same class situation. To take the case of the rural proletariat in East Elbe, the technical problems of organization were exceedingly difficult because these agricultural workers were dispersed far over the land. Weber explains that:

> The rural proletariat were able to develop an anti-landlord class consciousness under normal political conditions only in an isolated fashion against *individual* masters, who customarily combined a naive brutality

with camaraderie. (1979, p.180; emphasis in original)

Weber further accentuates the technical impediments to the organization of the isolated rural labourers—when he declares that even after the process of proletarianization has rendered the rural workers more equal, 'there is no possibility of a general union on the basis of common interests of the widely separated groups' (1979, p.200).[95]

As regards industrial workers, Weber maintains that it is also difficult to technically organize them in the modern capitalist factory. Despite the concentration of industrial workers in one workshop, they are still isolated from each other. Rather than entering into 'direct' relations with each other, the workers are integrated into the technical apparatus. This being so, Weber reasons that the so-called 'workshop community' 'basically, is not a community...' (1971a, p.155; see also 1970, p.368).

This is not tantamount to saying, though, that no kind of co-operation takes place between workers in a modern capitalist factory. In this connection, Marx observes that:

...the co-operation of wage-labourers is entirely brought about by the capital that employs them. Their unification into one single productive body, and the establishment of a connection between their individual functions, lies outside their competence. *These things are not their own act, but the act of the capital that brings them together and maintains them in that situation. Hence the interconnection between their various labours confronts them* ... as a plan drawn up by the capitalist, and, in practice, as his authority, *as the powerful will of a being outside them, who subjects their activity to his purpose.* (1976b, pp.449-50; emphasis added)

In short, the capitalist brings the individual workers (whose labour-power has been purchased for a fixed period of time) together in the modern factory, so that he can use them efficiently as a tool in the course of rational profit-making activity.

In addition to the technical problem of organizing isolated workers, Weber bequeaths the important insight that differences within the working class itself may also add to the technical difficulties of establishing a viable class-conscious organization. It is possible that status differentiation within the working class could seriously damage the effectiveness of a working class organization. Weber affirms that:

In the lands of the Anglo-Saxons there is often *not the slightest social contact* between skilled trade-unionists and lower classes of worker—it is well known that they sometimes find it hard to sit at the same table. (1971a, p.151; emphasis added)

Even though all workers are economically compelled to sell their labour-power in the modern capitalist market-economy, differences in type of occupation, degree of skill, level and type of education, intellectual and aesthetic interests and so on, may result in the emergence of distinct communal groupings isolated from each other within the working class. Similarly, political differences between workers can impede organizational effectiveness. Weber (1995, pp.65-70) in 'Bourgeois Democracy in Russia', for example, reflects upon the split within the Russian Social Democratic movement during the first decades of the twentieth century.

One final precondition identified by Weber for the success of class-conscious organization, relates to class members being 'led towards readily understood goals, which are imposed and interpreted by men outside their class (intelligentsia)' (Weber 1978a, p.305; see also 1994 p.298). In this light, it could be argued that workers by themselves are incapable of setting up a class-conscious organization to promote their interests. Rather, they are dependent upon the bourgeois intelligentsia to decide upon the objectives to be pursued. The importance of figures like Marx, Engels, Lenin and Trotsky would appear to confirm the crucial role played by the bourgeois intelligentsia in 'interpreting' and 'imposing' the goals to be pursued by working class organizations.

Given the preconditions for the success of class-conscious organization, Weber, however, provides little precise evidence of the circumstances under which the shared economic interests of workers give rise to a consciousness of mutual identity of interests and, thereby, to class-conscious organization. It is my contention that one of the major difficulties lies in the fact that workers' resistance has no theoretical foundation in Weber's sociology of action. Weber refers, it is true, to workers engaging in some forms of amorphous collective action. He speaks of, for instance, 'an increasingly typical phenomenon of precisely the latest industrial development, namely, the slowdown of laborers by virtue of tacit agreement' (1978a, p.929). Weber also describes the migration of German rural workers from the East Elbe region as 'a tacit strike' against the emergence of agricultural capitalists (1979, p.199). He even goes so far as to say that the 'class situation of the modern proletariat' represents the 'most important historical example' of a class reacting against the class structure 'in the form of rational association' (1978a, pp.929-30).

Although Weber refers to workers' opposition, the pertinent point, I would argue, is that the elaboration of workers' resistance as a sociological category is not undertaken in his conceptual exposition. It is not possible to conceptualize wage-labourers collectively acting together within the Weberian action schema. For these wage-labourers are hidden from Weber's sociological gaze except as a means of rational profit-making activity. In view of the fact that the individual worker does not constitute a rational economic agent acting on his own motives, it is, by the same token, inconceivable that a group of workers could collectively act on their own initiative by setting up some form of class-conscious organization. Workers within the Weberian action framework have no independent, sociological reality. Or as Bottomore pointedly remarks, 'it is the working class, not the bourgeoisie, which is "dissolved" in Weber's thought' (1985a, p.30).[96]

At this point in the discussion, it is necessary to ascertain the 'general cultural conditions' under which consciousness of a mutual identity of interests can emerge in the case of capitalist entrepreneurs. To begin with, the capitalist interest in rational profit-making is already securely entrenched in the 'rational capitalist *system*'. This interest is objectively defined by structural conditions. Seen in this light, the interest of any individual member of the capitalist class is, as Offe and Wiesenthal stipulate, 'far less likely to be ambiguous, controversial, or wrongly perceived' (1980, p.91). This is not to say, of course, that difficulties and uncertainties may arise concerning the most efficacious means of attaining the goal of profit. Another fundamental reason, as Offe and Wiesenthal observe, why the interest of any individual capitalist is far less liable to be equivocal— resides in the fact that the capitalist interest in rational profit-making is externally upheld by those institutional sectors of modern rational capitalism (especially, the modern state) which rely upon successful capital accumulation to carry out their own functions. Further, Offe and Wiesenthal (1980, p.91) indicate that the individual capitalist is not impelled to confer with his fellow capitalists to corroborate whether his interest in rational profit-making is really his 'true' interest. In this respect, the capitalist interest in rational profit-making is 'monological' rather than 'dialogical'.[97] And by the same token, the teleological model of action underpins the rational profit-making activity of each individual capitalist.

Bearing in mind that the development of a consciousness of mutual identity of interests is relatively easy to create among capitalists, Weber defines '"class action"' as 'social action by the members of a class' (1978a, p.929). 'Class action' on the part of capitalists is precisely the aggregation of the self-seeking interests of 'possessive' individuals.[98] Co-operation among capitalists concerns the intermingling of egoistic calculations of utility. Rational profit-making activity rules out anything other than temporarily expedient and individually based collective action. In this connection, Weber writes that:

> Participation in a market ... encourages *association* between the exchanging parties and a social relationship, above all that of competition, between the individual participants who must mutually orient their action to each other. But no further modes of association develop except in cases where certain participants enter into agreements in order to better their competitive situations, or where they all agree on rules for the purpose of regulating transactions and of securing favourable conditions for all. (It may further be remarked that *the market and the competitive economy resting on it form the most important type of the reciprocal*

determination of action in terms of pure self-interest, a type which is characteristic of modern economic life). (1978a, p.43, emphasis added; see also pp.30, 636)

The rational association of capitalists in a business organization simply entails the rationally motivated adjustment of egocentric calculations of utility. Capitalist co-operation merely involves a monological mode of intraorganizational communication. In short, capitalist co-operation is equivalent to instrumental collectivism.[99]

Pertinent to the issue at hand here also is that 'the kind of human relationship' which develops in the modern capitalist market-economy:

...is always exchange, market, goal-oriented associations, instead of personal brotherliness. It is always this as opposed to the other kind—that 'community' of acosmic love on a pure foundation of 'brotherhood'. (1973b, p.148; see also 1970, pp.331, 339, 357; 1978a, pp.107, 636-7)

At bottom, Weber is saying that a mode of collective action based upon a system of fraternal ethics is inconceivable in the modern capitalist market-economy. This market-economy is immune to an ethic of brotherhood. An ethic of brotherliness involves a communal relationship, that is, a kind of relationship 'based on a subjective feeling of the parties, whether affectual or traditional, that they belong together' (Weber 1978a, p.40). For Weber, as previously mentioned, a communal relationship is irrational because it is affection or tradition rather than reasons of expediency which bring individuals together.

Weber also mentions 'communist arrangements for the communal or associational organization of work' which are based 'on direct feelings of mutual solidarity' (1978a, pp.153-4). These include: the household communism of the family, the military communism of comrades in the army, and the communism grounded in love and charity in a religious community. None of these 'communist arrangements' are relevant to co-operation based on the rationally motivated adjustment of egocentric calculations of utility in the modern capitalist market-economy. In this same connection, Weber mentions 'associations' set up by Protestant sects in the United States. He declares that:

...*in those areas least touched by modern disintegration*, the association offered the member the ethical claim for brotherly help on the part of every brother who had the means. (1970, p.308; emphasis added)

Weber is once again underscoring the fact that an association grounded in brotherly love cannot be established in the modern capitalist market-economy.

The preceding discussion of the nature of capitalist co-operation bears on the industrial and commerical bourgeoisie. However, Weber also remarks on internal divisions which can impede the organizational effectiveness of the bourgeoisie. In the course of his appraizal of the prospects for liberal democracy in Tsarist

Russia, for instance, Weber states that 'political hostilities within the same social stratum or between rival social strata are often the most subjectively intense' (1995, p.106). The industrial and commercial bourgeoisie in Tsarist Russia strongly opposed the liberal reforms championed by the bourgeois intelligentsia in the late nineteenth and early twentieth centuries. The Russian industrialists and bankers never joined the Russian liberal parties. To the contrary, they supported pro-Tsarist associations.[100]

Finally, it is worthwhile considering Weber's understanding of the kind of co-operation to be found in an economic system organized on a socialist basis. Socialism in this instance is understood by Weber in terms of '"co-determination"', as opposed to individuals 'being administered "dictatorially"', that is, by autocratic determination from above in which they had no voice' (1978a, p.202). Weber once again insists that the self-seeking interests of individuals would prevail in an economic system organized on such a socialist basis. He writes that:

...it would be the interests of the individual, possibly organized in terms of the similar interests of many individuals as opposed to those of others, which would underlie all action. The *structure* of interests and the relevant situation would be different, and there would be other *means* of pursuing interests, but this fundamental factor would remain just as relevant as before. (1978a, p.203, emphasis in original; see also p.352)

The pivotal point is that although the 'structure of interests' and the 'means' of striving for these interests are different in an economy organized on what Weber deems to be socialist principles, co-operation would still entail the merging of egocentric calculations of utility. Weber goes on to say that economic action oriented 'to the interests of others does exist' (1978a, p.203). But, then, he also insists that 'it is an induction from experience' that most men cannot act in this manner and, in fact, 'never will' do so (ibid.).

It is my contention that Weber transgresses his own conception of 'social science' (i.e., concentrating on 'what is')—when he reads into the future in a deterministic manner the fact that economic action oriented 'to the interests of others', 'never will' arise. Another point especially pertinent here is that Weber's restriction of rational social action in general to the interplay of egoistic calculations of utility is, as already indicated, built into his action framework. This being the case, Weber's restriction of co-operation to individually based collective action in an economic system organized on a socialist basis (as he understands it), is much more than 'an induction from experience'. Weber's conceptual framework is such that he is debarred, in any case, from regarding any mode of social action oriented 'to the interests of others' as rational in modern capitalism.[101]

The discussion of Weber's understanding of classes as phenomena of the distribution of economic power within the modern capitalist market-economy has been quite extensive in this chapter. Rational capital accounting is, according to Weber, the most fundamental precondition for the existence of modern capitalism in the West. One of Weber's key arguments is that 'property' and 'lack of property' constitute the most important bases for the formation of classes in the modern capitalist market-economy. Weber develops a notion of 'property' understood in terms of legally guaranteed 'powers of control and disposal' over the means of production, human labour services and managerial functions. It is quite clear that the capital/wage-labour relationship always remained of compelling centrality for Weber. Weber's treatment of class relations also points to the emergence of the 'new middle class' of salaried possessors of marketable skills, distinct from both capitalist entrepreneurs and wage-labourers, during the first decades of the twentieth century. And Weber highlights the crucial role played by the modern nation-state, tailored to bureaucratic administration, in upholding the domination of capitalist interest in the market-economy. Besides Weber's core contention that 'property' and 'lack of property' structure class relations through the medium of the modern capitalist market, he also bequeaths the important insight that the class situation includes the necessity of complying with the discipline of the modern factory. Unlike domination by virtue of an aggregation of interests in the market-situation, capitalist domination in the factory takes the form of a formally regulated relationship of legal-rational authority. Finally, the consideration of class action highlights the fact that it is not possible to conceptualize workers collectively acting together with the Weberian action schema. For these workers are inaccessible to sociological analysis except as a means of rational profit-making activity. Capitalist co-operation, on the other hand, simply involves the rationally motivated adjustment of egocentric calculations of utility.

Notes

1 Cf. also Parsons 1928, pp.641-61; Sahay 1974, pp.25-40; Cohen 1981, pp.xv-lxxxiii; Bottomore 1985a, pp.22-34; Poggi 1983, pp.13-26; Collins 1980, pp.925-42; Kalberg 1983, pp.253-88; Seidman and Gruber 1977, pp.498-508; Birnbaum 1953, pp.125-41; Sayer 1991, pp.92-155.

2 'Budgetary management', on the other hand, involves 'the continual utilization and procurement of goods whether through production or exchange, by an economic unit for purposes of its own *consumption* or to procure others goods for *consumption...*' (Weber 1978a, p.87; emphasis in original).

3 Of particular relevance also is Cohen's (1981, pp.xxxiv-xxxv) underlining of the fact that for Weber the institutional locus of modes of economic activity oriented to profitability by the employment of rational capital

accounting, is the industrial enterprise and not the operation of the free market. True, Weber admits that 'enterprises based on capital accounting may be oriented to the exploitation of opportunities of acquisition afforded by the market...' (1978a, p.91). The crucial point, though, is that the kind of goods that are made available on the market, the nature of the labour services employed and so on, are determined by means of an *ex ante* calculation of the probable risks and chances of profit within the industrial enterprise itself. In this regard, Weber writes that 'the question, what type of demand is to be satisfied by the production of goods, becomes in turn dependent on the profitability of production itself' (1978a, p.94).

4 For Marx, on the other hand, the most fundamental feature of modern capitalism 'arises only when the owner of the means of production and subsistence finds the free worker available, on the market, as the seller of his own labour power. And this one historical pre-condition comprises a world's history. Capital, therefore, announces from the outset a new epoch in the process of social production' (1976b, p.274). The most integral feature of modern capitalism is its class character, exemplified in the relationship between capital and wage-labour. It is only as a 'mode of production' that one can conceptualize modern capitalism within a Marxian framework, because it is only, then, that the capital/wage-labour relationship is the major integrating force of society.

5 Cf. Mueller 1979, pp.156-68.

6 Regarding 'the commercialization of economic life' as one of the conditions making possible the maximization of the formal rationality of capital accounting, Weber writes that it essentially means 'the general use of commercial instruments to represent share rights in enterprise, and also in property ownership' (1981b, pp.277-8).

7 Cf. Graber 1985, pp.86-107; Trubek 1972, pp.720-53; Rheinstein 1954, pp.xxv-lxxii; Schluchter 1981, pp.82-138; Habermas 1984a, pp.243-71; Kronman 1983, pp.72-95; Turner 1981, pp.318-51.

8 Cf. Kronman 1983, pp.118-46; Trubek 1972, pp.739-50.

9 Although Weber contends that the calculable nature of modern rational law contributed to the maximization of the formal rationality of capital accounting in the modern profit-making enterprise, he nevertheless concedes that the development of modern rational capitalism in Britain was not contingent upon this type of legal system (see 1978a, pp.889-92). In Britain, according to Weber, 'the degree of legal rationality is essentially lower than, and of a type different from, that of continental Europe' (1978a, p.890). Even though the English legal system has a low level of calculability (i.e., an autonomous legal system with general universal rules), Weber argues that two aspects of the Common Law have been relevant for the development of capitalism in Britain. Firstly, legal training was the responsibility of the lawyers, that is, of a group 'active in the service of propertied, and particularly capitalistic, private interests and which has to

gain its livelihood from them' (Weber 1978a, p.892). Secondly, Common Law justice was almost completely denied to the underprivileged and the poor in Britain, since the administration of justice was concentrated in London and was extremely expensive. It was mainly the propertied and, especially capitalist interests, who had access to Common Law justice.

10   In this context, it is worthwhile noting that Lukács (1974, pp.83-222) appropriates Weber's conception of 'rationalization' by developing a Marxian inspired theory of 'reification'. In Lukács' view, 'rationalization' is a product of capitalist production which transforms individuals into objects of exploitation and administration.

11   In light of the preceding discussion, it is important to briefly consider how Weber's (1971b, pp.254-75; 1976b, pp.37-79) understanding of capitalism in Antiquity differs from his notion of modern rational capitalism. Cf. also Dibble (1968, pp.92-110), Finley (1977, pp.317-24), Wierner (1982, pp.389-401). See, esp., Love (1986, pp.152-72) who engages in a meticulous analysis of Weber's diverse conceptions of 'ancient capitalism'.

In the Introduction to one of his very early works, *The Agrarian Sociology of Ancient Civilizations* (originally written in 1896-1897), Weber declares that 'where we find that property is an object of trade and is utilized by individuals for profit-making enterprise in a market economy, there we have capitalism' (1976b, p.51). He goes on to say that capitalism understood in this manner 'shaped whole periods of Antiquity...' (ibid.). Weber's definition of capitalism in Antiquity is such that market exchange activity oriented to profit is the key feature. On the basis of this definition, Weber, for example, alleges that slave-based agriculture in the ancient world was capitalist, because both land and slaves were treated as objects of exchange and were obtained on the open market. Pertinent to the issue at hand here also is that the early Weber does not accept the notion that capitalism cannot exist because of the absence of free labour. To endorse such an idea is, according to the early Weber, 'to limit needlessly the concept of capitalist economy to a single form of valorization of capital—the exploitation of other people's labour on a contractual basis—and thus to introduce social factors' (1976b, pp.50-51). The crux of the matter, though, is that later in the Introduction to *The Agrarian Sociology of Ancient Civilizations*, Weber's understanding of the nature of capitalism in Antiquity begins to change. Weber now maintains that the most important forms of capital investment in the ancient world included: government contracts, mines, sea trade, plantations, banking, mortgages, overland trade, the capitalist exploitation of skilled slaves in cottage industries or craft workshops. Given these forms of capital investment, it is difficult to see how some of them (e.g., government contracts) can be easily accommodated to his other definition of ancient capitalism solely in terms of market exchange oriented to profit. In the later part of the Introduction to *The Agrarian Sociology of Ancient Civilizations,* Weber (1976b, pp.52-79), in fact, underlines the absence of 'capitalism' (now rendered more or less in terms of the absence of modern rational capitalism). Central features which now impede the development of capitalism in Antiquity include: the absence of mass markets, obstacles to the formation of capital, the technical limits to the exploitation of slave labour in large-scale enterprises, and the limited employment of cost accounting procedures due primarily to the impossibility of strict calculation in the exploitation of slave labour.

In view of the inconsistencies inherent in the early Weber's analysis of ancient capitalism, it is important to point out that the later Weber (1978a, pp.164-6; 1981b, pp.279-369) clearly separates 'ancient capitalism' from 'modern rational capitalism'. Weber now employs the term 'political capitalism' (or politically oriented capitalism) to describe non-market, irrational types of profit-making. Politically anchored capitalism is dependent upon the private exploitation of political relations of domination, rather than being principally oriented to the market. Political capitalism is orientated to a mode of profit-making which wields force. And by the same token, the incomes earned in 'political capitalism' 'are the return on *actual violence*' (Weber 1978a, p.206; emphasis in original). The various forms of political capitalism include: tax farming, capitalistic financing of wars and revolutions, sale of offices, trade speculation and so forth. Even though these activities are connected with the use of violence in the course of profit-making, they nevertheless can be categorized as 'capitalistic' because they are concerned with the systematic pursuit of profit by the deliberate investment of funds from which greater returns are expected. Moreover, the anticipated returns are calculated in monetary terms (of course, monetary calculation does not involve rational capital accounting). The different forms of 'political capitalism' have, on Weber's reading, been found throughout the world at various stages of history. However, these forms of 'politically oriented capitalism' were especially prevalent in Antiquity. As adumbrated above, market-oriented capitalism aligned to a rational type of profit-making (i.e., rational capital accounting) carried on peacefully, developed only in the modern Western world. In this connection, Weber proclaims that: 'it is only in the modern Western world that rational capitalistic enterprises with fixed capital, free labor, the rational specialization and combination of functions, and the allocation of productive functions on the basis of capitalistic enterprises, bound together in a market economy, are to be found' (Weber 1978a, p.165).

12 Weber (1949, pp.64-5) also gives a differentiated account of 'the economic'. He distinguishes between 'economic' phenomena, 'economically relevant' phenomena and 'economically conditioned' phenomena. 'Economic' phenomena relate to action directed towards a consciously economic end. 'Economically relevant' phenomena are not economic themselves, but they have indirect significance for economic life. And

'economically conditioned' phenomena have little economic effect, but can be more or less strongly influenced by economic factors in their formation.

13 'Utilities' include 'goods' and 'services' (Weber 1978a, pp.68-9).

14 Even when Weber does not directly mention the categories 'property' and 'lack of property' in some of his definitions of class situation, it is nonetheless important to bear in mind that these categories do condition class relations through the medium of the market. Weber, for instance, argues that 'the specific and typical cases of class situation today are ones determined by markets' (1970, p.301). Similarly, he contends that 'the kind of chance in the *market* is the decisive moment which presents a common condition for the individual's fate. Class situation is, in this sense, ultimately market situation' (1978a, p.928; emphasis in original).

15 See Poggi 1983, p.15; Kozyr-Kowalski 1982, pp.5-24; Curtis 1968, pp.93-8.

16 In a somewhat similar vein, Weber declares that: 'The category of "wealth" includes more than physical goods. Rather, it covers *all* economic advantages over which the budgetary unit has an assured control, whether that control is due to custom, to the play of interests, to convention, or to law' (1978a, p.89; emphasis in original).

17 This having been said, it is important to remember Weber's other point that 'it is by no means true that only the legal assurance of powers of disposal is decisive either for the concept or in fact' (1978a, p.72; see also p.68). Indeed, other economic modes of organization such as socialism entail, according to Weber, 'some kind of *de facto* distribution of powers of control and disposal' (1978a, p.67).

18 Weber labels 'economic advantages' as 'the opportunities of economic advantage, which are made available by custom, by the constellation of interest, or by a conventional or legal order for the purposes of an economic unit...' (1978a, pp.68-9).

19 Weber also speaks of 'the disposition over material property' (1978a, p.927).

20 For Weber, 'goods' are 'non-human objects which are the sources of potential utilities of whatever sort' (1978a, p.68).

21 Kozyr-Kowalski's reading of Weber is such that he also distinguishes between 'material goods property' and 'labour power property' (1982, p.14). In like manner, Marshall et al. claim that 'labour power, and the differing skills embraced by it, are simply forms of property which offer variable life-chances on the market' (1985, p.263).

22 See Kronman 1983, pp.137-46.

23 Or as Marx observes, capital does not directly appropriate the worker's labour-power. Rather, it is 'mediated through exchange' (1973, p.498).

24 Or as Marx puts it, the worker 'is free of all the objects needed for the realization of his labour-power' (1976b, pp.272-3).

25 Seen in this light, Giddens also maintains that it would be departing too much from the accepted terminology to consider both 'capital' and the 'labour-power' of the worker as 'property'. Therefore, he employs 'property' in the conventional sense (i.e., pertaining to ownership of the means of production). He uses 'market-capacity', on the other hand, in an inclusive sense 'to refer to all forms of relevant attributes which individuals may bring to the bargaining encounter' (1981b, p.103; emphasis removed). Possession of recognized skills is, for example, a key factor influencing 'market-capacity'.

Although Marx also speaks of the worker as 'the proprietor of labour-power' (1976b, p.271), he goes on to say that labour-power is a specific type of property. That is to say, the worker can treat his labour-power as his own property 'only by placing it at the disposal of the buyer, i.e. handing it over to the buyer for him to consume for a definite period of time, temporarily' (1976b, p.271).

26 On this score, Dahrendorf's view that the end-result of the 'managerial revolution' in advanced capitalism has been the replacement of 'the possession, or non-possession, of effective private property by the exercise of, or exclusion from, authority as the criterion of class formation' (1959, p.136), is thoroughly un-Weberian. For Dahrendorf, classes are now determined by authority and its distribution rather than by private property.

Similarly, Parsons (1954b, p.432) contends that the functions of 'management' and 'ownership' have become differentiated in the large business enterprises. In Parsons' view, the occupational functions of professionals are becoming more important than the ascriptive rights of ownership.

27 This point will be elaborated upon in the following chapter.

28 In this instance, Parsons' translation of 'class situation' as 'class status' in Weber (1964, pp.424-5) is confusing.

29 On Weber's notion of class, see: Cox 1950, pp.223-7; Walton 1971, pp.389-94; Barbalet 1980, pp.401-18; Parkin 1982, pp.90-96; Giddens 1981b, pp.41-52, 78-81; Burger 1985, pp.12-14; Kozyr-Kowalski 1982, pp.5-24; Jones 1975, pp.729-57; Valentine 1972, pp.64-8; Brewer 1989, pp.82-96; Holton and Turner 1989, pp.179-94; Jensen-Butler 1976, pp.50-60.

30 In a similar vein, Weber (1979, pp.177-205) offers an empirical analysis of different categories of agricultural labourers in his study of the East Elbe economy.

31 In this regard, it is also important to mention Marx's belief that the wage-labour/capital/landowner division was the fundamental class division in modern capitalist society. Marx purports that: 'The owners merely of labour-power, owners of capital, and landowners, whose respective sources of income are wages, profit and ground-rent, in other words, wage-labourers, capitalists and landowners, constitute then three big classes of modern society based upon the capitalist mode of production' (1959,

p.885). But Marx goes on to mention 'the infinite fragmentation of interest and rank into which the division of social labour splits labourers as well as capitalists and landlords...' (1959, p.886). It is possible that if Marx had further developed his chapter on 'Classes' at the end of *Capital* (Vol. III), he might have presented a much more meticulous analysis of the many divisions within the major classes in modern capitalism. Interestingly enough, Weber also maintains that 'the unfinished last part of Karl Marx's *Capital* apparently was intended to deal with the issue of class unity in the face of skill differentials' (1978a, p.305).

32 See Barbalet 1980, p.409; Parkin 1982, pp.93-4; Croix 1983, p.90.

33 See Giddens 1981b, p.79; Cox 1950, p.227; Barbalet 1980, p.409.

34 Other interpreters argue that Weber develops a wholly individualist notion of class at the expense of a structural explanation. See, e.g., Barbalet (1980, pp.410-18), Wenger (1987, pp.43-64), Burris (1987, pp.67-90). Atkinson (1972, pp.71-4), on the other hand, speaks of the equivocation between objective and subjective criteria in Weber's treatment of the 'class situation'. In light of the preceding discussion, and given that Weber's more general understanding of the relationship holding between social action and social structure is problematic—it is advisable not to place Weber either solely in the individualist or structural camp.

35 In a similar vein, Marx writes that: 'the class struggle in the ancient world ... took the form mainly of a contest between debtors and creditors, and ended in Rome with the ruin of the plebeian debtors, who were replaced by slaves. In the Middle Ages the contest ended with the ruin of the feudal debtors, who lost their political power together with its economic basis' (1976b, p.233).

36 If the modern proletariat as a class did not exist in the ancient world, this does not imply the non-existence of 'free' labour. Weber (1976b, pp.47-8; 1971b, p.258) points out that free artisans and free, unskilled wage-earners were to be found. Wage-earners were hired for harvesting and large numbers were also employed by the state for excavation work, construction and other public projects.

37 It is in this context that Weber speaks of 'the modern class struggle' (1970, p.125).

38 Briggs (1960, pp.43-73) likewise argues that the concept of 'class' with all its associated terminology, was the product of the major socio-economic changes that occurred in Europe in the late-eighteenth and nineteenth centuries. See also Bauman 1982, Cohen 1983.

39 It was stated in the previous chapter that Weber construes the ideal-typical concept of domination in a rather restrictive fashion. He excludes domination arising from the aggregation of interests from his typology of domination. For an usable concept of domination can only be defined by reference to power of command. It should be borne in mind, then, in the following discussion that capitalists' 'monopolistic domination in the

market' has nothing to do with a command-obedience relationship. It is in the modern capitalist factory, as we shall see in the next section, that domination is expressed in a formally regulated relationship of authority between employer and worker.

40 In contrast to the capitalist's 'true' interest in rational profit-making which is already objectively imposed by modern rational capitalism, the worker's interest in the sale of his labour-power does not 'factually', as opposed to 'formally', represent his 'true' interest. The worker's 'true' interests are not already firmly established in the modern capitalist market-economy. Hence, it is a much more difficult task to pinpoint these interests.

41 In this sense, Udéhn (1981, p.137) is incorrect to claim that the worker's initial act of entering a contract with the capitalist constitutes 'action'. The worker is not strictly speaking even 'acting' on his own motives, when he agrees to sell his labour-power for a fixed period of time. To reiterate, the worker is bound to sell his labour-power for a fixed period of time.

In this same connection, Marx writes that: *'The silent compulsion of economic relations sets the seal on the domination of the capitalist over the worker* ... In the ordinary run of things, the worker can be left to the "natural laws of production", i.e. it is possible to rely on his dependence on capital, which springs from the conditions of production themselves and is guaranteed in perpetuity by them' (1976b, p.899; emphasis added).

42 In a similar vein, Marx writes that 'since capital is the antithesis of the worker, this merely increases the *objective power* standing over labour' (1973, p.308, emphasis in original; see also p.831).

Foucault likewise underlines the anonymity and opaqueness of the exercize of what he calls 'disciplinary power' in modern society. Foucault affirms that: 'power is no longer substantially identified with the individual who possesses or exercises it by right of birth; it becomes *a machinery* that no one owns ... this is so much the case that class domination can be exercised just to the extent that power is dissociated from individual might' (1980, p.156; emphasis added).

43 Cf. Riesebrodt 1989, pp.131-57.

44 See Murphy 1985, pp.234-5.

45 Granted, Weber admits that 'through the payment of money wages on a large scale, the market for goods which are objects of mass consumption is broadened' (1978a, p.151).

46 Marx also reasons that: 'The illusion that the capitalists in fact practised "self-denial"—and became capitalists thereby' was 'a demand and a notion which only made any sense at all in the early period when capital was emerging from feudal etc. relations...' (1973, p.285).

47 Marx anticipates the consumer society when he states that: 'each capitalist does demand that his workers should save, but only *his own*, because they stand towards him as workers; but by no means the remaining world of workers, for these stand towards him as consumers. In spite of all "pious"

speeches he therefore searches for means to spur them on to consumption, to give his wares new charms, to inspire them with new needs by constant chatter etc.' (1973, p.287; emphasis in original).

48 Similarly, Weber speaks of 'the material struggle for existence' (1949, p.65), 'the economic death struggle for existence' (1980, p.428), 'the struggle of man against man' (1989, pp.218-19) and so on.

49 See Murphy 1985, pp.234-9.

50 Although the labour market predominates in modern capitalism, Weber (1978a, pp.138, 930-32; 1970, p.301) differentiates two other market-types, namely, the credit and commodity markets. With the development of modern rational capitalism, however, the commodity and labour markets are much more closely related, since 'labour' itself is treated as a 'commodity'. Cf. also Wiley 1967, pp.529-41; Jensen-Butler 1976, pp.50-60.

51 Weber does not mention this major difference between the sale of labour-power and capital goods.

52 See Rubery 1982, pp.330-48; Barbalet 1985b, pp.327-48.

53 In this instance, it is the order governing the market which is relevant.

54 In this context, Marx observes that: '*It is not individuals who are set free by free competition; it is, rather, capital which is set free.* As long as production resting on capital is the necessary, hence the fittest form for the development of the force of social production, the movement of individuals within the pure conditions of capital appears as their freedom...' (1973, p.650).

55 It needs to be noted, though, that the types of conflict in Weber's writings extend all the way from the extreme case of violent, unregulated conflict in the political sphere to peaceful and regulated conflict, that is competition, in the modern capitalist market-economy.

56 See Trubek 1972, pp.739-46.

57 It should be noted that a crucial feature of the emergence of modern industrial capitalism from the second half of the nineteenth century in Germany, was that it was directed 'from above' via much state involvement. See Lash and Urry 1987, pp.17-29.

58 The significance of Weber's understanding of himself as an '"economic nationalist"' can only be fully appreciated, when his intellectual debt to the nineteenth century German Historical School of Political Economy is taken into account. The science of political economy was closely linked to the state and administration. German economics was a *Staatswissenschaft*. Cf. Hennis 1988, pp.107-45.

59 It is interesting to note here that Weber's stipulation that 'the German character of the East ... *should* be protected', contravenes his espousal of the principle of value-freedom. Weber was well aware of this principle from the beginning of his career, since the distinction between 'what is' and 'what should be', as pointed out earlier, was first developed by the German Historical School of Political Economy.

60　Similarly, Weber appraized the importance of the stock exchange 'from the standpoint of Germanism'. He writes that: 'A strong exchange cannot be a mere club for "ethical culture", and the funds of the great banks are no more a "charitable device" than are rifles and canons. From the point of view of a national economic policy aimed at *this-worldly* goals; they could only be one thing—a weapon for achieving power in that economic struggle' (1978b, p.377; emphasis in original).

61　In his study of the emergence of a modern, capitalist, agricultural market-economy in East Elbe, Weber also recognized how 'a calculated "involvement in the world economy"' was 'substantial for the local class structure' (1979, p.194). Weber likewise (1989, pp.210-20) in his discussion of Germany as an industrial state, highlights the international character of modern capitalism.

62　Collins (1986b) and Wallerstein (1979) set out to further analyze the international character of modern capitalism which was treated only in a cursory manner by Weber.

63　See Marshall et al. (1985, pp.259-84) who also espouse a Weberian notion of class formation. Interestingly enough, Weber also wrote that 'classes are stratified according to their relations to the *production* and *acquisition* of goods...' (1978a, p.937; emphasis added). But he never developed a conception of classes understood strictly in terms of relations of production.

64　Interestingly enough, Lockwood (1958, p.15) also includes the following two factors under 'class position': 'market situation' and 'work situation'.

65　Cf. Schmidt 1976, pp.47-73; Eldridge 1971, pp.97-111; Oberschall 1965, pp.110-36; O'Neill 1986, pp.42-60; Greenspon 1963, pp.213-18; Lazarsfeld and Oberschall 1965, pp.188-90; Käsler 1988, pp.66-73.

66　In like manner, Marx remarks that '*the severe discipline of capital, acting on succeeding generations, has developed industriousness as the general property of the new species...*' (1973, p.325; emphasis added).

　　　Mann (1982, p.375) aptly calls the pragmatic accommodation to objective constraints 'pragmatic acceptance'. See also O'Neill 1986, p.55.

67　See also Collins 1986b, pp.77-80.

68　Marx likewise purports that: 'The technical subordination of the worker to the uniform motion of the instruments of labour, and the peculiar composition of the working group, consisting as it does of individuals of both sexes and all ages, gives rise to a *barrack-like discipline*, which is elaborated into a complete system in the factory...' (1976b, p.549, emphasis added; see also pp.544-64).

　　　In a similar vein, Foucault speaks of a kind of 'bipower' ('power over life') which is 'centered on the *body as a machine:* its disciplining, the optimization of its capabilities, the extortion of its forces, the parallel increase of its usefulness and its docility, its integration into systems of efficient and economic controls...' (1981a, p.139, emphasis added; see also 1980, pp.55-62). This 'controlled insertion of bodies into the machinery of production' was, in Foucault's view, a prerequisite for the development of modern capitalism.

69 Oberschall (1965, p.122) makes the interesting observation that Weber's use of the phrase, 'selection and adaptation', points to a parallelism between Weber's conception of industrial organization and the Darwinian world of struggle for survival. As a matter of fact, references to 'selection' are scattered throughout Weber's writings (see, e.g., 1976a, p.55; 1978a, p.935).

It is also worthwhile noting here that Weber's study of 'the technical peculiarity of the production process' in the modern capitalist factory directly determining the qualities developed in the workers involves, as Marianne Weber points out, 'the other side of the problems that are at the centre of the treatise on the spirit of capitalism' (1988, p.367). In the *Protestant Ethic* (1976a), Weber concentrates on the study of the spiritual factors moulding the type of individual required by modern rational capitalism.

70 On this score, Marx's work represents a forceful articulation of the relation holding between rational technology/science and the domination of capital. Marx claims, for instance, that 'it would be possible to write a whole history of the inventions made since 1830 for the sole purpose of providing capital with weapons against working-class revolt' (1976b, p.563). Marcuse also (1971, pp.133-51; 1978, pp.138-62) maintains that capitalist reason functions as technical reason. See also Braveman 1974.

71 Similarly, Marx observes that capital 'compels the working class to do more work than would be required by the narrow circle of its own needs' (1976b, p.425).

72 The following authors inquire into the resistance of traditionalism in the course of the transition to modern capitalism: Hearn 1978, Moore 1978, Bauman 1982.

73 Hobsbawn (1968, pp.344-70), for example, examines the transition in the nineteenth century from the workers' calculation of wages in a customary manner to the eventual application of market criteria in the determination of wage-rates. See also Thompson (1982, pp.299-309) who expatiates on the transition from the 'task-oriented' notion of time characteristic of peasant societies to the notion of 'timed labour' peculiar to modern industrial capitalism. 'Timed labour' has to do with the consumption of time in an instrumental manner. Similarly, Weber (1971a, p.109) refers to the 'saving' of time by mechanization in the modern capitalist factory.

74 Weber also points to the role of force in the rise of modern capitalism— when he writes that 'the concentration of workers within the shop was at the beginning of the modern era *partly compulsory*; the poor and homeless and criminals were *pressed into factories...*' (1981b, p.174; emphasis added).

75 See Wallace 1989, pp.86-90.

76   Weber further highlights the significance of the religious legitimation of rational profit-making, when he refers to the absence of any such legitimation during the era of 'political capitalism' in Antiquity. 'The ancient businessman remained no more than a "common tradesman" in his own eyes and in the eyes of his contemporaries' (1976b, p.67).

77   Parsons (1975, pp.666-7) argues that the relevant ascetic Protestant values have now been institutionalized in the occupational system. Marcuse (1971, p.137), on the other hand, commits an egregious error, when he accuses Weber of being unaware of the fact that Protestant asceticism no longer underpins modern capitalism. See also Forbes 1975, pp.219-36.

78   Cf. Littler 1978, pp.185-202; Kelly 1978, pp.203-7; Gramsci 1971, pp.306-13; Taylor 1912. Gramsci (1971, p.310) adroitly speaks of capital's aim to reduce the worker to a 'trained gorilla'. In this same connection, it needs to be noted that Foucault further extends our understanding of the role of disciplinary institutions in modern society when he examines institutions like the clinic (1976) and the prison (1979).

79   Weber is, of course, also underlining the importance of formal rationality in the modern capitalist factory. As Udéhn (1981, pp.139-40) points out, formal rationality is the precondition for *Zweckrationalität*. For what is promoted by formal rationality (i.e., a methodical ordering of activities in accordance with universally valid rules, regulations or laws): regularity, calculability, predictability, efficiency and impersonality—are crucial prerequisites for the precise calculation of means and ends.

80   See Burris 1987, pp.78-82.

81   Cf. Breuer 1982, pp.55-79; Luhmann 1982, pp.20-46.

82   Foucault (1980) has also expatiated on the fundamental importance of what he calls 'power-knowledge relations' in modern disciplinary society.

83   All of the following writers underline the workers' implicit and informal daily struggles at the level of the factory: Stark 1982, pp.310-29; Chinoy 1982, pp.87-100; Mackenzie 1982, pp.63-86; Castoriadis 1976-77, pp.3-42; Friedman 1977, pp.45-76.

84   Cf. also Oberschall's (1965, pp.134-6) discussion of Weber's 'non-ideal type of bureaucracy'. Oberschall refers to another source of Weber's views on the functioning of bureaucracy contained in the unfinished report of his experiences as a volunteer in military field hospitals during the first year of World War I. Marianne Weber includes this report in her biography (see 1988, pp.537-50).

85   Interestingly enough, Käsler (1988, p.36) pinpoints a case where the early Weber does, in fact, make a value-judgement. In the course of his analysis of the causes of the decline of the Roman empire, Weber writes that: '*In the depth of society organic structural changes occur (and had to occur) which*, if we look at them as a whole, *must be interpreted as an immense process of recovery.* Individual family life and private property were restored to the masses of unfree people; they themselves were raised again,

from the position of "speaking inventory" up into the circle of human beings' (1971b, p.274; emphasis added). In this context, Käsler comments that Weber evidently stood on the side of the weakest in the society of the late Roman empire, namely, the slaves.

86 It is Mueller's (1982, p.161) contention that Weber's conception of 'state-socialism' is not in substance socialism at all. Rather, it is 'state-capitalism'.

87 Cf. Bottomore 1985a, pp.22-34.

88 Marcuse (1958) in *Soviet Marxism* inquired into the nature of bureaucratic domination in the former Soviet communist societies. In *One-Dimensional Man* (1964), he identified increasing trends towards bureaucratization in contemporary capitalist, communist and Third World societies. In like manner, post-industrial society theorists like Bell (1973) pointed to the growing similarity between contemporary capitalist and communist societies. The salient point, though, is that Marcuse differs from these post-industrial society theorists by emphasizing the negative aspects of the increasing bureaucratization of modern societies.

89 Weber's attitude towards workers was rather ambivalent. Marianne Weber (1988, p.630) observed that her husband sympathized with the struggles of the workers for a life worthy of human beings. But, on the other hand, she acknowledged that one could be a 'Socialist' or a 'Christian', only if one were willing to give up a cultured existence underpinned by workers' labour. Marianne Weber continued that this was, of course, impossible for Weber—since his scholarly way of life depended upon unearned income. See also Simey 1966, pp.303-27.

90 See Roth 1971, p.233.

91 Cf. Roth 1971, pp.232-4; Beetham 1974, pp.144-7; Mommsen 1984, pp.101-23.

92 See Murphy 1986a, pp.262-3. Of particular relevance in the present context also is that Roth and Wittich translate one of Weber's sentences as follows: 'In our terminology, *"classes" are not communities*; they merely represent possible, and frequent, bases for social action' (Weber 1978a, p.927; emphasis added). Indeed, a great deal of confusion surrounds the translation of Weber's use of *Gemeinschaft*. Wenger (1987, p.55) interprets Weber's notion of 'class action' as 'communal action'. Marshall et al. claim that 'classes tend not to be groups or communities...' (1985, p.264). Giddens, on the other hand, clarifies the whole issue when he affirms that: 'classes and status communities represent *two possible, and competing, modes of group formation* in relation to the distribution of power in society' (1981b, p.44; emphasis added).

93 In this regard, Poggi's interpretation of Weber is such that the bourgeoisie can be understood as a 'collective actor' only in the sense of 'a number of discrete individuals ... oriented and propelled by shared interests' (1983, p.38; see also pp.92-113).

94 The 'talented author' in question seems to have been Weber's friend, Georg Lukács.

95 Weber's depiction of the dispersed East Elbian rural labourers brings to mind Marx's description of the French peasantry in *The Eighteenth Brumaire of Louis Bonaparte*. Marx asserts that the peasant's mode of production '*isolates them from one another* instead of bringing them into mutual intercourse ... In this way, the great mass of the French nation is formed by *simple addition of homologous magnitudes*, much as potatoes in a sack form a sack of potatoes' (1969, pp.478-9; emphasis added).

96 In this light, Murphy's contention that Weber was able to perceive classes 'in the form of constituents and alliances, as active creative subjects making history' (1986a, p.252), is spurious in the case of workers.

   Although I have argued that the elaboration of workers' resistance as a sociological category is not undertaken by Weber, I am not denying the fact that industrial workers engaged in collective action in Weber's Imperial Germany. See, e.g., Roth's (1963) interesting study of the working class in Imperial Germany.

97 Workers' interests, on the other hand, are not securely entrenched in modern rational capitalism. Therefore, the individual worker may find that his perception of his 'true' interest is not validated by his fellow workers. In this respect, Off and Wiesenthal correctly maintain that 'a "dialogical" process of definition of interest is required on the part of those who find themselves in an inferior power position and who do, therefore, depend upon a common and collective concept of their interest' (1980, p.91).

98 'Possessive individualism' is a term coined by MacPherson (1962). MacPherson argues that: 'the individual in a possessive market society *is* human in his capacity as proprietor of his own person; his humanity does depend on his freedom from any but self-interested contractual relations with others...' (1962, pp.271-2; emphasis in original).

99 Regarding 'free' persons in the sphere of circulation/commodity exchange, Marx likewise indicates that: 'The only force bringing them together, and putting them into relation with each other, is the selfishness, the gain and the private interest of each' (1976b, p.280).

100 For an assessment of Weber's writings on Russia, see Pipes 1955, pp.371-401; Murvar 1984, pp.237-72; Scaff and Arnold 1985, pp.190-214; Wells and Baehr 1995, pp.1-39.

101 In light of the foregoing, it is perplexing to discover that Weber in one instance purports that: 'the substitution of *any* form of common economic "solidarity" for today's selection on the principle of private economic viability ... within the factory ... would radically change the spirit found today in this great edifice, and no one can even surmise with what consequences' (1971a, p.155; emphasis in original). Weber is far less rigid here concerning his idea of a future, perhaps non-capitalist in character.

161

5 Status

In this chapter I consider Weber's understanding of mediaeval status groups, that is, estates as phenomena of the distribution of social power within the feudal social order in the West. In the first section of the chapter I briefly examine the meaning of *Stand* in Weber's writings. I focus attention on the 'individual' ideal-type of Western feudalism in the second section. The third section investigates the Weberian thesis that 'social honour' and 'lack of social honour' represent the key objective criteria in the formation of estates in the feudal social order in the Occident. In the fourth section I assess Weber's views on seigneurial proprietorship. The fifth section concentrates on the Weberian thesis that social honour is normally connected with the respective estate's legally guaranteed and monopolized claim to sovereign rights. In the final section of the chapter I consider Weber's views on the possibilities for collective traditional action on the part of estate groups in the feudal social order.

5.1 The meaning of stand

In translating Weber's term *Stand* most translators have employed the word 'status'. Although this is not incorrect, it is important to bear in mind the double meaning of the German *Stand* as 'estate' and 'status'.[1] In addition to this double meaning inherent in *Stand,* another salient point is that Weber himself gave more than one explanation of what he meant by this term in his writings.[2]

To begin with, Weber's designation of 'status situation' as 'every typical component of the life of men that is determined by a specific, positive or negative, social estimation of *honor...*' (1978a, p.932; emphasis in original), is used to analyze the distribution of power in historical societies in the past. Weber refers to the cities in Hellenic and Roman Antiquity during the '"status era"' (1978a, p.937). He also asserts that 'status groups arise within the framework of

162

organizations which satisfy their wants through monopolistic liturgies or in *ständisch*-patrimonial fashion' (1978a, p.306; see also p.937). Furthermore, Weber (1978a, pp.1340-49, 1354-59) compares the status structures of the ancient and mediaeval cities. And the rendering of *Stand* as 'estate' is not only used by Weber (1978a, pp.235-7, 255-9, 1070-1110) in his study of the feudal social order in the West, but also in his study (1979, pp.177-205) of the change from a society dominated by landed aristocrats, namely the Junkers, to a society dominated by a class of agricultural entrepreneurs in East Elbe. Regarding the status stratification of ancient societies in Asia (China and India), Weber (1951, 1958) points out that the acquisition and expression of social honour was dependent upon not only living a particular style of life, but also upon the performance of appropriate rituals. In fact, status groups in India evolved into closed castes. Physical contact with a member of any caste that was regarded as lower by the members of the higher case, was deemed to cause ritualistic impurity which could only be expiated by a religious act.

In addition to the utilization of *Stand* to study the distribution of power in historical societies in the past, Weber also declares that:

> Present-day society is predominantly stratified in classes, and to an especially high degree in income classes. But in the special *status* prestige of the 'educated' strata, our society contains a very tangible element of stratification by status. Externally, this status factor is most obviously represented by economic monopolies and the preferential social opportunities of the holders of degrees. (1970, p.301, emphasis in original; see also 1978a, pp.1000, 1400)

Weber (1978a, pp.140-44, 958-63, 998-1003) is thinking, in particular, here of the emergence of bureaucratic officials as a separate occupational status group with specific rights, duties and privileges within modern society. The development of bureaucratic administration throughout modern society creates a new status stratum of officials, distinguished by the new social barrier of educational qualifications. The introduction of specialized examinations, for example, was a consequence of the desire to limit the supply of candidates for certain positions in business offices and the public service, and to monopolize these positions for the holders of educational patents. Weber argues that 'the modern official, too, always strives for and usually attains a distinctively elevated *social esteem* vis-à-vis the governed' (1978a, p.959; emphasis in original). This having been said, it should be emphasized that Weber's understanding of modern officials as an occupational status group is not at all consistent. For Weber (1978a, p.304), as mentioned earlier, also includes 'public and private officials' in the 'middle classes' located between the positively privileged and negatively privileged commercial classes. And he speaks of the 'class position of ... a civil servant...' (1978a, p.306).

Another pertinent point made by Weber is that 'stratification by status groups on the basis of conventional styles of life evolves at the present time in the United States out of the traditional democracy' (1978a, p.933; see also p.932). Weber, furthermore, alludes to the 'status situation' influencing the 'class situation' (see, e.g., 1958, p.39; 1970, p.301; 1978a, p.306). Conversely, he makes reference to the 'status situation' resulting from the 'class situation' (see, e.g., 1978a, pp.301, 303, 306-7, 935). In effect, Weber is saying that status may be a precondition for the creation of classes in modern capitalist society whilst class, in turn, may be a precondition for the formation of status groups.

Weber, further, complicates our understanding of the relationship holding between class and status when he suggests a model of alternating tendencies. He proclaims that:

> When the bases of the acquisition and distribution of goods are relatively stable, stratification by status is favored. Every technological repercussion and economic transformation threatens stratification by status and pushes the class situation into the foreground. Epochs and countries in which the naked class situation is of predominant significance are regularly the periods of technical and economic transformations. And every slowing down of the change in economic stratification leads, in due course, to the growth of status structures and makes for a resuscitation of the important role of social honor. (1978a, p.938)

Weber is saying that when the acquisition and distribution of goods takes place in a relatively stable economic environment, stratification by status will prevail. But under conditions of technological and economic change, class stratification will predominate. Weber is not in this instance concerned with an historical movement from a 'status era' in the past to a 'class era' in modern society. Indeed, Weber's reference to 'epochs and countries in which the naked class situation is of predominant significance', implies that classes are no longer apprehended solely as bases of the aggregation of economic power within the modern capitalist market-economy. Similarly, Weber does not differentiate between 'status structures' in the past and in modern capitalist society. Moreover, the fact that Weber associates 'the growth of status structures' with a revival of the importance of social honour, suggests that social honour is not regarded as an historically limited concept.

In light of the aforesaid, it is obvious that the few comments made by Weber concerning the status factor in modern capitalist society are confusing. Firstly, it should be underlined that the concept of social honour cannot be applied to the study of status stratification in modern capitalist society. The idea of social honour is, as Berger (1973, pp.83-96) observes, an obsolete concept in the *Weltanschauung* of modernity. Social honour is usually understood as a noble, aristocratic concept, and is normally associated with traditional (i.e., pre-modern) societies like the feudal estate order in the West. This being so, it is rather perplexing when Weber maintains that:

Social honor can adhere directly to a class situation, and it is also, indeed most of the time, determined by the average class situation of the status-group members. (1958, p.39)

Contrary to Weber, the essential point is that social honour is a redundant concept in the class society that constitutes modern rational capitalism.

If the concept of social honour must be discarded in the treatment of status stratification in modern capitalist society, Weber's alternative argument that the status factor in modern society is represented by economic monopolies and the educational qualifications of certain social groups, is well-founded. Status groups form in modern capitalist society, for instance, through the capacity of professional associations and labour unions to allow only those holding particular educational patents entry into certain professions and trades. In this same connection, Barbalet (1980, p.413) makes the valid point that Weber cannot continue to make a clear-cut distinction of both a social and logical kind between class and status in his discussion of status in the class society that is modern capitalism. The sharp social and logical separation of class from status (i.e., status understood in terms of the possession of 'social honour' or the 'lack of social honour') is, in my view, most relevant in comparing the nature of stratification in a traditional society like the feudal estate order and the modern capitalist market-economy. However, Weber's proposition regarding class and status influencing each other in modern capitalist society, implies that they merge in some way. Weber does not think through this relationship holding between class and status. In order to conceptualize how class and status relate to each other in the modern capitalist market-economy, it would first of all have been necessary for Weber to give a detailed account of the changed nature of status.[3] However, Weber concentrates mainly on the study of status stratification in historical societies in the past.

Although I explore Weber's treatment of status groups in the feudal estate order in the West in the remainder of this chapter, his study of status stratification in various ancient socieities such as China (1951), India (1958), Greece and Rome (1976b) and Israel (1952) could be subject to a similar analysis.

5.2 Western feudalism

Weber's understanding of mediaeval estates as phenomena of the distribution of social power presupposes the framework of the feudal social order in the West. Weber is principally interested in Western feudalism which he considers as one major variant of traditional domination. His construction of the 'individual' ideal-type of Western feudalism is based on the form of landholding and on the relationship in which the vassal stood to his prince or sovereign.[4] The historical reality which corresponds most closely to Weber's 'individual' ideal-type of

Western feudalism is the feudal system found in Northern France between the ninth and twelfth centuries.[5]

Regarding the construction of the 'individual' ideal-type of Western feudalism on the basis of the form of landholding, Weber explains that:

> Appropriated seigneurial powers will be called a *fief* if they are granted primarily to particular qualified individuals by a contract and if the reciprocal rights and duties involved are primarily oriented to conventional standards of status honor, particularly in a military sense. If an administrative staff is primarily supported by fiefs, we will speak of (Western) *feudalism.* (1978a, p.235, emphasis in original; see also pp.255-9, 1070-1110; 1981b, p.62)[6]

At bottom, the feudal system of landholding in the West enabled traditional rulers to uphold their domination by making a contract with mounted warriors, namely, knights.[7] Traditional rulers created the economic conditions that made it possible for these mounted warriors to develop and practice their military skills. That is to say, these rulers bestowed upon the mounted warriors legally guaranteed (i.e., in a traditional sense) and monopolized claims to certain economic resources, especially land settled and cultivated by peasants. Weber also points out that 'in its Occidental beginnings, horse and arms were part of the fief; self-equipment came later when this institution became widespread' (1978a, p.1077). The fief had become hereditary by the later Middle Ages, subject only to the precondition that each new vassal have the necessary qualifications and be willing to pledge fealty to his lord.[8] Existing vassals were likewise expected to swear fealty to a new lord (see Weber 1978a, p.1074).

If the granting of a fief made certain economic resources available to the vassal, the onus was on the vassal in turn to place his military resources at the disposal of his sovereign. It is in this sense that Weber understands Western feudalism to be 'always domination by the few who have military skills' (1978a, p.1106; see also pp.1019, 1077-78; 1981b, pp.62-4). The mobilization of military service on the basis of fiefs in land was a crucial feature of Western feudalism between the ninth and twelfth centuries.[9] In the military society that constituted Western feudalism, the ruler valued land first and foremost as a source of mounted warriors.[10] Fiefs in land provided for the recruitment of vitally needed mounted warriors in a society which did not possess the liquid money to pay them in cash.

In addition to the fief, the second fundamental component built into Weber's 'individual' ideal-type of Western feudalism bears on the cult of personal fealty. In this regard, Weber affirms that:

> The contract of fealty is not an ordinary business contract, but establishes a solidary, fraternal relationship which involves reciprocal obligations of loyalty, to be sure, on a legally unequal basis. (1978a, p.255)

It is the profoundly personal nature of the feudal contract that distinguishes Western feudalism. The enfeoffment ceremony whereby the feudal vassal 'commended' himself to his lord, exemplifies the intensely personal ties of mutual loyalty and amity holding between the feudal vassal and his lord. In the course of this ceremony, the feudal lord promised to protect the vassal whilst the vassal in turn promised to help and advize his lord; and both promised to care for and respect each other. Fidelity was the essential bond between the lord and his vassal. Therefore, treachery was the most serious crime in the feudal code. On the other hand, loyalty and generosity were regarded as the highest virtues. The exceptional severity with which the treachery of a vassal was treated in feudal society in the West, is attested to by the fact that a name of great ignominy was coined for this offence. It was called a 'felony'.[11]

Another point especially pertinent here is that in contrast to a '"purposive" contract' (Weber 1978a, p.673) such as the labour contract entered into by the capitalist entrepreneur and the wage-labourer for a fixed period of time within the confines of the modern capitalist market, the 'status contract' entered into by the feudal lord and his vassal:

> ...meant that *the person would 'become' something different in quality (or status) from the quality he possessed before.* For unless a person voluntarily assumed that new quality, his future conduct in his role could hardly be believed to be possible at all. Each party must thus make a new 'soul' enter his body. (Weber 1978a, p.672; emphasis in original)

The feudal 'status contract' did not, according to Weber, simply entail the performance of specified reciprocally guaranteed obligations on the part of the lord and his vassal. It also involved a change in the total legal situation and social status of both the lord and his vassal.

Weber regarded feudal relations in the Occident as atypical, since they combined sentiments of loyal obedience on the part of the vassal with the same vassal's sense of high social rank.[12] The reason for the feudal vassal's association of personal loyalty with the pride of noble status inheres in the fact that Western feudalism originated in a cavalry of warriors. The feudal bond in the West always involved a bond between 'free' men. This being so, Weber contends that:

> Vassalage does not diminish honor and status of the vassal; on the contrary, it can augment his honor, and commendation is not submission to patriarchal authority, although its forms are borrowed from it. (1978a, p.1072)

When a feudal knight commended himself to a prince or sovereign, he did not become a personal dependent like the patrimonial official. Admittedly, loyalty and personal fealty are also intrinsic to many 'plebeian' forms of patrimonial or liturgical feudalism (e.g., slave armies, peasants or frontier guards). But the vital point is that 'they lack status honor as the integrating component' (Weber 1978a, p.1105). For Weber, then, *the feudatory relationship can only be an attribute of*

167

a ruling stratum, since it rests on emphatic notions of status honor as the basis of fealty and also of military fitness' (1978a, p.1081; emphasis added).[13] Knighthood and service were woven together in the feudal relationship in the West. Freedom implied a voluntary tie of dependence.[14]

Given Weber's construction of the 'individual' ideal-type of Western feudalism on the basis of the form of landholding and the relationship in which the vassal stood to his lord, it is clear that he apprehends Western feudalism as basically military in character.[15]   Weber argued that 'the decisive condition' leading to the development of feudalism in the Occident 'was the invasion of the Arabs and the necessity of opposing an army of Frankish horsemen to that of Islam' (1981b, p.63; see also 1978a, pp.1077-78). The emergence of personal relations of protection and dependence within the ruling stratum in the warlike society of Western Europe functioned mainly as a means of maintaining order and collective defence. During the anarchy of the early feudal period, the formation of highly personalized ties with economically and politically more powerful individuals was crucial for sheer survival. If the feudal bond served the need for security within the ruling stratum in a warlike society, the peasant was, as Weber (1981b, p.63; 1971b, pp.254-75) indicates, also forced to seek protection from individuals of superior power. Many peasants became serfs.

Weber also accentuates the political (i.e., ruler-centric) nature of Western feudalism when he refers to the rights of government attached to fiefs. It was the possession of rights of government by feudal vassals which distinguished Western feudalism. Weber writes that 'fully developed feudalism is the most extreme type of systematically decentralized domination' (1978a, p.1079). The granting of a fief by the feudal sovereign did not simply involve the transfer of landed resources. The vassals were also granted political powers which meant most of all judicial powers. This granting of political powers to individual vassals 'resulted in the fragmentation of powers into numerous individual rights, appropriated on different legal grounds, which traditionally limited one another' (Weber 1978a, p.1083). No central authority held a monopoly of legitimate power during the feudal era in the West. Public authority was what Strayer (1968, p.14) appropriately calls a 'private possession'. The feudal vassal monopolized the 'powers of rule' in his own locality. He exercized traditional authority in a 'private' capacity rather than as a representative of his sovereign.[16] Expressed another way, the most striking feature of Western feudalism was the dispersion of sovereignty. In line with Weber, Hintze understands Western feudalism as a system of personal means of lordship which led to 'the *reification* of dominion, instead of to its *objectification* as in the modern state' (1968, p.24; emphasis added). This meant, in effect, the division of state power according to the physical things over which power is wielded (i.e., land and people), rather than according to its functions.[17]

It is necessary at this point to consider the type of 'social action' corresponding to 'the feudal system' (Weber 1978a, pp.1102, 1105). For 'the

168

feudal system', in so far as it existed historically, could only be reproduced through human agency. 'Social action' can be regarded as a special case of 'socially oriented action'. The difficulty, though, is that unlike his definitions of 'economically oriented action' and 'economic action', Weber does not offer equivalent definitions of 'socially oriented action' and 'social action'.[18] All the same, Burger purports that 'the absence of a formal definition of "socially oriented" action does not necessarily mean the absence of its idea' (1985, p.25).

It is reasonable to assume that the feudal social order is comprised of the totality of 'socially oriented action'. What is at stake in the feudal social order, according to Weber, is social honour. Hence, 'socially oriented action' includes all primarily 'non-social action' which is influenced by 'social' considerations. That is to say, it includes all principally 'non-social action' concerned with individuals' attempts to acquire and express social honour. In this light, the pursuit of both wealth and 'rights of rule' to gain social honour in feudal society qualifies as 'socially oriented action'. 'Social action', on the other hand, is constitutive of a partial domain of the feudal social order. It is arguable that Weber would have defined the singular kind of 'social action' peculiar to feudal society in the West as action to gain and express social honour through living a specific style of life. 'Feudal social action' can be deemed meaningful in so far as it concerns the individual's endeavour to procure and express social honour. In other words, the feudal social order, in so far as it existed historically, could only be reproduced by virtue of 'feudal social action'. In the case of the connection between 'the feudal system' and 'feudal social action', it is the feudal upper stratum which is most consciously orientated to attaining and expressing social honour and, thereby, contributes directly to the reproduction of 'the feudal system'.

Another related point is that the feudal estate order is a modality of traditional action. That is to say, 'feudal social action' is a form of traditional action in the sense that the endeavour to acquire and express social honour is contingent upon living a knightly style of life largely rooted in custom. The fact that the great bulk of everyday action undertaken by the members of the various estates (e.g., the knighthood, the burghers and the peasantry) in feudal society involved abiding by the customary, does not necessarily imply that this society was static. Admittedly, Weber defines custom as:

...a typically uniform activity which is kept on the beaten track simply because men are 'accustomed' to it and persist in it by unreflective imitation. (1978a, p.319)

The members of the various feudal estates did collectively engage in habituated forms of activity to gain and express social honour. But Weber (1978a, p.25) also concedes, as earlier intimated, that tradition may be upheld with varying degrees of self-consciousness. It is quite clear (as we shall see throughout this chapter) that the various feudal estates, especially the knighthood, often

169

consciously championed tradition in the course of attempting to: gain and express social honour, acquire material resources compatible with the maintenance of a particular mode of life, and defend and extend their privileges and private rights.

5.3 'Social honour' and 'lack of social honour'

The ideal-type of status group that Weber regards as unique to Western feudalism, is the estate group. Estates are phenomena of the distribution of social power within the feudal social order in the West. The pivotal point is that Weber holds 'social honour'/'lack of social honour' to be the most important bases for the formation of these estates. 'Social honour' and 'lack of social honour' comprise the key objective criteria in the creation of estates. In this regard, Weber writes that:

> In contrast to the purely economically determined 'class situation', we wish to designate as *status situation* every typical component of the life of men that is determined by a specific, positive or negative, social estimation of *honor* ... In content, status honor is normally expressed by the fact that above all else a specific *style of life* is expected from all those who wish to belong to the circle. (1978a, p.932, emphasis in original; see also pp.305-6, 698, 937; 1958, p.39; 1970, p.300)

Essentially, Weber is saying that the opportunities for members of a status group like a mediaeval estate to acquire and express social honour, are dependent upon living a particular style of life. A specific style of life is a mark of social honour.[19] And because social honour is typically grounded in a particular mode of life, formal education and hereditary or occupational prestige are, on Weber's reading (1978a, pp.305-6), exceedingly important.[20] But why is a special way of life and, hence, formal education and hereditary or occupational prestige (as opposed to, for instance, the possession of wealth or rights of rule) held to be the foundation of social honour by Weber? More pertinently, why is there a peculiar affinity between a particular style of life and the feudal idea of social honour?

It is possible, I would argue, to draw together Weber's various comments on the feudal notion of social honour and, thereby, develop an understanding of the unique relationship holding between a special way of life and this specific conception of social honour. To begin with, the feudal idea of social honour is a noble concept deeply rooted in the social structure of Western feudalism. Weber explains that:

> The knight's conduct was molded by the feudal concept of honor and this in turn by the notion of vassalic fealty; this was the only type of status honor conditioned on the one hand by a common and internalized ethos

and on the other by an external relationship to the lord. (1978a, p.1069; see also pp.1074-75)

Social honour and personal fealty comprised the central values underpinning the knight's conduct. It was the struggle for and the acquisition and expression of social honour that rendered the knight's life meaningful. Stated otherwise, the feudal knight 'acted' in a value-rational manner. His life was a value-infused existence grounded in tradition. Social honour and personal fealty were the supreme values governing knightly conduct. Knightly conduct was distinguished by the need to fulfill the commands or demands of the feudal code of honour.

What is the exact meaning of the feudal concept of social honour? Weber begins to answer this question when he avers that:

> ...positively privileged feudal strata do not view their existence functionally, as a means for serving a mission, that is, an idea that should be realized purposively. Their typical myth is the value of their 'existence'. (1978a, p.1106, emphasis added; see also pp.934, 1104-09; 1970, p.276)

Positively privileged feudal strata such as the knights in solid possession of social honour claim an intrinsic and eminent quality of their own. The feudal knights' sense of dignity is an expression of their underived, ultimate and qualitatively unique being. Weber is principally saying that the basis of social honour in feudal society in the West is moral and social superiority. The knights claim high social honour because of the superiority of their 'being' or 'nature'.[21] Knightly existence is a value and end in itself. It is self-explanatory. It needs no justification.[22]

Furthermore, the intrinsic, inalienable value of knightly existence engenders an aloof conception of the self. Aloofness, as Poggi (1972, p.24) explains, involves a propensity for the individual to accentuate his distance from all other individuals, a contempt for all mundane and acquisitive affairs, and a strong sense of identification with the past and one's ancestors. Another essential point made by Weber (1978a, p.1106) is that the feeling of intrinsic, absolute worth characteristic of the knightly estate is diametrically opposed to bourgeois commercial utilitarianism. Because the feudal knight takes his own worth for granted, he does not, like the capitalist entrepreneur, view his existence as a means for the achievement of some goal in a purposive-rational fashion.[23] Feudal conduct, then, leads to the opposite of the rational profit-making activity which distinguishes modern capitalism.

If positively privileged feudal estates claim high social honour by virtue of 'their "beauty and excellence"' (Weber 1978a, p.934), the obvious implication is that this claim must be substantiated. Or as Burger (1985, p.32) remarks, this claim must be persuasively validated by reference to some visible features. In fact, positively privileged feudal strata uphold the superiority of their 'being' or 'nature' by living a knightly style of life rooted in tradition. A pattern of knightly living with a defined style of its own, is a prime honour-engendering resource that reinforces a feudal knight's sense of moral and social superiority. This knightly way of life has both a military and courtly aspect.

The military aspect of the knightly mode of life principally relates to the secular code of social honour of a martial estate. In this connection, Weber affirms that 'proprietors of military implements in their own right ... may be called "estates"' (1970, p.83). It is the idea of the necessity of war as a source of social honour that differentiates the knightly estate from the rest of feudal society in the West. The knightly estate lives solely by war and for war. What is more, the favourite amusements of this estate, namely hunting and tournaments, are also warlike. And the honourable qualities intrinsically associated with the knightly pattern of life are narrowly martial. These qualities include: loyalty, courage, bravery, valour, fealty, prowess, the pursuit of glory or praise and contempt for pain and death. Conversely, the primary dishonourable qualities instinctively linked with knightly existence include: breach of faith, cowardice and treason.[24]

If the knightly estate lends credence to the excellence of its 'being' or 'nature' by living a knightly style of life, it obviously follows that a military education is a crucial preparation for living this highly stylized way of life. On this account, Weber purports that:

The goal of military education is not, as in mass armies, drill for the sake of adaptation to an organized operation, but individual perfection in personal military skills. Therefore, one element finds a permanent place in training and general conduct ... the *game*. Under feudal conditions it is just as little a 'pastime' as in organic life, rather it is the natural form in which the psycho-physical capacities of the organism are kept alive and supple; the game is a form of 'training', which in its spontaneous and unbroken animal instinctiveness as yet transcends any split between the 'spiritual' and the 'material', 'body' and 'soul', no matter how conventionally it is sublimated. (1978a, p.1105; emphasis in original)

The 'game' is one of the primary forms of feudal education. It inculcates military ideals and trains the young members of the knightly elite to handle weapons skillfully and learn the fine arts of war. Moreover, the 'game' develops a thoroughly anti-rational and anti-utilitarian ethic. In the life of the knightly strata, the 'game' 'constitutes a counterpole to all economically rational action' (Weber 1978a, p.1106). Indeed, play is a way of life. The feudal knight understands war as a game with rules, played in hand-to-hand fights and duels. The tournament, of course, changes war into something even more playful.[25]

In addition to the importance of a military education as a preparation for living a knightly pattern of life, Weber also refers to hereditary prestige. As a matter of fact, there was no nobility of blood in the early Middle Ages. However, Weber

172

observes that by the later Middle Ages, 'the aspirant for a fief or prebend must not only live like a knight, but also be of knightly descent' (1978a, p.1081).[26] If a man cannot point to knights in his ancestry, he is no longer eligible to be made a knight. The positively privileged feudal strata now have recourse to hereditary prestige to support the pre-eminence of their 'being' or 'nature' and, thereby, their claim for high social honour. Of particular relevance also is that the mediaeval view of lineage does not focus only on birth. Lineage also appertains to family traditions of social honour founded on past achievements, especially military accomplishments. In short, then, a shared consciousness of knightly descent was a crucial element binding the positively privileged feudal strata together in the later Middle Ages.

Besides the military aspect of the knightly life-style, the courtly aspect also supported the knight's sense of moral and social superiority. The courts of the great feudal lords in Western Europe in the eleventh and twelfth centuries began to attract increasing numbers of knights. Opportunities for social advancement were growing in the various chambers of these courts. The end-result, as Elias (1978, 1982) points out, was that mounted warriors were transformed into a relatively pacified court nobility.[27] Chivalrous standards of conduct and sentiment are represented by a particular concept at the great feudal courts, namely, courtesy. Noble, courteous conduct involves stylistic conventions, particular forms of social intercourse, good speech and conversation, affect-moulding and the like. The concept of courtesy epitomizes the estate-consciousness of the knightly stratum at the great feudal courts. It designates what distinguishes the courtly circles of the knightly estate from the small knights and the peasants. Noble, courteous conduct is continually contrasted with coarse manners, the conduct of the peasantry.[28] It goes without saying that abiding by courteous standards of conduct reinforces the sense of moral and social superiority of the knights at court and, therefore, their claim for high social honour. Put somewhat differently, courteous conduct becomes a prestige instrument and, hence, an instrument of social power in the later Middle Ages.[29]

If the knights at the great feudal courts substantiate the excellence of their 'being' or 'nature' by adhering to a courteous code of conduct, systematic preparation for this highly stylized mode of life is indispensable. On this score, Weber declares that:

Wherever feudalism develops a status-oriented 'knightly' stratum, systematic preparation for a corresponding way of life emerges with all its consequences. Typically, certain *artistic* creations (in literature, music and the visual arts) ... become a means of self-glorification and establish and preserve the nimbus of the dominant stratum vis-à-vis the ruled. Thus 'refinement' is added to the at first purely military-gymnastic training; the result is that very complex type of 'cultivation' which is the polar opposite

173

of specialized education in a bureaucratic regime. (1978a, p.1090, emphasis in original; see also pp.1001-02)

With the courtization of the knightly estate in the later Middle Ages, the 'cultivated man' becomes another fundamental goal sought by feudal education. The fact that the knights believe in their own pre-eminence leads to the notion of feudal education as 'cultivation'. Latent noble/knightly qualities must be regenerated, that is, cultivated.[30] The arts play a crucial role in this process of cultivation. Literature, music and the visual arts become an expression of the intrinsic value of the knightly estate. They project the inate qualities of this estate.[31] Hence, no systematic attempt to master the arts is undertaken. Weber argues that among privileged status groups 'artistic and literary activity is ... considered degrading as soon as it is exploited for income, or at least when it is connected with hard physical exertion' (1978a, p.936; see also p.1081). Members of the knightly estate devote themselves to the cultivation of the arts because they have transcended the material conditions of existence. Thus, the main purpose of knowledge of the arts in feudal education in the later Middle Ages is to boost the social prestige of the knightly estate by creating culturally refined individuals.[32] The knights at the great feudal courts uphold the excellence of their 'being' or 'nature' and, therefore, their claim for high social honour by cultural exclusiveness, by the monopolization of ideal goods (Weber 1978a, p.935).[33] Or expressed in the language of Pierre Bourdieu, the courtly knights accumulate social honour by virtue of their monopoly of 'cultural capital'.[34]

In light of the aforesaid, it is rather marked that Weber considers the possession of the primary resource, social honour, as the direct expression of membership of the knightly estate in feudal society in the West. To lose one's honour is to forfeit membership of the knightly estate.[35] Indeed, if a knight loses his honour, he loses a constitutive element of his personal identity. For the feudal idea of social honour has fundamental consequences for the concept of personal identity. In this respect, Berger asserts that:

> The social location of honor lies in a world of relatively intact, stable institutions, a world in which *individuals can with subjective certainty attach their identities to the institutional roles that society assigns to them.* (1973, p.93, emphasis added; see also pp.83-96)

In the noble world of social honour, individual identity is connected to institutional roles. The individual finds his 'true' identity in the performance of the roles allotted to him by society. Personal identity in feudal society (and in all other aristocratic societies) is an objectively and subjectively given fact.[36]

In a similar vein, Weber maintains that:

> A sense of dignity is the precipitation in individuals of social honor and of conventional demands which a positively privileged status group raises for the deportment of its members. (1978a, p.934)

In the case of the knightly estate, the code of conduct demanded of its members bears, in the main, on living a knightly style of life anchored in tradition. The 'true' self of the feudal knight reveals itself either in battle or in adhering to courteous standards of conduct. In fact, a feudal knight would rather risk and even lose his life for his honour, for his self-esteem. The loss of his honour, his personal identity, is a fate worse than death for the feudal knight—since it relates to his membership of the knightly estate and, hence, to all that distinguishes him from his social inferiors, from those who lack honour.[37]

Pertinent to the general impetus of the present discussion also is the communal character of status groups. In this respect, Gerth's and Mills' translation of Weber reads as: 'In contrast to classes, *status groups* are normally communities' (1970, p.186; emphasis in original). Roth's and Wittich's translation, on the other hand, reads as: 'In contrast to classes, *Stände* (status groups) are normally groups' (1978a, p.932; emphasis in original). The former translation is the more correct. For Weber's crucial point, as previously mentioned, is that classes are not communities, whereas status groups usually are. A status group involves a communal relationship in the sense that it is 'based on a subjective feeling of the parties, whether affectual or traditional, that they *belong together*' (Weber 1978a, p.40; emphasis added). The fact that the members of a status group like the knightly estate have a strong sense of 'belonging together' means that:

> A status group is always somehow societalized, but it is not always organized into an association. *Commercium*, in the sense of 'social intercourse', and *connubium* among groups are the typical characteristics of the *mutual esteem* among status equals; their absence signifies status differences. (Weber 1970, p.300, emphasis in original; see also 1978a, pp.306, 932, 1139)

Weber is saying that the feeling of 'belonging together' among the members of a status group is demonstrated both by the great amount of time expended on social intercourse from which 'outsiders' are excluded, and by intermarriage within the status circle. The tournaments in feudal society, for instance, were a very important occasion for the social gathering of the members of the knightly estate. The knights shared a style of life which was value-permeated.

When Weber employs the term, 'status groups', and considers these 'status groups' as normally communities, he is also highlighting the fact that he is not interested in the issue of individual status. The status group as a social group possesses a group identity. It is in this sense that social honour is not an attribute of an individual person as such. Social honour in feudal society can only be understood in relation to the knightly estate. One had honour only as long as one was deemed to be a member of the knightly estate. Conversely, one lost honour if social opinion in the rather closed circles of the knightly estate judged one unworthy, because of a failure to adhere to the feudal code of honour. Social honour was bestowed and lost in communication among members of the knightly

175

estate.

It goes without saying that Weber's conception of 'status groups' is diametrically opposed to the treatment of status in much contemporary status-attainment research in the United States.[38] Isolated individuals rather than social groups are the units of analysis. Individuals are merely perceived as atomic units in a static society. The measurement of status distinctions basically involves the ranking of individuals in terms of occupational prestige scores. The status-attainment model is nothing more than a continuum of occupational positions of differential prestige on which individuals can be aligned. Social relationships are translated into a set of rank orders.[39]

So far, the present discussion has concentrated on Weber's understanding of the knightly estate in solid possession of the primary resource (and value), social honour, in feudal society. The feudal knight is already in a structural power position, because he can claim high social honour by virtue of the fact that he lives a knightly style of life grounded in tradition. On the other hand, the negatively privileged feudal estates, especially the peasants, lack social honour. The peasants are unable to live a value-infused, knightly way of life. Rather, they represent the economic foundation upon which the knightly estate lives.

It should, further, be underlined that differences in the distribution of social honour in the feudal social order are associated with expressions of deference by the morally and socially inferior towards their betters. Estates are phenomena of the distribution of social power in the sense that the positively privileged feudal strata can wrest from the negatively privileged feudal strata the acknowledgment of moral and social superiority. Deference in the feudal social context has to do with commitment by those who lack social honour to a moral and social order legitimating their own servility. Or expressed in the language of Pierre Bourdieu, positively privileged feudal strata such as the knights wield a 'symbolic power' proportionate to the recognition of their moral and social superiority as legitimate (i.e., not recognized as arbitrary) by their inferiors like the peasantry.[40]

Of paramount importance also is Newby's observation that deference is 'the form of social interaction which occurs in situations involving the exercise of traditional authority' (1975, p.146; emphasis removed). It involves legitimation by tradition of an hierarchical social structure like Western feudalism. For Weber (1978a, p.227), legitimation by tradition is, in fact, the most secure form of legitimation—because deference is not only accorded to tradition itself, but also to the person occupying the position of authority. The morally and socially inferior peasant in the feudal context submits to the morally and socially superior knight holding a position of authority by virtue of tradition. The peasant who lacks social honour is disciplined by dint of habit to obey the knight/lord in solid possession of social honour. In contrast to the impersonal, legal-rational character of the authority exerted by the entrepreneur in the modern capitalist factory, purely personal relations of superordination and subordination hold sway in the personalistic estate order that is Western feudalism. And because

176

traditional relations of domination have a purely personal character, they can be ethically regulated. In this respect, Weber observes that 'the lord of older social structures ... was moved by personal sympathy and favor, by grace and gratitude' (1978a, p.975; see also p.600).

Newby bequeaths another important insight when he argues that the ritual aspects of the deferential relationship are crucial to maintain social distance in 'the potentially polluting closely-knit interaction which characterises traditional authority' (1975, p.159). Bowing, curtseying and etiquette in general preserve social distance between the morally and socially superior party (e.g., the feudal knight) and the morally and socially inferior party (e.g., the mediaeval peasant).[41]

Writers like Parkin contend that 'deference as a general mode of understanding and responding to the facts of low status does not necessarily entail a sense of self-abnegation' (1972, p.85).[42] Deference is usually linked with a conception of the social order as an organic entity in which each individual/group has a role to play. Mediaeval thinkers, for example, expounded the justificatory theory of the trinitarian society. It was argued that society was comprised of three orders: those who pray, those who fight and those who labour.[43] The clergy, the knights and the peasantry all fulfilled complementary functions in the feudal estate order.

Weber also concedes that negatively privileged strata who accept a world-view customarily held to be deferential, have in reality their own feeling of dignity. He purports that:

> The sense of dignity of socially repressed strata or of strata whose status is negatively (or at least not positively) valued is nourished most easily on the belief that a special 'mission' is entrusted to them; their worth is guaranteed or constituted by an *ethical imperative*, or by their own functional *achievement*. (1970, p.276, emphasis in original; see also 1978a, p.934)

In opposition to the sense of dignity of positively privileged strata such as the feudal knighthood which is related to the excellence of their 'being' or 'nature' in the present, the sense of dignity of negatively privileged strata like the mediaeval peasantry bears on the value of their existence in a future, whether it is of this life or the next. This is tantamount to saying that the worth of the negatively privileged strata is founded upon a belief in a providential mission which must be carried out.

The millenarian movements which are found throughout Western Europe in the Middle Ages represent a very good example of how negatively privileged estates coped with their inferior position in the social hierarchy. Revolutionary millenarianism flourished, as Cohn (1970) contends, among those living on the margin of society, that is, among landless peasants or peasants with very little land, journeymen, unskilled labourers, beggars and vagabonds.[44] All of these marginal strata were liable to follow some inspired *propheta*. For what the *propheta* offered them, above all, was the prospect of accomplishing a divinely ordained mission. Passionate devotion to this mission functioned as an emotional compensation for the lowly position of the marginals in the social hierarchy of feudal society.

The creation of a sense of ethnic honour is another means by which negatively privileged strata like the Jews grappled with their inferior status in the feudal social hierarchy. Weber defines 'ethnic groups' as:

> ...those human groups that entertain a subjective belief in their common descent because of similarities of physical type or of customs or both, or because of memories of colonization and migration; this belief must be important for the propagation of group formation... (1978a, p.389; see also pp.385, 395)

The belief in the superiority of one's own customs and the inferiority of alien ones is crucial in upholding a sense of ethnic honour among ethnic groups. What is more, the sense of ethnic honour is, according to Weber (1978a, p.391), 'a specific honor of the masses', since it is a form of self-esteem accessible to every member of the ethnic group. For instance, the idea of the 'chosen people' has always been claimed equally by all Jews. The Jews, then, who cultivate a sense of their own distinctive ethnic honour in feudal society, are immune from the disparagement of 'outsiders' such as the knighthood located at the top of the feudal social hierarchy.

5.4 Seigneurial proprietorship

Hitherto, Weber's key argument regarding the positively privileged knightly estate in the feudal social order substantiating the pre-eminence of its 'being' or 'nature' and, hence, its claim for high social honour by living a traditional, knightly style of life, has been continually underlined. Of primary significane also is Weber's assertion that:

> ...social honor very frequently and typically is associated with the respective stratum's *legally guaranteed and monopolized claim ... to income and profit opportunities of a certain kind.* (1970, p.300, emphasis added; see also 1978a, pp.306, 935)

Weber is calling attention to the economic foundation of a style of life. If the onus is on a status group to reinforce its claim for high social honour by living a particular mode of life, it must in the first place possess the necessary material resources to live such a life.

Concerning the knights in the feudal social hierarchy, their capacity to live a knightly way of life was conditioned economically. To fully appreciate what this implies in the feudal estate order, it is first of all imperative to grasp the fact that the feudal economy was, to use Polanyi's terminology, an 'embedded' economy. Polanyi explains that:

> The outstanding discovery of recent historical and anthropological research is that man's economy, as a rule, is submerged in his social relationships. He does not act so as to safeguard his individual interest in the possession of material goods; he acts so as to safeguard his social standing, his social claims, his social assets. He values material goods only in so far as they serve this end. (1944, p.46)[45]

Generally, the economic process in the past in all societies was 'embedded' in non-economic institutions. Unlike the 'unembedded', modern, capitalist market-economy, the economy in pre-modern societies was not organized as a structurally independent sub-system of society.[46] Non-economic motives determined the nature of the economic system itself. Individuals sought not wealth as such, but rather the material resources that were compatible not only with the maintenance but the enhancement of their social standing, their social prestige. In like manner, Weber reasons that 'in the past the significance of stratification by status was far more decisive, above all, for the economic structure of societies' (1970, p.301; see also 1978a, pp.306, 927).

The main purpose of economic activity in the feudal social order was to enable each estate to live according to its appropriate mode of life. To begin with, let us take the case of the occupational estates. Weber declares that:

> ...an 'occupational status group', too, is a status group proper. For normally, it successfully claims social honor by virtue of the special style of life which may be determined by it. (1978a, p.937; see also pp.305-6)

Weber's definition of 'an "occupational status group"' in this instance in terms of the social honour it claims, suggests that it is most relevant in the feudal context.[47] The occupational estate groups in feudal society were primarily organized into craft guilds and merchant guilds. The craft guilds, in particular, wanted to earn an income that was compatible with the maintenance of their social standing in the feudal social hierarchy. In this connection, Weber points out that the notion of the mediaeval 'just price' 'was determined by the test (and occasionally experimentally) of whether or not at the given price the craftsmen in question could maintain the standard of living appropriate to their social status' (1978a, p.872; see also 1981b, pp.116, 118, 138). The craftsmen engaged in skilled labour were not interested in accumulating material goods as such.

In respect of the economic process in feudal society allowing the knightly estate to live a noble way of life, Weber affirms that:

> The full fief is always a *rent-producing* complex of rights whose ownership can and should maintain a lord in a manner appropriate to his style of life. (1978a, p.1072, emphasis in original; see also pp.256, 1093;

1970, p.369)

The feudal lord's primary economic motive is not capitalistic acquisition, but rather his organized want-satisfaction. He is a receiver of income rather than an entrepreneur. The rent-producing use of property rather than capital investment is crucial for the feudal seigneur. Income from rent-property is the precondition for living a value-permeated, knightly way of life.

Put somewhat differently, lordship over the land (i.e., *nulle terre sans seigneur*) was the economic basis of the knightly estate. Land worked by peasants (including serfs) was the principal form of rent-property from which the feudal lord derived his income for a long period during the Middle Ages. Weber explains that:

> Human beings (slaves and serfs) and fixed installations of all types which are used by seigneurial owners as sources of rent are, in the nature of the case, only rent-producing household property and not capital goods... (1978a, p.155; see also p.256)

That is to say, the rents which a feudal lord over land or persons receives from his dependents in payment for the obligations due him by reason of his seigneurial rights, are used for the consumption-oriented maintenance of himself and his lineage rather than for the creation of capital.[48] Another point especially pertinent here is that it is not rent-property *per se* which is recognized as a qualification for membership of the knightly estate in the feudal social order. Rather, it is the fact that rent-property provides the material resources requisite for living a value-inculcated, knightly mode of life. It is in this sense that Weber writes that it is 'not necessarily property itself that ennobles a person, but rather the style of life that is possible only on the basis of property' (1978a, p.1146; see also p.932).

The basic economic unit in feudal society was the manorial estate. Weber (1981b, pp.65-73) observes that two forms of landholding were found within this estate. The first was the seigneurial land or demesne which included the *terra salica* managed directly by the lord's officials, and the *terra indominicata* which were seigneurial landholdings in free peasant villages. The second form of landholding comprised the holdings or hide land of the peasants. This was subdivided into *mansi serviles* with unlimited services and *mansi ingenuiles* with limited services. Although the mediaeval peasants, by and large, 'possessed' their holdings, they did not 'own' them. They were tenants who rented the land from the legal owners, the feudal knighthood.

Another relevant point is Weber's (1981b, pp.69-70, 74-8) observation that the mediaeval peasantry was strongly differentiated. The richer peasants possessing one or even two plough teams, a full holding in the arable land in the village and full grazing rights in the commons, were differentiated from both the smallholders possessing inadequate plots of land and the landless labourers. The mediaeval serfs, as Hilton (1973, p.355) argues, were those peasants who were dependent upon the feudal lord by virtue of the fact that they were tenants on land which they did not own. These particular peasants were, furthermore, subject to legal restrictions concerning freedom of movement, freedom to buy and sell land, freedom to determine the use of their own labour, freedom to marry and freedom to pass on property to their heirs. The principal reason for the creation of these harsh rules of dependence was to make certain that the peasants remained on their landholdings and, thereby, paid their rents to the lord and provided the necessary labour services. Despite the stratification of the peasants in feudal society, they were nevertheless all part of the same negatively privileged estate, sharing a uniform way of life. In the final analysis, the various peasant strata could only be differentiated from one another in respect of the number of material goods they possessed.[49]

If all strata within the peasant estate, then, shared a similar mode of life, they were also all bound together by the fact that the feudal knighthood regarded them as nothing more than a source of revenue. The peasants shared an inescapable 'fate' as rent-payers. Indeed, Weber indicates that until the revolutions of 1789 and 1848, the European peasant 'was doomed to support the landlord, who possessed the higher ownership of the land and quite often the right to the peasant's body as well' (1970, p.365). The peasant was subject to structural compulsion. An objective inequality of conditions prevailed between the landlord and the peasant. The landlord's estate situation was such that he could 'exploit' the peasant by making him into a rent-payer. The landlord was already in a structural power situation. The 'feudal system'(Weber 1978a, pp.1102,1105) permitted him to exploit the peasant. When Weber makes reference to the 'exploitation of the subjugated peasantry by the lords...' (1981b, p.72), he is, of course, treating 'exploitation' as a neutral, technical term. Given Weber's commitment to a value-free social science, 'exploitation' cannot be construed as a normative category. The justice or injustice of utilizing the peasants as merely a source of revenue in the feudal estate order is an extra-scientific question.

Of particular relevance also is that feudal rent extraction was realized, in the main, through political means. Because the direct producers, the peasants, were in 'possession' of the means of production (i.e., the land), they had to be compelled by non-economic means to pay the rent which the feudal knight needed to fulfill his military/political obligations and to 'live like a lord'. No particular economic mechanism of rent extraction was at the disposal of the feudal lord. Or expressed in Marx's terminology, there was no specific economic means of exploitation available to the feudal lord. What distinguished the feudal economy was the absence of an instrument of exploitation springing from the system of production itself. The feudal rent paid by the peasant to his lord basically involved the forced transfer of surplus labour, the products of surplus labour or money made from the sale of these products.[50] Even though the feudal lord played no part as an agent in the process of production, his right to rent in labour, kind or money was sanctioned by the force of custom or law. The peasant faced a legally enforced deduction from his total product, a deduction which went to his seigneur. It is in this context also that Weber's statement regarding social honour being 'associated with the respective stratum's legally guaranteed and monopolized claim ... to income and profit opportunities of a certain kind', is understandable (1970, p.300). Rent, a primary source of a feudal lord's income, could only be extirpated from the mediaeval peasant through legal means.

Weber also concedes that 'ground rent is frequently the product of violent political subjection' (1978a, p.916). For example, the peasants in conquered territories like England and Ireland were compelled to pay ground rent to the Norman conquerors who became their landlords. However, the Norman landlord's violent extraction of the peasant's surplus acquired a veneer of legality grounded in tradition with the passage of time.

Rent was not the only source of income that made it possible for the feudal lord to fulfill his military/political obligations, and to 'live like a lord'. Weber (1970, p.378; 1978a, p.1100) states that seigneurial income was also derived from the lord's right to extort taxes, fees and tolls as well as from his monopoly and preemption rights and his right of patrimonial justice.[51] The origins of markets and towns in the Middle Ages, for instance, were 'to be found in speculation in taxes and rents by princes and lords' (Weber 1978b, p.300; see also pp.296-7; 1978a, pp.1331-33). The feudal seigneur's interest in markets and the affairs of the towns does not mean, though, that he had developed an interest in capital accumulation. Quite the contrary. His major interest always remained the consumption-oriented maintenance of himself and his lineage. Weber (1978a, p.155) argues that the goods which the mediaeval peasant or feudal lord puts up for sale were not 'capital goods' but 'commodities'. For economic activity in the feudal economy was not oriented to rational capital accounting. Seigneurial income derived from monopoly and exemption rights, included the lord's exclusive legal right to the natural products of the countryside (e.g., hunting and fishing rights) and his commercial monopolies (e.g., the processing of farm produce). Finally, seigneurial income gained from the profits of private justice mainly involved the imposition of fines in the seigneurial courts of law.

It is important to highlight the fact that the meaning which a feudal seigneur gave to the use of wealth is very different from that given by a capitalist entrepreneur during the emergence of modern rational capitalism. The early capitalist entrepreneur was primarily interested in the instrumental use of wealth to accumulate more wealth. He was oriented to the purposive-rational control of consumption. Weber notes that the Puritans were not engaged in 'a struggle against the rational acquisition, but against the irrational use of wealth' (1976a, p.171). They opposed what they perceived as 'all concessions to feudal "wastefulnesss"' (Weber 1978a, p.1202).[52]

On the other hand, Weber contends that:

The need for 'ostentation', glamor and imposing splendor, for surrounding one's life with utensils which are not justified by utility ... is primarily a feudal status need and an important power instrument for the sake of maintaining one's own dominance through mass suggestion. *'Luxury' in the sense of rejecting purposive-rational control of consumption is for the dominant feudal strata nothing superfluous: it is a means of social self-assertion.* (1978a, p.1106; emphasis added)[53]

In feudal society where every outward manifestation of the individual is significant, expenditure on prestige and social display is crucial. Pomp, circumstance and social display are invaluable weapons in the struggle for social honour.[54] Weber's statement that 'very frequently the striving for power is ... conditioned by the social honor it entails' (1978a, p.926), is especially pertinent here. The accumulation of social honour in feudal society is equivalent to the accumulation of social power. It is not surprising, then, that the craving for social honour and fear of its loss are primary motives underpinning the feudal knight's conduct. Each individual knight combats the obliteration of the social distinctions that separate him from his moral and social inferiors. The compulsion to openly display his rank in the feudal social hierarchy is relentless for the knight. Viewed in this light, the consumption of certain material goods in the feudal estate order is not principally the expression of wealth but of rank and social honour.[55] The prestige value of the knight's material goods overshadows their purely utilitarian value. The members of the knightly estate monopolize certain material goods like the right to bear arms and own an entailed estate (Weber 1978a, pp.698, 935, 937). The entailed estate, the social honour and the lineage of the knightly family were all intimately associated with one another.

Regarding the various occupational estates in feudal society, the consumption of certain material goods was likewise the expression of rank and social honour. Weber (1981b, p.233) observes that the trading members in the English guild system in the fourteenth century distanced themselves socially from the craft guilds as "'livery companies'". He continues that the members of these companies raised themselves above the poorer craft workers due to the cost of the livery or regalia which the latter could not meet.

Because the members of the knightly estate were, in particular, obliged to consume on a scale befitting their rank, it obviously follows, as Weber (1978a, pp.237-41, 1099-1102; 1981b, pp.93-4) reasons, that any notion of saving, let alone of capital accumulation, was inconceivable to the feudal mind. Wealth was for status-oriented consumption rather than for re-investment. Moreover, wealth in feudal society was redistributed by means of *largesse. Largesse* was one of the most honourable noble virtues. It basically involved, as Hilton explains, 'the downward redistribution of high aristocratic incomes, extracted from the peasants, to the military retainers and into the ever-open satchels of the clergy'

(1985, p.229). Given the use of wealth for status-oriented consumption and the importance of *largesse* in the feudal estate order, capital accumulation for investment in the extension of production was impossible. Hilton (1975b, p.196) estimates that no more than five per cent of total income was ploughed back into production by the landlords of the thirteenth century.[56]

Owing to the fact that wealth was used for status-oriented consumption in feudal society, it is not surprising that the knights, in particular, reacted strongly against the claims of purely economic acquisition. Weber purports that:

> Honor abhors hard bargaining among peers and occasionally it taboos it for the members of a status group in general. Therefore, everywhere some status groups, and usually the most influential, consider almost any kind of overt participation in economic acquisition as absolutely stigmatizing. (1978a, p.937; see also pp.306, 936,1106)

To take the case of the urban nobles in the Middle Ages, they often took part in mercantile enterprise, but only 'in the capacity of a shipowner, or as a limited partner, provider of *commenda* capital or of a "sea loan"' (Weber 1978a, p.1294). Weber accentuates the fact that the urban noble did not tarnish his honour by participating directly in economic acquisition. The actual voyage and the conduct of the trading operations were the responsibility of others. If the urban noble became too directly involved in economic acquisition, he was deemed to be '"not of the knightly kind"' (Weber 1978a, p.1295).[57] In point of fact, the feudal estate order would have been seriously endangered if naked economic power, still bearing the stigma of its extra-estate origin, could have bestowed upon the possessor the same or even greater social honour as the knights claimed for themselves by virtue of the superiority of their 'being' or 'nature'.

This total opposition on the part of the feudal knighthood to a distribution of power which is regulated exclusively through the market:

> ...motivates the *nouveaux riches* to invest their acquired wealth not in a capitalist venture but in land, in order to rise into the nobility if it be possible. All of this impedes the formation of productive capital; this was very typical of the Middle Ages, especially in Germany. (Weber 1978a, p.1101)

The *nouveaux riches* 'feudalize' their acquired wealth through the purchase of noble estates.[58] Bloch mentions the new power born in the twelfth century, namely the rich merchants, who aspired to '"the baldric of knighthood"' (1961, p.322). However, Weber (1978a, pp.936-7) points out that the purchase of a noble estate was not sufficient to be accepted among the members of the knightly estate in feudal society. Owing to the rigorous reactions against the pretensions of property *per se*, the *parvenu* was never accepted personally and without reservation in the rather closed circles of the knightly estate. To the contrary, the nobles will only accept the descendants of the *parvenu*, 'who have been educated in the conventions of their status group and who have never besmirched its honor by their own economic labor' (Weber 1978a, p.937). Weber mentions that the old knightly families of the cities in the late Middle Ages, at least in northern Europe, were not recognized as status equals by the rural knighthood—because they sat on the city council together with men of the craft guilds and, therefore, with entrepreneurs.[59]

Despite the efforts of the feudal nobles to limit the power of the *nouveaux riches* by making entry into their exclusive social circles exceedingly difficult, 'the paradox of unintended consequences' was such that:

> ...the more successfully the feudal stratum prevented the intrusion of *nouveaux riches*, excluded them from offices and political power, socially 'declassed' them and blocked their acquisition of aristocratic landed estates, the more it directed this wealth to purely bourgeois capitalist uses. (Weber 1978a, p.1102)

Weber is underscoring the fact that the feudal nobles contributed to their own eventual demise and, thereby, to the rise of modern market-oriented capitalism. For they socially ostracized the *nouveaux riches* like the rich merchants in the towns and cities, and refused to share political power (i.e., 'rights of rule') with them. Given this state of affairs, the *nouveaux riches* re-invested rather than consumed their wealth and, hence, contributed to capital accumulation.[60]

5.5 Private rights

Having unravelled the implications that follow from Weber's assertion that social honour is usually linked with the respective stratum's 'legally guaranteed and monopolized claim ... to income and profit opportunitites of a certain kind' (1970, p.300), it is now appropriate to consider Weber's statement that 'social honor very frequently and typically is associated with the respective stratum's legally guaranteed and monopolized claim to sovereign rights...' (1970, p.300). In the context of Weber's study of the nature of stratification in the feudal estate order, this statement implies that the unequal distribution of the prime resource, social honour, is also connected with a rights-based system of inequality. The unequal distribution of social honour in the feudal estate order is usually associated with differential relations of access to or exclusion from certain rights and privileges.

On this account, Mueller (1979, p.163) misreads Weber when he alleges that Weber fails to make sufficiently clear the fact that *Stände* are primarily defined by legal privileges and only secondarily by status honour and style of life. Omodei likewise misappropriates Weber when he maintains that status honour, style of life and other associated factors are 'derivative, not primary' (1982, p.200).

Omodei's interpretation of Weber is such that 'the critical defining characteristic' (1982, p.197) of status is access to or exclusion from rights, duties and privileges. But Weber himself states that:

Power, as well as honor, may be guaranteed by the legal order, but, at least normally, it is not their primary source. The legal order is rather an *additional factor* that enhances the chance to hold power or honor; but it can not always secure them. (1978a, pp.926-7; emphasis added)

Weber is underlining the fact here that the legal order is not the principal begetter of power and social honour. Rather, it is an 'additional factor' that augments one's chances of gaining power or social honour.

As to the relationship holding between social honour and the relevant estate's 'legally guaranteed and monopolized claim to sovereign rights...' in the feudal social order, Weber (1978a, p.933) affirms that all status honour in its beginnings rests on usurpation. Regarding 'the real origin' of many mediaeval cities (i.e., the burgher estates), for instance, Weber says that it 'is to be found in what is from the formal legal point of view a revolutionary usurpation of rights' (1978a, p.1250). In the case of the formation of the knightly estate, mounted warriors claimed moral and social superiority through various forms of social exclusion such as the necessity to live a highly stylized, knightly way of life. The emergence of the knightly estate was dependent upon how successful the knights were in actually convincing others of their moral and social superiority. This estate usurped its own moral and social superiority vis-à-vis those below, especially the peasantry, and also later the burghers in the towns and cities. This usurpation of superiority was, according to Weber (1978a, p.933), at first purely conventional since it was upheld only by social approval or disapproval.

But Weber adds that:

...the road to legal privilege, positive or negative, is easily traveled as soon as a certain stratification of the social order has in fact been 'lived in' and has achieved stability by virtue of a stable distribution of economic power. (1978a, p.933)

Legal privileges involve the sanctioning of usurpation. As a matter of fact, it was only from the twelfth century onwards that the feudal knighthood was solidified into a legal estate in the West.[61] The knighthood now wanted to make legally effective the moral and social superiority which it claimed for itself. One reason for this change in the character of the knighthood resides in the fact that noble status became hereditary in the later Middle Ages. It also became possible to acquire noble status through royal or princely decree. Monarchs began to monopolize the creation of new knights. This being so, both the old and new knighthood became interested in a set of legal privileges which would further reinforce the social distinctions separating the nobleman from the commoner (the peasant and the burgher).

A crisis of seigneurial revenues from the thirteenth century onwards was another fundamental reason for the feudal knighthood's interest in legal privileges.[62] It became more and more difficult for the knight to live a way of life consonant with his rank in the feudal social hierarchy. By the thirteenth century, the wealth of every feudal kingdom was no longer in its land but in its trade. Consequently, more and more money was put into circulation. But as money became more plentiful, its value diminished in proportion. The cost of living was continually rising. The knights were, however, restricted to fixed revenues rooted in immemorial custom. Many knights burdened with debts were economically ruined.[63] Given this state of affairs, the knights' response was to protect their social honour. For social honour was the unifying bond for the knightly estate as a whole. The knights sought to distinguish themselves from prospering burghers and peasants through the creation of legal privileges. The fact that economic instability was one reason for the knightly estate's interest in legal privileges, contravenes Weber's claim that the development of legal privileges is easily achieved as soon as a particular social order has attained stability by reason of a stable distribution of economic power.

The transformation of the feudal knighthood into a legal estate was only made possible by the consolidation of royal authority from the twelfth century onwards.[64] For it was this authority alone which could systematize the differences between the various estates by making them legal. The same legal codes were reproduced throughout feudal Europe in the twelfth and thirteenth centuries.

Weber also asserts that:

> In a formal legal sense the corporation of the burghers and its authorities had their 'legitimate' origin in (real or fictitious) privileges granted by the political and at times by the manorial powers. (1978a, p.1250; see also pp.1243, 1259; 1981b, p.148)

Weber (1978a, p.1250) goes on to make a distinction between a "'spontaneous'" and a "'derived'" formation of the corporations of burghers. In the "'spontaneous'" case, the city commune originated as a political association of the burghers in spite of, or in defiance of, the 'legitimate' power-holders. The 'legitimate' power-holders only later formally acknowledged the city commune by giving it the legal status of a corporation. However, city communes were not always accorded legal status by the 'legitimate' political powers. On the other hand, a "'derived'" burgher corporation was, according to Weber, created by means of a contracted or legislated grant of more or less limited rights of autonomy and autocephaly, issued by the political lords.

What was the nature of those legal privileges which further highlighted the social distinctions differentiating the various estates in feudal society? The heart of the matter is that legal privileges in the feudal estate order refer to rights vested in the individual as a member of a specific social group.[65] Weber explains that:

> ...in the medieval *Imperium,* every man was entitled everywhere to be judged by that tribal law by which he 'professed' to live. The individual carried his *professio iuris* with him wherever he went. Law was not a *lex terrae* ... but rather the privilege of the person as a member of a particular social group. (1978a, p.696; see also pp.694-704)

Feudal rights appear as the various privileges, liberties and immunities that are conferred upon the individual as a member of a given estate. It is in this sense that the members of the knightly estate and the burgher estate enjoy traditional, independent rights. The feudal estate order constitutes a synthesis of purely concrete rights and duties. Weber argues that this synthesis amounts 'to a "constitutional" state *(Rechtsstaat)* on the basis of "subjective" rights, not "objective" law' (1978a, p.1099). The knights and the burghers are each subject to their own special systems of law. The modern idea of a system of universal, formal, legal rules applicable to every citizen within the confines of the nation-state, is inconceivable in the feudal context.

Another point especially pertinent here is that the rights vested in the individual as a member of a given estate in feudal society, are sanctioned by tradition. These rights derive their validity from the sacredness of traditional law. Weber writes that:

> In the pure type of traditional authority it is impossible for law or administrative rule to be deliberately created by legislation. Rules which in fact are innovations can be legitimized only by the claim that they have been 'valid of yore', but have only now been recognized by means of 'Wisdom' ... Legal decisions as 'finding of the law' *(Rechtsfindung)* can refer only to documents of tradition, namely to precedents and earlier decisions. (1978a, p.227)

The assumption underpinning modern rational law, that is, the fact that laws are held to be legitimate if they have been enacted by the proper authorities adhering to specified legal procedures, is alien to the feudal mind. Feudal law cannot be 'deliberately created by legislation'. It is not possible to enact law in feudal society in a purposive-rational manner. Similarly, feudal rights can only be discovered in tradition. Unlike the civil, political and social rights which make up the separate components of citizenship in the modern nation-state, feudal rights could not be purposively formulated by legislation.[66]

Of decisive importance also is the fact that a unique conception of freedom was at the heart of the legal codes applying to the different estates in the feudal social order. Although Weber did not devote special attention to this issue, it is essential to briefly consider it. In fact, the most important legal distinction in feudal society was that between the 'free' and 'unfree'. Freedom in the feudal context meant a special legal status summed up in the word 'liberty'. Liberty

(Libertas) in feudal society could only be defined, as Southern (1953, pp.104-7) reasons, in relation to the law by which those who were free were governed. Subjection to a special law was not considered as an obstacle to the attainment of liberty. Quite the contrary. Liberty was a creation of feudal law itself. The greater the individual's liberty in the feudal estate order, the more was his conduct bound by law. The individual sought greater liberty by increasing the number of legal regulations governing his conduct.

In this same connection, Southern (1953, pp.106-7) points out that the idea of 'choice' was built into the feudal concept of liberty. What distinguished the feudal legal codes was the fact that adherence to them had to be voluntary. The submission of both the knights and the burghers to their respective legal codes had to involve free choice. Hence, the importance of the oath in feudal society. The oath was a very personal act embodied in a public ceremony. The enfeoffment ceremony whereby the vassal pledged fealty to his lord was one such key oath. In a somewhat similar vein, Weber describes the mediaeval city as a 'sworn *commune* which had the legal status of a corporation, although this was attained only gradually' (1978a, p.1248; emphasis in original).

In light of the preceding discussion, it is obvious that the knights/nobles represented the most positively privileged estate in the feudal social order. They were subject to many laws. In other words, they possessed the most extensive range of rights and, thereby, the greatest amount of liberty.[67] The symbol *par excellence* of noble liberty in the feudal estate order was 'the right to bear arms' (Weber 1978a, p.906). On the other hand, the mediaeval peasantry and, particularly the serfs, represented the most negatively privileged estate in feudal society. They were subject to the least number of laws. They possessed rudimentary rights and, therefore, had very little liberty. The deferential peasants and, above all the serfs, lived more 'outside' the law in the sense that they had to generally submit to 'the will' of another, that is, the feudal seigneur. They were judicially degraded.[68]

Even when non-noble freemen reappeared in Western Europe in the thirteenth and fourteenth centuries as a result of manumission from serfdom, the judicial distinction between the freemen of noble and commoner status persisted. The reason for this, as Genicot (1968, p.130) notes, inheres in the fact that all non-noble freemen still had to obey some noble functionary within the feudal estate order. In other words, they were 'mediatized' under private authority. However, noble liberty was distinguished throughout the Middle Ages by its two fundamental traits: immunity *(Immunitas)* and the right to have armed retainers.

It is appropriate at this point to mention some of the rights bestowed upon the members of the positively privileged knightly and burgher estates and the negatively privileged peasant estate in the feudal social order. With regard to the knightly estate, the fact that it possessed seigneurial rights to income has already been mentioned. These rights primarily concerned the private relationship between the feudal lord and his dependents and social inferiors.

In addition to seigneurial rights to income, the feudal knighthood was in solid possession of another set of seigneurial rights, that is, rights of rule. The feudal knights identified themselves as a legal estate ruling by private right.[69] The knight's exercize of governmental powers was a personal privilege. Weber (1978a, pp.641-4) observes that there was no distinction made between public and private law in pre-modern societies. Everything which in the modern nation-state falls within the sphere of public law made up the content of the private rights of individual power-holders, and was in this sense in no way different from a right in private law.

Under feudal conditions there was no monopoly of legitimate power, no central unified political authority. There was no state in the modern sense of the word. Rather, all powers of government were divided between the monarch and his vassals, each on the basis of his personal rights. Rule in the feudal sense was basically federal. For to each individual vassal belonged an autonomous rule over his dependents and social inferiors. Weber explains that:

> Feudalism is a 'separation of powers'... it is simply a quantitiative division of authority. The idea of the social contract as the basis of the distribution of political power, an idea which led to constitutionalism, is anticipated in a primitive fashion. Of course, not in the form of a pact between the ruler and the ruled or their representatives ... but in the essentially different form of a contract between the ruler and those whose authority derives from him. Type and distribution of powers are fixed through this contract, but there is no general *règlement* and no rational differentiation of individual jurisdiction. For the powers of the office are personal rights, contrary to the bureaucratic case; their extent is determined positively by the official's personal grant *and* negatively by the subjects' exemptions, immunities and privileges, whether they be granted or sanctified by tradition. Only this juxtaposition and the mutual limitation of the subjective right of *one* power-holder by the opposed rights of another produces ... that power distribution which would correspond to some extent to the bureaucratic notion of official jurisdiction. (1978a, p.1082, emphasis in original; see also pp.1083-85)[70]

The political organization of feudal society was such, then, that each individual power-holder pursued his own personal interests on the basis of his privately owned, inheritable authority. Similarly, Weber notes that feudal law was 'the law for the relation between lord and vassal and not the law of a "vassalic state" simply because such kind of state never existed' (1978a, p.700).

Weber also contends that the feudal form of government comes close to the ideal-type of estate-type patrimonialism. The estate-type of patrimonialism exists where 'the person exercising governing powers has personal control of the means of administration—if not all, at least of an important part of them' (Weber 1978a, p.234; see also pp.232-3).[71] The feudal knight fully controlled these means. The costs of administration were treated by the knight as personal expenditures identical with those of his own household. Another defining characteristic of the estate-type of patrimonialism, according to Weber, has to do with the fact that:

...the appropriation of judicial and military powers tends to be treated as a legal basis for a privileged status position of those appropriating them, as compared to the appropriation of purely economic advantages having to do with income from domains, from taxes, or perquisites. (1978a, pp.236-7)

The usurpation of judicial and military powers, as opposed to purely economic opportunities, was used by feudal knights as a legal basis for gaining more rights and social honour. Indeed, the right to rule over their dependents and social inferiors in their own locality was a key attribute of the feudal knights as a socially privileged estate.

Furthermore, the feudal knighthood's form of rule involves domination by *honoratiores*. According to Weber, this is a form of traditional authority which:

...exists wherever social honor ('prestige') within a group has become the basis of domination—and by no means does this happen in every case of social honor ... The specific authority of the notable—especially of one distinguished among his neighbors through property, education or style of life—derives from 'honor'. (1978a, p.1009; see also pp.290-92, 948-52)

The knight in solid possession of social honour in feudal society regarded himself (and was generally regarded) as the 'natural' ruler of his dependents and social inferiors in the locality. The knight's economic situation as a rentier was such that he was able to take part in policy-making and perform administrative functions continuously without (more than nominal) remuneration. In short, the feudal knight as a notable was able 'to live *for* politics without living *from* politics' (Weber 1978a, p.290; emphasis in original).

Another related point is the fact that the honourable feudal knights did not only regard themselves as the 'natural' rulers in their respective localities. They were also interested in the expansion of their rights of rule over other political structures. In this respect, Weber writes that 'the realm of "honor", which is comparable to the "status order" within a social strucutre, pertains also to the interrelations of political strucutres' (1978a, p.911). He is referring here to the 'power-oriented prestige' which derives from power over other political structures. Weber continues that feudal knights, like modern officers or bureaucrats, are 'the natural and primary exponents of this desire for power-oriented prestige for one's own political structure' (1978a, p.911). For the expansion of the feudal knight's rights of rule over other political structures, means the procurement of new objects for infeudation, more provisions for his lineage, and even more glory and social honour for himself and his descendents.[72]

What form did the rights of rule possssed by the feudal knighthood take? Essentially, these rights of rule enabled the feudal knighthood to control their dependents and social inferiors. These rights included, as Bush (1983, pp.157-85) indicates, the right of private jurisdiction, the right to determine tenancy, rights related to serfdom, the right to administer the fiscal and military demands which the royal power made of a seigneur's dependents, and the right to influence the appointment of public officials. The right of private jurisdiction was one of the most fundamental rights of rule possessed by the feudal knight. Indeed, Weber argues that the seigneur's right to wield judicial authority 'became far the most important single force in connection with the development of the West' (1981b, p.65). The seigneur's right to discharge justice in his own court included criminal and civil cases and misdemeanours. This right also frequently enabled the seigneur to mete out capital and corporeal punishment, to impose fines and to forefeit tenancies. Strayer aptly sums up the nature of the knight's 'private authority'—when he says that 'the feudal lord is not merely one of a group of men who influence the government; he *is* the government in his own area' (1968, p.14; emphasis in original).

It should be stressed that the peasants were not completely subordinated to 'the will' of the seigneur. In the first place, Weber notes that there was variation in property ownership in feudal society. He (1981b, pp.69-70) mentions that there were free peasants living outside the manorial estate on freehold land subject only to quit-rents. They were basically private owners over whom the feudal lord could not exercize judicial authority. These free peasants were known as '"odal"' peasants. Such peasants were found in large numbers in areas like Norway, the marsh lands of the North Sea, in parts of the Alps, Tyrol, Switzerland and England. What is more, manorial law developed as a result of the fact that free and unfree peasants were thrown together on the seigneurial landholdings. Weber writes that:

> Under these circumstances the free peasants were able to compel the lord to join with all his dependents in forming a manorial court in which the dependent persons functioned as magistrates. Thus the lord lost the power of arbitrary control over the obligations of his dependents and these became traditionalized... (1981b, p.68)

For instance, the fixed rents which the peasants were obliged to pay to their seigneur were now protected by manorial law. The development of manorial law reached its peak in the thirteenth century.

Another pivotal point made by Weber (1981b, p.70) is that the territorial princes adopted a policy of protecting the peasantry, and forbade the knighthood to confiscate peasant holdings. Differentiation in respect of liability to taxation was the reason for this policy. The knights/nobles were exempt from taxation. It was the peasants who had to bear the burden of taxation. Seen in this light, a decrease in the number of peasant holdings would have meant a substantial loss of revenue for the princes. One further point which I think bears mentioning here is that the crisis of seigneurial revenues from the thirteenth century onwards, and severe demographic decline resulting from some fatal plagues in the fourteenth and fifteenth centuries—gave both free and unfree peasants greater leverage to bargain with their seigneurs. In fact, serfdom had become a peripheral feature of the feudal agrarian system in the West by 1400.[73]

Besides the feudal warrior nobility exerting rights of rule over their dependents and social inferiors in their given localities, they also exercized rights of rule through rights of political participation with the royal/princely ruler in the governance of a particular national or regional territory. To understand how the warrior nobility of the later Middle Ages acquired the right to associate with the monarch/prince in ruling a national or regional territory, it is essential to briefly recall the nature of the relationship holding between the overlord and his vassal up to the twelfth century. Because the feudal estate order was a cosmos of concrete subjective rights and duties, anarchy was the norm. Chronic conflict was built into the overlord-vassal relationship. Weber explains that:

> It goes without saying that whenever *Lehensfeudalismus* is hightly developed, the overlord's authority is precarious. This is because it is very dependent on the voluntary obedience and hence the purely personal loyalty of the members of the administrative staff, who, by virtue of the feudal structure, are themselves in possession of the means of administration. Hence, the latent struggle for authority becomes chronic between the lord and his vassal, and *the ideal extent of feudal authority has never been effectively carried out in practice* or remained effective on a permanent basis. (1978a, p.257; emphasis added)

The fact that the overlord and his vassals monopolized the rights of rule in their respective localities, inevitably led in the concrete situation to jurisdictional disputes. Both the overlord and his vassals considered it quite legitimate to defend their private rights of rule by resorting to warfare or litigation. Litigation was second only to warfare as a form of conflict preferred in feudal Europe. Indeed, warfare and litigation were integral components of feudal politics. Whenever an overlord or a vassal opposed the violation of their 'private' rights of rule by force of arms or litigation, they believed that they were upholding the established social order. They were 'standing on their rights'.

By the later Middle Ages, great overlords like the French kings, Louis VI and VII (reigned 1108-1180) in the *ile de France*, were gaining the advantage over their feudal vassals in the struggle for authority. Faced with this gradual consolidation of royal/princely power, the lesser warrior noblemen took concerted action to gain royal recognition of their subjective rights. The end-result was that the warrior noblemen of various countries succeeded in exacting charters from their royal/princely overlords. These charters were to be the basis for the nobles' association with their royal/princely rulers in the governance of national/regional territories for centuries in Western Europe. Feudal principles such as: noble representation in the *curia regis*, consultation on issues of taxation, rule of law and so on were written into these charters.[74] These charters attest to the emergence of a corporate identity among the feudal nobility.

The nobles' right to participate with the royal/princely ruler in the governance of a national/regional territory was enshrined in a new system of rule which was widespread throughout Western Europe by the thirteenth century. This new system of rule is known as the *Ständestaat* in German scholarly discourse. The rise of the *Ständestaat* (the polity of Estates) signifies that the tenuous nature of the feudal contract entered into by the overlord and his vassal had been formalized. The mere agreed-upon action of the overlord and his vassal was transformed into a permanent political structure. On this score, Weber states that:

> Feudalism is oriented not only to characteristic patrimonial features such as tradition, privilege, customal and precedent, but also to *temporary alliances* between the various power-holders, as it was typical of and, in fact, the essence of the *polity of Estates (Ständestaat)* in the Occident ... These holders of privilege consociate with one another for the purpose of a concrete action which would not be possible without this collaboration. The existence of a *Ständestaat* merely indicates that this system of alliances, which was unavoidable because of the contractual guarantee of all rights and duties and because of the resulting inelasticity, has developed into a chronic condition, which under certain circumstances was legally perpetuated through an explicit association. (1978a, p.1086; emphasis in original)

Individual power-holders associated, more or less frequently, in the form of a corporative assembly, either to co-operate with, or if necessary, to oppose the royal/princely ruler or his agents. The typical *Ständestaat* was comprised of a variety of such assemblies.[75] The corporative assemblies were usually organized for the whole of the royal/princely ruler's territory or for significant regions or provinces within it.[76] The members of these assemblies represented not only the most privileged noble estate, but also the clergy and the towns (the burgher estate). The representatives of the different estates grouped themselves into separate chambers. The negatively privileged peasant estate was rarely represented in these assemblies. The noble chamber usually exerted great influence.[77] The nobles collaborated with the royal/princely ruler in governing a particular territory through the granting of taxes and also through participation in legislation.

Finally, the kind of rights possessed by the burgher estate in the feudal social order must be broached. The typical members of this estate included merchants and craftsmen. The rights of the city in feudal Europe took the form of the privileges of an estate.[78] Weber asserts that:

> ...the decisive common quality of the ancient Occidental and the typical medieval city lies in the institutionalized association, endowed with special

194

characteristic organs, of people who as 'burghers' are subject to a *special law* exclusively applicable to them and who thus form a legally autonomous status group. This quality of the *polis* or *commune* as a special status group *(Stand)* can be found, as far as is known, in all legal systems other than the Mediterranean and Occidental only in the most rudimentary form. (1978a, p.1240, emphasis in original; see also pp.1236-65; 1981b, pp.315-37) [79]

All the members of the burgher estate were deemed to have as a matter of group privilege the 'subjective' right to be treated under burgher law. The burgher law was an estate right of the members of the sworn fellowship of burghers.

The idea of freedom was intrinsic to burgher law. The judicial status of freeman was conferred on all burghers. Status differences, insofar as they concerned a legal differentiation between the 'free' and 'unfree', disappeared in the mediaeval city. Furthermore, Weber (1978a, p.1239; 1981b, p.330) observes that the principle, 'town air makes free' *(Stadtluft macht frei)*, stipulated that after a year and a day the feudal lord no longer possessed the right to recall his runaway serfs. Many runaway serfs were able in this way to break the chains of servitude that bound them to the feudal seigneur. The burghers had usurped the right to break the bonds of seigneurial domination. It goes without saying, then, that the mediaeval city constituted a unique political space of freedom protected by law. It enjoyed immunities which did not exist in the surrounding countryside.[80]

Of particular relevance also is Weber's comment that the mediaeval city was 'a place where *the ascent from bondage to freedom* by means of monetary acquisition was possible' (1978a, p.1238; emphasis in original). The burghers engaged in estate-conscious policies oriented towards this goal. They wanted to create a judicial environment that would make it both possible and profitable to take part in craftwork and trade. That is to say, the burghers sought the right to rule themselves so that they could pursue their own economic interests. The burghers' idea of rule was, as Poggi (1978, p.39) argues, a 'novelty' in the feudal context, since the right to rule 'over' others was a constitutive element of the nobles' identity as a legal estate.

Weber (1978a, pp.1322-31) contends that the burghers' attempt to gain legal recognition of their right to rule themselves achieved varying levels of success. To begin with, the elimination of obligations to those outside the city succeeded most fully in the case of the personal duties that derived from the burghers' former personal subjection to judicial or manorial lords. As regards autonomous law creation, this was a right fully exercized by the politically independent Italian cities and by a considerable number of the French and German cities. The urban courts with burghers as lay judges, applied a uniform system of law regarding urban landownership, market relations and trade to all the burghers of the relevant city. The right to hold markets and to formulate urban economic policy distinguished every mediaeval city. The right to supervize the markets had, by and large, been taken away from the city lord. However, rights to full autocephaly and taxing autonomy were rarely achieved by the corporations of burghers.

5.6 Estate action

Bearing in mind the importance of social honour in the feudal social order, conflict inevitably arose over the unequal distribution of this resource between the various estates. Moreover, the fact that the unequal distribution of social honour was usually associated with the unequal distribution of economic resources and a rights-based system of inequality, unavoidably led to dissension. If the members of the various estates in feudal society were to defend their ideal and material interests and their political rights, some form of concerted action was obviously required.

For Weber, status groups are, as previously intimated, usually communites. They experience a strong sense of 'belonging together'. The members of the knightly estate in feudal society shared a common identity. They lived a traditional, value-infused, noble way of life from which the burghers and, above all the peasantry, were excluded. The knights were the carriers of a distinct status honour. Weber also accentuates the communal character of the burgher estate when he describes it as a 'sworn *commune*' (1978a, p.1248; emphasis in original). And there was a strong feeling of community among the peasantry throughout mediaeval Europe.

Although status groups are normally communities, they do not necessarily act in concert to defend and even expand their traditional interests. There is no necessary correlation between status groups experiencing a profound sense of community and taking part in some kind of collective action. In this respect, Weber declares that 'a status group is always somehow societalized, but *it is not always organized into an association*' (1970, p.300; emphasis added). Weber is accentuating the problematic nature of collaborative action on the part of the members of a status group. This having been said, it could be argued that it is less difficult to mobilize the members of a status group for the attainment of collective goals. Since status groups (as opposed to classes) are communal groupings with a powerful sense of status consciousness, a mode of collective action grounded in tradition and in a system of fraternal ethics is possible. Stated otherwise, status groups can promote communal collectivism.

The way in which the members of a status group, in fact, set about collectively acting together is brought to light in Weber's discussion of the ideal-typical concept of social closure (see 1978a, pp.43-6, 339-48, 635-40). At bottom, Weber understands social closure as the process by which various groups seek to protect and improve their socio-economic situation by restricting access to resources and privileges to a select group of people. He writes that:

Usually one group of competitors takes some externally identifiable characteristic of another group of (actual or potential) competitors—race, language, religion, local or social origin, descent, residence, etc.—as a pretext for attempting their *exclusion.* It does not matter which characteristic is chosen in the individual case: whatever suggests itself most easily is seized upon. (1978a, p.342; emphasis added)

'Exclusionary social closure', to use Parkin's (1982, p.100) terminology, involves a form of concerted action by the members of a positively privileged status group to monopolize social and economic advantages to the detriment of other status groups.[81] Put another way, 'this monopolization ... is always the closure of social and economic opportunities to *outsiders*' (Weber 1978a, p.342; emphasis in original).

As a matter of fact, Weber (1978a, p.46) argues that there are three primary motives for the closure of a social relationship. Firstly, the participants want to preserve quality which is often linked with prestige and the consequent opportunities to enjoy social honour. The secular orders of chivalry found throughout feudal Europe are a very good example.[82] Secondly, the participants in a social relationship may exclude 'outsiders' because of the narrowing of advantages in relation to consumption needs. Weber refers here to the monopolies of consumption of which the most developed form in feudal Europe was the self-subsistent peasant village community. Finally, Weber maintains that a relationship may be closed because opportunities for acquisition are declining. This was one fundamental reason for the establishment of trading monopolies by the guilds in the Middle Ages.

If the members of a status group at first engage in some kind of joint action to restrict access to economic, social and political opportunities to a limited group of people, they may later set up an explicit association. Weber continues that:

...there is a growing tendency to set up some kind of association with rational regulations; if the monopolistic interests persist, the time comes when the competitors, or another group whom they can influence (for example, a political community), establish a legal order that limits competition through formal monopolies; from then on, certain persons are available as 'organs' to protect the monopolistic practices, if need be, with force. In such a case, the interest group has developed into a *'legally privileged group' (Rechtsgemeinschaft)* and the participants have become *'privileged members' (Rechtsgenossen).* Such closure, as we want to call it, is an every-recurring process; it is the source of property in land as well as of all guild and other group monopolies. (1978a, p.342; emphasis in original)

When Weber in this instance refers to the monopolistic interests of a status group being legally sanctioned, he is pointing to the crucial role played by the legal

197

apparatus of the state in the closure process. Strategies of social closure are made more secure when the monopolies are anchored in law. In the case of Weber's study of estate stratification in feudal society, the relevant 'political community' intervening in the closure process is represented by the royal/princely power sanctioning estate monopolies.

Pertinent to the general impetus of the present discussion also is Weber's point that the interest associations representing positively privileged status groups may not only be utilized to effectuate the closure of economic, social and political opportunities to 'outsiders'. They may also be used to bring about closure of such opportunities to 'insiders' (Weber 1978a, p.343). In addition to his concern with distributive struggles 'between' different status communities, Weber also allows for the possibility of similar struggles 'within' a status community itself. Certain members of a status group may not permit fellow-members access to particular economic, social and political advantages. Weber is highlighting the fact that status communities are not necessarily harmonious.[83] He purports that:

> The communal type of relationship is, according to the usual interpretation of its subjective meaning, the most radical antithesis of conflict. This should not, however, be allowed to obscure the fact that coercion of all sorts is a very common thing in even the most intimate of such communal relationships if one party is weaker in character than the other. Furthermore, a process of the selection of types leading to differences in opportunity and survival, goes on within these relationships just the same as anywhere else. (1978a, p.42)

Weber is saying that struggle will be part of any communal relationship where the more powerful party (i.e., possessing greater resources) is able to dominate the weaker party (i.e., lacking resources).

From the foregoing, it might appear that strategies of social closure are only the prerogative of positively privileged status groups. However, Weber maintains that restricting access to economic, social and political advantages 'may provoke a corresponding reaction on the part of those against whom it is directed' (1978a, p.342). The members of the negatively privileged status group may collectively resist and, thereby, limit the exercize of power by the members of the positively privileged status group. They may collectively oppose the monopolistic tactics of the positively privileged by attempting to increase their share of the economic, social and political resources available.[84] Quite simply, the negatively privileged may try to usurp some of the resources which have already been appropriated by the positively privileged through exclusionary practices.

When Weber states that exclusionary practices 'may provoke' opposition on the part of the negatively privileged strata, he is accentuating the fact that collective action is 'probable', not that it will 'necessarily' follow. If the attempts of the positively privileged strata to monopolize economic, social and political advantages are effective, it impedes the negatively privileged, as Neuwirth observes, 'from influencing the terms of their participation in the larger society'

(1969, p.152). To anticipate what I shall say later, the forms of social closure were such in feudal society that the negatively privileged peasant estate was excluded from participation in political power.

Weber employs the notion of social closure in the study of the concerted traditional action undertaken by the various estates in feudal society. Weber asserts that 'the essence of feudalism is *status consciousness,* and it increasingly perfects this very characteristic' (1978a, p.1081; emphasis added). Because the various feudal estates had a strong sense of communal identity, they were more disposed to defend their traditional interests by collectively acting together. This being the case, it is not surprising that estate struggles pervaded feudal society.[85]

To take the case of the mediaeval Italian city during the period of patrician domination, feuds continually raged 'within' the ranks of the urban patriciate (nobility). Even if all of the urban patricians in Italy shared a knightly style of life rooted in tradition, the few great families and their large followings were, according to Weber:

...always attempting to *exclude* each other (and each other's allies) from the offices and the economic opportunities of the urban administration and, if possible, to drive each other from the city altogether. (1978a, p.1273, emphasis added; see also pp.1266-76)

This interminable conflict 'within' the urban patrician estate resulted in the establishment of 'interlocal interest groups' represented by the Guelf and Ghibelline parties. Put another way, these parties were set up by rival groupings 'within' the urban nobility to effect the closure of economic, social and political opportunities to 'insiders'. As to the mediaeval cities in northern Europe during the period of patrician domination, a small number of privileged urban nobles likewise monopolized the council seats and, thereby, excluded the burghers (i.e., the 'outsiders') from political power (see Weber 1978a, pp.1281-82). Indeed, in all of the patrician cities, 'the principle of status closure became more rigid as the population and the importance of the monopolized offices increased' (Weber 1978a, p.1296).

The rule of the urban nobility in the mediaeval Italian cities and the cities of northern Europe was eventually broken by the burgher 'outsiders'. These burghers usurped the rights of rule monopolized by the urban nobility. Weber (1978a, pp.1301-07) observes that the next crucial stage in the estate struggles 'within' the mediaeval Italian cities involved the formation of the *popolo.* Like the German *Zünfte,* the Italian *popolo* was not only an economic community. It also constituted a separate political community within the urban commune. It had its own officials, finances and military organization. Weber describes the *popolo* as 'the first *deliberately nonlegitimate and revolutionary* political association' (1978a, p.1302; emphasis in original). The estate struggles 'between' the *popolo* and the urban nobility were violent and often long drawn-out. On this account, Weber writes that:

199

Even more inciting seem to have been the personal insults and threats dealt out to the *popolani* by the militarily superior nobility, which continued to recur everywhere after the formation of the separate political association of the *popolo*. *The status pride of the knighthood and the natural resentment of the bourgeoisie forever made for collisions.* (1978a, p.1307; emphasis added)

The *popolo* employed varied 'means of power' to defeat the urban knighthood. The urban artisans were used as a tactical force. They were what Weber calls 'the crack troops of the opposition' (1978b, p.294; see also 1978a, p.1301). The entrepreneurial crafts provided the necessary finance. And the jurists, especially the notaries and often also the judges, comprized the 'intellectual and administrative backbone of the *popolo*...' (Weber 1978a, p.1306). Weber (1981b, pp.324-5) highlights the fact that the guild army of disciplined infantry played a crucial role in the overthrow of the urban knighthood dedicated to the feudal idea of heroic combat between heroes. Wherever the *popolo* was wholly successful in usurping political power in the mediaeval cities, the urban nobility 'was from a purely formal point of view, left with only negative privileges' (Weber 1978a, p.1304). In fact, Weber (1978a, pp. 1294, 1296, 1347; 1978b, p.293; 1981b, p.324) observes that during the period of the craft guilds' rule, the urban nobility was compelled to enrol in the guilds, if it wanted to take part in the governing of the city.

If all the members of the burgher estate were initially united in the course of their struggle with the urban nobility, the upper guilds (e.g., merchants, judges, notaries, bankers) in cities like Florence later excluded the lower guilds (e.g., craftsmen) from participation in the governance of the city (see Weber 1978a, p.1305). In other words, rights of political participation were now closed even to 'insiders'.

Political rights were not the only bone of contention in the struggle 'between' and 'within' estates in the mediaeval cities. Conflict over access to social and economic opportunities was another source of bitter dissension. It is in this context that Weber mentions the mediaeval Western guild. He explains that:

The spirit of the medieval Western guild is most simply expressed in the proposition, *guild policy is livelihood policy.* It signifies the maintenance of a substantial burgherly prosperity for the members of the guild, in spite of increased competition in consequence of the narrowing of the opportunities of life; the individual guild member must obtain the *traditional standard of life* and be made secure in it. This conception of the traditional standard of life is the analogue of the 'living wage' of the present day. (1981b, p.138, emphasis added; see also pp.136-43)

The mediaeval guilds, then, were organized for the purpose of monopolizing the economic opportunities requisite for maintaining the 'traditional standard of life'.

The craft guild, for example, was an association of craft workers principally interested in earning an income consonant with their traditional social status in the feudal estate order. Accordingly, this type of guild performed two specific functions: the internal regulation of work and monopolization against 'outsiders'.

The internal regulation of work by the craft guild meant that processes of work were traditionally regulated, the number of apprentices and labourers in a particular craft was controlled, the provision of raw materials was regulated, and the relations between the individual craftsmen were supervized (see Weber 1981b, pp.138-9). Moreover, Weber calls attention to the fact that the craft guild attempted to procure and maintain equality of opportunity for all members. This form of guild also regulated the economic relations of the relevant industry by limiting any master's ability to accumulate capital, by prohibiting guild members to work for other masters, by controlling buying opportunities, by disallowing the sale of the products of outsiders, and by regulating marketing through price schedules in order to maintain the traditional standard of life. Finally, Weber (1981b, pp.141-2) argues that the craft guild monopolized economic opportunities against 'outsiders' by establishing industrial courts in many instances to police the industry, by aiming at compulsory membership in the guild, and by creating a guild district where no industry other than that of the guild could be set up. In sum, then, the monopolistic practices of the craft guild in the feudal estate order are diametrically opposed to capitalist monopolies in the modern market-economy. For whereas a member of a craft guild maintains his economic power 'against' the market, the economic monoplies of the modern capitalist entrepreneur are acquired 'through' the market.[86]

Owing to the monopolistic practices of the craft guilds, it is not surprising that economic strife occurred throughout feudal society. Some of the economic struggles mentioned by Weber (1978a, p.931; 1981b, pp.149-52) include: craft guilds fighting with consumers over pricing policies in the commodity market, craft guilds opposing the craft workers of the landed estates, and craft guilds grappling with labourers and merchants.

In this same connection, Fourquin (1978, pp.60-61) remarks that up to the thirteenth century conflict between craft guilds and between master artisans (i.e., 'horizontal conflict') was often more frequent and more acrimonious than that between masters and journeymen. However, after the thirteenth century, bitter strife between masters and journeymen (i.e., 'vertical conflict') occurred much more often.[87] To be more precise, access to the mastership of a craft was usually strictly regulated by the end of the fourteenth century. The raising of the entrance tax for a mastership was a guarantee that only the sons of masters could acquire it. The opportunity of rising in the feudal social hierarchy was now denied to journeymen. Moreover, the fact that the creation of a masterpiece *(chef d'oeuvre)* became necessary for a mastership, restricted the economic opportunities of journeymen. Expressed in Weberian terms, social and economic advantages were being closed to 'insiders'. Indeed, this particular closure process may account to a certain extent, as Fourquin (1978, pp.61-2, 147-60) notes, for the increasing number of urban disturbances throughout feudal Europe from the fourteenth century onwards.

Besides the kind of concerted traditional action undertaken by the various estates 'within' the mediaeval city to defend or increase their economic, social and political advantages, estate struggles were also endemic in the countryside throughout feudal Europe. The diverse exclusionary practices employed by the rural knighthood to defend their material and ideal interests and their political privileges, have been alluded to in different contexts throughout this chapter. The most effective form of social closure at the disposal of the rural knighthood (and the urban knighthood) was descent and lineage. If a man could not point to knights in his ancestry, he was excluded from the knightly estate and, hence, from the possession of high social honour. What is more, the rural knighthood monopolized a primary resource in feudal society, namely land, by the closure of eligibility for fiefs to those of knightly descent. The estate consciousness of the rural knighthood was also determined by its possession of rights of rule. These rights were vigorously defended, especially when threatened by the strengthening of royal/princely authority from the twelfth century onwards. The feudal knights exacted charters from their royal/princely rulers. They also became the king's associates in rule.

Regarding the type of collective traditional action engaged in by the peasantry in feudal Europe, Weber makes a few brief comments. Given Weber's principal interest in the political (i.e., ruler-centric) aspect of Western feudalism, this lack of concern for the peasantry is not at all surprising. Essentially, Weber apprehends Western feudalism as a variant of traditional domination. When characterizing the 'validity' of the feudal system of domination, Weber concentrates on the bases of 'claims to legitimacy' on the part of the rulers (i.e., the prince/sovereign and the administrative staff of feudal vassals) at the expense of the bases of compliance on the part of the ruled (primarily, the peasants). To be sure, the 'belief in legitimacy' on the part of the subordinate peasantry is built into Weber's ideal-type of Western feudalism. But the pivotal point is that belief merely reflects the traditional ruler's claim to legitimacy in the case of the ruled peasantry. Weber does not concern himself with 'how' the compliance of the subjugated peasantry is 'actually' achieved. Rather, he apprehends obedience in ruler-centric terms. The vital point in Weber's construction of the ideal-type of the feudal system of domination, bears on what form and to what extent obedience can be marshalled by the ruling stratum. The feudal ruling stratum legitimizes its exercize of rule by having recourse to tradition. Of particular relevance also is that the validity of the claim to legitimacy in feudal society, is more important for providing the 'means' to administer rule than it is to gain support from the objects of rule, the peasantry.

Even if the ruler-centric bias is intrinsic to Weber's treatment of Western feudalism as a variant of traditional domination, it is important to call attention to

202

his brief commentary on the nature of resistance under a system of traditional domination. Weber proclaims that:

> The exercise of power is oriented towards the consideration of how far master and staff can go in view of the subjects' traditional compliance without arousing their resistance. When resistance occurs, it is directed against the master or his servant personally, the accusation being that he failed to observe the traditional limits of his power. *Opposition is not directed against the system as such—it is a case of 'traditionalist revolution'.* (1978a, p.227; emphasis added)

Weber is saying that a "'traditionalist revolution'" does not challenge the established order of things as such. To the contrary, individuals/groups rebel against established authority—because the traditional ruler is deemed to have failed in the fulfillment of his customary obligations (whatever they might be). Dissident subjects oppose traditional authority not because of its existence, but rather because it is not functioning properly. Accordingly, traditional rebels demand the 'replacement' of the 'bad' ruler (or his agent) by a 'good' ruler, that is, by one who will adhere to valid tradition. It is in this sense that traditional insurgents like the mediaeval peasantry fight for issues such as the restoration of the 'good old law'.[88]

Similarly, when Weber describes the struggles of the craft guilds against the urban nobility in the mediaeval cities as "'craft" revolutions' (1978a, p.1282), he is referring to a "'traditionalist revolution'". The various members of the burgher estate did not oppose the urban knighthood in order to dismantle the political organization of feudal society. They simply demanded recognition for their own new autonomous jurisdiction 'within' the feudal political framework. In short, then, traditional insurgents take on the character of the society against which they rebel.[89] They jointly participate in traditional action.

Of cardinal importance also for an understanding of rebellion in feudal society is that the ambiguity built into traditional authority can be a source of great dissension between traditional rulers and their subjects. Weber (1978a, p.227) highlights the ambivalence inherent in traditional authority—when he affirms that the commands of a traditional ruler (e.g., feudal seigneur ruling in his own locality) are legitimate not only when they abide by tradition, but also when they emanate from the arbitrary will of the ruler. The traditional ruler is placed in a dilemma. Certainly, he may have the subjective right to disregard tradition because of the absolute nature of his will. But, on the other hand, this very unrestrained exercize of his will can jeopardize his traditional authority.[90] The traditional ruler may have to deal with calls for substantive justice on the part of his subjects. His subjects who are in the 'ideal' situation held to be deferential, can claim that their traditional rights are being infringed upon. Hence, they may in the 'concrete' situation rebel to defend these rights.

Peasant rebellions were endemic in feudal society. The distinctive feature of these rebellions in the early Middle Ages was that they, as Hilton (1973, pp.61-95) contends, concentrated on fulfilling the basic needs of the peasantry, were localized geographically, and were restricted in scope. In order to realize their basic material needs, mediaeval peasants struggled with their seigneurs over the level of rents, labour services, access to natural resources (e.g., grazing rights in the commons) and the like. Indeed, one of the most acrimonious and bloody peasant rebellions of the early Middle Ages took place in Normandy in 996 over the question of rights to common land.[91] Expressed in Weber's language, the Normandy peasants were bitterly opposed to the seigneurs' attempts to 'exclude' them from enjoying a crucial economic resource in a traditional, agricultural society. Mediaeval peasants justified their opposition to increases in rents and labour services by claiming that their economic obligations to the lord were anchored in immemorial custom and, therefore, could not be tampered with. Weber notes that peasants in West and South Germany were very successful in their struggle with their seigneurs. One reason for this had to do with the power of manorial law and the traditionalism associated with it. Weber, furthermore, states that in West and South Germany 'landholding, judicial authority, and liege-lordship were in different hands, and the peasant was able to play off one against the other (1981b, p.76). The chief advantage which the peasants gained from this situation was the appropriation of large tracts of the common mark and, to a much smaller degree, of the common pasture.[92]

Members of the peasant estate in the early Middle Ages also fought their feudal lords over the question of political rights. Feudal society 'excluded' the majority of the population from the exercize of political rights which depended upon grants of immunity. Peasants, as Bendix (1977, p.51) argues, participated in feudal politics only indirectly, that is, when they were called upon as subjects of their seigneur to assist him in military struggles. Therefore, when the peasants fought for political rights in feudal society, they demanded (like the burghers in the cities) the recognition of a new autonomous jurisdiction 'within' the traditional political framework. Peasant communities consciously organized themselves to attain grants of immunity.

The movement for village enfranchizement was very strong in France in the twelfth and thirteenth centuries. On this account, Weber avers that:

The village community organized itself as a corporation which assumed a joint obligation for the rents of the lord, in return for full autonomy in administration, which autonomy was also protected by the king. Both sides obtained an advantage from the arrangement: the lord because he had only one debtor to deal with, and the peasants because their power was enormously increased. (1981b, pp.74-5)

Various village communities wrested liberties and charters from their lords by means of collective traditional action and offers of money. The success of village communities in acquiring the legal status of corporations meant that they were

204

exempted from various exactions, and their seigneurial obligations were also fixed by custom rather than being arbitrary. The village corporations (like the city corporations) created their own judicial and administrative organs. Furthermore, they set up popular assemblies for determining village policies. Weber (1981b, p.75) adds that the French peasant estate was even temporarily summoned to the Estates General. When Weber asserts that the French peasants' usurpation of rights of rule in their own villages was protected by the king, he is pointing to the role of the central political authority in the closure process. That said, it should be stressed that even if some mediaeval peasant communities were able to develop their own judicial and administrative structures, the warrior nobility was still the dominant force in rural society.[93]

The discussion of Weber's understanding of estates as phenomena of the distribution of social power within feudal society, has been quite extensive in this chapter. Weber's study of estates involves the examination of stratification in a premodern, traditional society, whereas his study of classes and parties bears on the analysis of stratification in modern, rationalized society. Hence, the content of this chapter differs somewhat from the fourth and sixth chapters. Weber's concern with value-rationality, traditional action and traditional domination pervades his exploration of estate stratification in feudal society. Another salient point is that Weber's analysis of the feudal estate order takes place against the backdrop of *Zweckrationalität*. Weber's study of feudal society against this backdrop implies, of course, that this society is understood as the negative of instrumental rationality.

Concerning the unequal distribution of power in feudal society, Weber's key argument, as shown in this chapter, is that the unequal distribution of the primary resource, social honour, is decisive for the formation of estates. The positively privileged knights, in solid possession of social honour, uphold the superiority of their 'being' or 'nature' by living a knightly style of life. A pattern of knightly living anchored in tradition is, according to Weber, the prime honour-engendering resource in the feudal estate order. The feudal knight is already in a structural power position, because he can claim high social honour by virtue of the fact that he lives a traditional, knightly mode of life. Conversely, the negatively privileged peasants lack social honour. The estate situation of the peasant is such that he cannot live a knightly way of life. Moreover, the unequal distribution of social honour in the feudal social order is associated with expressions of deference by the morally and socially inferior towards their 'betters'. Weber's second crucial argument is that the unequal distribution of social honour is usually associated with the unequal distribution of economic resources (primarily, land) in feudal society. Although the negatively privileged peasant estate 'possesses' the land, the knightly estate legally 'owns' it. Weber, in particular, highlights the fact that the feudal economy (unlike the modern capitalist market-economy) is not organized as a structurally independent sub-system of society. That is to say, non-economic motives determine the nature of the economic system itself. The warrior nobility and the various occupational estates sought not wealth as such, but the material resources that were compatible with the maintenance and enhancement of their social prestige in the feudal social hierarchy. Weber's third key argument is that the possession of social honour in the feudal social order is usually linked with the respective estate's legally guaranteed and monopolized claim to private rights. Feudal rights appear as the various privileges, liberties and immunities that are conferred upon the individual as a member of a given estate. It is in this sense that the members of the knightly estate, the burgher estate and, to a much lesser extent, the peasant estate enjoy independent rights. Finally, the manner in which the estate groups in feudal society act in concert to defend their economic, social and political advantages grounded in tradition, is brought to light in Weber's discussion of social closure. The members of the positively privileged estates may not only effect the closure of economic, social and political opportunities to 'outsiders', but also to 'insiders'. Weber, further, states that exclusionary practices may evoke a corresponding reaction on the part of the excluded. Weber's study of social closure testifies to the fact that estate struggles were endemic in feudal society.

Notes

1   See Dahrendorf 1959, p.7; Bendix 1966, p.85; Williams 1976, pp.251-2.
2   Cf. Neuwirth 1969, pp.148-63; Omodei 1982, pp.196-213; Croix 1983, pp.85-96; Cox 1950, pp.225-6; Wenger 1980, pp.361-9; Brewer 1989, pp.89-96; Barbalet 1980, pp.411-14; Barbalet 1986b, pp.560-64; Parkin 1982, pp.96-104; Burger 1985, pp.24-35; Giddens 1981b, pp.78-80; Rex 1970, pp.144-6.
3   Cf. Barbalet (1986b, pp.557-75) for an interesting discussion of the relationship holding between class and status in modern capitalist society. See also Turner 1988.
4   Many definitions of Western feudalism and other types of feudalism (e.g., Oriental feudalism) have been offered. For example, Ward (1985, pp.40-67), Mukherjee (1985, pp.25-39) and Brown (1974, pp.1063-88) discuss the varied definitions of feudalism available in the secondary literature.
5   It is also worthwhile noting that the nature of the feudal system found in the Norman and crusading states was similar to that found in Northern France. The reason for this resides in the fact that Northern France played a major role in the colonization of these states.
6   The word 'feudal' is derived from the Latin *feodalis* which means 'of or appertaining to a fief (*feodum*)'. The word *feodum* was not generally used until about the mid-eleventh century. It should also be noted that it was the Old Regime which gave rise to the 'concept' of feudalism. The word

féodalite was coined in the seventeenth century. At first, it only referred to the body of feudal law. It was a legal concept.

7   These mounted warriors were called *Milites* in Latin, *Chevaliers* in French and *Ritter* in German.

8   Weber observes that the 'benefice', on the other hand, 'is a lifelong, not a hereditary, remuneration for its holder in exchange for his real or presumed services; the remuneration is an attribute of the office, not of the incumbent' (1978a, pp.1073-74). Essentially, benefice-holders are only rentiers with specific official duties. In fact, they stand closer to a bureaucratic official than a feudal vassal.

9   It is noteworthy that the lord valued his land just as much as a source of money by the twelfth century. Knight service was, in fact, in many cases commuted for a money payment. This was called 'scutage' in England.

10 Pirenne (1939, p.157) makes the pertinent point that it was not until the thirteenth century that the plebeian was debarred from the possession of a fief.

11 Cf. Dessau's (1968, pp.192-7) discussion of the notion of 'treason' in the Middle Ages.

12 Weber (1978a, p.1105) also mentions that Japanese 'vassalic' feudalism combined status honour and fealty.

13 Thus far, the 'individual' ideal-type of Western feudalism which Weber constructed in *Economy and Society* (1978a), has been examined. However, it is important to remember that the early Weber gave a much wider definition of feudalism in the course of his discussion of the agrarian systems of ancient civilizations. He asserts, for instance, that: 'it appears unnecessary and unwise to limit the use of the concept "feudalism" to its mediaeval form ... There is no reason why the concept of feudalism should not be used to characterize all those social institutions whose basis is a ruling class which is dedicated to war or royal service and is supported by privileged landholdings, rents, or the labour services of a dependent, unarmed population' (1976b, p.38). This particular Weberian definition of feudalism brings to mind Marx's notion of feudalism as a mode of production. Weber also speaks of 'city feudalism' in Mediterranean Antiquity. These 'feudal cities' were 'fortified centers settled by professional warriors' (1976b, p.39).

14 See also Hintze 1968, p.27; Borst 1968, pp.180-91; Bosl 1968, p.359.

15 Cf. Bendix (1966, pp.360-84), Poggi (1988, pp.211-27) and Zeitlin (1960, pp.203-8) for an appraizal of Weber's conception of feudalism.

16 Cf. Poggi's (1978, pp.16-35) discussion of the feudal system of rule.

17 It is also essential at this stage to mention Hintze's (1968, p.30) point that different aspects of feudalism remained relevant in Western Europe for different periods of time. The military/political aspect (i.e., the fief-holding mounted warriors/knights bound to a lord by fidelity) prevailed, as already indicated, from the ninth century to the end of the twelfth century.

Concerning warrior noblemen monopolizing 'rights of rule' in the form of lordships in their respective localities, this lasted until the sixteenth or seventeenth century (see Section 5.5). The social (Section 5.3) and economic (Section 5.4) aspects of Western feudalism continued in many areas until the French revolution. Indeed, the landlord-peasant economy persisted in many areas until the nineteenth century.

18 'Social' is understood here in the sense of a 'social occasion' or a 'social event'.

19 Weber also uses the expressions, 'conduct of life' (see, e.g., 1970, pp.268, 426) and 'ways of life' (see, e.g., 1958, p.133). Toennies (1967, pp.13-14) likewise maintains that a 'way of life' is a mark of social honour.

20 The vital significance of the idea of a 'style of life' in Weber's thought, is attested to by the fact that each chapter of his sociology of domination (Chapters X-XVI) contains a section dealing with the 'ethos and education' of status groups (see Weber 1978a, pp.941-1372).

21 In a somewhat similar vein, Toennies defines noble pride as 'a heightened awareness of prominence, of adornment and beauty, which are based on one's estate...' (1967, p.13). See also Speier (1952, pp.36-52) and Burger (1985, pp.30-35) for a similar rendering of the idea of social honour.

22 In like manner, Elias reasons that the mode of being of the French aristocracy in the seventeenth and eighteenth centuries was distinguished by 'this self-sufficiency of mere social existence, this unreflective existentialism' (1983, p.103).

23 Weber (1978a, p.1106) adds, though, that the crusading knight fighting for the 'true' faith had a different orientation. This particular type of knight was dedicated to the Christian 'cause' (as he understood it).

24 Cf. Bloch 1961, pp.312-19; Tocqueville 1954, pp.242-55; Pirenne 1939, pp.154-60; Pitt-Rivers 1965, pp.21-39; Bumke 1982; Keen 1984.

25 The importance of the 'game' in the military education of the knightly estate in the feudal social order in the West brings to mind the fundamental significance of the *agon* (contest) in Hellenic Antiquity. Weber writes that 'the *agon* (contest), a product of the individual knightly combat and the glorification of knightly heroism, was the source of the most important traits of Hellenic education' (1978a, p.1367).

26 Similarly, Bloch (1961, p.320) points out that it was only between 1130 and around 1250 that the right to be made a knight had been transformed into a hereditary principle. See also Keen 1984, pp.143-4, 151-3.

27 This having been said, it is important to emphasize Elias' (1982, p.68) point that the great majority of the small knights continued to live solely by the sword. Elias (1978) undertakes a perspicacious study of the development of chivalrous standards of conduct and sentiment at the mediaeval courts. He (1982) also engages in another penetrating study of the economic, social and political conditions that caused these changes in standards of conduct.

28 Similarly, Heer (1974, p.34) makes reference to 'domesticated court aristocracies'.

29 In this connection, it should also be noted that knighthood and nobility came to be almost complementary in the later Middle Ages. In the early Middle Ages, the knights were distinguished from other strata in society by their military function. For instance, these knights, many of whom had only moderate or small landholdings, were differentiated from the economically and politically more powerful counts and castellans, who were regarded as nobles. Keen (1984, pp.27-8) observes that by the later Middle Ages many of these nobles also identified themselves as knights. The implication is that the lesser knighthood and the greater nobility were becoming more socially cohesive, despite disparities of wealth and political power. This being so, knighthood and nobility will be used as interchangeable terms in the remainder of this book.

30 It is worthwhile mentioning that the German bourgeois intelligentsia from the second half of the eighteenth century developed a different notion of cultivation, namely *Bildung*, which constituted a serious threat to the claims of uniqueness and intrinsic worth on the part of the nobility. For neo-humanists like Lessing and von Humboldt, the acquisition of *Bildung* basically involved the cultivation of capacities already present in the individual. But in opposition to the noble standpoint, the neo-humanists believed that the possession of these capacities was not confined to individuals from any particular stratum in society.

31 The *chansons de geste* were the principal channel for the expression of the cultural attitudes of knightly society, especially in the period between 1120 and 1160. These epics went back to the *Chanson de Roland*. The noble Franks were celebrated as invincible warriors in these epics. The courtization of the knightly estate brought about a change in mediaeval literature in the later Middle Ages. With the work of Chrétien of Troyes writing in the later part of the twelfth century, we enter the more refined, cultivated world of the great feudal court. Both the lyric and the courtly epic or romance were the product of courtly culture. This new literary culture was educational in intention. The fundamental goal was the creation and moulding of the cultivated man. Cf. Southern's (1953, pp.209-44) incisive discussion of mediaeval literature.

32 In a similar vein, Weber (1951, pp.107-70; 1978a, pp.1047-51) describes the Chinese literati as a cultivated status group. However, they were never an autonomous status group of scholars like the Brahmins in India (see Weber 1958), but rather a stratum of officials and aspirants to office. Weber explains that: 'For twelve centuries social rank in China has been determined more by qualification for office than by wealth. This qualification, in turn, has been determined by education, and especially by examinations. China has made literary education the yardstick of social prestige in the most exclusive fashion...' (1951, p.107). In the form of

literary education, Confucianism appealed to the key values of piety and propriety as constitutive motives for action. The conventionally educated gentleman was expected to participate in the old ceremonies with great respect. Furthermore, he had to control all his activities, physical gestures and movements with politeness and grace in conformity with the status mores and the rules of propriety (see Weber 1951, p.156). In short, then, Confucianism was a systematization of rules of etiquette befitting to a dignified status group, the members of which had undergone literary training. Cf. Duncan's (1969, pp.3-31) appraizal of Weber's treatment of the Chinese literati.

33   If the feudal knights support the intrinsic and inalienable worth of their 'being' or 'nature' by living a chivalrous style of life, it is rather surprising that Weber does not pay much attention to charisma as a primary honour-engendering resource in the feudal estate order (see Poggi 1988, pp.221-2). Weber defines charisma as 'a certain quality of an individual person by virtue of which he is considered extraordinary and treated as endowed with supernatural, superhuman, or at least specifically exceptional powers or qualities' (1978a, p.241). The 'ordinary' person cannot possess these qualities. On the other hand, all the martial and courtly qualities attributed to the knight in feudal society substantiate the 'extraordinary' nature of his mode of 'being'. Admittedly, Weber states that 'the feudal allegiance between lord and vassal must also be interpreted as a routinization of a charismatic relationship...' (1978a, p.1070). He (1978a, p.1136) also refers to the transferability of charisma through blood ties, that is, lineage charisma. And interestingly enough, Weber claims in one of his essays on religion that: 'all intensive religiosity has a tendency towards a sort of status stratification, in accordance with differences in the charismatic qualifications. "Heroic" or "virtuoso" religiosity is opposed to mass religiosity' (1970, p.287; emphasis removed).

34   For Bourdieu, cultural or symbolic goods (e.g., literature, music) differ from material goods in the sense that individuals can 'consume' them only by understanding their meaning. And individuals, by the very same token, can appropriate these goods, can grasp their meaning, only if they have already procured the required schema of appreciation and comprehension. The concept of 'cultural capital', then, connotes the complex of cultivated predispositions that comprises such a schema. The notion of status distinctions in modern society (especially, in French society) being upheld by cultural exclusiveness, has been developed in a meticulous fashion by Bourdieu (1984) in his exemplary study, *Distinction*.

35   For instance, the knightly nobility living in the countryside only recognized those urban patricians living a knightly mode of life as part of their estate. The urban patricians living a knightly style of life were eligible to participate in tournaments, to receive a fief and the like (see Weber 1978a, p.1267).

36 Elias (1983) also contends that social honour was a constitutive element of personal identity in the society of courtly absolutism in the seventeenth and eighteenth centuries.

37 With regard to personal identity in modern society, Berger (1973, pp.83-96; 1974, pp.159-81) asserts that it is largely independent of institutional roles. Similarly, Habermas speaks of 'the modern problem of identity' as 'the disremption of the "I" from society' (1974b, p.95; see also pp.91-103). The modern discovery of human dignity bears on the intrinsic humanity of each individual person, devoid of all institutional roles. The feudal idea of dignity, on the other hand, concerns the possession of a particular rank within an hierarchically ordered society, and adherence to a code of conduct in line with this rank. The individual in modern society can only find his 'true' identity by liberating himself from his institutional roles. The modern individual apprehends his objectively assigned identity as a major impediment to the discovery of his 'true' self. Instead of the individual being assigned an identity in the form of socially imposed roles, the onus is on the modern individual to create his own personal identity. Or expressed in Weberian terms, the modern individual as a cultural/value-implementing being must endow the world with meaning. Viewed in this light, the modern individual has, as Berger (1974, p.173) states, an inherently unstable identity. He is continually trying to find himself. Cf. also Elias (1978, pp.221-63) for a penetrating analysis of the development of the modern individual.

38 However, Eisenstadt claims that 'the central concept in later sociological analysis of stratification, largely derived from Weber, is that of prestige' (1968, p.xxxiii).

39 The literature available on the status-attainment model is extensive. See, e.g., Treiman 1975, pp.563-83; Treiman and Terrell 1975, pp.174-200; Featherman et al. 1975, pp.329-60; Featherman and Hauser 1976, pp.621-51; Kerckhoff 1976, pp.368-81; Blau and Duncan 1978.

40 Cf. Bourdieu's (1977, pp.112-19) succinct discussion of his notion of 'symbolic power'. Essentially, Bourdeiu apprehends this kind of power as 'the power to constitute the given by stating it, to create appearances and belief, to confirm or transform the vision of the world and thereby action in the world...' (ibid., p.117).

41 See also Shils 1968, pp.104-32.

42 Cf. also Newby 1975, p.145; Tocqueville 1954, pp.187-95.

43 Cf. Fourquin 1978, pp.38-48; Duby 1980.

44 See also Fourquin 1978, pp.83-107.

45 Cf. also Polanyi 1944, pp.43-55; Polanyi 1957, pp.243-70; Hopkins 1957, pp.271-300.

46 Indeed, it was only at the end of the eighteenth century that a name was coined to describe the organization of the material conditions of existence. It

was French thinkers who coined the name '*économie*' and called themselves '*économistes*'.

47 Weber's comments on the idea of occupation are confusing. Weber (1978a, p.304) in one instance regards occupational differentiation as part of the class structure (e.g., public and private officials). He (1978a, pp.141-2) states in another context that occupational status depends on both the amount of training required for the relevant specialized functions, and the chances available for earnings from these functions. My own conclusion is that Weber's definition of an occupational status group quoted above pertains to occupational estates in the feudal social order, whereas his comments on occupational status alluded to in this note, bear on occupational differentiation in modern capitalist society. However, it has already been mentioned that Weber never undertook a detailed study of occupational status groups in the context of modern capitalism and how such groups relate to classes.

Weber's failure to work through the relationship holding between class and status in modern capitalist society has created much confusion in the secondary literature. Bourdieu, for example, says that his study, *Distinction*, is 'based on an endeavour to rethink Max Weber's opposition between class and *Stand*...' (1984, p.xii). Alexander (1983, pp.117-22) argues that Weber reduces status group to class. Status becomes a residual category. Rex's (1970, pp.136-55) development of the concept of status (including Weber's concept) is such that status becomes the means by which a class legitimates its own position. Marxists like Therborn (1980b, pp.138-43) contend that the Weberian dichotomy between class and status impedes an analysis of the functioning of ideology in capitalist class societies.

48 Contemporary overtones of the word 'consumption' must be avoided. The feudal notion of 'consumption' has to do with how far the economy was dependent on wealth generated by rents, taxes and tolls.

49 Taking account of the fact that Weber considers 'social honour' and 'lack of social honour' to be the key objective criteria in the formation of estates in the feudal social order, the mediaeval peasantry cannot within a Weberian framework be conceptualized other than as a negatively privileged estate, devoid of the primary resource, social honour. Hilton, on the other hand, defines the mediaeval peasantry 'as a class, as determined by its place in the production of society's material needs; not as a status group determined by attributed esteem, dignity, or honour' (1975a, p.12; see also pp.3-19).

50 In contradistinction to Weber's rendering of Western feudalism, Marx conceptualizes Western feudalism, first and foremost, as a mode of production. Cf. Marx's (1959, pp.782-802) discussion of labour-rent, rent in kind and money-rent. It is also important to mention that Marx views with extreme scepticism the contention that the growth of money-rent *per se* was symptomatic of the breakdown of feudal relations. He makes a

fundamental distinction between 'feudal rent' and 'capitalist ground rent'. For Marx, 'feudal rent' is comparable with the 'surplus-value' 'pumped out' of the wage-labourer by the capitalist. 'Capitalist ground rent', on the other hand, is simply a super-profit procured by the landlord from the capitalist farmer by reason of his legal monopoly of the land.

51   Cf. Bush (1983, pp.144-85) for a detailed discussion of seigneurial rights.

52   In fact, the Puritans' deep-seated aversion for what they regarded as feudal extravagance led them to develop, as Poggi (1983, pp.109-10) notes, their own unique style of life characterized by sobriety, solidity and austerity.

53   Elias (1983, p.38) says that one of the objectives of his study of the 'court society' of the Old Regime is to test the correctness of this Weberian view.

54   Similarly, Tocqueville observes that 'honor acts solely for the public eye...' (1954, p.253). Bloch in his study of feudal society also refers to 'this struggle for prestige through extravagance...' (1961, p.311).

55   In advanced capitalism, on the other hand, the notion of consumption has very different connotations. Advanced capitalism relies as much on the production of needs and consumers as on the production of goods. The functioning of this form of capitalism is contingent upon a form of society which evaluates individuals in terms of both their ability to consume (i.e., their life-style) and to produce. This being the case, the consumption of certain material goods in advanced capitalism is an expression of wealth. Put another way, advanced capitalism leads to the development of a status order based on the prestige accorded by wealth *per se*. Veblen (1970) in his study, *The Theory of the Leisure Class* (first published in 1899), was one of the first social thinkers to examine the nature of status-oriented consumption in modern capitalist society. He speaks of 'conspicuous consumption' which essentially involves putting one's wealth on social display. Weber did not, as already intimated, fully appreciate the fundamental importance of the consumption ethic for the further development of modern market-oriented capitalism. But he did briefly mention the status factor in modern capitalist society. He writes, for example, that 'in the so-called pure modern democracy ... it may be that only the families coming under approximately the same tax class dance with one another' (1978a, p.932). It is reasonable to assume that Weber is pointing to a concept of status rooted in wealth in modern society.

56   Similarly, Pirenne (1939, pp.98-105) describes the domain economy characteristic of feudal Europe as an '"economy without outlets"'. Since the feudal economy could not regulate production in order to export and sell goods outside the domain, it had to regulate it, as Pirenne (1939, p.99) explains, with a view to the distribution and consumption of the relevant goods within the confines of the domain. See also Hilton (1975b, pp.174-214) and Brenner (1976, pp.30-75) on the nature of the feudal economy.

57 The equivalent name for the urban noble who became too directly enmeshed in economic acquisition in Antiquity was *banausos* (Weber 1978a, p.1295).

58 As a matter of fact, the feudal ethos remained influential throughout Western Europe for many centuries. By the last decades of the ninteenth century, for instance, the entire German industrial and commercial bourgeoisie were subject to the pervasive influence of the noble Junkers. The bourgeoisie tried to emulate the Junkers' noble mode of life. It is in this context that Weber (1989, pp.215-16) refers to 'the feudalization of bourgeois capital'. The Prussian government published a bill as late as 1903 contemplating statutory measures that would allow rich bourgeois citizens to buy extensive landed estates. What is more, this bill put forward measures that would protect the entailed estates of the Junkers by the imposition of special tariffs for agricultural products (see Munters 1972, p.139). Another essential point is that the German bourgeoisie were assimilated to the Junker style of life through the introduction of the reserve officer system.

59 On the other hand, Weber (1978a, p.1240) indicates that in southern Europe, particularly in Italy, almost all of the nobility settled in the cities as the power of the municipalities increased. He adds that this was even more characteristic of the ancient world, where the city arose as the seat of the nobility.

60 In a similar vein, Weber states that 'precisely because the Prussian "Junker" despises that urban possession of money, capitalism makes a debtor of him' (1970, p.369; see also pp.363-85). Weber fully understood that the agrarian basis of Junkerdom was crumbling. More to the point, he argued that since the fall of grain prices in the 1870s, the Junkers' 'fate was sealed, for the average knightly holding of 400 to 500 acres can no longer support a lordly aristocratic existence' (1981b, p.110). The onset of modern market-oriented capitalism meant that the Junker could no longer 'live like a lord'.

61 Cf. Bloch 1961, pp.320-31.

62 See Pirenne (1939, pp.231-7) for an analysis of this economic crisis.

63 In the fourteenth and fifteenth centuries the consequences of the economic crisis in feudal society were rendered even more acute by other factors: severe demographic decline resulting from the famines of 1314-1317 and a series of fatal plagues, the wastage of agricultural land through interminable warfare, a rise in the price of labour and so forth.

64 Cf. Elias' (1982, pp.91-225) incisive discussion on the sociogenesis of the monopoly of power by the royal mechanism from the twelfth century onwards in Western Europe.

65 See Marshall 1977a, pp.193-204.

66 On the development of the modern notion of citizenship, see, e.g., Marshall 1977b, pp.71-134; Turner 1986; Turner 1988, pp.42-64; Barbalet 1988.

67 Pirenne (1939, p.155) makes the interesting point that the word *liber* took on the meaning of *nobilis* from the tenth century onwards.

68 Of course, the conception of freedom in the democratic-constitutional nation-state differs radically from the feudal rendering of liberty. Freedom in the democratic-constitutional nation-state does not derive from rights which are vested in the individual as a member of a particular positively privileged status group, but from rights conferred on all citizens. Freedom is now apprehended as universal equality before the law of the nation-state (at least in the ideal situation).

69 Similarly, Toennies (1967, p.13) identifies the nobility as one of the 'ruling estates'.

70 Or to use Hintze's terminology, Western feudalism constituted 'a "put-together state", a simple personal union under the king, whose "person" alone held the whole together' (1968, p.24).

71 In his discussion of the relationship between patrimonialism and status honour, though, Weber stresses that the feudal relationship is best dealt with as 'an extreme marginal case of patrimonialism, since it is so much shaped by the purely personal loyalty bond with the lord...' (1978a, p.1069).

72 Weber (1978a, p.911) makes the interesting point that Pope Urban II concentrated on these opportunities in his speech promoting the crusades (see also Davis 1970, pp.278-94). The Norman knights played a major role in these crusades.

73 See Bush 1983, pp.164-5; Fourquin 1978, p.57.

74 Some of the charters include: the *Magna Carta* granted to the English baronage in 1215, the Golden Bull awarded by Andrew II to the Hungarian nobility in 1222, and the diploma for the nobility of the empire ceded by the Emperor Sigismund in 1422 (see Myers 1975, p.14).

75 It is important to underline the difference between 'estates' and 'Estates' (see Poggi 1978, p.43). So far in the present chapter, Weber's views on 'estates' as phenomena of the distribution of power within feudal society have been examined. Weber constructs the ideal-type of estates to study the nature of structural social inequality in the feudal social order. The operation of 'Estates' (*Stände*), on the other hand, in feudal society pertains to 'public' bodies set up to fulfill specific political functions.

76 These assemblies were known by different names in different countries: the Commons of England, the Estates-General of France, the *Cortes* of Aragon, the States-General of the Netherlands, the *Riksdag* of Sweden and so forth.

77 However, Weber (1978a, pp.1254, 1324) remarks that although the representatives of the burgher estate were allocated 'a formally subordinate position' in the late-mediaeval assemblies, they often played a decisive role because of their financial power. The Commons of England provide the best example of burgher influence in the corporative assemblies of the late Middle Ages.

78 The word 'burgher' referred to a member of a town corporation in feudal Europe. This word, however, gained the meaning of master artisan or industrial entrepreneur during the seventeenth and eighteenth centuries. This

change in the meaning of 'burgher' finally led to it being identified with 'capitalist' or 'bourgeois' (see Brunner 1968, p.40). Cf. Poggi (1983, pp.94-113) and Hahn (1995, pp.139-74) for an interesting discussion of the history of the *Buergertum.*

79 It is important to bear in mind, though, Weber's (1978a, p.1323) point that there were 'very significant structural differences' among mediaeval cities.

80 Cf. Heer 1974, pp.63-95; Spencer 1977, pp.507-25; Poggi 1978, pp.36-42; Käsler 1988, pp.42-8.

81 Weber uses the notion of social closure to study the kind of collective action engaged in by status groups. However, Parkin (1974, pp.1-18; 1981) enlarges upon Weber's original usage in order to study the nature of class action in modern capitalist society. Cf. also Murphy (1984, pp.547-67; 1985, pp.225-43; 1986a, pp.247-64; 1986b, pp.21-41) for a further development of closure theory.

The term, collective/collaborative/joint/concerted action, will be used continually in this section in the context of my discussion of Weber's ideas on how estates mobilize themselves to defend their economic, social and political advantages grounded in tradition.

82 See Keen 1984, pp.178-99.

83 Neuwirth (1969, pp.148-63) underlines this point in her appropriation of Weber's notion of social closure.

84 The idea of status groups exercizing social closure to monopolize resources has been completely ignored in studies of status stratification in the United States. American studies of status stratification (e.g., the Warner School, structural functionalism, status-attainment research) have all placed the emphasis on consensus, as opposed to conflict. I have already indicated that Parsons layed the theoretical foundation for this consensus perspective, when he emphasized the importance of social ranking in terms of a common value system. To take the case of status-attainment research, occupations are represented merely by their prestige scores. The criteria for the differential evaluation of a set of occupations is assumed to derive from an underlying common value system. This evaluation of an occupation is considered sufficient for an understanding of the stratification system.

85 Weber (1951, 1952, 1958, 1970, pp.267-359) was also very conscious of the struggles between various status groups in his sociology of religion. The Chinese literati, for example, were engaged in a constant struggle to defend their monopolization of official positions. They had to fight the purchasers of office and the administration's interest in an expert officaldom. In the final analysis, though, there remained only one major and enduring enemy opposing the literati, namely, sultanism and the eunuch system. The Hindu Brahmins had to contend with the pretensions of the warrior caste, the Kshatriyas. Finally, the Jewish prophets were in continual strife with the royal prophets, oracle-givers and other groups.

86 Cf. also Weber (1981b, pp.215-22, 230-35) for a discussion of the mercantile guilds.

In this context, it is also worthwhile noting Marx's (1976a, p.74) comment on the nature of feudal capital. Capital in the towns of feudal Europe was 'a naturally evolved capital' comprising a house, the tools of the craft and the natural hereditary customers. Marx continues that in contrast to 'modern capital' which can be evaluated in monetary terms and which may be indifferently invested in this thing or that, feudal capital 'was directly connected with the particular work of the owner, inseparable from it and to this extent *estate* capital' (1976a, p.74; emphasis in original). Marx (1976a, pp.76-7), furthermore, observes that the first advance beyond 'natural capital' was made possible by the emergence of merchants in the Middle Ages, whose capital was from the outset moveable. The second advance was provided by the rise of manufacture which also mobilized a mass of 'naturally derived estate capital'.

87 This is not to say, though, that 'horizontal rivalry' ceased.

88 Similarly, the peasants in Tsarist Russia often yearned for what they perceived as the 'good Tsar'.

89 It should be noted here that Weber's use of the term '"traditionalist revolution"' is not strictly correct. The modern concept of 'revolution' was unknown prior to the two great revolutions at the end of the eighteenth century. Arendt remarks that: 'only where change occurs in the sense of a *new beginning,* where *violence* is used to constitute an altogether different form of government, to bring about the formation of *a new body politic,* where the liberation from oppression aims at least at the constitution of *freedom* can we speak of revolution' (1973, p.35, emphasis added; see also pp.21-58). Novelty, beginning and violence are inherent in the modern idea of revolution. Seen in this light, revolution is unthinkable in a traditional society where traditional relations of domination prevail. The notion of revolution was alien to the feudal mind. In like manner, Fourquin (1978) refuses to employ the term 'revolution' in his study of the nature of social conflict in the Middle Ages. Instead, he utilizes the term 'rebellion'.

90 See Bendix 1965, pp.19-20; Bendix 1977, p.40.

91 See Hilton 1973, p.70; Heer 1974, p.44.

92 See (Weber 1981b, pp.74-8) on the condition of the peasants in various Western countries before the advent of modern capitalism.

93 The fact that the rights-based system of inequality in feudal society was the source of great strife—had a profound influence on the form taken by the European revolutions of the late eighteenth and early nineteenth centuries. Because feudal rights appeared as the various privileges, liberties and immunities conferred upon the individual as a member of a given estate, injustice was, as Bush (1983, p.24) notes, defined by the European revolutionaries as a discrepancy of judicial right rather than of wealth. The question of judicial right was built into the demand for *égalité*. In other words, *égalité* had a judicial rather than a material meaning.

6 Political leadership, party organization and the masses

In this final chapter I consider Weber's understanding of the unequal distribution of political power (i.e., 'powers of rule') between responsible political leaders, democratic parties and the electoral masses within the confines of the German nation-state. In the first section of the chapter I focus attention on the 'historical individual', the modern nation-state, and I also appraise Weber's notion of 'political action'. In the second section I investigate Weber's conception of the role of the modern democratic party in the German nation-state with a parliamentary-democratic system of government. In this particular section I also underline the fact that Weber regards the docile, inactive, electoral masses in a parliamentary democracy merely as a 'means' of procuring votes and, thereby, of rule. Weber, however, became increasingly disillusioned with the parliamentary-democratic politics he witnessed in the early days of the Weimar republic set up in November 1918. Hence, his later advocacy of plebiscitary leadership democracy. The third section of the chapter engages in an evaluation of this type of democracy. The final section revolves around an assessment of Weber's rendition of political emancipation. One of the central themes pervading the discussion is the paradox of freedom built into Weber's political thought.

6.1 The modern nation-state

Weber's analysis of political leadership, the modern democratic party and the role of the masses in modern democratic politics presupposes the framework of the modern nation-state. According to Weber:

> A 'ruling organization' will be called 'political' insofar as its existence and order is continuously safeguarded within a given *territorial* area by the threat and application of physical force on the part of the administrative staff. A compulsory political organization with continuous operations will

218

be called a 'state' insofar as its administrative staff successfully upholds the claim to the *monopoly* of the *legitimate* use of physical force in the enforcement of its order. (1978a, p.54, emphasis in original; see also pp.314, 640; 1970, pp.78, 82; 1949, p.46)

Essentially, Weber's construction of the ideal-type of the state involves an administrative staff which is able to successfully defend its claim to the legitimate monopoly of the means of violence within a given territory.[1] This particular type of state has 'only in modern times reached its full development...' (Weber 1978a, p.56).[2] The modern state as a 'compulsory organization with a territorial basis' (Weber 1978a, p.56) can involve the legitimate employment of violence of the most extreme kind.[3]

Although the monopoly of the legitimate use of physical force constitutes one key element in the 'individual' ideal-type of the modern state, Weber does not say anything about the purposes/ends for which force is utilized. Indeed, the modern state's monopoly of the legitimate use of physical force can be employed for the most diverse ends ranging from the oppression of a minority group within the boundaries of the modern state to protecting the human rights of its citizens. Bearing in mind these varied ends, Weber contends that 'sociologically, the state cannot be defined in terms of its *ends*' (1970, p.77, emphasis added; see also p.334; 1978a, p.55). It is not possible within a Weberian framework to identify different types of the modern state such as capitalist and socialist states pursuing different goals.[4] The modern state can only be defined in terms of the 'means' peculiar to it, namely, the legitimate use of physical force.[5]

Given Weber's understanding of the modern state, it would appear that he rejects traditional German theories in which the state is constituted as a substantial being.[6] Weber explains that 'the *national state* is not ... an indeterminate entity raised higher and higher into the clouds in proportion as one clothes its nature in mystical darkness...' (1980, p.438, emphasis in original; see also 1978a, p.1394). The difficulty, though, was that the average German treated what he regarded as supra-personal authorities with the most profound respect. 'The purely emotive state metaphysics, flourishing on this ground, has had far-reaching political consequences' (Weber 1978a, p.1141). One major consequence, according to Weber, was the political passivity of the majority of the German population.[7] This being the case, Weber constructs an ideal-type of the modern state on a purely individual and legal basis. In opposition to the traditional, German, supra-individual view of the state, Weber avers that:

...one of the important aspects of the existence of a modern state, precisely as a complex of social interaction of individual persons, consists in the fact that the action of various individuals is oriented to the belief that it exists or should exist, thus that it acts and laws are valid in the legal sense. (1978a, p.14)

The modern state exists only as a series of individual actions with particular

219

subjective meanings. Moreover, laws in the modern state are deemed valid simply because they are legally sanctioned.

Of particular relevance also is the Puritan influence on Weber's construction of the 'individual' ideal-type of the modern state. The Puritans, on Weber's interpretation, did not consider secular power-holders to 'have any inwardly binding authority since they are merely parts of an order *made by and for man*. The office is functionally necessary...' (1978a, p.1141; emphasis added). It goes without saying, then, that a state-office is not a mystical, supra-individual entity transcending mundane political events.

This having been said, it seems, as Poggi (1978, pp.99-100) observes, that Weber cannot totally escape the influence of the traditional German conception of the state. Certain comments made by him in 'Religious Rejections of the World and Their Directions' (1970, pp.333-40) appear to support the view of the modern state as a spiritual, supra-individual entity. Weber alleges, for example, that 'as the consummated threat of violence among modern polities, war creates a pathos and a sentiment of community' (1970, p.335). The soldier's death on the battlefield today (as in the times of 'the warrior') is a consecrated one. This almost mystical idea of warfare between modern states is not, I would suggest, consonant with Weber's other notion of the modern state as a 'temporal power-organization' (1980, p.438) involved in the mundane affairs of daily political struggles.

Another salient issue concerns the legitimacy of the modern state (see Weber 1978a, pp.875-6, 880-95). Weber explains that for the purpose of threatening and exercizing its monopoly of the legitimate use of physical force within a given territory, the modern state 'has developed a system of casuistic rules to which that particular "legitimacy" is imputed. This system of rules constitutes the "legal order"...' (1978a, p.904; see also pp.56, 317). More to the point, the legitimacy of the modern state rests 'on a belief in the legality of enacted rules and the right of those elevated to authority under such rules to issue commands (legal authority)' (Weber 1978a, p.215). Laws in the modern state are deemed legitimate, according to Weber, if they have been enacted by the proper authorities (i.e., the elected political leader and his government of ministers, secretaries of state and the like) on the basis of procedures which have the sanction of law. The legitimacy of the modern state tailored to bureaucratic administration is dependent upon the commands of its political leader and government being accepted as valid, because they are legal.[8] Or as Habermas succinctly puts it, 'the belief in legitimacy thus shrinks to a belief in legality; the appeal to the legal manner in which a decision comes about suffices' (1976, p.98).[9]

Owing to the value-free nature of modern rational law, legitimation by procedure does not allow for the normative evaluation of the newly proclaimed laws. For Weber, it is by definition impossible to assess the normative validity of positive law by invoking some intrinsically binding substantive ideal like the

'Rights of Man'. Workers, for instance, challenge legal formalism by demanding 'a "social law" to be based upon such *emotionally colored ethical postulates* as "justice" or "human dignity"...' (Weber 1978a, p.886; emphasis added). But in view of Weber's defence of value-free social science, the authority of positive law cannot be wielded to justify the workers' claims for substantive justice in the modern state. The juristic precision of scientific (i.e., value-free), legal concepts would be seriously undermined by the introduction of normative (i.e., non-scientific) claims into the body of modern rational law. Seen in this light, scientific-legal criticism in the modern state is purely of a technical nature. Such criticism is solely concerned with procedural correctness. Correct legal procedures cannot be judged illegitimate. It should be highlighted that the formally correct enactment of even the most pernicious law in the modern state cannot within the Weberian schema be deemed illegitimate. In effect, Weber espouses an 'authoritarian legalism'.[10]

Weber's argument that the legitimacy of the modern state is based upon sheer legality is, in fact, circular—because the belief in legality, as Habermas reasons, 'can produce legitimacy only if we already presuppose the legitimacy of the legal order that lays down what is legal' (1984a, p.265).[11] Legitimation by procedure cannot *per se* produce legitimacy, it cannot alone attest to an underlying legitimacy. It is essential that legitimation by procedure is itself subject to rational justification. However, Weber ignores the question of rational justification for a more positivistic conception of law that is valid merely by virtue of decisions.[12]

One further issue relevant to Weber's grounding of the legitimacy of the modern state in sheer legality, has to do with the restraints imposed on the modern state's exercize of legal power. Weber maintains that the modern state:

...is a consociation of bearers of certain defined *imperia*; these bearers are selected according to established rules; their *imperia* are delimitated from each other by general rules of separation of powers; and internally each of them finds the legitimacy of its power of command defined by set rules of limitation of power. (1978a, p.652)

Legal rules pertaining to the 'separation of powers' exist where one *imperium* (i.e., state-office) is engaged in conflict with another *imperium* 'either equal or in certain respects superior to it, but the legitimate validity of which is fully recognized as limiting the extent of its authority' (Weber 1978a, p.652). Legal rules relating to 'limitation of power', on the other hand, mean that the legal authority of various state-offices (e.g., the police, military administrators of justice) is restricted by the 'rights' of subjects. However, if the only limit to what can be enforced by positive law in the modern constitutional state (whether it takes a monarchic, liberal or parliamentary-democratic form) is vested in the law itself, and if laws can be changed, there is no reason why this type of state cannot expand its legal power. In opposition to Weber, then, it is my contention that the modern constitutional state cannot ultimately be constrained by its own legal procedures, since it is its own legal procedures.[13]

Bearing in mind the ideal-typical nature of Weber's concept of the modern state, it follows that the legitimacy of this type of state may not 'in reality' rest upon a belief in the legality of enacted rules.[14] To begin with, the tenuous nature of the belief in the legality of enacted rules as a means of legitimizing the modern state in the 'concrete' situation is underlined by Weber when he declares that:

> *In the case of 'legal authority', it is never purely legal.* The belief in legality comes to be established and habitual, and this means it is partly traditional. Violation of the tradition may be fatal to it. Furthermore, it has a charismatic element, at least in the negative sense that persistent and striking lack of success may be sufficient to ruin any government, to undermine its prestige, and to prepare the way for charismatic revolution. (1978a, p.263; emphasis added)

At bottom, Weber is saying that the legal government of any modern state is 'in reality' strengthened through appeals to elements of traditional and charismatic authority. For the present, it is only necessary to add that Weber (1978a, pp.1381-1419) himself advocated in the summer of 1917 the combination of legal-parliamentary government with the value-setting charisma of a responsible political leader in the German nation-state.

The weak legitimizing powers of pure formal legalism are also accentuated by Weber (1978a, pp.395-8, 921-6) when he claims that commitment to the nation is an essential support for the modern state.[15] In the first instance, a nation means that '*it is proper* to expect from certain groups a specific sentiment of solidarity in the face of other groups. Thus, the concept belongs in the sphere of values' (Weber 1978a, p.922; emphasis in original). There is no consensus, according to Weber, as to how these groups are to be demarcated. Nationhood is often associated with a common factor like language or ethnicity. But nationhood is not necessarily identical with the solidarity of language or ethnic groups. Swiss nationalism, for example, cuts across three different language-speaking groups.

Owing to the ambiguity surrounding the ideal-typical concept of the nation, Weber posits a notion of 'cultural mission' as a precondition of nationhood. That is to say:

> ...the idea of the nation for its advocates stands in very intimate relation to 'prestige' interests. The earliest and most energetic manifestations of the idea ... have contained the legend of a providential 'mission' ... Therewith, in so far as its self-justification is sought in the value of its content, this mission can consistently be thought of only as a specific 'culture' mission. *The significance of the 'nation' is usually anchored in the superiority, or at least the irreplacability of the culture values that are to be preserved and developed only through the cultivation of the peculiarity of the group.* (Weber 1978a, p.925; emphasis added)

222

The sense of *Kultur* that Weber is dealing with here involves those specific values differentiating one group (or society) from others.[16] Such values are usually articulated in a self-conscious manner in human products like music, art, literature and philosophical systems. This concept of *Kultur* exemplifies the self-consciousness of a national community. Indeed, it was as an embodiment of *Kultur* that the German nation represented a fundamental value for Weber in all of his political writings.[17]

At this point, it is necessary to ask: How can a commitment to the nation as an embodiment of *Kultur* legitimize the modern state? Weber's answer is that the nation can only preserve its *Kultur*, its peculiar identity against outsiders, by relying on the modern state which is the repository of the most drastic means of exercizing physical force. And the modern state, by the very same token, makes use of the sentiments of solidarity found in the national community to legitimize its power-position. The fragility of the legal-rational order supporting the modern state is offset in the 'concrete' situation by the existence of emotional commitments to the nation. For Weber, nationalism, one of the most irrational elements in modern social life, props up the modern state. Weber (1980, pp.428-49), for example, justified the employment of state violence to safeguard Germany's cultural identity against the inflow of Poles into East Elbe in the 1890s. He goes so far as to say that 'the more power is emphasized, the closer appears to be the link between nation and state' (1978a, p.398).[18] Regarding nations like Switzerland and Luxemburg, Weber proclaims that 'we hesitate to call them "nations" ... because these neutralized states have purposively forsaken power' (1978a, p.397).[19] In light of the foregoing, it is obvious that the 'individual' ideal-type of the modern power-state (*Machtstaat*) grounded in means-end rationality and the 'individual' ideal-type of the nation grounded in value-rationality and emotionalism, complement each other within a Weberian framework. When speaking of the German state, Weber claims that 'our state is a *national state*...' (1980, p.436; emphasis in original).

Another pivotal point reinforcing the weak legitimizing powers of formal legalism, is that one particular type of political leader, namely, a charismatic plebiscitary leader:

> ...will attempt to consolidate the loyalty of those he governs either by winning glory and honor in war or by promoting their material welfare, or under certain circumstances, by attempting to combine both. (1978a, p.269)

When Weber purports that a charismatic plebiscitary leader will try to make secure the compliance of the ruled 'by winning glory and honor in war', he is stipulating that the 'internal' legitimacy of the modern state is connected to its power-position in the international political arena. Weber (1978a, pp.910-12) is stating that a major factor buttressing the modern state is imperialism in the sense of foreign military intervention into other states.[20] The military success of a charismatic plebiscitary leader in the international political arena enhances the 'power-prestige' (i.e., 'the glory of power over other communities') of the modern state over which he rules and, concomitantly, strengthens domestic legitimacy.[21] The 'Great Powers' (e.g., Britain, France, Germany and Russia) in the nineteenth century were the natural exponents of such pretensions to power-prestige. Conversely, the military defeat of a plebiscitary leader in a war and the consequent loss of 'power-prestige' for the modern state he governs, endangers domestic legitimacy.[22]

As to Weber's other assertion that a charismatic plebiscitary leader will try to consolidate the support of the governed by advancing their 'material welfare', he is pointing to the indispensability of modern rational capitalism as a means of legitimizing the modern state. For the 'material fate' of the masses, as previously intimated, is more and more predicated upon the correct functioning of the modern capitalist market-economy. The material well-being of the masses is increasingly dependent upon the opening-up of external markets in the course of Western capitalist expansion abroad. Weber (1978a, pp.913-21) is, in fact, referring to the expansion of imperialist capitalism in the early decades of the twentieth century. In this respect, he writes that:

> ...under the present economic order, the tribute to 'creditor nations' assumes the forms of interest payments on debts or of capital profits transferred from abroad to the propertied strata of the 'creditor nation'. Were one to imagine these tributes abolished, it would mean for countries like England, France, and Germany a very palpable decline of purchasing power for home products. *This would influence the labor market in an unfavorable manner.* (1978a, p.920; emphasis added)

If a charismatic plebiscitary leader's attempt, then, to win 'glory and honor in war' points to military imperialism as a means of consolidating the support of the ruled within the modern nation-state, his endeavour to promote the 'material welfare' of the ruled likewise brings to bear the fundamental role of modern capitalist imperialism as a means of bolstering the modern nation-state. In short, Weber is indicating, as Collins (1986b, pp.145-66) emphasizes, that the dynamics of domestic legitimacy grounding the modern nation-state are based upon the principles of geopolitics.

Besides treating violence as the modern nation-state's principal instrument and dealing with the problem of state legitimacy, Weber also considers the social basis of this type of state. He, in the main, analyzes the modern state in terms of 'who' controls it rather than in terms of what 'kind' of state it is.[23] Concerning the Wilhelmine, monarchic-constitutional nation-state, in particular, Weber (1978a, p.1405) believes that it lacks direction by a politician. The kernel of the problem is that 'the actual ruler is necessarily and unavoidably the bureaucracy, since power is exercised ... through the routines of administration' (Weber

1978a, p.1393). State officials monopolize the 'powers of rule'. The enormous political power of professional bureaucrats in the Wilhelmine state is further accentuated by Weber, when he affirms that the setting up of the so-called 'revolutionary state' in the course of the November 1918 revolution signified 'nothing new in practice' (1970, p.92). The revolutionary regime did not dispense with the professional bureaucrats. Quite the contrary. This regime would, according to Weber, have liked to employ these bureaucrats simply as 'executive heads and hands' (1970, p.92; see also 1978a, p.266), that is, as the administrative 'means' for the achievement of its own revolutionary goals.

When Weber speaks of professional bureaucrats being in control of the Wilhelmine state, he is not referring to the functioning of a non-partisan bureaucracy. To the contrary, Weber avers that:

Our conditions can teach everyone that rule by career officials is not tantamount to the absence of party rule ... every government and its representatives must be 'conservative', with only a few concessions to the patronage of the Prussian bourgeoisie and of the Center party. This and nothing else is meant by the 'impartiality' of the bureaucracy ... The partisan interests of the conservative bureaucracy and of its allied interest groups dominate the government. (1978a, p.1426)

To be more precise, 'the partisan interests of the conservative bureaucracy' pertain to the interests of the Junkers residing east of the Elbe. Even though the Junkers as a class of agricultural entrepreneurs were 'economically' in decline, they were 'politically' dominant (see Weber 1980, pp.428-49). A major source of the Junkers' political power in the Wilhemine state lay in their complete control over recruitment to the civil service and the army. These Junkers monopolized the 'powers of rule' in the German state until the downfall of the *Kaiserreich* in November 1918.

For Weber, the major problem was that the 'economically dominant' class, the industrial bourgeoisie, did not 'rule' in Wilhelmine Germany. They lacked the 'powers of rule'. However, the big industrialists concentrated in Western Germany were able to exert great influence on government policy through the activity of employers' associations. Moreover, there was an increasing *rapprochement* between the 'politically dominant' Junkers and the 'economically dominant' industrial bourgeoisie from the 1880s onwards in the Wilhelmine state. There were two principal reasons, as Roth (1963, p.145) indicates, for this *rapprochement*: the Junkers' recognition by the 1880s of the constitutional monarchy and the *Kaiserreich* as established by Bismarck, and the bourgeois achievement of a major constitutional goal, that is, the legal-constitutional taming of the authoritarian state. The end-result of this *rapprochement* between the 'politically dominant' East Elbian agricultural interests and the 'economically dominant' Western industrialists was the policy of *Sammlungspolitik* (i.e., the alliance of 'iron and rye') for the defense of the existing political order.[24] This policy continued until the end of the *Kaiserreich* in November 1918.[25] At this point, it is only necessary to add that Weber vehemently opposed the policy of *Sammlungspolitik*. For, in his view, the narrow sectional class interests of both the Junkers and the industrial bourgeoisie were given priority at the expense of what he apprehended as the 'power-political interests' of the German nation-state (1980, p.438; see also 1989, pp.210-20).[26]

In view of the fact that the modern nation-state, in so far as it exists historically, can only be reproduced through human agency, it is necessary at this stage to consider the corresponding type of 'political action'. 'Political action' is understood by Weber as a special case of '"politically oriented" action'. The political order is comprised of the totality of '"politically oriented" action'. In other words, 'it aims at *exerting influence on the government of a political organization*; especially at the appropriation, expropriation, redistribution or allocation of the powers of government' (Weber 1978a, p.54, emphasis added; see also p.55) For example, wholly peaceful groups trying to influence government policy are engaged in '"politically oriented" action'.

'Political action', on the other hand, takes place only 'within' a partial domain of the political order, namely, the nation-state. On this score, Weber writes that:

> ...we generally mean by 'political', things that have to do with *relations of authority within* what is, in the present terminology, a political organization, *the state*. The reference is to things which are likely to uphold, to change or overthrow, to hinder or promote, these authority relations as distinguished from persons, things, and processes which have nothing to do with it. (1978a, p.55, emphasis added; see also 1970, pp.77-128)

If the modern state is distinguished by its monopoly of the legitimate use of violence, it obviously follows that violence is likewise intrinsic to Weber's notion of 'political action'. Weber, indeed, states that 'politics operates with very special means, namely, power backed up by violence' (1970, p.119, emphasis in original; see also pp.121, 126; 1978a, p.1188). Only those actions which are bolstered by the threat or actual use of physical force are deemed 'political' within the Weberian schema.[27] The fact that there is an inbuilt bias towards violence in Weber's idea of 'political action' also suggests that this kind of action involves struggle. 'Politics means conflict' (Weber 1978a, p.1399; see also pp.1414-50). Politics presupposes conflict in the sense of 'striving to share power, either among states or among groups within a state' (1970, p.78; see also 1978a, pp.1399, 1414, 1450).

Weber's claim that violence is built into political action, implies that all individuals and groups utilize the same means of violence. Weber does not consider whether individuals or groups differ in the degree of violence employed. Terror, for example, involves the most intensive use of violence. Furthermore, Weber does not ask, as Parkin (1982, p.73) points out, whether the employment of violence is selective in the sense that the possibility of certain individuals or groups being subjected to violence is greater, as opposed to others.[28]

If violence is central to Weber's construction of the ideal-type of political action, a concern for the character and quality of leadership is also built into this type of action. Weber states that:

> We wish to understand by politics only the leadership or the influencing of the leadership, of a *political* association, hence today, of a *state*. (1970, p.77, emphasis in original; see also p.115; 1980, p.442; 1995, p.245)

Weber's definition of political action in terms of 'leadership' of a state or the 'influencing of' this leadership implies, I would suggest, that the majority of individuals do not 'act' in a political sense. Indeed, 'political action is always determined by the "principle of small numbers", that means, the superior political maneuverability of small leading groups' (Weber 1978a, p.1414; see also pp.952, 1421). Political leaders are, according to Weber, the principal political actors. The masses, on the other hand, merely engage in reactive behaviour. To anticipate what I shall say later, the masses have no independent, sociological reality in Weber's political thought. They are located below the level of sociological detection except as a means of rule.

Let us examine Weber's understanding of leadership in more detail. The political leader is 'ideally' a professional politician. Three fundamental personal qualities are decisive for such a politician: passion, a feeling of responsibility and a sense of proportion. Weber apprehends passion 'in the sense of *matter-of-factness*, of passionate devotion to a "cause"...' (1970, p.115; emphasis in original). Such passionate commitment, in turn, entails 'responsibility' to the 'cause'. And 'responsibility' necessitates a 'sense of proportion' in the sense of '*distance* to things and men' (ibid., emphasis in original). The 'responsibile' political leader, then, is totally dedicated to a 'cause' (*Sache*). Furthermore, such a leader calculates and accepts the consequences of pursuing a particular 'cause'. He knows that one must 'give an account of the foreseeable results of one's actions' (Weber 1970, p.120). Weber sums up his notion of political leadership when he purports that the ethic of conviction and the ethic of responsibility are not 'absolute contrasts but rather supplements, which only in unison constitute a genuine man—a man who *can* have the "calling for politics"' (1970, p.127; emphasis in original). In other words, the ethic of responsibility involves an attempt by Weber, as Brubaker (1984, p.108) underlines, to integrate *wertrational* and *zweckrational* action, the passionate devotion to a 'cause' (value) with the dispassionate assessment of the alternative means of realizing it.[29] This ethic of responsibility is *par excellence* the ethic of matter-of-fact power-politics.

Weber's ideal-type of responsible political leadership ultimately rests upon his concept of 'personality'. 'Personality' is 'a concept which entails a constant and intrinsic relation to certain ultimate "values" and "meanings" which are forged into purposes and thereby translated into rational-teleological action' (Weber 1975a, p.192). In line with the logical principle of value-relevance, Weber is saying that a 'personality', just like any other social object, exists to the extent that it embodies cultural values. Given that a segment of social reality can be subject to social-scientific analysis only by reference to cultural values, the 'individual', by the same token, can attain personality only if his conduct is rationally consistent with cultural values. For Weber, a personality 'can only be an "entity" synthetically produced by a *value* relation' (Weber 1975a, pp.183-4, emphasis in original; see also 1949, pp.5, 55). It is in this sense that the political personality is 'synthetically produced' by reference to the cause/ultimate value of the German nation-state. The other crucial component built into Weber's ideal-type of personality, of course, relates to the fact that instrumental rationality is the *sine qua non* for the realization of the freely chosen cultural values. The political personality must translate his core value, the promotion of the interests of the German nation-state, into means-end rational action.[30]

Another point especially pertinent here is that the responsible political leader's commitment to a 'cause', attests to the charismatic nature of his leadership. Weber explains that:

The term 'charisma' will be applied to a certain quality of an individual personality by virtue of which he is considered extraordinary and treated as endowed with supernatural, superhuman, or at least *specifically exceptional powers or qualities*. (1978a, p.241, emphasis added; see also pp.242-5, 1111-20)

The fact that the responsible political leader is a 'personality' completely dedicated to a 'cause'/'mission', in contradistinction to the mass of 'ordinary' individuals, suggests that he must be endowed with 'specifically exceptional powers or qualities'.[31] Devotion to such a leader 'means that the leader is personally recognized as the innerly "called" leader of men. Men do not obey him by virtue of tradition or statute but because they believe in him' (Weber 1970, p.79).[32]

It is obvious, then, that conduct tied to 'directives' is not, on Weber's interpretation, reconcilable with the political leader's commitment to the ethic of responsibility. For 'the honor of the political leader ... lies precisely in an exclusive *personal* responsibility for what he does, a responsibility he cannot and must not reject or transfer' (Weber 1970, p.95; emphasis in original).[33] In contrast to political leadership, 'administration', on Weber's reading, involves the subjection of one's will to another. The bureaucratic official is dedicated to an ethic of obedience. This is tantamount to saying that he is 'disciplined', he merely 'behaves'. To take an example, 'the honor of the civil servant is vested in his ability to execute conscientiously the order of the superior authorities, exactly as if the order agreed with his own convictions' (Weber 1970, p.95; see also 1978a, pp.1393-1416).[34] For Weber, the difficulty, as already shown, was that the

228

governmental bureaucracy 'ruled' in Wilhelmine Germany.[35] It goes without saying that this exercize of 'powers of rule' by the civil servants was 'illegitimate', since within a Weberian framework these civil servants should 'obey' (behave) rather than 'rule' (act). In a word, then, Wilhelmine Germany lacked leadership.

Some significant implications follow from the fact that there is a predisposition towards responsible political leadership built into Weber's ideal-type of political action. To begin with, I would argue that the notion of responsible political leadership is ambivalent, since Weber does not specify the standards by means of which the leader evaluates the consequences of his actions. The ethic of responsibility simply deals with the political leader's ability and willingness to confront consequences. Stated otherwise, Weber in his role as a value-free social scientist comprehends political responsibility as merely a technical question regarding the means to be employed by the political leader in pursuit of his freely chosen cause/value. The criteria for assessing the results flowing from a certain course of action reflect the political leader's choice of cause. But 'what the cause in the service of which the politician strives for power and uses power, looks like is a *matter of faith*' (Weber 1970, p.117; emphasis added). There is no rational basis for a political leader being passionately devoted to one cause as opposed to another. Simply put, Weber is a decisionist in the sense that normative valuation in the political realm is ultimately a question of a pre-rational (and, hence, irrational) decision. Rationality in the selection of means for the realization of a chosen cause, and avowed irrationality in the case of the normative appraizal of this same cause belong together.[36]

Even though Weber affirms that the leader's choice of cause is 'a matter of faith', the pivotal point, as Smith (1986, pp.50-51) observes, is that Weber (see, e.g., 1980, pp.428-49) identified his own faith, namely the 'power-political interests' of the German nation-state, with the ethic of responsibility.[37] Political responsibility is not a neutral, technical term, because it embodies Weber's commitment to what he regards as the higher value of the German nation-state. The more responsible political leader is the one most passionately dedicated to promoting the 'power-political interests' (Weber 1980, p.438) of the German nation-state. In this light, the syndicalist's commitment to the advancement of the cause of proletarian brotherhood is held to be 'irresponsible' and, thereby, 'apolitical' by Weber. Syndicalism simply promotes 'the unpolitical and anti-political heroic ethos of brotherhood...' (Weber 1978a, p.1428). Weber fully appreciated the fact that devotion to the 'international' cause of brotherhood amongst workers was opposed to the 'national' cause of promoting the 'power-political interests' of the German nation-state.

Another related point is that it was this total devotion to the 'national cause' that gave the political leader the 'right' to rule. Indeed, Weber transformed the 'liberal' cause in Wilhelmine Germany into the 'national' cause. Thus, a responsible political leader within the Weberian schema is defined not only by his capacity to confront consequences, but by the specific value in which he believes. For all this, Weber never overtly acknowledged that his understanding of the ethic of responsibility expressed his commitment to the advancement of the 'power-political interests' of the German nation-state. Such a candid admission would have been opposed to the methodological principle of value-freedom.

Yet another pivotal point is that Weber, as Sharp (1964, pp.304-17) stresses, evaluates political responsibility in terms of a leader's willingness to employ violence to realize his cause. Owing to the fact that the 'tasks of politics can only be solved by violence' (Weber 1970, p.126), it follows that the responsible political leader must be in favour of using violence to serve his cause. This, in turn, involves a readiness to face the possibility or even the probability of evil consequences. Weber affirms that:

> Everything that is striven for through political action operating with violent means and following an ethic of responsibility endangers the 'salvation of the soul'. (1970, p.126)

Viewed in this light, the 'peculiarity of all ethical problems of politics' (Weber 1970, p.124) inheres in the fact that the responsible political leader must be prepared to use morally dubious means like violence to attain 'good' ends like the promotion of the 'power-political interests' of the German nation-state.

If Weber regards a leader as politically responsible on account of his willingness to use violence to actualize his cause, he, by the very same token, considers an individual committed to the 'ethic of ultimate ends' alone as politically irresponsible. The convinced syndicalist is held to be politically irresponsible by Weber, since he pursues the ultimate end of 'protesting against the injustice of the social order' (1970, p.121), without making use of violent means to achieve this end. Expressed another way, the syndicalist can never attain his political goal because only violent conduct is politically effective. As a matter of fact, the reluctance of the proponent of the 'ethic of ultimate ends' to use violent means, entails that 'goals may be damaged and discredited for generations...' (Weber 1970, p.126).[38]

Although a political leader's preparedness to employ violence to pursue a cause is one major criterion by means of which Weber evaluates political responsibility, the importance of violence is accentuated more in the discussion of relations 'between' nation-states (see, e.g., Weber 1978a, pp.901-26, 1431-42). Weber, on the other hand, pays more attention to the various types of legitimate domination in the analysis of domestic political issues 'within' the confines of the nation-state.

Weber's identification of political responsibility with a leader's readiness to make use of violence to serve the cause of promoting the 'power-political interests' of the German nation-state is, in my view, absolutely invalid in the late twentieth century. Because all of humankind is now compelled to live in the shadow of atomic annihilation, a most extreme use of violence to promote the interests of national power, as in the case of war, can only be deemed utterly irresponsible. In this regard, Aron (1962, pp.452-7; see also pp.445-51) suggests that responsible, effective leadership in the nuclear age can only advocate a strategy of deterrence. A responsible leader's goal is the prevention of war, not victory. In other words, 'it is on the fear of atomic apocalypse that we must base our hope that the directors of the great powers will be wise' (Aron 1962, p.453).[39]

Of primary importance in the context of this discussion also is that Weber is not, as Eden (1983, p.208) contends, espousing a personality cult. He is not promoting an arbitrary subjectivism. Weber dismisses 'the mere "power-politician"'. For:

> ...there is no more harmful distortion of political force than the parvenu-like braggart with power, and the vain self-reflection in the feeling of power, and in general every worship of power *per se*. (Weber 1970, p.116; see also p.78; 1978a, p.1457)

The responsible political leader's utilization of the means of political violence is justified only in the service of a cause like the advancement of the 'power-political interests' of the German nation-state.[40] Interpreted in this light, it is apparent that Weber separated himself from mere *Machtpolitikers* like the Prussian historian, Treitschke (1978), for whom the securing of political power for the German nation-state was an end in itself. Even so, it could still be argued that Weber's understanding of political responsibility is such that *Wertrationalität* which involves adhering to a value like the 'national' cause for its own sake, degenerates into mere expediency, since the use of violence is required to realize the value.

One final ramification to be drawn from the conception of responsible political leadership intrinsic to Weber's ideal-type of political action, has to do with the non-materialist character of this kind of action. True, the satisfaction of material interests is a precondition for political action. But Weber insists that the responsible political leader should not make material interests the cause of politics. Quite the contrary. He proclaims that:

> The political enterprise is an *enterprise of interested persons*. (We do not mean those materially interested persons who influence politics in every form of state, but those politically interested men who strive for political power and responsibility in order to realize certain political ideas.) This very pursuit of interests, then, is the essential part of the matter. (1978a, p.1457, emphasis in original; see also p.285; 1970, p.78)

Indeed, Weber (1970, pp.84-6; 1978a, pp.1447-48) argued that in the ideal situation only economically independent individuals who lived 'for' and not 'by' politics, should be called to political leadership. Living 'for' politics presupposed a secure economic existence.[41]

However, Weber (1980, pp.428-49) also conceded that the Wilhelmine, monarchic-constitutional state was characterized by a crisis of political leadership—because the political rulers of Germany, the Junkers, were using their traditional monopoly of the 'powers of rule' to prop up their declining economic position as a class of agricultural entrepreneurs.[42] These Junkers were no longer the bearers of a distinctively political *Weltanschauung*. That is to say, the 'power-political interests' of the German nation-state were now viewed by the Junkers as ancillary to their sectional class interests. This being so, what Germany desperately needed, according to Weber, was an economically independent, responsible political leader to advance the 'power-political interests' of the German nation-state.[43] Weber is pointing to the relationship holding between economic and political power. He is underlining the economic foundations of rule. He stipulates that:

> It is dangerous, and in the long term incompatible with the interests of the nation when an economically declining class is politically dominant. (1980, p.442)

On this account, Weber inquired whether the 'power-political interests' of the German nation-state could be advanced by the development of a political consciousness among the economically dominant bourgeoisie. The *locus classicus* of what Weber understood as 'the political immaturity of broad strata of the German bourgeoisie' lay in their 'unpolitical past' (1980, p.445). The liberal bourgeoisie's 'will to power' and to national leadership had been curbed by the 1848 revolution and by the prolonged dominance of Bismarck in German politics.[44] All the same, Weber hoped that political leaders in the future could be recruited from a more politically mature bourgeoisie.

6.2 Parliamentary leadership and party organization

The modern type of party, according to Weber, 'does not arise except in the legal state with a representative constitution' (1978a, p.287).[45] More to the point, it is a parliamentary-democratic system of government which is the necessary precondition for the existence of modern parties. Weber explains that:

> ...the most modern forms of party organizations ... are the children of democracy, of mass franchise, of the necessity to woo and organize the masses, and develop the utmost unity of direction and the strictest discipline. (1970, p.102; see also p.100)

When Weber maintains that 'the most modern forms of party organizations' are the product of democracy, he is referring to a very 'individual' ideal-type of democracy.[46] Weber (1978a, pp.1381-1419; 1994, pp.80-129) argued for the creation of a parliamentary-democratic system of government in post-war Germany in a series of articles published during 1917. These articles were written against the background of the impending defeat of the Wilhelmine state in the First World War. If Weber described himself as 'the resolute follower of democratic institutions' (1970, p.370), it was not because he favoured the establishment of a parliamentary-democratic system of government in the post-war German nation-state to ensure a maximum degree of free determination 'by' the people. He writes that 'such notions as the "will of the people" ... are *fictions*' (cited in Mommsen 1984, p.395; emphasis in original).

Weber advocated the creation of a parliamentary democracy in the post-war German nation-state for the purpose of selecting and training responsible political leaders and enabling them to rule. He declares that committee work in a strong parliament is especially important:

Only such intensive training, through which the politician must pass in the committees of a powerful *working* parliament, turns such an assembly into a recruiting ground not for mere demagogues but for positively participating politicians. (1978a, p.1420, emphasis in original; see also pp.1427-28; 1970, p.107)

Professional politicians undertaking committee work are in a position to exercize personal responsibility. A 'powerful *working* parliament' can also, on Weber's (1978a, p.1409) interpretation, lead to the emergence of responsible, political, parliamentary leaders—since the competitive struggle for political power (i.e., 'powers of rule') tends to thrust the more competent politicians into the leading positions.

Modern parties play a crucial role in this competitive struggle for political power in a 'powerful *working* parliament'. As a matter of fact, Weber assesses the role of parties in a parliamentary democracy solely in terms of whether they 'permit at all the rise of men with leadership capacities?' (1978a, p.1458). What is more, he hoped that the rise to prominence of responsible political leaders in the course of this competitive parliamentary struggle, would advance the 'power-political interests' of the German nation-state in the post-war era. Parliamentary democracy is a means for the production of responsible political leaders to promote the interests of national power.[47] Quite simply, 'the vital interests of the nation stand ... above democracy and parliamentarism' (Weber 1978a, p.1383).[48]

Weber's (1994, pp.80-129) advocacy of equal suffrage adds further weight to the argument that parliamentary democracy was understood by him as a tool for the promotion of the interests of the German nation-state. Weber stipulated that equal suffrage should be implemented so that the soldiers returning from the war, would find that 'purely formal political rights have *already* been so ordered that they can turn their hands immediately to the material reconstruction of the structure of the state' (1994, p.107; emphasis in original). Indeed, Weber (1994, p.126) goes so far as to say that the German nation-state could never again be mobilized for war in the way it had been during the First World War, if equal suffrage was not put into effect.

How, then, does Weber define the ideal-typical concept of the modern party? He states that:

> The term 'party' will be employed to designate associations, membership in which rests on formally free recruitment. The end to which its activity is devoted is to secure power within an organization for its leaders in order to attain ideal or material advantages for its active members. (1978a, p.284; see also pp.285-8, 938-9, 1395-99; 1994, pp.98-100)

The principle of formally voluntary solicitation is central to the notion of a modern party.[49] For Weber (1978a, pp.287, 1395-96), this principle differentiates modern parties from all organizations with a clearly defined membership enacted by law or contract.[50] Lawyers comprise a substantial proportion of the membership of a modern party. The work-situation of lawyers (as opposed to other free entrepreneurs like the industrial entrepreneur) is such that they can devote a large proportion of their time to politics. On this score, Weber asserts that:

> Besides the knowledge of the law and, more importantly, the preparation for fighting an opponent which this profession affords ... a purely material element is decisive: the possession of a private office—today an absolute necessity for the professional politician. (1978a, p.1448)

The second crucial component built into Weber's ideal-type of the modern party relates to the goals pursued by a such a party. 'By definition a party can exist only *within* an organization, in order to influence its policy or gain control of it' (Weber 1978a, p.285; emphasis in original). Every modern party, according to Weber, is committed to attaining political power ('powers of rule') 'within' a parliamentary-democratic nation-state for its leaders in order to procure 'material' advantages for its active members. Modern democratic parties 'are merely interested in putting their leader into the top positions so that he can turn over state offices to his following, the regular and the campaign staffs of the party' (Weber 1978a, pp.1397-98; see also pp.1409, 1421).[51] In short, these parties are 'essentially *organizations for job patronage...*' (Weber 1978a, p.1397; emphasis in original). They are purely organizations of job-hunters.[52]

When Weber, on the other hand, speaks of a modern democratic party being concerned with securing political power for its leaders in order to obtain 'ideal' advantages for its active members, he is referring to an ideological party. This kind of modern party intends 'to accomplish the realization of *substantive* political ideals' (Weber 1978a, p.1398, emphasis in original; see also p.287). The

234

German Social Democratic Party represented such a party before it became bureaucratized. In general, modern democratic parties combine 'material' and 'ideal' goals. They want to achieve substantive goals and to control job patronage. Even so, Weber concedes that 'setbacks in participating in offices are felt more severely by parties than is action against their objective goals' (1970, p.87). 'Ideal' goals are insignificant in the face of 'material' interests.[53]

Bearing in mind Weber's understanding of modern democratic parties as political organizations concerned mainly with procuring material (and ideal) advantages for their active members, it follows that they cannot, in my view, be regarded as directly analogous to classes and estates.[54] Whilst the formation of classes and estates depends on the principles governing the 'distribution' of power in the modern capitalist market-economy (i.e., private property and marketable skills) and the feudal social order (i.e., social honour) respectively, '"*parties*" reside in the sphere of power' (Weber 1978a, p.938; emphasis in original).[55] That is to say, parties as goal-oriented political organizations are, in the main, interested in the 'acquisition' of political power ('powers of rule') for their own leaders.

Of pivotal importance also is that Weber in the later part of *Economy and Society* incorporates parties into the sociology of domination (see 1978a, pp.284-8), and treats classes and status groups (including estates) in the following chapter (see 1978a, pp.302-7). Weber is stressing here, as Schluchter (1981, p.30) points out, that classes and status groups belong to 'the societal level of social life', whereas parties are located 'on the level of organizations'. Even if classes and status groups (including estates) belong to 'the societal level of social life', this does not mean, of course, that goal-oriented organizations cannot be established to pursue their respective interests.

In fact, Weber's contention that parties reside 'in the sphere of power' has led to much confusion in the secondary literature. This confusion could possibly have been avoided, if Weber had written that parties reside 'in the sphere of political power'. For instance, Weber's statement that '"*parties*' reside in the sphere of power', misled Bendix and Lipset (1967) into identifying 'party' and 'power'. Power is held to be merely a political phenomenon. The end-result was that the concept of 'party' was assimilated directly to the concept of 'power' as one of the three dimensions of social stratification. The concept of power became a mere internal dimension of social stratification relegated to a place next to class and status.

As to the title of their reader, *Class, Status and Power*, Bendix and Lipset acknowledge in the introduction to the second edition that:

...we are uncomfortably aware that in choosing it originally we were swayed by its euphonious appeal and failed to pay attention to the fact that classes and status groups are themselves bases of aggregations of power. (1967, p.xvi)[56]

But in view of the fact that they did not change the title of their very influential reader, the misappropriation of Weber's notion of social stratification was simply perpetuated in much English-language sociology. Besides, Bendix's and Lipset's crucial admission concerning the egregious error of identifying 'party' and 'power' was concealed in an inconspicuous footnote.

If modern parties, then, cannot be regarded as the direct parallel in the political sphere of what classes and estates are in their respective spheres, this does not mean that political formations equivalent to classes and estates do not exist within a Weberian framework. Taking account of the unequal distribution of 'powers of rule' in the modern nation-state, the political formations corresponding to classes and estates within the Weberian schema are, as Burger (1985, p.16) suggests, 'rulers' and 'ruled'. The constitution of 'rulers' and 'ruled' (the leaders and the masses) is predicated upon the unequal distribution of 'powers of rule' in the modern nation-state.[57]

Another issue relevant to Weber's conceptualization of modern democratic parties bears on the specific means employed to attain their goals. Professional politicians in a parliamentary democracy 'strive for power through sober and "peaceful" party campaigns in the market of election votes' (Weber 1970, p.100; see also 1978a, p.1396). The electoral campaigns of modern democratic parties are '"peaceful"' in the sense that they presuppose the monopoly of the legitimate use of violence by the modern nation-state. The basis of the political power of modern democratic parties resides, according to Weber, in control of a primary resource in a parliamentary democracy, namely, votes. Therefore, these parties 'are primarily organizations for the attraction of votes' (Weber 1978a, p.285).

The bureaucratization of modern democratic parties is crucial for the attraction of votes.[58] Weber asserts that 'the power of the parties rests primarily on the organizational effectiveness of these bureaucracies' (1978a, p.1399). For the strictly bureaucratic type of administration, as previously indicated, is 'formally the most rational means of exercising authority over human beings' (Weber 1978a, p.223). It is in this sense that a modern party bureaucracy in the ideal situation, represents the most rational means of wooing and organizing the electoral masses into voting for particular party candidates. Or as Michels pointedly remarks, the modern democratic party 'is the methodical organization of the electoral masses' (1915, p.367). The 'caucus' in England, the rise of the 'machine' in the United States and 'party officialdom' in Germany all testified to the bureaucratization of modern democratic parties in the last decades of the nineteenth century.

Bureaucratization, in Weber's view, leads to the development of a strict hierarchical structure within every modern democratic party. Similarly, Michels maintains that 'organization implies the tendency to oligarchy' (1915, p.32; see also pp.365-92).[59] The party leader is located 'at the top' of the bureaucratic organization that is the modern democratic party. The next major group are the 'active party members' who, according to Weber, 'have for the most part merely

236

the function of acclaiming their leaders' (1978a, p.285). There is, however, a 'hard core' of 'active party members' (i.e., the party officials) responsible for financing the modern democratic party by gaining the support of rich sponsors, due-paying members and the like. What is more, this 'hard core' determines the party programme, the selection of party candidates, and the tactics to be employed for the attraction of votes in the electoral campaign (see Weber 1978a, pp.287, 1396). Below the 'active party members' are located the 'inactive masses of electors or voters' who are 'merely objects whose votes are sought at election time' (Weber 1978a, p.285; see also pp.1444-45).

The fact that the electoral masses are merely regarded as a tool for securing votes by the party leader and party officialdom, is corroborated by, for instance, the use of oratory in modern electoral campaigns. In this connection, Weber purports that:

...the rhetoric has the same meaning as the street parades and festivals: to imbue the masses with the notion of the party's power and confidence in victory and, above all, to convince them of the leader's charismatic qualification. (1978a, p.1130; see also 1970, pp.95-6)

The content of the rhetoric is not significant. Rather, what is of the utmost importance is the emotional influence of the words spoken, in particular, by a charismatic party leader. Or as Michels puts it, 'the fineness of the oratory exercises a suggestive influence whereby the crowd is completely subordinated to the will of the orator' (1915, p.69). In other words, the use of oratory in an electoral campaign is such that the masses are nothing more than reflexes of 'the will' of the charismatic party leader.

It is in this same context that Weber refers to 'the suggestive appeal of advertising' (1978a, p.288) and, further, to the fundamental role of the press. He, for example, holds the journalist to be 'nowadays the most important representative of the demogogic species' (1970, p.96; see also pp.97-9). Interestingly enough, Weber also points to the increasing role which capitalist interests play in modern democratic politics—when he avers that 'for all modern states, apparently the journalist worker gains less and less as the capitalist lord of the press ... gains more and more political influence' (1970, p.97).

In light of the foregoing, it is obvious that the political role assigned to the electoral masses by Weber is that of 'objects of solicitation by the various parties' (1978a, p.287; see also pp.1129, 1445). The docile, electoral masses are within the Weberian action schema located below the level of sociological identification except as a means of obtaining votes and, thereby, of rule. Weber observes, for example, that the Social Democrats in Imperial Russia inure the electoral masses 'to a "hysterical indulgence in emotion", which takes the place of economic and political thought and action' (1995, p.110). The masses are not rational, political agents 'acting' on their own motives. They are not free to choose means and ends.[60]

If the electoral masses are employed merely as a means of procuring votes by the party leader and party officialdom, the party officials themselves are the administrative tool in the hands of the party leader to gain the votes of the electoral masses. On this score, Weber writes that:

In order to be a useful apparatus, a machine in the American sense— undisturbed either by the vanity of notables or pretensions to independent views—*the following of such a leader must obey him blindly* ... This is simply the price paid for guidance by leaders. (1970, p.113, emphasis added; see also p.103)

The obedient, disciplined party officials are simply viewed as reflexes of the party leader's will. These officials, like the electoral masses, are not rational, political agents 'acting' on their own motives. The party leader is the only 'real' subject of political action within a Weberian action framework. He is the one 'personality' capable of exercizing individual responsibility and 'acting' on his own motives. The responsible party leader is the one self-assertive personality in the administered, dehumanized world that is the modern democratic party. It was Weber's ultimate hope that such a responsible party leader would become the parliamentary leader as a result of the electoral success of his party. He hoped that such a parliamentary leader would, in turn, promote the 'power-political interests' of the German nation-state.

If it is the goal of the party leader to simply use party officialdom as the administrative means to win the votes of the electoral masses and, thereby, gain control of the nation-state, Weber nevertheless recognizes the independent power base of the party bureaucracy itself. He affirms, as shown earlier, that 'bureaucratic administration means fundamentally domination through knowledge' (1978a, p.225). In this light, the party leader's capacity to exert 'control by means of a particular kind of administrative staff' (Weber 1978a, p.222), is limited to the extent that he is 'in reality' dependent upon his party officials (monopolizing 'technical knowledge' and 'official information') to secure the votes of the electoral masses. Even in the case of a so-called revolutionary leader, Weber proclaims that:

He who wants to establish absolute justice on earth by force requires a following, a human 'machine'. He must hold out the necessary internal and external premiums, heavenly or worldly reward, to this 'machine' or else the machine will not function. Under the conditions of the modern class struggle, the internal premiums consist of the satisfying of hatred and the craving for revenge ... The external rewards are adventure, victory, booty, power, and spoils. *The leader and his success are completely dependent upon the functioning of his machine and hence not on his own motives.* (1970, p.125; emphasis added)

238

The 'dictatorship of the official' (Weber 1978b, p.260), then, in a modern democratic party restricts individually differentiated activity on the part of the party leader himself.

The fact that the 'dictatorship of the official' limits the ability of the party leader 'at the top' of the party bureaucracy to exercize his legitimate authority raises, I would argue, a fundamental problem for Weber's typology of legitimate domination. Ideally, bureaucratic officialdom within a Weberian framework is committed to an ethic of obedience (i.e., the subjection of one's will to another). But if bureaucratic officialdom tries to exert authority itself (on account of its monopoly of 'technical knowledge' and 'official information'), it infringes upon the legitimate authority of the party leader. Or as Parkin astutely remarks, the bureaucracy 'uses its power illegitimately' (1982, p.89). On Weber's account, then, the party bureaucracy cannot be understood as a form of legitimate domination. If Weber wants to remain consistent, only a party bureaucracy championing the ethic of obedience can be considered 'legitimate'. Conversely, a party bureaucracy exercizing authority on its own behalf is 'illegitimate'.[61]

Another fundamental point made by Weber is that:

The more bureaucratization advances and the more substantial the interests in benefices and other opportunities become, the more surely does the party organization fall into the hands of experts, whether these appear immediately as party officials or at first as independent entrepreneurs—witness the American boss. (1978a, p.1131)

Weber acknowledges, though, that 'in times of great public excitement, charismatic leaders may emerge even in solidly bureaucratized parties, as was demonstrated by Roosevelt's campaign in 1912' (1978a, p.1132). The goal of such leaders is to make electoral success less contingent upon the functioning of the party bureaucracy by, for example, imposing plebiscitary designation. It goes without saying that such charismatic leaders are vehemently opposed by the party officials whose material interests (e.g., the government jobs obtained upon the electoral success of the party) are at stake. On the other hand, party officials appreciate the demagogic talents of charismatic leaders who do not wish to impose plebiscitary designation. For such officials:

...expect that the demagogic effect of the leader's *personality* during the election fight will increase votes and mandates and thereby power, and, thereby, as far as possible, will extend opportunities to their followers to find the compensation for which they hope. (Weber 1970, p.103, emphasis in original; see also 1978a, pp.1397-98, 1446-47, 1459)

In the final analysis, Weber believed that only exceptional circumstances could 'bring about the triumph of charisma over the organization' (1978a, p.1132). In fact, he became very disillusioned about the prospect of 'men with leadership capacities' (1978a, p.1158) emerging in solidly bureaucratized, modern, democratic parties.

If party officialdom impeded the rise of 'men with leadership capacities', a greater threat, according to Weber, was posed by what he calls 'interest organizations'. On this account, he asserts that:

> In fact, party officialdom presents the relatively smaller danger of bringing about a domination by the 'bureaucratic spirit' to the disadvantage of real leaders. This danger emanates much more from the compulsion to take account of interest organizations for the sake of vote-getting; this leads to the infiltration of their employees into the list of party candidates ... A parliament composed of such employees would be politically sterile. (1978a, p.1448; see also p.1128; 1970, pp.94, 114; 1986, pp.130-31; 1994, p.105)

Weber is once again pointing to the prevalence of material interests in modern democratic politics. However, he never specifies in any detail whose material interests are represented in a modern democratic party. Certainly, he admits that parties may 'predominantly and consciously act in the interests of a status group or a class...' (1978a, p.285; see also pp.287, 931; 1970, p.372). But, on the other hand, parties 'need be neither purely class nor purely status parties; in fact, they are more likely to be mixed types and sometimes they are neither' (Weber 1978a, p.938).[62] One reason why Weber may not have enumerated in any detail the material interests of the various groups represented in modern democratic parties, lies in his fundamental conviction that only those interests transcending conflicts of material interests should be pursued in politics. He (1994, p.111) argued, for instance, that modern capitalist entrepreneurs were too directly involved in 'the struggle of economic interests' to be 'politically useful'. Quite simply, Weber wants responsible political leaders to rule in the German nation-state 'who stand above party and class' (cited in Beetham 1974, p.223).

6.3 Plebiscitary leadership and the masses

Since party officialdom and 'interest organizations' hindered the rise of 'men with leadership capacities', Weber became dissatisfied with parliamentary democracy as a viable means for the production of responsible political leaders to advance the 'power-political interests' of the German nation-state. He (1986, pp.128-32), in particular, grew increasingly disillusioned with the parliamentary politics he witnessed in the early days of the Weimar republic set up in November 1918. The national unity which the beginning of the First World War fostered in the Wilhelmine state, was gradually replaced in the latter years of the war and in the Weimar republic by conflicts of economic interests (i.e., class conflict), regional conflicts and so on.

240

This being so, Weber began to speak up publicly from 1918 in favour of a popularly elected president with substantial independent powers. He at this point considers 'the right to the direct election of the leader' as 'the Magna Carta of democracy' (Weber, 1986, p.132). For Weber, 'true democracy' is now rendered as 'subjection to leaders chosen by the people themselves' (ibid.). The reason for this resides in the fact that:

...only the President of the Reich could become the *safety valve of the demand for leadership if he were elected in a plebiscitarian way* and not by Parliament. (Weber 1970, p.114, emphasis added; see also 1986, pp.123-32)[63]

Such a plebiscitary president/leader, with an independent basis of support in the mass electorate, would represent the unity of the German nation-state and promote its 'power-political interests'. A president/leader elected, on the other hand, 'by means of particular constellations and coalitions of parties is politically a dead man when these constellations shift' (Weber 1986, p.132). The popularly elected president/leader was to be the head of the executive branch of government. If conflict arose between the parliament and the government, the plebiscitary president/leader was, according to Weber, to be empowered to appeal directly to the people. What is more, the popular election of the president/leader involved restricting the influence of political parties in the selection of ministers. And political patronage was to be limited.

It could also be argued that Weber's advocacy of plebiscitary leadership democracy, corroborates the fact that he offers a political solution to the problem of value-conflict endemic in the rapidly developing capitalist market-economy of early twentieth century Germany. The conflict between capitalist entrepreneurs and wage-labourers over the meaning of rationality, for instance, can be understood as a struggle between different values. The maximum of formal rationality in capital accounting is espoused by capitalist entrepreneurs interested in rational profit-making activity. Substantive rationality, on the other hand, is championed by the workers concerned with the satisfaction of human needs (see Weber 1978a, p.138). The confrontation between capital and labour could manifest itself politically through 'interest organizations' in parliament.

Given this inexorable value-conflict built into modern capitalist society, Weber reasoned that a plebiscitary leader with an independent power base in the mass vote, was the means of transcending it. The plebiscitary leader dedicated to the advancement of the 'power-political interests' of the German nation-state, had the capacity to preserve national unity in the face of the inescapable struggle between capital and labour. Weber envisaged commitment to the cultural value of the nation generating 'a specific sentiment of solidarity' (1978a, p.922), which could overcome what he regarded as the narrow sectional class interests of capital and labour. Weber had claimed some years earlier that the success of the proletariat in undermining the notion of nationhood 'is rather diminishing at the present time' (1978a, p.924).[64]

Let us now examine Weber's individual ideal-type of plebiscitary leadership democracy in more detail. Weber purports that:

> Plebiscitary democracy—the most important type of *Führer Demokratie*—is a variant of charismatic authority, which hides behind a legitimacy that is *formally* derived from the will of the governed. The leader (demagogue) rules by virtue of the devotion and trust which his political followers have in him personally. (1978a, p.268, emphasis in original; see also pp.266-71, 1111-20, 1451-59; 1986, pp.128-32)

The plebiscitary, as opposed to the parliamentary selection of a responsible charismatic leader, involves the direct popular election of the leader by the masses. Expressed more precisely, the plebiscitary selection of a charismatic leader is not an 'election'. Weber explains that:

> We are not at all dealing with an election, of course, when voting for a political ruler has a plebiscitary and hence charismatic character; when instead of a real choice between candidates *only the power claims of a pretender are being acknowledged.* (1978a, p.1129, emphasis added; see also pp.1126, 1451)[65]

The plebiscite is simply a tool employed by the political leader to derive 'the legitimacy of authority from the confidence of the ruled, even though the voluntary nature of such confidence is only formal or fictitious' (Weber 1978a, p.267).

Recognition on the part of the ruled is in the ideal-typical sense crucial for the validity of the charismatic plebiscitary leader's authority. But 'in reality' '*it is not the politically passive "mass" that produces the leader from its midst,* but the leader recruits his following and wins the mass through demagogy' (Weber 1978a, p.1457; emphasis added). The politically inert mass is, on Weber's reading, incapable of engaging in political action.[66] It cannot act on its own motives, since 'it is ... always exposed to direct, purely emotional and irrational influence' (Weber 1978a, pp.1459-60).[67] Put another way, the mass can only engage in affectual action, that is, action 'determined by the actor's specific affects and feeling states...' (Weber 1978a, p.25).

On this account, the emotional, irrational mass can only become involved in democratic politics, on Weber's account, as a result of initiative 'from above'. This is tantamount to saying that the charismatic plebiscitary leader gains the faith and trust of the masses in him personally by exploiting mass emotionalism. Emotionalism props up plebiscitary leadership democracy. Weber stipulates that:

> It is characteristic of the *Führerdemokratie* that there should in general be a highly emotional type of devotion to and trust in the leader. This accounts for a tendency to favor the type of individual who is most spectacular, who

promises the most, or who employs the most effective propaganda measures in the competition for leadership. (1978a, p.269)

The charismatic relationship of domination holding between the plebiscitary leader and the electoral masses is simply an emotional and irrational one.

In light of the aforesaid, it might appear that Weber regards plebiscitary leadership democracy as nothing more than 'a variant of charismatic authority' (1978a, p.268). But Weber also affirms that:

There are very important types of rational domination which, with respect to *the ultimate source of authority*, belong to other categories. This is true ... of the pure charismatic type of a president chosen by a plebiscite. (1978a, p.219; emphasis added)

Plebiscitary leadership democracy, then, is a form of legal-rational domination which is 'ultimately' legitimized by virtue of the charismatic quality of the leadership. Weber refers to the legal-rational nature of the plebiscitary leader's authority, when he maintains that:

If a ruler is dependent on recognition by plebiscite he will usually attempt to support his regime by an organization of officials which functions promptly and efficiently. (1978a, p.269)

Bureaucratic officialdom bolsters the plebiscitary leader's rule. Recall also Weber's point that passion, a feeling of responsibility and a sense of proportion are essential personal attributes for all political leaders. Therefore, the responsible plebiscitary leader tries to integrate *wertrational* and *zweckrational* action, the passionate commitment to a cause/value (like the promotion of the 'power-political interests' of the German nation-state) with the rational, dispassionate appraizal of the alternative means of realizing it.

It is against this backdrop that the irrational, emotional masses are rationally assessed by the plebiscitary leader as a means for obtaining a primary resource requisite for rulership in a modern mass democracy, namely, votes. The onus is on the plebiscitary leader to rationally discipline and organize 'the unorganized "mass"—the democracy of the streets' (Weber 1978a, p.1460) into voting for him. For Weber, then, legal-rational domination grounded in value- and purposive-rational action is constitutive of plebiscitary leadership. But, on the other hand, the inclusion of the irrational, charismatic form of authority as 'the ultimate source' of the plebiscitary leader's legitimacy—shows clearly that Weber did not in the concrete situation consider sheer rational legality an adequate source of legitimacy under the conditions of modern mass democracy. That said, it is important to remember that Weber is aware of the limitations of a highly emotional type of commitment to and trust in a plebiscitary leader as a source of legitimacy in the modern legal-rational state. He observes, for example, that 'even in America it has not *always* come up to expectations' (1978a, p.269; emphasis in original).

Some fundamental implications can be drawn from Weber's espousal of plebiscitary leadership democracy. Firstly, it is my contention that Weber's employment of the term 'mass' is sociologically amorphous. Subordinate political groupings are simply equated with the general category, the 'mass'. The 'mass' represents an undifferentiated whole. The use of the term 'mass' makes it impossible to consider the differential relations of domination that may hold between a political leader and different subordinate political groups. Weber's identification of all subordinate political groupings with the 'mass' entails that all such groups can be treated as given, as not requiring further examination.[68]

Furthermore, Weber's use of the term 'mass' implies that it is *a priori* impossible to consider 'ordinary' individuals as political 'subjects' capable of acting in concert in the German nation-state. 'Ordinary' individuals dissolved into the amorphous 'mass' are nothing more than passive political 'objects' of manipulation at the disposal of an 'outstanding' plebiscitary leader. Weber's employment of the term 'mass' leads to the depoliticization of the majority of the population in the German nation-state. The participation of the obedient, disciplined masses in 'democratic' politics is reduced to a minimum, that is, to the acclamation of the charismatic plebiscitary leader.[69] The 'outstanding' plebiscitary leader is the only 'real' subject of political action.

As a matter of fact, Weber's voluntaristic overestimation of the individual is rather marked in his political writings. For Weber, as Beetham (1974, p.112) points out, can only apprehend an individual personality performing great political acts.[70] Weber was never interested in elitist theory in the strict sense. His concern is not impersonal elites engaged in collective action but always individual leaders undertaking political action and, thereby, ruling.[71]

Because only individual leaders rule within the Weberian schema, it, furthermore, follows that the notion of a ruling class cannot be formulated. Admittedly, an individual leader cannot rule if he does not possess the necessary economic resources. The economic foundations of rule are crucial. Weber states, for example, that 'the charismatic party leader requires the material means of power' (1978a, p.244). Under modern capitalist conditions, this can only mean that a political leader is very much dependent upon the financial support of the capitalist class. However, Weber was adamant, as previously stated, that a responsible political leader should not make 'material interests' the 'cause' of politics. A secure economic existence was the 'precondition' for but not the 'cause' of politics.

Another fundamental ramification that can be drawn from Weber's defence of plebiscitary leadership democracy as a viable form of government for the post-war German nation-state, relates to the fact that this kind of government points in the direction of political absolutism, that is, political dictatorship.[72] In the first place, Weber's constitutional proposals enhanced and expanded the political power of the popularly elected leader. Weber (1986, pp.131-2) proposed that such a leader should be equipped with a suspensory veto and the authority to dissolve parliament and to call referenda. In this same connection, it is interesting to consider how far the Weimar constitution reflected Weber's constitutional proposals for a popularly elected leader. Weber himself stated in a letter to his wife that the provisions of the new constitution were 'very similar to my proposals' (cited in Weber 1988, p.640; emphasis in original). The popularly elected Weimar president was, in fact, sanctioned to call a referendum, and he was equipped with the power to dissolve parliament. However, Wells (1986, p.127) points out that Article 48 of the Weimar constitution, the 'dictatorship paragraph', whereby the president was empowered to suspend basic rights in periods of emergency, was not part of Weber's constitutional proposals.

Even if this 'dictatorship paragraph' was not part of Weber's constitutional proposals, I would still urge the view that his defence of plebiscitary leadership democracy points in the direction of political dictatorship. For the politically inert, compliant, disciplined masses are inaccessible to sociological analysis except as a means of rational, political action on the part of a leader. It is not possible to conceptualize subordinate political groupings in the German nation-state collectively acting together within the Weberian action framework. More pointedly, it is impossible to envisage such groups opposing a despotic, plebiscitary leader.

Surprisingly enough, Weber alleges that the charismatic plebiscitary leader should be answerable to 'the people'. He declares that:

We must ensure that whenever the President of the Reich attempts to tamper with the laws or to govern autocratically, he sees the 'noose and gallows' before his eyes. (1986, p.129)

He, further, states that 'we must restrict the power of the popularly elected President as always...' (1986, p.131). The pivotal point, though, is that these assertions are wholly unwarranted. For political resistance 'from below' to limit the power of a dictatorial, plebiscitary leader (or, indeed, the power of an autocratic leader elected by parliament) has no foundation in Weber's conceptualization of legal-rational domination. Weber's plebiscitary leader is immune to pressures 'from below'. In a somewhat similar vein, Gouldner accuses Weber of being 'an ideologist ... of quiescence and neutralism' (1969, p.485).

Another point especially pertinent here is that it is not possible, in any case, to oppose an autocratic, charismatic, plebiscitary leader, since Weber's defence of the methodological principle of value-freedom makes it impossible to distinguish such a leader from a leader who does not rule autocratically. Weber asserts, for instance, that value-free sociological analysis treats the charisma of a '"berserk"' or a '"shaman"' 'on the same level as it does the charisma of men who are the "greatest" heroes, prophets, and saviors according to conventional judgments' (1978a, p.242). It is not possible to speak of a despotic charismatic leader, because Weber does not recognize the existence of any supervening principle of political morality that would support the accusation of a charismatic leader's tyrannical rule. For Weber, a normative evaluation of a charismatic leader's political conduct is beyond the realm of scientific criticism. Normative questions cannot be adjudicated rationally.[73]

From the foregoing, it is evident that resistance 'from below' has no independent, sociological reality in Weber's political thought. This is not to say, though, that Weber does not refer to such resistance. When he speaks of political intransigence, he does not consider it in relation to the experience of the ruled. Rather, such defiance is viewed from a ruler-centric vantage-point, that is, from a vantage-point of control. Opposition 'from below' is, as Beetham (1974, p.111) indicates, a dangerous phenomenon that must be tightly controlled.[74] Weber conveys his ruler-centric pattern of thinking in a striking fashion in the following statement:

> The industrial proletariat ... is a force which is at least *capable* of being ordered and led by its trusted representatives, which is to say by politicians who think rationally. As far as the politics of the state are concerned, the most important thing of all is to increase the power of these leaders—in our case the union leaders—over momentary instincts, and beyond this, *generally* to increase the importance of *responsible* leaders, indeed of political leadership as such ... *only* the orderly *leadership* of the masses by responsible politicians is at all capable of breaking *unregulated* rule by the street and leadership by chance demagogues. (1994, pp.124-5; emphasis in original)

From the vantage point of 'the politics of the state', the responsible, calculating, rational leader must exert control over the unruly, emotional, irrational masses. He must undertake the political taming of the masses. For Weber, equal suffrage guarantees the 'involvement' of the masses in 'democratic' politics in a regulated, disciplined and organized manner. In a word, Weber's 'theory' of democratic politics is, as Prager (1981, pp.918-50) reasons, a 'theory' of political control.[75] Weber's authoritarian conception of democratic politics is succinctly summed up in a conversation with Ludendorff in 1919:

> In a democracy the people choose a leader in whom they trust. Then the chosen leader says 'Now shut up and obey me'. People and party are then no longer free to interfere in his business. (cited in Bottomore 1985b, p.85; emphasis added)

Once the political leader has been elected, he assumes exclusive personal responsibility for his actions. He has to answer to no one except himself.[76]

Thus far, the fact that Weber regards the masses in the German nation-state as a passive object to be disciplined and manipulated by the responsible political leader (whether elected in a parliamentary or plebiscitarian manner), has been continually underlined. However, it is important to mention at this stage that

Weber's attitude towards the masses is not always clear-cut. Weber (1985, pp.7-13) perceived the masses in North America in a different light in the article, "'Churches' and "Sects" in North America: An Ecclesiastical Socio-Political Sketch', first published in the *Frankfurter Zeitung* in April 1906 (see also Weber 1973a, pp.140-49; 1978a, pp.1204-11).[77]

In opposition to the notion of a politically passive mass at the disposal of a responsible political leader, Weber declares that:

> Whoever represents 'democracy' as a mass fragmented into atoms ... is fundamentally mistaken so far as the American democracy is concerned ... The genuine American society—and here we include especially the 'middle' and 'lower' strata of the population—was never such a sandpile. (1985, p.10; see also 1978a, p.1207)

It was the Protestant sects that gave 'American democracy its own flexible structure and its individualistic stamp' (Weber 1985, p.10). The Protestant sects, on Weber's reading, instilled a very strong sense of individual responsibility in the masses and, particularly, in the modern workers. The fundamental axiom of all types of ascetic Protestantism was that only proving oneself in life, especially in one's calling, provided certainty of grace and exoneration. The corollary of this was that the 'proven' Christian was the person who was 'proven' in his 'calling'. When this particular kind of individual responsibility cultivated by the Protestant sects was transferred to the political sphere, it became the foundation stone of American 'participatory' democracy. American 'participatory' democracy facilitated individuals to exercize individual initiative and responsibility. Moreover, Weber argues that the 'individualism' championed by the Protestant sects led to the establishment of cohesive social groups open to all social strata in American society. Of course, qualification for membership of such groups (as of the Protestant sects) was based solely on individual achievement and the exercize of individual responsibility.

For all this, Weber conceded that it was impossible to establish sect-democracy in the German nation-state where church-religion predominated. This form of religion did not favour 'the energy of the individual but the prestige of the "office"' (Weber 1985, p.11). It did not encourage the individual to exercize individual responsibility. What is more, Weber (1985, p.7) argued that the onset of 'Europeanization' (i.e., the 'church' model of social organization) in North America itself was leading to the decline of sect-democracy. Given this state of affairs, the theme of sect-democracy increasingly receded in Weber's political writings.

Pertinent to Weber's conceptualization of the masses also is that he hoped for the emergence of an active, politically sophisticated citizenry in the German nation-state. Weber took citizenship rights in the public sphere for granted. Indeed, he (1978a, p.1403) acknowledged, as stated earlier, that it would not be possible to go on living in modern society without 'the achievements of the age

247

of the Rights of Man'. The crux of the problem, though, was the powerlessness of the citizenry, especially the bourgeoisie, in the German nation-state. This crisis in citizenship pervades Weber's (1980, pp.428-49) thought as early as the Freiburg inaugural lecture. One of the principal reasons for the political impotence of the bourgeoisie, of course, was the prolonged dominance of Bismarck in German politics. The political legacy left behind by Bismarck, when he departed from the political stage in 1890, was 'a nation *without any political will of its own*, accustomed to the idea that the great statesman at the helm would make the necessary political decisions' (1978a, p.1392; emphasis in original). In essence, the form of government created by Bismarck was a caesarist regime propped up by bureaucracy.

It is against this backdrop that Weber (1994, pp.80-129) promoted the idea of an active, responsible, self-reliant citizenry in his article, 'Suffrage and Democracy in Germany', published in December 1917. He argued that the vote, in particular, was a mechanism for raising the political consciousness of the bourgeoisie and facilitating their political participation in the German nation-state. To use Weber's own words:

> ...the ballot slip is the *only* instrument of power which is at all *capable* of giving the people who are subject to bureaucratic rule a minimal right of co-determination in the affairs of the community for which they are obliged to give their lives. (1994, pp.105-6; emphasis in original)

Weber's espousal of citizenship as an active political force, would seem to contravene the idea of the politically inert mass as a means of rule at the disposal of the 'democratic' leader (whether elected in a parliamentary or plebiscitarian fashion).

My first response to this ambivalence in Weber's political thought, is to highlight the fact that Weber's advocacy of an active citizenry is closely linked with the goal of promoting the 'power-political interests' of the German nation-state. He insists that:

> There are only two choices: either the mass of citizens is left without freedom or rights in a bureaucratic, 'authoritarian state' which has only the appearance of parliamentary rule, and in which the citizens are 'administered' like a herd of cattle; or the citizens are integrated into the state by making them its *co-rulers*. A *nation of masters (Herrenvolk)*—and only such a nation can and may engage in 'world politics'—has *no* choice in this matter. (1994, p.129; emphasis in original)

Weber is stipulating here that a body of responsible, internally motivated citizens, as opposed to a politically passive mass, is the precondition for the German nation-state's participation in international politics. It is not far-fetched to claim that an independent citizenry is not a value in itself for Weber. Rather it is defended on purely instrumental grounds. It is the promotion of the interests of national power that remains as one of Weber's core political values. He stresses that without the integration of the mass of citizens into the nation-state, 'the price to be paid ... would be the entire future of Germany' (1994, p.129).

Another related point is that most of the textual evidence given by Weber, would suggest that the electoral masses are conceptualized, in the main, as an instrument of rule. Furthermore, Weber's defence of active, self-reliant responsible citizens fits uncomfortably with his simultaneous championing of the manipulation of these citizens by a democratic leader solely responsible to himself.

Finally, it will be recalled that since Weber conceptualizes most individuals as a 'means' of rational action rather than actors in their own right in modern society, it obviously follows that a notion of citizens in the modern nation-state 'acting' on their own motives, has likewise no theoretical foundation in his political thought. More to the point, Weber's definition of political action in terms of leadership suggests that the majority of individuals do not 'act' in a political sense.

6.4 Political emancipation

In addition to the advancement of the 'power-political interests' of the German nation-state, Weber also declares that 'politicians must be *the countervailing force against bureaucratic domination*' (1978a, p.1417; emphasis added). The onus is on the responsible charismatic leader to secure the predominance of 'the political' over 'the bureaucratic'. Weber was deeply disturbed about 'the basic fact of the irresistible advance of bureaucratization...' (1978a, p.1403). Bureaucratization was an historic inevitability. There was no safety-hatch available to escape from the bureaucratic inferno. Indeed, Weber declares that 'this passion for bureaucracy ... is enough to drive one to despair' (1954, p.97). Modern bureaucracy is '"escape-proof"' (Weber 1978a, p.1401).[78] Weber, in particular, indicts the process of bureaucratization (i.e., the administrative expression of formal rationality) in the modern capitalist factory and the modern nation-state. For the impersonal regulation of human conduct according to fixed rules and regulations was leading to what Levine (1981, p.16) calls 'situational unfreedom', that is, it was increasingly delimiting the chances available to the capitalist entrepreneur and the political leader to act on their own motives.[79] The capitalist entrepreneur and the political leader had less opportunities to exercize genuine acts of responsibility.

That said, it is worthwhile recalling Weber's point (1978a, p.1402; 1994, pp.104-5) that in the face of the inescapable advance of bureaucratization, the tension between the economic bureaucracy of private capitalism and the political bureaucracy of the modern nation-state maintained an element of dynamism in modern society. If this Weberian thesis had some validity at an earlier stage in the development of modern rational capitalism, it is no longer tenable under the conditions of advanced capitalism dominated by large corporations. For it is much more likely, as Bottomore (1984, pp.126-7) reasons, that the economic sector and the state sector will bolster each other under the conditions of advanced capitalism and, thereby, accelerate the process of bureaucratization.[80]

Weber accentuates the impersonal, dehumanizing nature of modern bureaucratic administration by the continual employment of the metaphor of machinery. Weber writes that the performance of each individual worker 'is mathematically measured, each man becomes *a little cog in the machine* and, aware of this, his one preoccupation is whether he can become a bigger cog' (1954, p.96; emphasis added). Similarly, 'the professional bureaucrat is *chained* to his activity in his entire economic and ideological existence. In the great majority of cases he is only *a small cog* in a ceaselessly moving mechanism which prescribes to him an essentially fixed route of march' (Weber 1978a, p.988; emphasis added). Weber, further, states that 'there is nothing, no machinery in the world, which works so precisely as does this *human machine*—nor so cheaply' (1954, p.95; emphasis added).[81] It is increasingly impossible for autonomous, self-reliant individuals to emerge in this 'human machine' that is modern bureaucracy. The 'shell of bondage' (Weber 1978a, p.1402) created by the unrelenting march of bureaucratization more and more 'restricts the importance of charisma and of individually differentiated conduct' (Weber 1978a, p.1156). This being the case, Weber's fundamental question is: 'How can one possibly save *any remnants* of "individualist" freedom in any sense?' (1978a, p.1402; emphasis in original).

To begin to answer this question, it is first of all important to appreciate the fact that '"individualist" freedom', in Weber's view, can only be secured 'within' the 'iron cage' (1976a, pp.181-2) that is modern bureaucracy. For the modern bureaucratic apparatus:

...makes 'revolution', in the sense of the forceful creation of entirely new formations of authority, more and more impossible—technically because of its control over the modern means of communication (telegraph etc.), and also because of its increasingly rationalized inner structure. (Weber 1978a, p.988)

The fact that chaos results if the modern bureaucratic apparatus ceases to function reinforces, according to Weber, the 'objective indispensability' (1978a, p.988) of this apparatus. What is more, 'the material fate of the masses' is more and more dependent upon 'the continuous and correct functioning of the ever more bureaucratic organizations of private capitalism ...' (Weber 1978a, p.988).

Owing to the 'objective indispensability' of the 'iron cage' that is modern bureaucracy, some *'remnants* of "individualist" freedom' can only be saved, according to Weber, by an heroic individual opposing the inescapable advance of bureaucratization from 'within' the 'iron cage' itself.[82] The possibilities for '"individualist" freedom' are confined 'within' boundaries determined by the existence of the 'practically indestructible' (Weber 1978a, p.987), modern bureaucratic apparatus.[83] In other words, a 'tragic vision' pervades Weber's political discourse. Gouldner explains that the 'tragic vision' summons men 'to transcend tragedy by *the courageous endurance of the unchangeable*' (1976, p.76; emphasis added). Such transcendence is understood essentially as individual heroism.[84] Individual heroism is the only way of coping with an unalterable fate. Stated otherwise, the tragic *Weltanschauung* reconciles men to 'what is'. It quells any consciousness of 'what may be possible'.

The heroic individual who can oppose the ineluctable onset of bureaucratization 'from inside' the 'iron cage' is the charismatic leader. Weber explains that:

> *Since it is 'extra-ordinary', charismatic authority is sharply opposed to rational, and particularly bureaucratic, authority* ... Bureaucratic authority is specifically rational in the sense of being bound to intellectually analysable rules; while charismatic authority is specifically irrational in the sense of being foreign to all rules ... Within the sphere of its claims, charismatic authority repudiates the past, and is in this sense *a specifically revolutionary force*. (1978a, p.244, emphasis added; see also pp.245, 1115-17)

Charismatic authority is '"extra-ordinary"' in the sense that the charismatic leader (as opposed to the mass of 'ordinary' individuals) possesses a special quality, namely, passionate commitment to a cause/mission/ultimate value. Weber believes that this serving of a cause, this attempt to actualize a value, allows the charismatic leader to retain his autonomy in the face of the bureaucratic leviathan. Being driven by a sense of mission gives the charismatic leader greater 'inner strength' (Weber 1970, p.117). It is Weber's contention that charisma, the most irrational political force, is the only way in which the individual personality can exert influence on the anonymous bureaucratic machine. Charismatic leadership 'in its most potent forms disrupts rational rule...'[85] (Weber 1978a, p.1117). Only irrational charisma can personalize and humanize a society subject to the irreversible onslaught of bureaucratization.[86]

Important ramifications follow from the Weberian thesis that some 'remnants of "individualist" freedom' can be safeguarded within the bureaucratic cage by a charismatic heroic leader serving a certain cause/mission/ultimate value. To begin with, I would argue that Weber's rendering of political freedom is such that domination is the prerequisite for freedom. The paradox of freedom in Weber's political thought is such that the charismatic leader procures his freedom at the expense of the politically inert, disciplined, docile masses. The charismatic leader's dedication to the cause of advancing the 'power-political interests' of the German nation-state presupposes the use of the politically passive masses as a means of obtaining votes and, hence, of rule. This particular leader can attain the freedom to act on his own motives and realize his cause within the 'iron cage' only by subverting the freedom of the mass of ordinary individuals. The precondition for the overinflated autonomy of the charismatic leader is the manipulation and subjugation of the compliant masses.[87] Therefore, Weber's rendition of political freedom is such that rare, charismatic, heroic leaders constitute the sole 'portion of mankind' to be emancipated from 'this supreme mastery of the bureaucratic way of life' (1954, p.97). It is *a priori* impossible for a charismatic leader to liberate himself by assisting in the liberation of the masses. The charismatic leader's sole concern as a value-implementing being is to achieve liberation of the self. He is inwardly responsible only to himself and his own cause. In other words, Weber is expounding an ascetic notion of freedom, freedom understood as an inner quality.

What is darkly ironic is that in addition to the charismatic leader's freedom being contingent upon the use of others (the electoral masses) as a means of political action, his freedom is also dependent upon the utilization of his own self as a tool. It will be recalled that a particular notion of 'personality' underpins Weber's (1975a, pp.191-8) conceptualization of political leadership. A 'personality' can only be constituted by reference to a value. Moreover, this value must be shaped into a purpose and, thereby, translated into means-end rational action. For Weber, only the domination of the 'natural' self (the emotional, irrational self) and its employment as an instrument in the service of an impersonal cause/higher value through the pursuit of a calling/vocation, could create the inwardly free, self-reliant 'personality' to act as a bulwark against the 'human machine' that is modern bureaucracy. Only a 'personality' (i.e., the 'ascetic' self), the product of serving impersonal causes/ultimate values, could confront the modern, bureaucratized, dehumanized world.[88] Viewed in this light, the charismatic leader could only become the autonomous personality required to oppose the unrelenting march of bureaucreatization by the subjugation of his own 'natural' self, and its mobilization in the service of the higher value of the German nation-state. Weber's response, then, to the inexorable onslaught of bureaucratization, and more generally of rationalization, was to recommend a self-depreciating commitment to the ultimate value of the German nation-state on the part of the charismatic leader.

Of paramount importance also is that Weber's understanding of political freedom as the inner freedom of a charismatic heroic leader, supports the fact that he apprehends political freedom in a non-negative way. This is tantamount to saying that he defends a unique German idea of political freedom as freedom within the confines of the state.[89] The positive German conception of political freedom received its classic formulation in Treitschke's article on 'Freedom' in 1861. Treitschke affirms that:

Whoever sees the state as only a means for the ends of the citizens must logically demand ... freedom *from* the state, not freedom *in* the state. (cited in Krieger 1957, p.367; emphasis added)

The distinct Anglo-Saxon idea of political freedom has traditionally been construed in a negative way as personal freedom 'from' interference by the state. Political freedom in the Anglo-Saxon world has always entailed the power of the state being restricted as much as possible.[90] Treitschke, on the other hand, defends a peculiar German concept of freedom as freedom 'in' the state. That is to say, 'inner freedom ... forms the firm basis upon which a free national state will be raised' (cited in Krieger 1957, p.369). The fundamental presupposition underpinning Treitschke's argument, as Krieger (1957, p.368) indicates, was the primary association between the autonomous ideal of personal freedom and the autonomous validity of the state. The citizen's claims for personal freedom 'from' the state were granted by the state itself. This meant, in effect, the incorporation of personal freedom 'into' the German state.[91] In the case of Weber, the absorption of inner freedom into the German state involved the charismatic leader retaining his autonomy by committing himself to the cause/ultimate value of the German nation-state.

The difficulty, though, is that charisma itself undergoes a process of depersonalization and routinization. In this regard, Weber declares that:

In its purest form charismatic authority has a character specifically foreign to everyday routine structures. The social relationships directly involved are strictly personal, based on the validity and practice of charismatic personal qualities. If this is not to remain a purely transitory phenomenon ... it is necessary for the character of charismatic authority to become radically changed. Indeed, in its pure form charismatic authority may be said to exist only in *statu nascendi.* It cannot remain stable, but becomes either traditionalized or rationalized, or a combination of both. (1978a, p.246, emphasis added; see also pp.247-54, 1121-48; 1970, p.125)

The 'paradox of unintended consequences' is such that charismatic authority, personal, emotional, unstable and irrational in character, is inevitably routinized. The principal reason for this transformation, in Weber's view, lies in the fact that charisma is exposed to the conditions of everyday life and to the powers controlling it. This means, in effect, that 'the process of routinization of charisma is in very important respects identical with adaptation to the conditions of the economy, since this is the principal continually operating force in everyday life' (Weber 1978a, p.254). Charisma is inevitably altered 'under the weight of material interests...' (Weber 1978a, p.1120). Weber points out, for instance, that the transition to depersonalized forms of charisma like hereditary charisma or the charisma of office functions, in the main, as 'a means of legitimizing existing or recently acquired powers of control over economic goods' (1978a, p.254).[92]

Owing to the fact, then, that charismatic authority is, on Weber's account, inevitably routinized, I would argue that an inwardly free, charismatic leader cannot in the long term be considered as a viable countervailing force to the irresistible advance of bureaucratization.

In light of the preceding discussion, it is quite clear that Weber simply offers a subjectivist solution to the inescapable advance of bureaucratization. He engages in what Habermas aptly calls *'an existential-individualistic critique of the present age'* (1984a, p.244; emphasis added). Weber does not envisage a new type of society, but a new type of personality with the capacity to achieve his own internal liberation by dint of service to some cause/mission/ultimate value. It is my contention that Weber's equation of political emancipation with decisionist self-assertion in the face of the bureaucratic leviathan is sociologically defunct. The Weberian paradox of political freedom culminates in a radical stratification of people into a few inwardly free, charismatic, heroic, personalities monopolizing the powers of rule in the modern nation-state and the mass of ordinary individuals located below the level of sociological detection except as a means of rule.[93] In sum, the kernel of the problem, as Jacobson contends, is that Weber's idea of political emancipation 'does not account for the possibility (or impossibility) of emancipation at the level of society and its institutions—at a genuinely sociological level' (1976, p.27).[94]

I would, further, urge the view that Weber's reduction of the fundamental problem of political freedom to the existential concerns of a few heroic individuals is, especially, bizarre in the context of the last decades of the twentieth century. If Weber's primary goal in the first decades of the twentieth century was to safeguard some *'remnants* of "individualist" freedom' within the 'iron cage', the crucial issue in the last decades of the twentieth century is the fact that all of mankind is locked into what Haferkamp (1987, p.38) appropriately calls an 'atomic cage'. The political reality of nuclear weapons and the threat of total destruction they entail, demonstrates conclusively the political bankruptcy of Weber's individualist understanding of human freedom. The annihilation of every individual (including, of course, Weber's rare charismatic heroes) is now a real possibility. Weber's free charismatic leaders and the unfree masses now share a common fate. They are all compelled to live in the shadow of atomic destruction.

In this same connection, the contemporary French philosopher, Michel Foucault, astutely reasons that:

For millennia, man remained what he was for Aristotle: a living animal with the additional capacity for a political existence; *modern man is an animal whose politics places his existence as a living being in question.* (1981a, p.143, emphasis added; see also pp.139-45)

The very biological existence of mankind is now at stake. It is a question of what Foucault calls 'biopower'. 'Biopower' concentrates on the 'species body', that is, 'the body imbued with the mechanics of life and serving as the basis of the biological processes...' (1981, p.139).[95] The technology of 'biopower' in the form of nuclear armaments is at present endangering the very biological survival of human civilization.[96]

To be sure, Weber could never have envisaged the development of this totally new terrifying political reality in the first decades of the twentieth century. He assumed that there would be history in the future. Weber refers, for instance, to the 'concern for the *future*, for *those who will come after us*' (1980, p.437, emphasis in original; see also 1970, p.118; 1995, p.110). Similarly, he speaks of 'the sense of our responsibility *before history*' (1980, p.447, emphasis in original; see also 1994, p.75).[97] But, as Roth points out, it is mandatory to develop a new kind of responsibility in the nuclear age, namely a responsibility 'for' history, a responsibility '*for* the very possibility that new generations will be able to live...' (1984, p.508; emphasis in original).

Taking account of the fact that a new kind of responsibility is called for in the nuclear age, it goes without saying that Weber's reduction of the problem of political freedom to the existential concerns of a few heroic charismatic leaders is wholly untenable. Moreover, the fact that these exceptionally rare individuals achieve emancipation at the cost of the emancipation of the mass of people is, in my view, totally unacceptable. Weber's depoliticization of the masses by restricting their role in 'democratic' politics to that of objects of manipulation at the disposal of those rare, heroic, charismatic leaders is, indeed, very serious in an age when all of humanity lives in the shadow of atomic apocalypse. Politics in the nuclear age must be, as Roth (1984, p.509) insists, 'everybody's vocation' rather than just a question of responsible political leadership (as Weber understands it).

In a similar vein, the contemporary German philosopher, Karl-Otto Apel (1978, p.99), observes that for the first time in human history survival is a problem that concerns all of humanity and, therefore, can only be solved collectively. The compelling issue of political freedom and responsibility must be salvaged from the Weberian realm of irrational decisionism. Weber's existential notion of freedom is politically impotent. What is required, according to Apel, is some kind of ethics of collective responsibility. In contrast to Weber's existential ethic of responsibility concerned solely with liberation of the self, it is important, in Apel's view, to develop a collective ethic of responsibility understood as 'the demand for a responsible *care* for the survival of humanity...' (1979, p.338; emphasis added). Moreover, the development of some kind of ethics of collective responsibility would involve the 'communicative mediation of interests and deliberate discussion of world problems' (Apel 1978, p.88).[98]

I would, further, add that the mass of individuals committed to an ethic of collective responsibility would obviously engage in forms of collective action to try and ensure the very survival of human civilization in the nuclear age. Contemporary social movements like the environmental and anti-nuclear movements attest to the vital importance of collective action for human beings trapped in an atomic cage.

Given Weber's rendering of political freedom, the political ineffectiveness of the tragic vision pervading his political discourse must be highlighted. For Weber, the tragic vision reconciles individuals to an essentially unchangeable fate, that is, to 'the *sober fact* of universal bureaucratization...' (1978a, p.1400; emphasis added). Individual heroism on the part of a few charismatic leaders is the only way of coping with this inescapable fate. But the pivotal point (as Weber himself continually stressed) is that the social-scientific analysis of existing economic, social and political conditions of life in any society is historical. That is to say, it is concerned with the temporality of all institutions. The temporality of all institutions, in turn, signifies, I would suggest, that social change cannot be ruled out, no matter how remote it may appear at a particular historical juncture. Viewed in this light, the transformation of the nature of modern bureaucracy always remains a possibility.

If the temporality of all institutions implies the possibility of their transformation, it also means that an orientation to the future is crucial. We cannot afford to remain trapped within Weber's politically ineffective tragic vision, particularly, when the very biological survival of humanity is at stake in the nuclear age. What is required now, I would suggest, is an utopian vision. A consciousness of 'what may be possible' must not be quelled. At bottom, the notion of utopia, as Bauman (1976, p.17) contends, conjures up a vision of a future and better world which is still held to be unfulfilled and requires an extra effort to be brought into existence. This vision of a future and better world is also considered desirable in the sense that it should come about. Furthermore, this vision, as Bauman continues, promotes criticism of the existing society. And, finally, championing an utopian vision involves an element of risk in the sense that a vision of the future cannot come into being unless fostered by planned collective action.

The idea of a future and better world (of the 'not-yet') built into the utopian vision is not a mere ideal which is, after all, the ideal of just anyone. Neither does this idea of the future appertain to the exploration of unreal human possibilities. Rather, a consciousness of 'what may be possible' in a future society must be drawn from and rooted in the present social reality. Outlining future possibilities involves extrapolating from objective tendencies already present in contemporary society. However, such an extrapolation must not be confused with the projection of particular forms of life. On this account, Habermas reasons that:

> ...the only utopian perspectives in social theory which we can straightforwardly maintain are of a procedural nature. For the utopian lineaments of any future emancipated society can be no more than *necessary general conditions* of it. They cannot be in the nature of a design for a form of life. (Habermas 1986b, p.212; emphasis added)

It is not the task of the social theorist to determine what the 'content' of a future and better world 'will be'. It is in this sense that Habermas insists on making '*a*

256

clean conceptual cut between utopian perspectives in general and the projection of particular forms of life' (1986b, p.213; emphasis added). For example, the socialist vision basically refers to the 'general conditions' requisite for the creation of a socialist society rather than providing a blueprint for the institutionalization of socialist principles of organization as such. Indeed, Marx and Engels did not wish to go beyond predictions of the downfall of capitalism. They did not deliberate on the specific details of the organization of a future society, non-capitalist in character.

Of particular relevance in the present context also is that projections of 'what may be possible' in a future society are more than just extrapolations from objective tendencies already present in social reality. These projections also involve, as Marković (1974, p.212) maintains, an utopian component in the sense of a *"'Seins-tranzcendente'"* and *"'Seins-sprengende'"* orientation. That is to say, commitment to fundamental values like social justice, equality, freedom and individual autonomy cannot be legitimized simply by having recourse to scientific (positive) knowledge. The realization of these values cannot be ultimately guaranteed. There is always an element of risk involved in the effort to create a better world in the future.[99] This being so, the indiscriminate merger of an utopian vision (reflection) and praxis (practical commitment) perverts both. The utopian vision does not have the capacity to legitimize 'what is to be done'. Put another way, a consciousness of the general conditions indispensable for the creation of an emancipated society in the future, does not prejudge the future action of those concerned.[100]

Another salient point is that in contrast to the Weberian tragic vision which reconciles individuals to an essentially unchangeable fate, the utopian consciousness relativizes the present and, thereby, fosters criticism of existing society. The utopian consciousness can envisage a future with different possibilities. Social reality is not synonymous with what is. And of course, the utopian consciousness has a normative dimension in the sense of a model of what ought to be. It summons individuals to transcend existing social conditions by appropriate collective action to bring about what should be.

In light of the discussion of Weber's treatment of the unequal distribution of political power (i.e., 'powers of rule') within the confines of the German nation-state in this chapter, it is quite clear that Weber's principal interest always remained the question of responsible political leadership. The most responsible political leader, on Weber's reading, is the one most passionately committed to promoting the 'power-political interests' of the German nation-state. Weber insists that the responsible political leader should not make material interests the cause of politics. Rather, the onus is on this leader to secure the predominance of 'the political' over 'the economic'. Hence, Weber evaluates forms of government like parliamentary democracy and plebiscitary leadership democracy primarily in terms of whether they allow men with leadership capacities to emerge. Similarly, Weber regards the modern democratic party in a parliamentary democracy, in the main, as a political organization for the selection and training of responsible political leaders. Furthermore, Weber's voluntaristic overestimation of the individual suffuses his political discourse. For Weber can only apprehend an individual personality performing great political acts. Political action of a collective nature in the German nation-state cannot be conceptualized within the Weberian action schema. It is not possible to envisage a group of political leaders (i.e., a political elite) acting together. And of course, the idea of a group of subordinate individuals acting in concert to defend their political interests (whatever they might be), or to resist the rule of an individual political leader or a political elite, cannot be formulated within a Weberian action framework. For the electoral masses in modern 'democratic' politics are hidden from Weber's sociological gaze except as a means of securing votes and, thereby, of rule. Weber's ruler-centric pattern of thinking leads to the depoliticization of the mass of people within the confines of the German nation-state. The other fundamental problem associated with Weber's study of the unequal distribution of 'powers of rule', bears on his rendition of political emancipation. It is only a few responsible charismatic leaders, by reason of their passionate devotion to a cause/mission/higher value, who can retain their autonomy in the face of the bureaucratic leviathan. The paradox of freedom in Weber's political thought is such that only the inner freedom of a few charismatic leaders within the confines of the bureaucratic nation-state is secured by subverting the freedom of the politically inert masses.

Notes

1   It is important to remember that Weber's (1978a, p.286) proposed Sociology of the State was never written.
2   But Weber confuses the situation when he says that it is best to define the state 'in terms appropriate to the modern type of state but at the same time, in terms which abstract from the values of the present day, since these are particularly subject to change' (1978a, p.56). The difficulty is that this procedure would diminish the differences between the modern state and other types of state.
3   The emergence of the modern state characterized by its monopoly of the legitimate use of violence within a given territory, presupposed the earlier separation of 'society' and 'state'. The emancipation of 'civil society' was first achieved in England on the basis of the revolution of 1688. Accordingly, 'civil society' became a consciously entertained theme in the eighteenth century during the reign of parliamentary absolutism resting on capitalist interests. The moral philosophers of the Scottish Enlightenment (i.e., Adam Smith, Adam Ferguson and John Millar) thematized the new and autonomous sphere of 'the social'. The separation of 'civil society' from the

'body politic' meant that 'the social' was conceptualized as that sphere which is constituted and held together by the production, distribution and consumption of goods as well as the organization of social labour. In other words, the emergence of 'civil society' in the eighteenth century was synonymous with the emergence of 'economic society'. (see, e.g., Therborn 1980a, pp.72-5, 115-44, 343-53; Polanyi 1944, pp.111-29).

Even though the separation of 'civil society' from the 'state' occurred in the eighteenth century, the 'state'/'society'distinction, as Poggi (1978, p.120) observes, ultimately originated in the gradual disengagement of the Western state from the Church and Christianity.

4   See also Parkin 1982, p.73.

5   Elias (1982) develops an interesting argument concerning the historical process that led towards the centralization and monopolization of the use of violence by the modern state. He declares that: '*the hour of the strong central authority within a highly differentiated society strikes when the ambivalence of interests of the most important functional groups grows so large, and power is distributed so evenly between them, that there can be neither a decisive compromise nor a decisive conflict between them*' (1982, p.171; emphasis in original). The conflict, for example, between the bourgeois groups and aristocratic groups went through an historical phase prior to the French revolution of 1789, when both groups balanced each other out in political power. Since neither group could completely dominate 'the other', they had to 'leave to a central ruler all the decisions that they cannot bring about themselves' (Elias 1982, p.180). The conflict between the aristocracy and the bourgeoisie was a major source of the king's power in the age of absolutism. At bottom, then, the kernel of Elias' argument is that the power of the central authority increases when none of the competing groups in a society can attain preponderance. The central authority has to intervene to establish order.

Cf. also Giddens (1985) for a meticulous analysis of the modern nation-state as the purveyor of violence.

6   See Roth 1963, pp.147-8.

7   On this score, it is worthwhile noting Weber's point that the political passivity of the German population was also due to the influence of Lutheranism in German society. Within the Lutheran tradition the onus is on the secular authority, whose sphere is not influenced by the axioms of religion, to determine, for example, whether political wars are just or unjust. The individual subject is called upon to obey the secular authority in all matters that 'do not destroy his relationship to God' (Weber 1978a, p.596; see also 1970, p.124). Weber also claims that the political passivity of the German population was related to 'that internalized devotion to authority which has remained an almost ineradicable legacy of unrestrained patrimonial rule in Germany... (1978a, p.1108). Cf. also Hahn 1995, pp.27-55.

8   In this same connection, Weber writes that: 'the State itself, in the sense of a political association with a rational, written constitution, rationally ordained law, and an administration bound to rational rules or laws, administered by trained officials, is known, in this combination of characteristics, *only in the Occident*, despite all other approaches to it' (1976a, pp.16-17, emphasis added; see also 1981b, pp.338-43).

9   See also Habermas 1984a, pp.254-71; Poggi 1978, pp.104-7; Gronow 1988, pp.321-5; Bendix 1966, pp.417-23.

10 The term, 'authoritarian legalism', is borrowed from Habermas. Habermas (1985, pp.95-116) coins this term in his discussion of civil disobedience in the democratic-constitutional state.

11 See also Poggi 1978, p.105; Grafstein 1981, p.469; Turner 1982, p.374; Barbalet 1986a, p.13.

12 It is interesting to note that Weber's grounding of the legitimacy of the modern state in sheer legality represents a continuation of the *Rechtsstaat* tradition in Germany. The *Rechtsstaat* doctrine was the outcome of the events that occurred in Germany between 1815 and 1830. Its basic function in German political thought was, as Krieger (1957, p.252) points out, the practical reconciliation of the traditional political authorities (the nobility) with the demands for popular rights (i.e., private, civil and political) on the part of groups like the bourgeoisie. It was the traditional political authorities who carried through the process of liberalization (i.e., permitting to the individual 'rights' apart from the state). After 1870, Rudolf Gneist's particular doctrine of *Rechtsstaat* gave expression to the new legal reality of the Wilhelmine state. The political power of the *Rechtsstaat* was articulated in legal rules. *Recht* became a formal attribute of *Staat*.

13 Cf. also Trubek 1972, p.749; Poggi 1978, pp.104-7.

14 See Turner 1982, pp.367-91; Barbalet 1986a, pp.12-19.

15 See Mommsen 1984, pp.35-67; Beetham 1974, pp.119-50; Smith 1986, pp.27-31.

16 The concept of *Kultur* has, as already adumbrated, a much wider meaning in Weber's epistemological-methodological writings. Weber employs the notion of *Kultur* in these writings to differentiate the 'cultural sciences' from the 'natural sciences'.

17 Elias (1978, pp.3-34) expatiates on the socio-genesis of the concept of *Kultur* in Germany. This concept received its specific German imprint and tenor from the bourgeois intelligentsia. See also Hahn 1995, pp.92-9.

18 Weber also speaks of 'the lasting power-political interests' of the German nation (1980, p.438) and the 'nation's power' (1980, pp.439, 442). In this same connection, Marianne Weber indicates that Max Weber 'regarded the state only as the framework of the *nation*...' (1988, p.587; emphasis in original).

19 In contrast to Weber's understanding of the German 'nation' as a tool employed by the modern state to legitimize its power-position, Ehmke

observes that 'in the context of European history the concept of "nation" originally had an enlightening, progressive significance' (1984, p.328). 'Liberty', 'equality' and 'fraternity' were built into the idea of the French 'nation' that emerged in the course of the 1789 revolution. The emergence of nationhood in former colonies like India and Ireland was inextricably intertwined with the notion of liberation.

20 Collins (1986b, pp.145-66), in particular, extends Weber's point that a military theory of imperialism is an integral component of a theory of domestic legitimacy.

21 In this respect, it is interesting to refer to Weber's ruler-centric observation that the support of the masses is, especially, consolidated in the case of war—because the masses 'become conscious of the significance of national power. Then it emerges that the national state rests on deep and elemental psychological foundations within the broad economically subordinate strata of the nation...' (1980, p.442).

22 Weber perspicaciously sums up the reactions of various groups within the modern state to defeat in war when he avers that: 'In case of a lost war, the *monarch* has to fear for his throne; *republican power-holders* and groups having vested interests in a republican constitution have to fear their own victorious general. The majority of the *propertied bourgeoisie* have to fear economic loss from the brakes being placed upon business as usual ... The "*masses*" as such, at least in their subjective conception and in the extreme case, have nothing concrete to lose but their lives' (1978a, p.921; emphasis added).

23 Two fundamental sociological approaches to the study of the modern state are at issue here. The Weberian procedure concentrates on establishing 'who' controls the 'compulsory political organization' that is the modern state. Elite theorists like Mills (1959) and Domhoff (1967, 1979) are located within this Weberian tradition. The classic Marxist method, on the other hand, examines particular 'forms' of state (e.g., the capitalist state). The state is defined not only in terms of the 'means' at its disposal (i.e., the monopoly of violence), but in terms of the 'ends' it pursues (e.g., class domination). See, e.g., Wright (1974-1975, pp.69-108) who compares Weber's and Lenin's respective concepts of the modern state.

24 On this score, it is important to recall Weber's point that 'big capitalist interests', in any case, favour monocracy, that is, a bureaucratic organization at the top of which is a single individual rather than a group of individuals (i.e., a collegial body). The 'big capitalist interests' prefer monocracy because, in their view, 'the monocratic chief is more open to personal influence and is more easily swayed, thus making it more readily possible to influence the administration of justice and other governmental activity in favor of such powerful interests. This is also in accord with German experience' (Weber 1978a, pp.283-4).

25 The German historian, Eckart Kehr (who died in 1933), was deeply influenced by Weber's insistence on the importance of *Sammlungspolitik* for an understanding of the politically and economically dominant interest groups in the Wilhelmine state. The thesis of the *Sammlungspolitik* became influential again in the study of the Wilhelmine state in West German historiography through the 'Kehr-revival' in the 1960s and 1970s. See, esp., Eley (1978, pp.737-50) for an assessment of the thesis of *Sammlungspolitik*.

Cf. also Tribe's (1983, pp.181-226) interesting discussion of the importance of the Prussian agricultural problem for German politics.

26 In this context, Marianne Weber makes the pertinent point that her husband suspected all political metaphysics as a means by which privileged groups (e.g., the Junkers) defended themselves against a redistribution of the spheres of power. Indeed, she goes so far as to say that Weber in this respect 'shared Karl Marx's conception of the state and its ideology' (1988, p.587).

27 See Nicholson (1984, pp.33-45) who apprehends politics in a similar manner.

28 See also Smith 1986, p.48.

29 Cf. also Stark 1968, pp.380-92; Schluchter 1981, pp.58-9; Levine 1981, p.20.

30 For a critical appraizal of Weber's ideal-type of personality, see, e.g., Brubaker 1984, pp.91-8; Mommsen 1965, pp.23-45; Sica 1990, pp.131-68; Portis 1978, pp.113-20; Portis 1986; Bologh 1990; Goldman 1991.

31 Expressed another way, the responsible political leader is committed to what Weber calls 'the "heroic" ethic, which imposes on men demands of principle to which they are generally *not* able to do justice, except at the high points of their lives, but which serve as signposts pointing the way for man's endless *striving*' (1978b, p.385; emphasis in original). The mass of 'ordinary' individuals, on the other hand, champion what Weber refers to as 'the "ethic of the mean", which is content to accept man's everyday "nature" as setting a maximum for the demands which can be made' (1978b, pp.385-6).

32 There is an enormous amount of literature available on Weber's concept of charisma. See, e.g., Wolpe 1968, pp.305-18; Friedland 1964, pp.18-26; Spencer 1973, pp.341-54; Bensman and Givant 1975, pp.570-614; Dow 1969, pp.306-18; Dow 1978, pp.83-93; Sennett 1978, pp.271-7.

33 In fact, Weber contends that personal responsibility 'is the lifeblood of the politician as well as of the entrepreneur' (1978a, p.1404).

34 The Prussian administration served as a model for Weber's construction of the 'individual' ideal-type of modern bureaucracy.

35 As a matter of fact, Weber differentiates two ideal-types of official: 'political' and 'administrative'. 'Political' officials can be identified by the fact 'that they can be transferred any time at will, that they can be dismissed, or at least temporarily withdrawn' (1970, p.90). The

'administrative' official, on the other hand, 'should engage in impartial "administration"' (1970, p.95).

36   See also Blum 1959, pp.1-20.

37   Cf. also Wright 1974-1975, pp.101-2; Bottomore 1984, pp.123-34; Mommsen 1984, pp.35-67; Aron 1971, pp.83-100.

38   If an advocate of the 'ethic of ultimate ends' is considered politically 'irresponsible' by Weber, this, of course, does not mean that this particular ethic is identical with 'irresponsibility' in every sense (see Weber 1970, p.120).

39   Similarly Giddens (1985) stipulates that the tactics of survival in the atomic age point to the prevention of warfare involving nuclear armaments.

Interestingly enough, Sharp (1964, pp.311-13) expounds a 'politics of nonviolent action'. He understands nonviolent action as 'a technique by which people who reject passivity and submission, and who see struggle as essential, can wage their conflict without violence' (1973, p.64). In opposition to Weber, Sharp maintains that non-violent means of political action exist which can generate the power to effectively influence political events. This is tantamount to saying that non-violent political action can be 'responsible' in Weber's terms. For example, the downfall of entrenched Communist regimes throughout Eastern Europe in 1989 has clearly demonstrated the political viability of non-violent action. The non-violent means of political action employed by social movements like Civic Forum generated the power to 'effectively' influence political events.

40   In his study of Ancient Judaism, Weber (1952) likewise expatiates on the prophet Jeremiah's passionate devotion to the 'cause' of Yahweh.

41   In this regard, it is important to note that Weber (1970, pp.84-6; 1978a, pp.1447-48) identifies two ideal-types of professional politician: those who live materially 'off' a political party and other political activities, and those who live 'for' politics, having independent economic means. Interestingly enough, Gunlicks (1978, pp.498-500) suggests that Weber also includes a 'part-time politician' in his typology of politicians.

42   Weber alleges that 'only in the realm of private capitalism is there today anything approaching a selection of men with leadership talents' (1978a, p.1413). The capitalist entrepreneur 'at the top' of the bureaucratic organization of the modern factory is such a 'leader'.

43   Weber (1980, p.446) was concerned, in particular, with strengthening the German nation-state's 'external' position as a world power. Hence, his interest in the promotion of both military imperialism and imperialist capitalism.

44   Habermas also comments on the German bourgeoisie's 'unpolitical past'. He argues that the slow emergence of a political consciousness among the German bourgeoisie was related to the fact that a bourgeois public sphere arose belatedly in Germany and, even then, only to a limited degree. However, the bourgeois public sphere was well established in the

Anglo-Saxon countries. This particular public sphere evolved into an institution between 'state' and 'society' (see Habermas 1974c, pp.49-55). It was comprised of '"private individuals" who were excluded from public authority, because they held no office' (Habermas 1974c, p.51). These private individuals (e.g., capitalist entrepreneurs, the bourgeois intelligentsia) assembled in a public body to engage in rational public discussion. The principal goal of these 'private individuals' was the 'supervision' of the 'public authority' (the state). The bourgeoisie, in particular, demanded that all political proceedings be made public. Cf. also Habermas 1992.

45 Weber 'also designates as parties the ancient and medieval ones, despite the fact that they differ basically from modern parties' (1978a, p.939).

46 In view of the fact that Weber's idea of democracy has been subject to a meticulous examination in the secondary literature, the following discussion will be very brief. See, e.g., Mommsen 1984; Beetham 1974; Eden 1983; Wright 1974-1975, pp.69-108; Falk 1935, pp.373-93; Bottomore 1984, pp.123-35; Kilker 1984, pp.55-65; Prager 1981, pp.918-50; Cohen 1985, pp.274-99; Baehr 1988, pp.149-64; Giddens, 1972.

47 In a somewhat similar vein, Schumpeter (1976, pp.269-302) apprehends modern democracy as a mere technical apparatus for the selection of political leaders. More pointedly, he understands modern democracy as a social instititution akin to that of the modern capitalist market in which various politicians compete for the votes of the electorate.

48 In like manner, Marianne Weber contends that, for Weber, 'the *nation* and its future in the world "towered" over all questions of the form of government...' (1988, p.585; emphasis in original).

In this same connection, it is important to remember that although Weber is primarily interested in a strong parliament as a 'recruiting ground for leaders' (1978a, p.1411) to advance the interests of national power, he also calls attention to other important functions of such a parliament. Weber stipulates, for example, that a 'powerful *working* parliament' contains built-in mechanisms of accountability in the sense that 'the politician and, above all, the party leader who is rising to public power is exposed to public scrutiny through the criticism of opponents and competitors and can be certain that, in the struggle against him, the motives and means of his ascendancy will be utterly publicized' (1978a, p.1450). Furthermore, Weber affirms that 'a working parliament ... is one which supervises the administration by continuously sharing its work' (1978a, p.1416). A 'working parliament' controls the state bureaucracy, in particular, through the investigations carried out by parliamentary committees.

49 Toennies (1967, p.12) likewise states that parties are formed by virtue of a 'free decision' on the part of individuals.

50 Weber observes that 'there is a *formal* similarity between the party system and the system of capitalistic enterprise which rests on the recruitment of

formally free labor' (1978a, p.288; emphasis in original). However, this similarity is, in my view, irrelevant in the 'concrete' situation. For whereas the wage-labourer is 'in reality' compelled to sell his labour-power on the capitalist market in order to simply survive, the individual citizen, for instance, in the democratic-constitutional state is not forced to join a political party.

51 It goes without saying that modern democratic parties, on Weber's interpretation, are not interested in overthrowing the modern nation-state.

52 Weber, further, argues that in a non-parliamentary system like the Wilhelmine, monarchic-constitutional state, political parties did not control the patronage of the top state-offices. However, the most influential parties were usually able to pressure the government bureaucracy into giving jobs to their followers. Such parties exercized what Weber calls '"subaltern"-patronage' (1978a, p.1398).

53 In a similar vein, Michels (1915) in his study of the Social Democrats in Imperial Germany observed that the struggle carried on by the socialists against the bourgeois parties was no longer a question of 'principle', but merely one of 'competition'. The German Social Democrats simply became the rivals of the bourgeois parties for the conquest of state-offices.

54 See also Wild 1978a, p.21; Barbalet 1980, p.417, note 7; Burger 1985, p.15.

55 Weber is not strictly correct, then, to describe parties as 'phenomena of the distribution of power within a community' (1978a, p.927).

56 On this score, it is also worthwhile noting Calvert's point that the apprehension of power as such as a political phenomenon can only be fully understood in the context of American society. Calvert observes that in the United States 'the nature of political power was essentially separable from that of the economic organization of society in a way that it was not in the older unitary states of Europe' (1982, p.107). The geographical size of the United States, the federal system of government, and the association of political activity with the urban environment combined, according to Calvert, 'to separate in the minds of American writers the concept of power from the concept of class or status' (ibid.). Party was deemed the fundamental instrument for the organization of political power, whereas class and status could only exert political influence through party. The end-result was that the notion of party was assimilated directly to the concept of political power as one of the three dimensions of social stratification. Cf. also Pease et al. (1970, pp.127-37) for a discussion of ideological currents in American stratification literature.

Mokken and Stokman (1976, p.47), furthermore, call attention to the fact that the identification of power as such as a political phenomenon has been prevalent among American political scientists since the beginning of the Chicago School of political science in the thirties.

57   Admittedly, the categorization of human individuals in terms of 'rulers' and 'ruled' is not peculiar to the modern nation-state. But I am primarily interested in Weber's understanding of the unequal distribution of 'powers of rule' in the German nation-state in this chapter.

58   Weber was strongly influenced by Ostrogorski's (1902) monumental study on *Democracy and the Organization of Political Parties.* Ostrogorski analyzed the emergence of modern party organization in England and the United States. He demonstrated in a meticulous fashion how mass suffrage and industrialization led to the establishment of party machines mobilizing the masses in a quasi-military manner.

59   Michels' 'iron law of oligarchy' maintains that all large-scale bureaucracies inevitably develop oligarchic controls. This creates a serious dilemma for democratic-socialist parties. The stated goal of such parties is the liberation of the masses. The crux of the problem, though, is that the party leaders tend to serve their own interests through skill monopoly, the control of the means of communication and so on.

60   In a similar vien, Schumpeter writes that 'party and machine politicians are simply the response to the fact that the electoral mass is incapable of action other than a stampede...' (1976, p.283).

61   Of course, the preceding comments on the ambivalence surrounding Weber's understanding of the party bureaucracy also apply to private officialdom usurping the legitimate authority of the capitalist entrepreneur in the modern factory.

62   On this score, Michels (1915, p.16) makes the interesting observation that no matter how much political parties may be founded upon narrow class interests, they usually prefer to portray an image of themselves as co-operating with all the citizens of the modern state. Michels, further, points out that it was only socialist leaders who sometimes declared that their party was a specifically class party.

63   However, Weber (1978a, pp.1455-57) had earlier in a 1917 article discussed the limitations of the plebiscite itself as a means of election and legislation.

64   This quotation from Weber appears in the earlier Part II of *Economy and Society* which was written between 1910 and 1914.

65   But Weber argues, as already shown, that even an 'election' in a mass democracy does not involve a 'real' choice between candidates. That is to say, 'normal "elections", too, can only be a decision between several candidates who have been screened before being offered to the voters' (Weber 1978a, p.1129).

66   In his sociology of religion, Weber likewise underlines the fact that the masses by themselves are culturally inert. He alleges, for example, that 'by themselves, the masses ... have everywhere remained engulfed in the massive and archaic growth of magic—unless a prophecy that holds out specific

promises has swept them into a religious movement of an ethical character' (1970, p.277).

67 Michels likewise maintains that 'the incompetence of the masses is almost universal throughout the domains of political life, and this constitutes the most solid foundation of the power of the leaders' (1915, p.86).

68 Although contemporary elitists do not share Weber's ideological commitment to the treatment of the masses as a 'means' of rule, the difficulty is that they are obsessed with the study of what they call the 'governing elite' at the expense of any examination of the masses. Elitists contend that elites and interaction among them comprise the focal point for the analysis of political conduct. Elite theory is, in the main, concerned with the tendency for political power to devolve into small, well-organized elite groups.

69 Interestingly enough, Weber also maintains that 'the dictatorship of the proletariat for the purpose of carrying out the nationalization of industry requires an individual "dictator" with the confidence of the masses' (1978a, p.278; see also 1986, p.129).

70 It is noteworthy that in the course of his discussion of 'Bourgeois Democracy in Russia' (1995, pp.41-147), Weber writes that 'the situation of Russia "cries out", it is true, for a "statesman"...' (p.107; see also p.231).

71 In this sense, Weber's position differs markedly from the sociological theories of elites expounded by classic elitists like Pareto (1968) and Mosca (1939). The notion of a great leader did not play an important role in their theories.

72 See Midgley 1983, p.153; Bottomore 1984, p.132; Wolpe 1968, p.312; Mommsen 1984, p.424.

73 Cavalli (1987, pp.317-33) in his discussion of 'Charisma and Twentieth-Century Politics', makes a distinction between 'plebiscitary democracy' and 'dictatorship'/'tyranny'/'charismatic tyranny'. He grounds this differentiation in the quality of the 'acknowledgement' given by the masses to a political leader. For Cavalli, 'plebiscitary democracy' involves what he calls 'a free dialectic between leader's performance (success, in cultural terms) and acknowledgement (personal trust)' (1987, p.326). In the case of 'dictatorship'/'tyranny'/'charismatic legitimacy', on the other hand, the masses are manipulated in plebiscites.

74 Cohen (1985, pp.284-95) also observes that Weber defines subordinate groupings from a position of advantage and control.

75 It is worthwhile noting that Michels and Weber assess the problem of political leadership from different standpoints. Michels' (1915) key concern is how to control the elected leaders' propensity to perpetuate their own vested interests at the expense of the electoral masses. Weber, on the other hand, is primarily interested in the establishment of systems of government (e.g., parliamentary democracy and plebiscitary democracy) conducive to the emergence of responsible political leaders. In this light, the fate of the

politically passive masses is not an issue for Weber. Cf. Beetham (1981, pp.81-99), Mommsen (1981, pp.100-116) and Scaff (1981, pp.1269-86) for a comparison of Michels and Weber.

76 Cf. Struve (1973) for an exemplary study of elitism in bourgeois political thought in Germany between 1890 and 1933.

77 "'Churches" and "Sects'" appeared in a revised form in *Christliche Welt* in June 1906. The text translated by Loader (1985, pp.7-13) is the second, most complete version. See also Loader and Alexander 1985, pp.1-6; Harrison 1960, pp.232-7.

78 In contrast to Weber's thesis of increasing bureaucratization and disenchantment in the modern Occident, the early Frankfurt School of the 1930s expounded the thesis of growing unreason. Modern Western society was undergoing a process of 'remystification' rather than 'disenchantment'. Adorno and Horkheimer (1979) in the *Dialectic of Enlightenment* argued that the process of technical rationalization in modern Western society was, in fact, inculcating 'irrationality' throughout the society. For example, the spread of fascism and other irrational ideologies attested to this proliferation of mass irrationality.

79 Weber maintains that the capitalist entrepreneur 'is the only type who has been able to maintain at least relative immunity from subjection to the control of rational bureaucratic knowledge' (1978a, p.225). He has been able to maintain 'relative' rather than 'absolute' immunity because he is, after all, also dependent upon the bureaucratic organization of the modern factory to attain his goal, profit.

80 If the process of bureaucratization (i.e., formal rationality) contributes to a loss of freedom for the capitalist entrepreneur in the modern factory and for the political leader in the modern nation-state, this is not to say that formal rationality circumscribes individual freedom in all spheres. Weber asserts, for example, that: 'Juridical formalism enables the legal system to operate like a technically rational machine. Thus it guarantees to individuals and groups within the system a relative maximum of freedom, and greatly increases for them the possibility of predicting the legal consequences of their actions. Procedure becomes a specific type of pacified contest, bound to fixed and inviolable "rules of the game"' (1978a, p.811). The establishment of a formally rational juridical system, for instance, guarantees the individual a 'relative maximum of freedom' in the form of 'rights' (see Weber 1978a, pp.666-8).

Another point which bears mentioning here is that rational intellectualism (i.e., conceptual rationality), on Weber's reading (1970, p.139), enhances individual freedom in the sense that it liberates the individual from the fetters of mysterious, incalculable forces. On this account, Alexander (1987, pp.187-92) comments on the internal connection between rationalization and individuation in Weber's thought.

81 In addition to 'cogs', Weber constantly uses other machine metaphors like: 'switchmen' and 'tracks' (see, e.g., 1970, p.280) and 'iron cage' (see, e.g., 1976a, pp.181-2; 1978b, p.281). Cf. Tiryakian (1981, pp.27-33) for a discussion of the source of Weber's use of the 'iron cage' metaphor. See also Turner 1982, pp.84-7; Baum 1977, pp.309-30; Kent 1983, pp.297-320.

Interestingly enough, Heidegger (1978, pp.287-317) also appealed to an image similar to Weber's image of being enclosed in an 'iron cage', when he speaks of modern technology in terms of 'enframing' (*Gestell*). For Heidegger, modern technology demands that all beings be available for sheer manipulation.

Finally, the machinery metaphor is also central to Michel Foucault's exposition. In *Discipline and Punish* (1979), the analysis of power in modern society is conducted in terms of disciplinary techniques, technologies of power and machines. In like manner, Foucault describes the cell in the prison at Attica as 'a terrifying *animal cage*' (1974, p.157; emphasis added). He, further, describes modern power 'as a machine working by a complex system of *cogs* and *gears*...' (1980, p.158; emphasis added).

82 Weber's advocacy of individualistic opposition 'from within' the 'iron cage' itself belongs within the tradition of Puritan asceticism. The Puritans' concern with 'activities leading to salvation may require participation within the world (or more precisely: *within the institutions of the world but in opposition to them*) on the basis of the religious individual's piety and his qualifications as the elect instrument of god' (Weber 1978a, p.542; emphasis added).

83 Cf. Löwith 1982, pp.52-60; McIntosh 1983, pp.69-109; Swatos 1984, p.210; Greisman 1976, pp.495-507; Simey 1965, pp.45-64; Beetham 1974, pp.268-9; Marcuse 1971, p.138.

84 Cf. Gouldner (1976, pp.67-90) for a comparative analysis of the 'ideologic vision' and the 'tragic vision'. See also Rossides 1972, pp.207-10.

85 See Hearn 1985, pp.74-85.

86 Because Weber only allows for opposition to the irreversible onset of bureaucratization, and more generally of rationalization, from 'within' the 'iron cage', he (1970, pp.323-59) in the *Zwischenbetrachtung* dismisses other responses such as: an absolutist ethics of brotherliness, aestheticism and eroticism. An absolutist ethics of brotherhood is deemed utopian (i.e., politically irresponsible) by Weber, since it promises transcendence 'above' an increasingly rationalized world in the realm of direct and personal human relations. Similarly, Weber considers aestheticism and eroticism as apolitical responses to modern rationalized society. In essence, both asceticism and eroticism are manifestations of the 'subjectivist culture' constitutive of modernity. For Weber, flights into the aesthetic and erotic realms of culture involve a retreat into the 'inwardness' or 'interiority'

(*Innerlichkeit*) of the modern subject. The escape-routes provided by aestheticism and eroticism result in what Weber (1970, p.346) calls 'inner-worldly salvation from rationalization'. See, esp., Scaff (1991, pp.73-120) for an enlightening discussion of Weber's treatment of the cultural responses to rationalization.

87 See Udéhn 1981, pp.132-4; Hennis 1988, pp.177-8.

88 The influence of Puritanism is rather marked in Weber's conceptualization of 'personality' in terms of the 'ascetic' self. The Puritan notion of selfhood pervades *The Protestant Ethic and the Spirit of Capitalism*. Weber writes, for instance, that: 'The Puritan, like every rational type of asceticism, tried to enable a man to maintain and act upon his constant motives, especially those which it taught him itself, *against the emotions*' (1976a, p.119; emphasis added). The conquest of the emotional, irrational self facilitated the Puritan to serve God in a calling/vocation (*Beruf*).

Cf. Goldman's (1991) incisive analysis of Weber's concept of personality.

89 Cf. Factor and Turner 1984, pp.39-54.

90 See, e.g., Mill (1974) for a classic statement of the Anglo-Saxon, liberal rendition of political freedom.

91 In his exemplary study of *The German Idea of Freedom*, Krieger (1957) shows that the political history of Germany from the sixteenth to the twentieth century was characterized by the gradual absorption of the diverse demands for personal freedom into the structure of monarchical government of the various principalities. See also Hahn 1995, pp.56-81.

In this context, it is also necessary to stress the fact that the development of the singular German notion of inner freedom was the product of the political situation of the German bourgeoisie. Essentially, the German bourgeoisie (including the intelligentsia and commercial and professional groups) were debarred from the political realm. The structure of the absolutist society of the various German principalities excluded them from any share in the exercize of political power. Moreover, they were ostracized from the 'society' of the courtly aristocracy. This being the case, the German bourgeois intelligentsia could, as Elias indicates, merely '"think and write" independently; they could not act independently' (1978, p.18). The bourgeois intelligentsia legitimized themselves from the second half of the eighteenth century onwards by having recourse to the purely spiritual. That is to say, the self-image of the German bourgeois intelligentsia manifested itself in scholarship, religion, art, philosophy, the emphasis on the intellectual formation (*Bildung*) of the individual, inner freedom, depth of feeling and so on. This 'inwardly' rich bourgeois tradition was an integral part of Weber's intellectual inheritance.

92 In this respect, critics of Weber like Andreski (1984, p.108) and Friedrich (1961, p.22) make the valid point that Weber uses the term, 'charisma', in a contradictory manner. It makes little sense to speak of 'routinized' charisma

because 'routine' and 'charisma' are contradictory terms. It is rather difficult to comprehend how charisma, antiroutine and personal in character, could be routinized and depersonalized. If Weber wants to remain consistent, he should, as Andreski indicates, state that charisma vanishes at some point and is replaced by other forms of authority.

93   Weber's political bifurcation of people into a few free, heroic, charismatic leaders and the unfree, politically inert masses, finds a striking philosophical parallel in Heidegger's (1962) radical separation of those rare 'authentic' individuals from the falleness of the 'they' who dwell in the everyday world of 'idle talk', 'curiosity' and 'ambiguity'. Being-in-the world is characterized by this great gap separating 'authenticity' and the 'they'. Heidegger has no concept of mediation by means of which the 'they' might rise to the level of 'authenticity'.

94   See also Eisen 1978, pp.66-7.

95   In fact, 'biopower' is, according to Foucault (1981a, pp.135-59), made up of two poles. One of these poles is centred on the body as a 'machine', whereas the other is concentrated on the 'species body'. Interestingly enough, Foucault's study of 'biopower' is characterized by a shift from a microphysical orientation to power (i.e., the study of individualizing power structures like the prison and the clinic) to a macrophysical orientation (i.e., the study of the exercize of power at the level of whole societies and populations).

96   Of course, it is not only the existence of nuclear weapons that threatens the very biological survival of humanity. The intensification of the human exploitation of nature as a result of continual technological expansion is also endangering the very biological existence of mankind through: environmental pollution, depletion of energy resources and so forth.

97   Weber also speaks of 'the participation of our nation in *the responsibility for the future of the earth...*' (cited in Portis 1986, p.123; emphasis added).

98   An evaluation of Apel's advocacy of some kind of ethics of collective responsibility is beyond the scope of this book. All that can be said is that one of Apel's primary goals is to demonstrate rationally the intersubjective validity of such an ethic. See, esp., Apel 1978, pp.81-101; Apel 1979, pp.307-50; Apel 1980, pp.225-300.

99   Interestingly enough, Weber himself alleges in one instance that even if successful political action is always the '"art of the possible"', 'the possible is often reached only by striving to attain the impossible that lies beyond it' (1949, p.24).

100   For an insightful discussion of the difficulties inherent in the attempt to link theory and praxis, see Habermas 1974a, pp.1-4

Conclusion

It has been the principal intention of this book to retrieve the essential form and significance of Weber's conceptualization of social stratification. An internal reconstruction of Weber was undertaken by elucidating the inconsistencies and contradictions in his thought on social stratification, whilst simultaneously conceding its intrinsic unity. This internal *explicatio* necessitated a detailed textual scrutiny of some of Weber's key writings. Textual exegesis was considered a necessary intellectual strategy to unravel the 'analytic structure' underpinning the Weberian thesis that '"classes", "status groups", and "parties" are phenomena of the distribution of power within a community' (1978a, p.927).

Given the detailed textual exposition undertaken in this book, it is worthwhile at this point briefly recapitulating some of the principal issues dealt with in the various chapters.

In order to tease out the 'analytic structure' underlying Weber's conceptualization of power inequalities in various societies, it was necessary in the first chapter to focus attention on Weber's epistemological-methodological principles. What emerged was the importance of Weber's neo-Kantian notion of scientific knowledge. In accordance with the logical principle of value-relevance, Weber makes specific constellations of empirical phenomena like modern capitalism and the modern nation-state the embodiment of the general cultural value, instrumental rationality. Weber's primary interest in *Zweckrationalität* and, concomitantly the process of rationalization, was one of the main themes pervading the book.

The importance of the ideal-typical mode of concept formation for Weber's analysis of power inequalities was also underscored in the first chapter. Weber's study of the famous *triumvirate* of 'class status and party' essentially involves conceptual representations of power inequalities in various societies.

Finally, the ethically neutral nature of Weberian social science was accentuated. Since normative questions cannot be adjudicated rationally, Weberian social science, in effect, denies them. It has been continually emphasized throughout the

272

book that Weber's espousal of value-freedom frustrates a sociologically effective critique of power inequalities in the modern capitalist market-economy, the feudal estate order and the German nation-state.

Weber's credentials as the theorist of social action *par excellence* were critically investigated in the second chapter. It was argued that Weber's line of sociological reasoning is such that the majority of individuals in modern society are not 'actors' at all. They are merely a 'means' of action. Only 'extraordinary' individuals like capitalist entrepreneurs and charismatic leaders can act and attain their freedom by subverting the freedom of 'ordinary' individuals like workers and citizens in modern society. In a similar vein, when evaluated against the backcloth of *Zweckrationalität*, the members of the various estates engaged in habituated forms of activity in a pre-modern (i.e., traditional) society like the feudal social order are deemed to be acting irrationally by Weber. Finally, the restricted notion of 'the social' built into Weber's rendering of action was drawn out in Chapter 2. It became quite clear that Weber's conceptualization of 'the social' in terms of the intertwining of egocentric calculations of utility is constitutive of modern society. The relationship of Weber's *triumvirate* of 'class, status and party' to his conceptualization of social action was one of the main threads woven through the fabric of the discussion in the book.

Key ideal-typical concepts central to Weber's study of power differentials were examined in the third chapter. Even though Weber continually employs the terminology of power, it was demonstrated that the ideal-types of legitimate domination (i.e., legal-rational domination, traditional domination and charismatic domination) represent the 'more precise' concepts used by Weber to analyze classes, status groups and parties as bases of the aggregation of power. Weber's focus on discipline as a crucial prerequisite for the exercize of legitimate domination in both modern and traditional societies was also accentuated.

Finally, three important implications teased out of Weber's sociology of domination, were fundamental to my interpretation of Weber's *triumvirate* of class, status and party in the remainder of the book. To begin with, the ideal-typical nature of the three forms of legitimate domination was highlighted. Although Weber incorporates 'belief in legitimacy' into the ideal-types of legitimate domination, he nevertheless concedes that subordinates in the 'concrete' situation may yield to the imposition of orders for many reasons like fear, the use of force, the manipulation of mass emotionalism and so forth. The second implication drawn out of the typology of legitimate domination pertains to Weber's ruler-centric perspective, namely, that power inequalities are always viewed by Weber from the vantage point of the power holder(s). And it is this elitist perspective, in turn, that denies the possibility of resistance (collective action) 'from below' in a relationship of legal-rational domination in modern society. Simply put, Weber promotes a sociology of domination 'from above' rather than 'from below'.

Once the epistemological-methodological and sociological principles underpinning the Weberian thesis that '"classes", "status groups", and "parties" are phenomena of the distribution of power within a community' had been disentangled, the remainder of the book explored some of Weber's historically oriented studies of structural social inequalities.

Chapter 4 examined Weber's conceptualization of classes as phenomena of the distribution of economic power within the modern capitalist market-economy. It was first of all made clear that Weber considers rational capital accounting as the most fundamental precondition for the existence of modern capitalism in the West. It was, then, argued that one of Weber's main theses is that 'property' and 'lack of property' structure class relations thorough the medium of the modern capitalist market. It was underlined that Weber develops a notion of 'property' understood in terms of legal guaranteed 'powers of control and disposal' over the means of production, human labour services and managerial functions. It is evident from the fourth chapter that the capital/wage-labour relationship always remains one of Weber's principal concerns. For Weber, class power is always relational in the sense that it facilitates control over conditions in which other individuals/groups are implicated. Weber's study of class relations also points to the emergence of the 'new middle class' of salaried possessors of marketable skills distinct from both capitalist entrepreneurs and wage-labourers during the first decades of the twentieth century. And Weber further underscores the central role played by the modern nation-state in upholding the domination of capitalist interests in the market-economy.

Besides the primary contention that 'property' and 'lack of property' structure class relations through the medium of the modern capitalist market, it was established that the class situation for Weber also includes the necessity of complying with the discipline of the modern capitalist factory. In contradistinction to domination by virtue of a constellation of interests in the market-situation, capitalist domination in the factory takes the form of a formally regulated relationship of legal-rational domination.

Finally, the discussion of class action accentuated the fact that it is not possible to conceptualize workers engaging in collective action within the Weberian action schema. For these workers are located below the level of sociological detection except as a means of rational profit-making activity. It is Weber's contention that collective action on the part of capitalist entrepreneurs, on the other hand, merely involves the intermingling of egocentric calculations of utility.

In the context of the discussion of some of Weber's historically oriented studies of structural social inequalities, Chapter 5 explored Weber's understanding of estates as phenomena of the distribution of power within the feudal social order in the West. In order to clarify the focus of this chapter, it was first of all necessary to underscore the fact that Weber gives more than one explanation of what he means by status in his far-flung writings. It was suggested that Weber's rendering of status in terms of social honour is more relevant in the study of pre-modern, traditional societies like the feudal estate order. It was, then, shown that Weber's construction of the ideal-type of Western feudalism is based on the form of landholding and on the relationship in which the vassal stood to his lord.

Concerning the unequal distribution of power in feudal society, Weber's principal thesis, as demonstrated in the fifth chapter, is that the unequal distribution of the primary resource, social honour, is decisive for the formation of estates. The positively privileged feudal knights, in solid possession of social honour, uphold the superiority of their 'being' or 'nature' by living a knightly style of life anchored in tradition. Conversely the negatively privileged peasants lack social honour.

Weber's second thesis relating to the fact that the unequal distribution of social honour in feudal society is usually associated with the unequal distribution of economic resources (primarily, land), was next examined. Weber, in particular, accentuates the fact that the feudal economy (unlike the modern capitalist market-economy) is not organized as a structurally independent sub-system of society. That is to say, non-economic motives determine the nature of the economic system itself. The feudal knighthood and the various occupational estates sought not wealth as such, but the material resources that were compatible with the maintenance and enhancement of their social prestige in the feudal social hierarchy.

Weber's third thesis is that the possession of social honour in the feudal social order is usually linked with a rights-based system of inequality. Feudal rights appear as the various privileges, liberties and immunities that are conferred upon the individual as a member of a given estate. It is in this sense that the members of the knightly estate, the burgher estate and, to a much lesser extent, the peasant estate enjoy private rights rooted in tradition.

Finally, the way in which the members of the various estate groups in the feudal social order collectively engage in traditional action to defend their economic, social and political rights and advantages, was brought to light in the discussion of Weber's treatment of social closure.

The final chapter of the book dealt with Weber's analysis of the unequal distribution of political power (i.e., 'powers of rule') within the confines of the German nation-state. Key issues assessed included: Weber's understanding of the modern state as a ruling organization with a claim to the monopoly of the legitimate use of violence within a given territory, the question of state legitimacy, and the social basis of the Wilhelmine state.

The corresponding type of political action leading to the reproduction of the nation-state was, then, considered. A distinct form of political leadership is built into the Weberian conceptualization of political action. The most responsible political leader is the one most passionately committed to advancing the 'power-political interests' of the German nation-state. Moreover, Weber insists that material interests should not be made the cause of politics. One of the central themes pervading the discussion in the final chapter was the voluntaristic over-estimation of the individual in Weber's rendition of political action. For Weber can only apprehend an individual personality performing great political acts. Political action of a collective nature cannot be formulated within the Weberian action schema. It is not possible to envisage a group of political leaders (i.e., a political elite) acting in concert. What is more, the idea of a group of subordinate individuals (i.e., the electoral masses) acting together to defend their political interests (whatever they might be) or to resist the rule of an individual political leader or a political elite, cannot be conceptualized within a Weberian action framework.

Another major focus of interest in the final chapter was Weber's analysis of the role of the modern democratic party in the German nation-state with a parliamentary-democratic system of government. Although Weber regarded the modern democratic party primarily as a political organization for the selection and training of responsible political leaders, the difficulty (from Weber's standpoint) was that this particular type of party was mainly concerned with procuring material and ideal advantages for its own members. The fact that Weber considers the docile, disciplined, inactive citizens in a parliamentary-democratic nation-state simply as a means of securing votes and, thereby of rule, was also underlined. Weber's elitist line of reasoning leads to the depolitization of the mass of citizens.

Weber became increasingly disillusioned with the parliamentary-democratic politics that he witnessed in the early days of the Weimar republic set up in November 1918. It is in this context that his later advocacy of plebiscitary leadership democracy is discussed. One of the main threads running through this discussion was that Weber's advocacy of plebiscitary leadership democracy points in the direction of political absolutism, that is, political dictatorship. Political opposition 'from below' to a despotic leader has no theoretical foundation in Weber's political thought. In a word, Weber is a proponent of democratic elitism rather than participatory democracy. The electoral masses in modern democratic politics are hidden from Weber's sociological gaze except as a means of gaining votes and, thereby, of rule.

The final issue considered in the course of appraizing Weber's analysis of the unequal distribution of 'powers of rule' within the German nation-state, bears on the notion of political emancipation. The principal contention was that Weber's conceptualization of political emancipation is sociologically defunct. For it is only the inner freedom of a few charismatic leaders within the bureaucratic nation-state that is secured by subverting the freedom of the politically inert electoral masses.

In the light of this overview of the principal issues dealt with in the book, a few final key points need to be reinforced. One of the principal justifications for writing this book is my fundamental belief that interpretative work that takes the texts of a great social thinker like Max Weber as its object of empirical investigation, plays a crucial role in sociological research. Some of the principal goals of such interpretative work include: laying bare the foundations of concepts (including their logic and the various languages in which they have been formulated), uncovering the cultural and historical contexts in which concepts emerged and developed, unravelling the implications of propounding a particular set of concepts, and teasing out authorial intent. Given the textual exposition undertaken in this book, it is rather marked that a whole hidden mass of implicit meanings and presuppositions, historically specific applications, and value-standpoints hold up any particular cluster of concepts. It was this very failure, in my view, to undertake interpretative work grounded in careful textual exegesis that led many American theorists of social stratification to misappropriate Weber's conceptualization of the *triumvirate* of 'class, status and party'.

It should also be clear at this point that contrary to the many books which have been written 'for' Weber, I have engaged in a process of 'deheroizing' Weber throughout this book. It goes without saying that Weber made a major contribution to the comparative, historical analysis of different structures of social inequality. However, he does not treat social inequality as a normative category. His various studies of structures of social inequality simply supply us with 'scientific'/'empirical' ('value-free') knowledge regarding the unequal distribution of power in various societies. His 'scientific' analysis of power inequalities does not take place against the backcloth of normative claims like distributive justice and social equality. In effect, Weber's study of structures of social inequality leaves them intact without any possibility of transcending or going beyond them being envisaged at the level of society and its institutions, that is, at a genuinely sociological level.

In a somewhat similar vein, Weber's restricted understanding of the nature of 'social' action in modern society is such that collective action 'from below' on the part of 'ordinary' individuals like workers and citizens to bring about a more egalitarian, just and humane society cannot be conceived. Weber only conceptualizes collective action 'from above' on the part of 'extraordinary' individuals like capitalist entrepreneurs in modern society. This form of collective action merely entails a rationally motivated adjustment of egocentric calculations of utility, an aggregation of self-seeking interests.

The elitist strand in Weber's sociological thought also distorts his 'scientific' analysis of structures of social inequality. Weber never ceases to conceptualize the exercize of power exclusively from the vantage point of those in authority. He is concerned with the state of play between contending knights, capitalist entrepreneurs, political leaders and so forth. This ruler-centric approach accords little or no significance to the role of underdogs like workers and citizens. For Weber, knights, capitalist entrepreneurs and political leaders command, the underdogs merely obey.

Finally, it is necessary to reiterate the fact that Weber's understanding of classes, status groups and parties as bases of the aggregation of power within society does not constitute a theory of social stratification in the sense of a set of consistent and systematically related statements of universal validity. To the contrary, Weber regarded society as an historical process analyzed by the open-ended nature of concepts. Concepts are inherently historical and must, therefore, be continually criticized and reformulated. Accordingly, Weber's study of structures of social inequality involves an historically oriented analysis of power differentials in various societies. This book has, I would hope, served to demystify much of Weber's contribution to the sociology of social stratification by relocating his analysis of structures of social inequality in the relevant historical and cultural contexts.

One final point is that given Weber's understanding of society as an historical process, he would have advocated the development of a new cluster of intrinsically historical concepts to investigate the new forms of social inequality emerging in contemporary 'late' capitalist societies. With the emergence of new structures of social inequality, it is timely that the massive shadow cast by Weber over the sociology of social stratification should be receding.

Bibliography

Cited works of Weber

Weber, M. (1949), *The Methodology of the Social Sciences*, Shils, E.A. and Finch, H.A. (trs and eds), Free Press, New York.

Weber, M. (1951), *The Religion of China: Confucianism and Taoism*, Gerth, H.H. (trans. and ed.), Free Press, Glencoe, Ill.

Weber, M. (1952), *Ancient Judaism*, Gerth, H.H. and Martindale, D. (trs and eds), Free Press, Glencoe, Ill.

Weber, M. (1954), 'Max Weber on Bureaucratization in 1909', Mayer, J.P. (trans.), in Mayer, J.P., *Max Weber and German Politics: A Study in Political Sociology*, Faber and Faber, London, pp.95-9.

Weber, M. (1958), *The Religion of India: The Sociology of Hinduism and Buddhism*, Gerth, H.H. (trans. and ed.), Free Press, Glencoe, Ill.

Weber, M. (1961), 'The Three Types of Legitimate Rule', Gerth, H.H. (trans.), in Etzioni, A. (ed.), *Complex Organizations*, Holt, Rinehart and Winston, New York, pp.4-14.

Weber, M. (1964), *The Theory of Social and Economic Organization*, Henderson, A.M. (trans.) and Parsons, T. (ed.), Free Press, New York.

Weber, M. (1970), *From Max Weber: Essays in Sociology*, Gerth, H.H. and Mills, C.W. (trs and eds), Routledge and Kegan Paul, London.

Weber, M. (1971a), 'Methodological Introduction for the Survey of the Society for Social Policy Concerning Selection and Adaptation (Choice and Course of Occupation) for the Workers of Major Industrial Enterprises (1908)', Hÿtch, D. (trans.), in Eldridge, J.E.T. (ed.), *Max Weber: The Interpretation of Social Reality*, Michael Joseph, London, pp.103-55.

Weber, M. (1971b), 'The Social Causes of the Decay of Ancient Civilization', Mackauer, C. (trans.), in Eldridge, J.E.T. (ed.), *Max Weber: The Interpretation of Social Reality*, Michael Joseph, London, pp.245-75.

279

Weber, M. (1972), 'Georg Simmel as Sociologist', Levine, D.N. (trans.), *Social Research*, vol. 39, pp.158-63.

Weber, M. (1973a), 'The Power of the State and the Dignity of the Academic Calling in Imperial Germany', Shils, E. (trans.), *Minerva*, vol. XI, no. 4, pp.574-632.

Weber, M. (1973b), 'Max Weber on Church, Sect and Mysticism', Gittleman, J.L. (trans.), *Sociological Analysis*, vol. 34, no. 2, pp.141-9.

Weber, M. (1975a), *Roscher and Knies: The Logical Problems of Historical Economics*, Oakes, G. (trans.), Free Press, New York.

Weber, M. (1975b), 'Marginal Utility Theory and "The Fundamental Law of Psychophysics"', Schneider, C. (trans.), *Social Science Quarterly*, vol. 56, pp.24-36.

Weber, M. (1976a), *The Protestant Ethic and the Spirit of Capitalism*, Parsons, T. (trans.), 2nd edn, Allen and Unwin, London.

Weber, M. (1976b), *The Agrarian Sociology of Ancient Civilizations*, Frank, R.I. (trans.), New Left Books, London.

Weber, M. (1977), *Critique of Stammler*, Oakes, G. (trans.), Free Press, New York.

Weber, M. (1978a), *Economy and Society*, 2 vols, Roth, G. and Wittich, C. (trs and eds), University of California Press, Berkeley.

Weber, M. (1978b), *Selections in Translation*, Matthews, E. (trans.) and Runciman, W.G. (ed.), Cambridge University Press, Cambridge.

Weber, M. (1978c), 'Anticritical Last Word on "The Spirit of Capitalism"', Davis, W.M. (trans.), *American Journal of Sociology*, vol. 83, no. 5, pp.1110-31.

Weber, M. (1980), 'The National State and Economic Policy (Freiburg Address)', Fowkes, B, (trans.), *Economy and Society*, vol. 9, no. 4, pp.428-49.

Weber, M. (1981a), 'Some Categories of Interpretive Sociology', Graber, E.E. (trans.), *The Sociological Quarterly*, vol. 22, pp.151-80.

Weber, M. (1981b), *General Economic History*, Knight, F.H. (trans.), Transaction Books, New Brunswick.

Weber, M. (1983a), 'The Failure of Capitalism in the Ancient World', Frank, R.I. and Andreski, S. (trs), in Andreski, S. (ed.), *Max Weber on Capitalism, Bureaucracy and Religion*, Allen and Unwin, London, pp.30-58.

Weber, M. (1983b), 'The End of Capitalism', Frank, R.I. (trans.), in Andreski, S. (ed.), *Max Weber on Capitalism, Bureaucracy and Religion*, Allen and Unwin, London, pp.158-9.

Weber, M. (1985), '"Churches" and "Sects" in North America: An Ecclesiastical Socio-Political Sketch', Loader, C. (trans.), *Sociological Theory*, vol. 3, no. 1, pp.7-13.

Weber, M. (1986), 'The Reich President', Wells, G.C. (trans.), *Social Research*, vol. 53, no. 1, pp.128-32.

Weber, M. (1989), 'Germany as an Industrial State', Tribe, K. (trans.), in Tribe, K. (ed.), *Reading Weber*, Routledge, London, pp.210-20.

Weber, M. (1994), *Political Writings*, Speirs, R. (trans.) and Lassman, P. and Speirs, R. (eds), Cambridge University Press, Cambridge.

Weber, M. (1995), *The Russian Revolutions*, Wells, G.C. and Baehr, P. (trs and eds), Polity Press, Cambridge.

Secondary works

Aaronovitch, S. (1979), *The Ruling Class*, Greenwood Press, Westport, Connecticut.

Abel, T. (1948), 'The Operation Called *Verstehen*', *American Journal of Sociology*, vol. 54, pp.211-18.

Abel, T. (1967), 'A Reply to Professor Wax', *Sociology and Social Research*, vol. 51, pp.334-6.

Abercrombie, N. and Turner, B.S. (1982), 'The Dominant Ideology Thesis', in Giddens, A. and Held, D. (eds), *Classes, Power, and Conflict: Classical and Contemporary Debates*, Macmillan, London/Basingstoke, pp.396-414.

Abrahamson, M. et al. (1976), *Stratification and Mobility*, Collier-Macmillan, London.

Adorno, T. and Horkheimer, M. (1979), *Dialectic of Enlightenment*, Cumming, J. (trans.), Verso, London.

Albrow, M. (1972), 'Weber on Legitimate Norms and Authority: A Comment on Martin E. Spencer's Account', *The British Journal of Sociology*, vol. 23, pp.483-7.

Albrow, M. (1975), 'Legal Positivism and Bourgeois Materialism: Max Weber's View of the Sociology of Law', *The British Journal of Law and Society*, vol. 2, no. 1, pp.14-31.

Albrow, M. (1987), 'The Application of the Weberian Concept of Rationalization to Contemporary Conditions', in Lash, S. and Whimster, S. (eds), *Max Weber, Rationality and Modernity*, Allen and Unwin, London, pp.164-82.

Albrow, M. (1990), *Max Weber's Construction of Social Theory*, Macmillan, London/Basingstoke.

Alexander, J.C. (1983), *Theoretical Logic in Sociology: The Classical Attempt at Theoretical Synthesis: Max Weber*, Vol. III, Routledge and Kegan Paul, London.

281

Alexander, J.C. (1987), 'The Dialectic of Individuation and Domination: Weber's Rationalization Theory and Beyond', in Lash, S. and Whimster, S. (eds), *Max Weber, Rationality and Modernity*, Allen and Unwin, London, pp.185-206.

Andreski, S. (1984), *Max Weber's Insights and Errors*, Routledge and Kegan Paul, London.

Apel, K.-O. (1978), 'The Conflicts of Our Time and the Problem of Political Ethics', in Dallmayr, F.R. (ed.), *From Contract to Community: Political Theory at the Crossroads*, Marcel Dekker, New York/Basel, pp.81-102.

Apel, K.-O. (1979), 'Types of Rationality Today: The Continuum of Reason between Science and Ethics', in Geraets, T.F. (ed.), *Rationality Today*, University of Ottawa Press, Ottawa, pp.307-50.

Apel, K.-O. (1980), *Towards a Transformation of Philosophy*, Adey, G. and Frisby, D. (trs), Routledge and Kegan Paul, London.

Archer, M.S. and Giner, S. (eds) (1971), *Contemporary Europe: Class, Status and Power*, Weidenfeld and Nicolson, London.

Arendt, H. (1973), *On Revolution*, Penguin, Harmondsworth.

Aron, R. (1962), 'Political Action in the Shadow of Atomic Apocalypse', Klein, R.H. (trans.), in Lasswell, H.D. and Cleveland, H. (eds), *The Ethic of Power*, Conference on Science, Philosophy and Religion in their Relation to the Democratic Way of Life, New York, pp.445-57.

Aron, R. (1970), *Main Currents in Sociological Thought*, Vol. I, Howard, R. and Weaver, H. (trs), Penguin, Harmondsworth.

Aron, R. (1971), 'Max Weber and Power-Politics', in Stammer, O. (ed.), *Max Weber and Sociology Today*, Basil Blackwell, Oxford, pp.83-100.

Ashcraft, R. (1972), 'Marx and Weber on Liberalism as Bourgeois Ideology', *Comparative Studies in Society and History*, vol. 14, no. 2, pp.130-68.

Atkinson, D. (1972), *Orthodox Consensus and Radical Alternative: A Study in Sociological Theory*, Heinemann, London.

Avineri, S. (1974), *Hegel's Theory of the Modern State*, Cambridge University Press, Cambridge.

Baehr, P. (1988), 'Max Weber as a Critic of Bismarck', *European Journal of Sociology*, vol. 29, no. 1, pp.149-64.

Baldus, B. (1979), 'An Alternative Approach to the Study of Power', in Curtis, J.E. and Scott, W.G. (eds), *Social Stratification: Canada*, 2nd edn, Prentice-Hall of Canada Ltd, Scarborough, Ontario, pp.170-90.

Banton, M. (1972), 'Authority', *New Society*, vol. 22, no. 523, pp.86-8.

Barbalet, J.M. (1980), 'Principles of Stratification in Max Weber: An Interpretation and Critique', *The British Journal of Sociology*, vol. 31, no. 3, pp.401-18.

Barbalet, J.M. (1982), 'Social Closure in Class Analysis: A Critique of Parkin', *Sociology*, vol. 16, no. 4, pp.484-97.

Barbalet, J.M. (1985a), 'Power and Resistance', *The British Journal of Sociology*, vol. 36, no. 4, pp.531-48.

Barbalet, J.M. (1985b), 'Class Theory and Earnings Inequality', *Australian and New Zealand Journal of Sociology*, vol. 21, no. 3, pp.327-48.

Barbalet, J.M. (1986a), 'Weber and Marshall on the State', *Politics*, vol. 21, no. 2, pp.12-19.

Barbalet, J.M. (1986b), 'Limitations of Class Theory and the Disappearance of Status: The Problem of the New Middle Class', *Sociology*, vol. 20, no. 4, pp.557-75.

Barbalet, J.M. (1987), 'Power, Structural Resources and Agency', *Current Perspectives in Social Theory*, vol. 8, pp.1-24.

Barbalet, J.M. (1988), *Citizenship: Rights, Struggle and Class Inequality*, Open University Press, Milton Keynes.

Barker, M. (1980), 'Kant as a Problem for Weber', *The British Journal of Sociology*, vol. 31, no. 2, pp.224-45.

Baum, R.C. (1977), 'Beyond the "Iron Cage"', *Sociological Analysis*, vol. 38, no. 4, pp.309-30.

Bauman, Z. (1976), *Socialism*, Allen and Unwin, London.

Bauman, Z. (1982), *Memories of Class: The Pre-History and After-Life of Class*, Routledge and Kegan Paul, London.

Beetham, D. (1974), *Max Weber and the Theory of Modern Politics*, Allen and Unwin, London.

Beetham, D. (1981), 'Michels and His Critics', *European Journal of Sociology*, vol. 22, no. 1, pp.81-99.

Bell, D. (1973), *The Coming of Post-Industrial Society*, Basic Books, New York.

Bendix, R. (1965), 'Max Weber's Sociology Today', *International Social Science Journal*, vol. 17, pp.9-22.

Bendix, R. (1966), *Max Weber: An Intellectual Portrait*, Methuen, London.

Bendix, R. (1974), 'Inequality and Social Structure: A Comparison of Marx and Weber', *American Sociological Review*, vol. 39, no. 2, pp.149-61.

Bendix, R. (1977), *Nation-Building and Citizenship*, University of California Press, London.

Bendix, R. (1984), 'What Max Weber Means to Me', in Glassman, R.M. and Murvar, V. (eds), *Max Weber's Political Sociology: A Pessimistic Vision of a Rationalized World*, Greenwood Press, Westport, Connecticut, pp.13-24.

Bendix, R. and Lipset, S.M. (1967), *Class, Status and Power: Social Stratification in Comparative Perspective*, rev. edn, Routledge and Kegan Paul, London.

Benhabib, S. (1981), 'Rationality and Social Action: Critical Reflections on Weber's Methodological Writings', *The Philosophical Forum*, vol. XII, no. 4, pp.356-74.

Bensman, J. and Givant, M. (1975), 'Charisma and Modernity: The Use and Abuse of a Concept', *Social Research*, vol. 42, no. 4, pp.570-614.

Benton, T. (1981), '"Objective" Interests and the Sociology of Power', *Sociology*, vol. 15, no. 2, pp.161-84.

Berger, P.L. (1973), 'On the Obsolescence of the Concept of Honor', in Berger, P.L. et al. (eds), *The Homeless Mind: Modernization and Consciousness*, 1st edn, Random House, New York, pp.83-96.

Berger, P.L. (1974), 'Modern Identity: Crisis and Continuity', in Ditton, W.S. (ed.), *The Cultural Drama: Modern Identities and Social Ferment*, Smithsonian Institution Press, City of Washington, pp.159-81.

Betts, K. (1986), 'The Conditions of Action, Power and the Problem of Interests', *The Sociological Review*, vol. 34, no. 1, pp.39-64.

Birnbaum, N. (1953), 'Conflicting Interpretations of the Rise of Capitalism: Marx and Weber', *The British Journal of Sociology*, vol. 4, pp.125-41.

Blau, P.M. (1963), 'Critical Remarks on Weber's Theory of Authority', *The American Political Science Review*, vol. 57, no. 2, pp.305-16.

Blau, P.M. (1964), *Exchange and Power in Social Life*, John Wiley and Sons, London.

Blau, P.M. and Duncan, O.D. (1978), *The American Occupational Structure*, Free Press, New York.

Bloch, M. (1961), *Feudal Society*, Manyon, L.A. (trans.), Routledge and Kegan Paul, London.

Blum, F.H. (1959), 'Max Weber: The Man of Politics and the Man Dedicated to Objectivity and Rationality', *Ethics*, vol. 70, pp.1-20.

Bologh, R.W. (1984), 'Max Weber and the Dilemma of Rationality', in Glassman, R.M. and Murvar, V. (eds), *Max Weber's Political Sociology: A Pessimistic Vision of a Rationalized World*, Greenwood Press, Westport, Connecticut, pp.175-86.

Bologh, R.W. (1990), *Love or Greatness: Max Weber and Masculine Thinking*, Unwin and Hyman, London.

Borst, A. (1968), 'Knighthood in the High Middle Ages: Ideal and Reality', in Cheyette, F.L. (ed.), *Lordship and Community in Medieval Europe*, Holt, Rinehart and Winston, New York, pp.180-91.

Boskoff, A. (1971), 'Stratification, Power and Social Change', in Turk, H. and Simpson, R.L. (eds), *Institutions and Social Exchange*, Botts Merrill, Indianapolis, pp.289-308.

Bosl, K. (1968), 'Ruler and Ruled in the German Empire from the Tenth to the Twelth Century', in Cheyette, F.L. (ed.), *Lordship and Community in Medieval Europe*, Holt, Rinehart and Winston, New York, pp.357-75.

Bottomore, T. (1984), 'Max Weber and the Capitalist State', in Bottomore, T. (ed.), *Sociology and Socialism*, Wheatsheaf Books, Brighton, Sussex, pp.123-34.

Bottomore, T. (1985a), 'Max Weber on Capitalism and Rationality', in Bottomore, T. (ed.), *Theories of Modern Capitalism*, Allen and Unwin, London, pp.22-34.

Bottomore, T. (1985b), 'Vote, Shut Up and Obey', *Times Literary Supplement*, 19th April, pp.84-5.

Bourdieu, P. (1977), 'Symbolic Power', in Gleeson, D. (ed.), *Identity and Structure: Issues in the Sociology of Education*, Studies in Education Ltd, Driffield, Nafferton, England, pp.112-19.

Bourdieu, P. (1984), *Distinction: A Social Critique of the Judgement of Taste*, Nice, R. (trans.), Routledge and Kegan Paul, London.

Bourricaud, F. (1981), *The Sociology of Talcott Parsons*, Goldhammer, A. (trans.), University of Chicago Press, Chicago/London.

Brand, A. (1977), 'Interests and the Growth of Knowledge - A Comparison of Weber, Popper and Habermas', *The Netherlands Journal of Sociology*, vol. 13, pp.1-20.

Braude, L. (1964), 'Ethical Neutrality and the Perspective of the Sociologist', *The Sociological Quarterly*, vol. 5, pp.396-9.

Braverman, H. (1974), *Labor and Monopoly Capital: The Degradation of Work in the Twentieth Century*, Monthly Review Press, New York/London.

Brenner, R. (1976), 'Agrarian Class Structure and Economic Development in Pre-Industrial Europe', *Past and Present*, vol. 70, pp.30-75.

Breuer, S. (1982), 'The Illusion of Politics: Politics and Rationalization in Max Weber and George Lukács', *New German Critique*, vol. 26, pp.55-79.

Brewer, J.D. (1989), 'Max Weber and the Royal Irish Constabulary: A Note on Class and Status', *The British Journal of Sociology*, vol. 40, no. 1, pp.82-96.

Briggs, A. (1960), 'The Language of "Class" in Early Nineteenth Century England', in Briggs, A. and Saville, J. (eds), *Essays in Labour History*, Vol. I, Macmillan, London, pp.43-73.

Brown, D. (1976), 'The Problem of *Laissez-Faire* Bias in Weber's Concept of Formal Rationality: A Reply', *Sociological Analysis and Theory*, vol. 6, pp.205-9.

Brown, E.A.R. (1974), 'The Tyranny of a Construct: Feudalism and Historians of Medieval Europe', *American Historical Review*, vol. 79, no. 4, pp.1063-88.

Brubaker, R. (1984), *The Limits of Rationality: An Essay on the Social and Moral Thought of Max Weber*, Allen and Unwin, London.

Brunner, O. (1968), 'Feudalism: The History of a Concept', in Cheyette, F.L. (ed.), *Lordship and Community in Medieval Europe*, Holt, Rinehart and Winston, New York, pp.32-61.

285

Bruun, H.H. (1972), *Science, Values and Politics in Max Weber's Methodology*, Munksgaard, Copenhagen.

Bumke, J. (1982), *The Concept of Knighthood in the Middle Ages*, AMS Press, New York.

Burger, T. (1976), *Max Weber's Theory of Concept Formation: History, Laws and Ideal Types*, Duke University Press, Durham, North Carolina.

Burger, T. (1977a), 'Max Weber's Interpretive Sociology, and the Sense of Historical Science: A Positivistic Conception of *Verstehen'*, *The Sociological Quarterly*, vol. 18, no. 2, pp.165-75.

Burger, T. (1977b), 'Max Weber's Interpretive Sociology, the Understanding of Actions and Motives, and a Weberian View of Man', *Sociological Inquiry*, vol. 47, pp.127-32.

Burger, T. (1985), 'Power and Stratification: Max Weber and Beyond', in Murvar, V. (ed.), *Theory of Liberty, Legitimacy and Power*, Routledge and Kegan Paul, London, pp.11-39.

Burris, V. (1987), 'The Neo-Marxist Synthesis of Marx and Weber on Class', in Wiley, N. (ed.), *The Marx-Weber Debate*, Sage, London, pp.67-90.

Bush, M.L. (1983), *Noble Privilege*, Manchester University Press, Manchester.

Butts, S. (1975), 'Parsons, Weber and the Subjective Point of View', *Sociological Analysis and Theory*, vol. 5, no. 2, pp.185-217.

Calvert, P. (1982), *The Concept of Class: An Historical Introduction*, Hutchinson, London.

Castoriadis, C. (1976-77), 'On the History of the Workers' Movement', *Telos*, no. 30, pp.3-42.

Cavalli, L. (1987), 'Charisma and Twentieth-Century Politics', in Lash, S. and Whimster, S. (eds), *Max Weber, Rationality and Modernity*, Allen and Unwin, London, pp.317-33.

Chinoy, E. (1982), 'Control and Resistance on the Assembly Line', in Giddens, A. and MacKenzie, G. (eds), *Social Class and the Division of Labour*, Cambridge University Press, Cambridge, pp.87-100.

Clarke, S. (1982), *Marx, Marginalism and Modern Sociology: From Adam Smith to Max Weber*, Macmillan, London/Basingstoke.

Clegg, S. (1975), *Power, Rule and Domination*, Routledge and Kegan Paul, London.

Cohen, I.J. (1981), 'Max Weber on Modern Western Capitalism', in Weber, M., *General Economic History*, Transaction Books, New Brunswick, pp.xv-lxxxiii.

Cohen, I.J. (1985), 'The Underemphasis on Democracy in Marx and Weber', in Antonio, R.J. and Glassman, R.M. (eds), *A Weber-Marx Dialogue*, University Press of Kansas, Lawrence, Kansas, pp.274-99.

Cohen, J. (1972), 'Max Weber and the Dynamics of Rationalized Domination', *Telos*, no. 14, pp.63-86.

Cohen, J. (1983), *Class and Civil Society: The Limits of Marxian Critical Theory*, Martin Robertson, Oxford.

Cohen J. et al. (1975), 'De-Parsonizing Weber: A Critique of Parsons' Interpretation of Weber's Sociology', *American Sociological Review*, vol. 40, no. 2, pp.229-41.

Cohn, N. (1970), *The Pursuit of the Millennium: Revolutionary Millenarians and Mystical Anarchists of the Middle Ages*, rev. edn, Temple Smith, London.

Collins, R. (1980), 'Weber's Last Theory of Capitalism: A Systematization', *American Sociological Review*, vol. 45, no. 6, pp.925-42.

Collins, R. (1986a), *Max Weber: A Skeleton Key*, Sage, London.

Collins, R. (1986b), *Weberian Sociological Theory*, Cambridge University Press, Cambridge.

Cox, O.C. (1950), 'Max Weber on Social Stratification', *American Sociological Review*, vol. 15, no. 2, pp.223-7.

Croix, G.E.M. de (1983), *The Class Struggle in the Ancient Greek World*, 2nd imp. (corrected), Duckworth, London.

Curtis, J.E. and Scott, W.G. (eds) (1979), *Social Stratification: Canada*, 2nd edn, Prentice-Hall of Canada Ltd, Scarborough, Ontario.

Curtis, T.D. (1968), 'Marshall and Weber on Wealth and Property: A Comparative Appraizal', *American Journal of Economics and Sociology*, vol. 27, pp.89-98.

Dahl, R.A. (1961), *Who Governs? Democracy and Power in an American City*, Yale University Press, New Haven/London.

Dahrendorf, R. (1959), *Class and Class Conflict in Industrial Society*, Routledge and Kegan Paul, London.

Danzger, M.H. (1964), 'Community Power Structure: Problems and Continuities', *American Sociological Review*, vol. 29, pp.708-17.

Davis, K. and Moore, W.E. (1967), 'Some Principles of Stratification', in Bendix, R. and Lipset, S.M. (eds), *Class, Status and Power: Social Stratification in Comparative Perspective*, Routledge and Kegan Paul, London, pp.47-53.

Davis, R.H.C. (1970), *A History of Medieval Europe: From Constantine to Saint Louis*, rev. edn, Longman, London.

Dawe, A. (1971), 'The Relevance of Values', in Sahay, A. (ed.), *Max Weber and Modern Sociology*, Routledge and Kegan Paul, London, pp.37-66.

Dessau, A. (1968), 'The Idea of Treason in the Middle Ages', in Cheyette, F.L. (ed.), *Lordship and Community in Medieval Europe*, Holt, Rinehart and Winston, New York, pp.192-7.

287

Dibble, V.K. (1968), 'Social Science and Political Commitments in the Young Max Weber', *Archives Européennes de Sociologie*, vol. 9, no. 1, pp.92-110.

Domhoff, G.W. (1967), *Who Rules America?*, Prentice-Hall, Englewood-Cliffs, N.J.

Domhoff, G.W. (1979), *The Powers That Be: Processes of Ruling-Class Domination in America*, Vintage Books, New York.

Doorn, J.A.A. van (1962-63), 'Sociology and the Problem of Power', *Sociologia Neerlandica*, vol. 1, no. 1, pp.3-51.

Dow, T.E. (1978), 'An Analysis of Weber's Work on Charisma', *The British Journal of Sociology*, vol. 29, no. 1, pp.83-93.

Duby, G. (1980), *The Three Orders, Feudal Society Imagined*, Goldhammer, A. (trans.), Chicago University Press, Chicago.

Duncan, H.D. (1969), 'The Works of Max Weber', in Duncan, H.D. (ed.), *Symbols and Social Theory*, Oxford University Press, New York, pp.3-49, 85-98.

Eden, R. (1983), *Political Leadership and Nihilism: A Study of Weber and Nietzsche*, University Press of Florida, Tampa.

Ehmke, H. (1984), 'What is the Germans' Fatherland?', in Habermas, J. (ed.), *Observations on 'The Spiritual Situation of the Age'*, MIT Press, Cambridge, Mass., pp.309-32.

Eisen, A. (1978), 'The Meanings and Confusions of Weberian "Rationality"', *The British Journal of Sociology*, vol. 29, no. 1, pp.57-70.

Eisen, A. (1979), 'Called to Order: The Rule of the Puritan *Berufsmensch* in Weberian Sociology', *Sociology*, vol. 13, no. 2, pp.203-18.

Eisenstadt, S.N. (1968), 'Introduction: Charisma and Institution Building: Max Weber and Modern Sociology', in Eisenstadt, S.N. (ed.), *On Charisma and Institution Building: Selected Papers*, University of Chicago Press, Chicago/London, pp.ix-lvi.

Eldridge, J.E.T. (1971), 'Weber's Approach to the Sociological Study of Industrial Workers', in Sahay, A. (ed.), *Max Weber and Modern Sociology*, Routledge and Kegan Paul, London, pp.97-111.

Eley, G. (1978), 'Capitalism and the Wilhelmine State: Industrial Growth and Political Backwardness in Recent German Historiography, 1890-1918', *The Historical Journal*, vol. 21, no. 3, pp.737-50.

Elias, N. (1978), *The Civilizing Process: The History of Manners*, Vol. I, Jephcott, E. (trans.), Basil Blackwell, Oxford.

Elias, N. (1982), *The Civilizing Process: State Formation and Civilization*, Vol. II, Jephcott, E. (trans.), Basil Blackwell, Oxford.

Encel, S. (1970), *Equality and Authority: A Study of Class, Status and Power in Australia*, Cheshire, Melbourne.

Etzioni, A. (1961), 'Compliance as a Comparative Base', in Etzioni, A. (ed.), *A Comparative Analysis of Complex Organizations: On Power, Involvement and Their Correlates*, Free Press of Glencoe, New York, pp.3-22.

Factor, R.A. and Turner, S.P. (1979), 'The Limits of Reason and Some Limitations of Weber's Morality', *Human Studies*, vol. 2, pp.301-34.

Factor, R.A. and Turner, S.P. (1984), 'Weber, the Germans, and the "Anglo-Saxon Convention": Liberalism as Technique and Form of Life', in Glassman, R.M. and Murvar, V. (eds), *Max Weber's Political Sociology: A Pessimistic Vision of a Rationalized World*, Greenwood Press, Westport, Connecticut, pp.39-54.

Falk, N. (1935), 'Democracy and Capitalism in Max Weber's Sociology', *The Sociological Review*, vol. 27, no. 4, pp.373-93.

Featherman, D.L. and Hauser, R.M. (1976), 'Changes in the Socioeconomic Stratification of the Races 1962-73', *American Journal of Sociology*, vol. 82, no. 3, pp.621-51.

Featherman, D.L. et al. (1975), 'Assumptions of Social Mobility Research in the US: The Case of Occupational Status', *Social Science Research*, vol. 4, pp.329-60.

Ferguson, A. (1971), *Essay on the History of Civil Society*, Garland, New York.

Ferrarotti, F. (1982), 'Max Weber and the Destiny of Reason', *International Journal of Sociology*, vol. 12, no. 1, pp.3-132.

Field, G.L. and Higley, J. (1980), *Elitism*, Routledge and Kegan Paul, London.

Finley, M.I. (1977), 'The Ancient City: From Fustel de Contanges to Max Weber and Beyond', *Comparative Studies in Society and History*, vol. 19, pp.305-27.

Forbes, R.P. (1975), 'The Problem of *"Laissez-Faire"* Bias in Weber's Concept of "Formal Rationality"', *Sociological Analysis and Theory*, vol. 5, no. 2, pp.219-36.

Foucault, M. (1973), 'The Intellectuals and Power: A Discussion between Michel Foucault and Gilles Deleuze', Seem, M. (trans.), *Telos*, no. 16, pp.103-9.

Foucault, M. (1974), 'Michel Foucault on Attica: An Interview', *Telos*, no. 19, pp.154-61.

Foucault, M. (1976), *The Birth of the Clinic*, Sheridan, A.M. (trans.), Tavistock, London.

Foucault, M. (1977a), 'Revolutionary Action: "Until Now"', Bouchard, D. and Simon, S. (trs), in Bouchard, D.F. (ed.), *Language, Counter-Memory, Practice: Selected Essays and Interviews*, Basil Blackwell, Oxford, pp.218-33.

289

Foucault, M. (1977b), 'Power and Sex: An Interview with Michel Foucault', Parent, D.J. (trans.), *Telos*, no. 32, pp.152-61.

Foucault, M. (1979), *Discipline and Punish: The Birth of the Prison*, Sheridan, A. (trans.), Penguin Books, Harmondsworth.

Foucault, M. (1980), *Power/Knowledge: Selected Interviews and Other Writings 1972-77*, Gordon, C. et al. (trs), Pantheon Books, New York.

Foucault, M. (1981a), *The History of Sexuality: An Introduction*, Vol. I, Hurley, R. (trans.), Penguin Books, Harmondsworth.

Foucault, M. (1981b), 'Is It Useless To Revolt?', Bernauer, J. (trans.), *Philosophy and Social Criticism*, vol. 8, no. 1, pp.5-9.

Foucault, M. (1981c), 'Omnes et Singulatim Towards a Criticism of "Political Reason"', in McMurrin, S. (ed.), *The Tanner Lecture on Human Values, II*, University of Utah Press, Salt Lake City, pp.223-54.

Foucault, M. (1982), 'The Subject and Power', *Critical Inquiry*, vol. 8, pp.777-95.

Fourquin, G. (1978), *The Anatomy of Rebellion in the Middle Ages*, Chesters, A. (trans.), North-Holland, Oxford/Amsterdam.

Freund, J. (1972), *The Sociology of Max Weber*, Ilford, M. (trans.), Penguin, Harmondsworth.

Friedland, W.H. (1964), 'For a Sociological Concept of Charisma', *Social Forces*, vol. 43, pp.18-26.

Friedman, A.L. (1977), *Industry and Labour: Class Struggle at Work and Monopoly Capitalism*, Macmillan, London/Basingstoke.

Friedrich, C.J. (1961), 'Political Leadership and the Problem of Charismatic Power', *The Journal of Politics*, vol. 23, no. 1, pp.27-33.

Genicot, L. (1968), 'The Nobility in Medieval France', Cheyette, F.L. (trans.), in Cheyette, F.L. (ed.), *Lordship and Community in Medieval Europe*, Holt, Rinehart and Winston, New York, pp.128-36.

Gerth, H.H. and Mills, C.W. (1970), 'Introduction: the Man and His Work', in Weber, M., *From Max Weber: Essays in Sociology*, Routledge and Kegan Paul, London, pp.3-74.

Giddens, A. (1968), '"Power" in the Recent Writings of Talcott Parsons', *Sociology*, vol. 2, no. 3, pp.257-72.

Giddens, A. (1972), *Politics and Sociology in the Thought of Max Weber*, Macmillan, London.

Giddens, A. (1976a), *New Rules of Sociological Method: A Positive Critique of Interpretative Sociologies*, Hutchinson, London.

Giddens, A. (1976b), 'Introduction', in Weber, M., *The Protestant Ethic and the Spirit of Capitalism*, Allen and Unwin, London.

Giddens, A. (1979a), 'Max Weber on Facts and Values', in Giddens, A., *Studies in Social and Political Theory*, Hutchinson, London, pp.89-95.

Giddens, A. (1979b), *Central Problems in Social Theory: Action, Structure and Contradiction in Social Analysis*, Macmillan, London/Basingstoke.

Giddens, A. (1981a), *A Contemporary Critique of Historical Materialism: Power, Property and the State*, Vol. I, Macmillan, London/Basingstoke.

Giddens, A. (1981b), *The Class Structure of the Advanced Societies*, Hutchinson, London.

Giddens, A. (1982), 'Power, the Dialectic of Control and Class Structuration', in Giddens, A. and MacKenzie, G. (eds), *Social Class and the Division of Labour: Essays in Honour of Ilya Neustadt*, Cambridge University Press, Cambridge, pp.29-45.

Giddens, A. (1985), *A Contemporary Critique of Historical Materialism: The Nation-State and Violence*, Vol. II, University of California Press, Berkeley/Los Angeles.

Goddard, D. (1973), 'Max Weber and the Objectivity of Social Science', *History and Theory*, vol. 12, pp.1-22.

Goldman, H. (1991), *Max Weber and Thomas Mann: Calling and the Shaping of the Self*, University of California Press, Berkeley/Los Angeles.

Goldthorpe, J.H. (1972), 'Class, Status and Party in Modern Britain: Some Recent Interpretations, Marxist and Marxisant', *Archives Européennes de Sociologie*, vol. 13, no. 2, pp.342-72.

Gordon, M.M. (1963), *Social Class in American Sociology*, McGraw-Hill, New York/London.

Gouldner, A.W. (1969), 'Metaphysical Pathos and the Theory of Bureaucracy', in Coser, L.A. and Rosenberg, B. (eds), *Sociological Theory: A Book of Readings*, Macmillan, New York/London, pp.484-94.

Gouldner, A.W. (1975), 'Anti-Minotaur: The Myth of a Value-free Sociology', in Gouldner, A.W., *For Sociology: Renewal and Critique in Sociology Today*, Penguin, Harmondsworth, pp.3-26.

Gouldner, A.W. (1976), *The Dialectic of Ideology and Technology: The Origins, Grammar and Future of Ideology*, Macmillan, London/Basingstoke.

Graber, E.E. (1975), 'Interpretive Sociology Is Not Part of a Psychology', *Sociological Inquiry*, vol. 45, pp.67-70.

Graber, E.E. (1985), 'Law and Society in Max Weber's Sociology', in Murvar, V. (ed.), *Theory of Liberty, Legitimacy and Power*, Routledge and Kegan Paul, London, pp.86-107.

Grafstein, R. (1981), 'The Failure of Weber's Conception of Legitimacy: Its Causes and Implications', *The Journal of Politics*, vol. 42, no. 2, pp.456-72.

Gramsci, A. (1971), *Selections From Prison Notebooks*, Hoare, Q. and Smith, G.N. (trs and eds), Lawrence and Wishart, London.

Greenspon, S.P. (1963), 'Some Theoretcal Contributions Made by Marx, Weber and Durkheim to the Field of Industrial Sociology', *The Journal of Educational Sociology*, vol. 26, pp.213-18.

Greisman, H.C. (1976), "'Disenchantment of the World": Romanticism, Aesthetics and Sociological Theory', *The British Journal of Sociology*, vol. 27, no. 4, pp.495-807.

Gronow, J. (1988), 'The Element of Irrationality: Max Weber's Diagnosis of Modern Culture', *Acta Sociologica*, vol. 31, no. 4, pp.319-31.

Gunlicks, A.B. (1978), 'Max Weber's Typology of Politicians: A Reexamination', *The Journal of Politics*, vol. 40, pp.498-509.

Habermas, J. (1971a), 'Discussion on Value-freedom and Objectivity', in Stammer, O. (ed.), *Max Weber and Sociology Today*, Basil Blackwell, Oxford, pp.59-66.

Habermas, J. (1971b), *Toward a Rational Society*, Shapiro, J.J. (trans.), Heinemann, London.

Habermas, J. (1974a), *Theory and Practice*, Viertel, J. (trans.), Heinemann, London.

Habermas, J. (1974b), 'On Social Identity', *Telos*, no. 19, pp.91-103.

Habermas, J. (1974c), 'The Public Sphere', *New German Critique*, vol. 3, pp.49-55.

Habermas, J. (1976), *Legitimation Crisis*, McCarthy, T. (trans.), Heinemann, London.

Habermas, J. (1977), 'Hannah Arendt's Communications Concept of Power', *Social Research*, vol. 44, no. 1, pp.3-24.

Habermas, J. (1979a), 'Aspects of the Rationality of Action', in Geraets, T.F. (ed.), *Rationality Today*, University of Ottawa Press, Ottawa, pp.185-205.

Habermas, J. (1979b), *Communication and the Evolution of Society*, McCarthy, T. (trans.), Heinemann, London.

Habermas, J. (1984a), *The Theory of Communicative Action: Reason and the Rationalization of Society*, Vol. I, McCarthy, T. (trans.), Heinemann, London.

Habermas, J. (ed.) (1984b), *Observations on 'The Spiritual Situation of the Age'*, Buchwalter, A. (trans.), MIT Press, Cambridge, Mass./London.

Habermas, J. (1985), 'Civil Disobedience: Litmus Test for the Democratic Constitutional State', *Berkeley Journal of Sociology*, vol. 30, pp.95-116.

Habermas, J. (1986a), 'Conservative Politics, Work, Socialism and Utopia Today', in Habermas, J., *Autonomy and Solidarity: Interviews*, Dews, P. (trans.), Verso, London, pp.131-47.

Habermas, J. (1986b), 'Life Forms, Morality and the Task of the Philosopher', in Habermas, J., *Autonomy and Soldiarity: Interviews*, Dews, P. (trans.), Verso, London, pp.191-216.

Habermas, J. (1992), *The Structural Transformation of the Public Sphere*, Burger, T. and Lawrence, F. (trs), Polity Press, Cambridge.

Haferkamp, H. (1987), 'Beyond the Iron Cage of Modernity? Achievement, Negotiation and Changes in the Power Structure', *Theory, Culture and Society*, vol. 4, no. 1, pp.51-3.

Hahn, H.J. (1995), *German Thought and Culture*, Manchester University Press, Manchester.

Harrison, P.M. (1960), 'Weber's Categories of Authority and Voluntary Associations', *American Sociological Review*, vol. 25, pp.232-7.

Hearn, F. (1975), 'The Dialectical Use of Ideal-Types', *Theory and Society*, vol. 2, no. 4, pp.531-61.

Hearn, F. (1978), *Domination, Legitimation, and Resistance: The Incorporation of the Nineteenth-Century English Working Class*, Greenwood Press, Westport, Connecticut.

Hearn, F. (1985), *Reason and Freedom in Sociological Thought*, Allen and Unwin, Boston.

Heer, F. (1974), *The Medieval World: Europe from 1100 to 1350*, Sondheimer, J. (trans.), Cardinal, London.

Hegel, G.W.F. (1967), *Philosophy of Right*, Knox, T.M. (trans.), Oxford University Press, London.

Hegy, P. (1974), 'Words of Power: The Power of Words', *Theory and Society*, vol. 1, pp.329-39.

Heidegger, M. (1962), *Being and Time*, Macquarie, J. and Robinson, E. (trs), Basil Blackwell, Oxford.

Heidegger, M. (1978), 'The Question Concerning Technology', in Heidegger, M., *Basic Writings*, Routledge and Kegan Paul, London, pp.287-317.

Hekman, S.J. (1979), 'Weber's Concept of Causality and the Modern Critique', *Sociological Inquiry*, vol. 49, pp.67-76.

Hekman, S.J. (1983), *Max Weber and Contemporary Social Theory*, Martin Robertson, Oxford.

Heller, C.S. (1972), *Structured Social Inequality*, Collier-Macmillan, London.

Hennis, W. (1988), *Max Weber: Essays in Reconstruction*, Tribe, K. (trans.), Allen and Unwin, London.

Herva, S. (1988), 'The Genesis of Max Weber's *Verstehende Soziologie*', *Acta Sociologica*, vol. 31, no. 2, pp.143-56.

Hilton, R.H. (1973), *Bond Men Made Free: Medieval Peasant Movements and the English Rising of 1381*, Temple Smith, London.

Hilton, R.H. (1975a), 'The Peasantry as a Class', in Hilton, R.H., *The English Peasantry in the Later Middle Ages*, Clarendon Press, Oxford, pp.3-19.

Hilton, R.H. (1975b), 'Rent and Capital Formation in Feudal Society', in Hilton, R.H., *The English Peasantry in the Later Middle Ages*, Clarendon Press, Oxford, pp.174-214.

Hilton, R.H. (1985), *Class Conflict and the Crisis of Feudalism*, Hambledon Press, London.

Hindess, B. (1977), 'Humanism and Teleology in Sociological Theory', in Hindess, B. (ed.), *Sociological Theories of the Economy*, Macmillan, London/Basingstoke, pp.157-89.

Hindess, B. (1982), 'Power, Interests and the Outcomes of Struggles', *Sociology*, vol. 16, no. 4, pp.498-511.

Hindess, B. (1987), 'Rationality and the Characterization of Modern Society', in Lash, S. and Whimster, S. (eds), *Max Weber, Rationality and Modernity*, Allen and Unwin, London, pp.137-53.

Hinkle, G.J. (1986), 'The Americanization of Max Weber', *Current Perspectives in Social Theory*, vol. 7, pp.87-104.

Hintze, O. (1968), 'The Nature of Feudalism', in Cheyette, F.L. (ed.), *Lordship and Community in Medieval Europe*, Holt, Rinehart and Winston, New York, pp.22-31.

Hirst, P.Q. (1976a), *Social Evolution and Sociological Categories*, Allen and Unwin, London.

Hirst, P.Q. (1976b), 'Book Review: "Roscher and Knies: The Logical Problem of Historical Economics"', *The British Journal of Sociology*, vol. 27, no. 3, pp.407-8.

Hobsbawn, E.J. (1968), 'Custom, Wages and Work-Load in Nineteenth Century Industry', in Hobsbawn, E.J. (ed.), *Labouring Men: Studies in the History of Labour*, Weidenfeld and Nicolson, London, pp.344-70.

Hodges, D.C. (1964), *Social Stratification*, Schenkman, Cambridge, Mass.

Holton, R.J. and Turner, B.S. (1989), *Max Weber on Economy and Society*, Routledge, London/New York.

Honigsheim, P. (1968), 'Max Weber in American Intellectual Life', in Honigsheim, P., *On Max Weber*, Free Press, New York, pp.135-50.

Hopkins, T.K. (1957), 'Sociology and the Substantive View of the Economy', in Polanyi, K. et al. (eds), *Trade and Market in the Early Empires*, Free Press, New York, pp.271-306.

Horowitz, I.L. (1961), 'Max Weber and the Spirit of American Sociology', *The Sociological Quarterly*, vol. 5, pp.344-54.

Huff, T.E. (1984), *Max Weber and the Methodology of the Social Sciences*, Transaction Books, New Brunswick.

Hunter, F. (1959), *Top Leadership, USA*, University of North Carolina Press, Chapel Hill.

Ingham, G.K. (1970), 'Social Stratification: Individual Attributes and Social Relationships', *Sociology*, vol. 4, no. 1, pp.105-13.

Jackson, J.A. (ed.) (1968), *Social Stratification*, Cambridge University Press, Cambridge.

Jacobson, D.C. (1976), 'Rationalization and Emancipation in Weber and Habermas', *Graduate Faculty Journal of Sociology* (New School for Social Research), vol. 1, pp.18-31.

Jensen-Butler, B. (1976), 'An Outline of a Weberian Analysis of Class with Particular Reference to the Middle Class and the NSDAP in Weimar Germany', *The British Journal of Sociology*, vol. 27, no. 1, pp.50-60.

Jones, B. (1975), 'Max Weber and the Concept of Social Class', *The Sociological Review*, vol. 23, no. 4, pp.729-57.

Kalberg, S. (1980), 'Max Weber's Types of Rationality: Cornerstones for the Analysis of Rationalization Processes', *American Journal of Sociology*, vol. 85, no. 5, pp.1145-79.

Kalberg, S. (1983), 'Max Weber's Universal-Historical Architectonic of Economically-Oriented Action: A Preliminary Reconstruction', in McNall, S.G. (ed.), *Current Perspectives in Social Theory*, Vol. IV, JAI Press, Greenwood, Conn., pp.253-88.

Kalberg, S. (1994), *Max Weber's Comparative-Historical Sociology*, Polity Press, Cambridge.

Käsler, D. (1988), *Max Weber: An Introduction to his Life and Work*, Hurd, P. (trans.), Polity Press, Cambridge.

Keen, M. (1984), *Chivalry*, Yale University Press, New Haven/London.

Keller, S. (1963), *Beyond the Ruling Class: Strategic Elites in Modern Society*, Random House, New York.

Kelly, J.E. (1978), 'Understanding Taylorism: Some Comments', *The British Journal of Sociology*, vol. 29, no. 2, pp.203-7.

Kelsall, R.K. and Kelsall, H.M. (1974), *Stratification: An Essay on Class and Inequality*, Longman, London.

Kent, S.A. (1983), 'Weber, Goethe, and the Nietzschean Allusion: Capturing the Source of the "Iron Cage" Metaphor', *Sociological Analysis*, vol. 44, pp.297-320.

Kerckhoff, A.C. (1976), 'The Status Attainment Process: Socialization or Allocation', *Social Forces*, vol. 55, pp.368-81.

Kilker, E. (1984), 'Max Weber and the Possibilities for Democracy', in Glassman, R.M. and Murvar, V. (eds), *Max Weber's Political Sociology: A Pessimistic View of a Rationalized World*, Greenwood Press, Connecticut, London/Westport, pp.55-65.

Kocka, J. (1985), 'The Social Sciences between Dogmatism and Decisionism: A Comparison of Karl Marx and Max Weber', in Antonio, R.J. and Glassman, G.M. (eds), *A Weber-Marx Dialogue*, University Press of Kansas, Lawrence, Kansas, pp.134-66.

Körner, S. (1955), *Kant*, Penguin, Harmondsworth.

Kozyr-Kowalski, S. (1982), 'Ownership and Classes in Max Weber's Sociology', *The Polish Sociological Bulletin*, no.1-4, pp.5-24.

Krauss, I. (1976), *Stratification, Class, and Conflict*, Free Press, New York.

295

Krieger, C. (1957), *The German Idea of Freedom*, Beacon Press, Boston.

Kronman, A.T. (1983), *Max Weber*, Edward Arnold, London.

Landmann, M. (1976), 'Critiques of Reason from Max Weber to Ernst Bloch', *Telos*, no. 29, pp.187-98.

Lane, D. (1982), *The End of Social Inequality: Class, Status and Power under State Socialism*, Allen and Unwin, London.

Lane, J.-E. (1976), 'On the Use of the Word "Political"', in Barry, B. (ed.), *Power and Political Theory: Some European Perspectives*, John Wiley, London, pp.217-44.

Lash, S. and Urry, J. (1987), *The End of Organized Capitalism*, Polity Press, Cambridge.

Lassman, P. and Velody, I. (eds) (1989), *Max Weber's 'Science as a Vocation'*, Unwin Hyman, London.

Lazarsfeld, P.F. and Oberschall, A.R. (1965), 'Max Weber and Empirical Social Research', *American Sociological Review*, vol. 30, no. 2, pp.185-99.

Levine, D.N. (1981), 'Rationality and Freedom: Weber and Beyond', *Sociological Inquiry*, vol. 51, no. 1, pp.5-25.

Levine, D.P. and Levine, L. (1975), 'Social Theory and Social Action', *Economy and Society*, vol. 4, no. 2, pp.162-93.

Littlejohn, J. (1972), *Social Stratification*, Allen and Unwin, London.

Littler, C.R. (1978), 'Understanding Taylorism', *The British Journal of Sociology*, vol. 29, no. 2, pp.185-202.

Loader, C. and Alexander, J.C. (1985), 'Max Weber on Churches and Sects in North America: An Alternative Path Toward Rationalization', *Sociological Theory*, vol. 3, no. 1, pp.1-6.

Lockwood, D. (1958), *The Blackcoated Worker: A Study in Class Consciousness*, Allen and Unwin, London.

Love, J. (1986), 'Max Weber and the Theory of Ancient Capitalism', *History and Theory*, vol. 25, no. 2, pp.152-72.

Löwith, K. (1982), *Max Weber and Karl Marx*, Bottomore, T. and Outhwaite, W. (eds), Fantel, H. (trans.), Allen and Unwin, London.

Luhmann, N. (1982), 'Ends, Domination, and System', in Luhmann, N., *The Differentiation of Society*, Columbia University Press, New York, pp.206-46.

Lukács, G. (1972), 'Max Weber and German Sociology', *Economy and Society*, vol. 1, no. 4, pp.386-98.

Lukács, G. (1974), *History and Class Consciousness: Studies in Marxist Dialectics*, Livingstone, R. (trans.), Merlin Press, London.

Lukes, S. (1979), 'Power and Authority', in Bottomore, T. and Nisbet, R. (eds), *A History of Sociological Analysis*, Heinemann, London, pp.633-76.

MacKenzie, G. (1982), 'Class Boundaries and the Labour Process', in Giddens, A. and MacKenzie, G. (eds), *Social Class and the Division of Labour*, Cambridge University Press, Cambridge, pp.63-86.

MacPherson, C.B. (1962), *The Political Theory of Possessive Individualism: Hobbes to Locke*, Clarendon Press, Oxford.

Mann, M. (1982), 'The Social Cohension of Liberal Democracy', in Giddens, A. and Held, D. (eds), *Classes, Power, and Conflict: Classical and Contemporary Debates*, Macmillan, London/Basingstoke, pp.373-95.

Marcuse, H. (1958), *Soviet Marxism*, Colombia University Press, New York.

Marcuse, H. (1964), *One-Dimensional Man: Studies in the Ideology of Advanced Industrial Society*, Beacon Press, Boston.

Marcuse, H. (1971), 'Industrialization and Capitalism', in Stammer, O. (ed.), *Max Weber and Sociology Today*, Basil Blackwell, Oxford, pp.133-51.

Marcuse, H. (1978), 'Some Implications of Modern Technology', in Arato, A. and Gebhardt, E. (eds), *The Essential Frankfurt School Reader*, Basil Blackwell, Oxford, pp.138-62.

Markovic, M. (1974), *From Affluence to Praxis: Philosophy and Social Criticism*, University of Michigan Press, Michigan.

Marshall, G. et al. (1985), 'Class, Citizenship and Distributional Conflict in Modern Britain', *The British Journal of Sociology*, vol. 36, no. 2, pp.259-84.

Marshall, T.H. (1977a), 'The Nature and Determinants of Social Status', in Marshall, T.H., *Class, Citizenship, and Social Development*, University of Chicago Press, Chicago/London, pp.191-219.

Marshall, T.H. (1977b), 'Citizenship and Social Class', in Marshall, T.H., *Class, Citizenship and Social Development*, University of Chicago Press, Chicago/London, pp.71-134.

Martin, R. (1977), *The Sociology of Power*, Routledge and Kegan Paul, London.

Marx, K. (1959), *Capital: A Critique of Political Economy*, Vol. III, Anonymous (trans.), Progress Publishers, Moscow.

Marx, K. (1969), 'The Eighteenth Brumaire of Louis Bonaparte', Anonymous (trans.), in Marx, K. and Engels, F., *Selected Works*, Vol. I, Progress Publishers, Moscow, pp.394-487.

Marx, K. (1973), *Grundrisse: Foundations of the Critique of Political Economy*, Nikolaus, M. (trans.), Penguin in association with New Left Books, Harmondsworth.

Marx, K. (1976a), *The German Ideology*, Anonymous (trans.), 3rd rev. edn, Progress Publishers, Moscow.

Marx, K. (1976b), *Capital: A Critique of Political Economy*, Vol. I, Fowkes, B. (trans.), Penguin in association with New Left Books, Harmondsworth.

Matheson, C. (1987), 'Weber and the Classiciation of Forms of Legitmacy', *The British Journal of Sociology*, vol. 38, no. 2, pp.199-215.

Mayrl, W.W. (1985), 'Max Weber and the Causality of Freedom', in Murvar, V. (ed.), *Theory of Liberty, Legitimacy and Power*, Routledge and Kegan Paul, London, pp.108-24.

Merquior, J.G. (1980), *Rousseau and Weber: Two Studies in the Theory of Legitimacy*, Routledge and Kegan Paul, London.

Michels, R. (1915), *Political Parties: A Sociological Study of the Oligarchical Tendencies of Modern Democracy*, Paul, E. and Paul, C. (trs), Free Press, Glencoe, Ill.

Midgley, E.B.F. (1983), *The Ideology of Max Weber*, Gower, Aldershot, Hants.

Miliband, R. (1973), *The State in Capitalist Society*, Quartet Books, London.

Mills, J.S. (1974), *On Liberty*, Penguin, Harmondsworth.

Millar, J. (1960), 'The Origin of the Distinction of Ranks', in Lehmann, W.C., *John Millar of Glasgow 1735-1801*, Cambridge University Press, Cambridge, pp.167-322.

Mills, C.W. (1959), *The Power Elite*, Oxford University Press, Oxford.

Mokken, R.J. and Stokman, F.N. (1976), 'Power and Influence as Political Phenomena', in Barry, B. (ed.), *Power and Political Theory*, John Wiley, London, pp.33-54.

Mommsen, W.J. (1965), 'Max Weber's Political Sociology and His Philosophy of World History', *International Social Science Journal*, vol. 17, pp.23-45.

Mommsen, W.J. (1974), *The Age of Bureaucracy: Perspectives on the Political Sociology of Max Weber*, Basil Blackwell, Oxford.

Mommsen, W.J. (1977), 'Max Weber as a Critic of Marxism', *Canadian Journal of Sociology*, vol. 2, pp.373-98.

Mommsen, W.J. (1981), 'Max Weber and Robert Michels: An Asymmetrical Relationship', *European Journal of Sociology*, vol. 22, no. 1, pp.100-116.

Mommsen, W.J. (1984), *Max Weber and German Politics 1890-1920*, Steinberg, M.S. (trans.), University of Chicago Press, Chicago/London.

Moore, B. (1978), *Injustice: The Social Bases of Obedience and Revolt*, Macmillan, London/Basingstoke.

Mosca, G. (1939), *The Ruling Class*, Kahn, H.D. (trans.), McGraw-Hill, New York.

Mueller, G.H. (1979), 'The Notion of Rationality in the Work of Max Weber', *Archives Européennes de Sociologie*, vol. 20, no. 1, pp.149-71.

Mueller, G.H. (1982), 'Socialism and Capitalism in the Work of Max Weber', *The British Journal of Sociology*, vol. 33, no. 2, pp.151-71.

Mukherjee, S.N. (1985), 'The Idea of Feudalism, from the Philosphers to Karl Marx', in Leach, E. et al. (eds), *Feudalism*, Association for Studies in Society and Culture, Sydney, pp.25-39.

Munch, P.A. (1975), '"Sense" and "Intention" in Max Weber's Theory of Social Action', *Sociological Inquiry*, vol. 45, no. 4, pp.59-65.

Münch, R. (1988), *Understanding Modernity: Toward a New Perspective Going Beyond Durkheim and Weber*, Routledge and Kegan Paul, London.

Munters, Q.J. (1972), 'Max Weber as Rural Sociologist', *Sociologia Ruralis*, vol. 12, no. 2, pp.129-45.

Murphy, R. (1982), 'Power and Autonomy in the Sociology of Education', *Theory and Society*, vol. 11, no. 2, pp.179-203.

Murphy, R. (1984), 'The Structure of Closure: A Critique and Development of the Theories of Weber, Collins and Parkin', *The British Journal of Sociology*, vol. 35, no. 4, pp.547-67.

Murphy, R. (1985), 'Exploitation or Exclusion', *Sociology*, vol. 19, no. 2, pp.225-43.

Murphy, R. (1986a), 'The Concept of Class in Closure Theory: Learning from Rather than Falling into the Problems Encountered by Neo-Marxism', *Sociology*, vol. 20, no. 2, pp.247-64.

Murphy, R. (1986b), 'Weberian Closure Theory: A Contribution to the Ongoing Assessment', *The British Journal of Sociology*, vol. 37, no. 1, pp.21-41.

Murvar, V. (1964), 'Some Reflections on Weber's Typology of "Herrschaft"', *The Sociological Quarterly*, vol. 5, no. 4, pp.374-84.

Murvar, V. (1983), *Max Weber Today - An Introduction to a Living Legacy*, Max Weber Colloquia and Symposia at the University of Wisconsin-Milwaukee, Brookfield, Wisconsin.

Murvar, V. (1984), 'Epilogue: Max Weber and the Two Nonrevolutionary Events in Russia 1917: Scientific Achievements or Prophetic Features?', in Glassman, R.M. and Murvar, V. (eds), *Max Weber's Political Sociology: A Pessimistic Vision of a Rationalized World*, Greenwood Press, London/Westport, Connecticut, pp.237-72.

Murvar, V. (1985), 'Introduction: Theory of Liberty, Legitimacy and Power: New Directions in the Intellectual and Scientific Legacy of Max Weber', in Murvar, V. (ed.), *Theory of Liberty, Legitimacy and Power*, Routledge and Kegan Paul, London, pp.1-7.

Myers, A.R. (1975), 'The Parliaments of Europe and the Age of the Estates', *History*, vol. 61, pp.11-27.

McIntosh, D. (1970), 'Weber and Freud: On the Nature and Sources of Authority', *American Sociological Review*, vol. 35, pp.901-11.

McIntosh, D. (1977), 'The Objective Bases of Max Weber's Ideal Types', *History and Theory*, vol. 16, no. 3, pp.265-79.

McIntosh, D. (1983), 'Max Weber as a Critical Theorist', *Theory and Society*, vol. 12, no. 1, pp.69-109.

Neuwirth, G. (1969), 'A Weberian Outline of a Theory of Community: Its Application to the "Dark Ghetto"', *The British Journal of Sociology*, vol. 20, pp.148-63.

Newby, H. (1975), 'The Differential Dialectic', *Comparative Studies in Society and History*, vol. 17, no. 2, pp.139-64.

Nicholson, P.P. (1984), 'Politics and Force', in Leftwich, A. (ed.), *What is Politics? The Activity of Its Study*, Basil Blackwell, Oxford, pp.33-45.

Oakes, G. (1982), 'Methodological Ambivalence: The Case of Max Weber', *Social Research*, vol. 49, no. 3, pp.589-615.

Oberschall, A.R. (1965), 'Max Weber and the Problem of Industrial Work', in Oberschall, A., *Empirical Social Research in Germany 1848-1914*, Mouton and Co., Paris/The Hague, pp.110-36.

Offe, C. and Wiesenthal, H. (1980), 'Two Logics of Collective Action: Theoretical Notes on Social Class and Organizational Form', *Political Power and Social Theory*, vol. 1, pp.67-115.

Omodei, R.A. (1982), 'Beyond the Neo-Weberian Concept of Status', *Australian and New Zealand Journal of Sociology*, vol. 18, no. 2, pp.196-213.

O'Neill, J. (1986), 'The Disciplinary Society: From Weber to Foucault', *The British Journal of Sociology*, vol. 37, no. 1, pp.42-60.

Ostrogorski, M. (1902), *Democracy and the Organization of Political Parties*, Clarke, F. (trans.), Macmillan, London/New York.

Owen, C. (1968), *Social Stratification*, Routledge and Kegan Paul, London.

Owen, D. (1994), *Maturity and Modernity: Nietzsche, Weber, Foucault and the Ambivalence of Reason*, Routledge, London.

Pareto, V. (1968), *The Rise and Fall of the Elites: An Application of Theoretical Sociology*, Anonymous (trans.), The Bedminster Press, Totowa, New Jersey.

Parkin, F. (1972), *Class Inequality and Political Order*, Paladin, St Albans, Herts.

Parkin, F. (1974), 'Strategies of Social Closure in Class Formation', in Parkin, F. (ed.), *The Social Analysis of Class Structure*, Tavistock, London, pp.1-18.

Parkin, F. (1979), 'Social Stratification', in Bottomore, T. and Nisbet, R. (eds), *A History of Sociological Analysis*, Heinemann, London, pp.599-632.

Parkin, F. (1981), *Marxism and Class Theory: A Bourgeois Critique*, Tavistock, London.

Parkin, F. (1982), *Max Weber*, Ellis Horwood Ltd, Chichester, Tavistock, London.

Parsons, T. (1928), "'Capitalism" in Recent German Literature: Sombart and Weber', *The Journal of Political Economy*, vol. 36, pp.641-61.

Parsons, T. (1942a), 'Max Weber and the Contemporary Political Crisis', *Review of Politics*, vol. 4, no. 1, pp.61-76.

Parsons, T. (1942b), 'Max Weber and the Contemporary Political Crisis', *Review of Politics*, vol. 4, no. 2, pp.155-72.

Parsons, T. (1949), *The Structure of Social Action*, Free Press, Glencoe, Ill.

Parsons, T. (1954a), 'An Analytical Approach to the Theory of Social Stratification (1940)', in Parsons, T., *Essays in Sociological Theory*, Free Press, Glencoe, Ill., pp.69-88.

Parsons, T. (1954b), 'A Revised Analytical Approach to the Theory of Social Stratification (1953)', in Parsons, T., *Essays in Sociological Theory*, Free Press, Glencoe, Ill., pp.386-439.

Parsons, T. (1960), 'Max Weber', *American Sociological Review*, vol. 25, no. 5, pp.750-52.

Parsons, T. (1964), *The Social System*, Free Press, New York.

Parsons, T. (1967), 'On the Concept of Political Power', in Bendix, R. and Lipset, G.M. (eds), *Class, Status, and Power: Social Stratification in Comparative Perspective*, Routledge and Kegan Paul, London, pp.240-65.

Parsons, T. (1975), 'On "De-Parsonizing Weber"', *American Sociological Review*, vol. 40, no. 5, pp.666-9.

Parsons, T. (1976a), 'Social Structure and the Symbolic Media of Interchange', in Blau, P.M. (ed.), *Approaches to the Study of Social Structure*, Open Books, London, pp.94-120.

Parsons, T. (1976b), 'Comments: Reply to Cohen, Hazelrigg and Pope', *American Sociological Review*, vol. 41, pp.361-5.

Parsons, T. (1977), 'Equality and Inequality in Modern Society, or Social Stratification Revisited', in Parsons, T., *Social Systems and the Evolution of Action Theory*, Free Press, Glencoe, Ill., pp.321-80.

Parsons, T. et al. (1953), *Working Papers in the Theory of Action*, Free Press, Glencoe, Ill.

Pease, J. et al. (1970), 'Ideological Currents in American Stratification Literature', *The American Sociologist*, vol. 5, no. 2, pp.127-37.

Pipes, R. (1955), 'Max Weber and Russia', *Politics*, vol. 7, no. 3, pp.371-401.

Pirenne, H. (1939), *A History of Europe*, Miall, B. (trans.), Allen and Unwin, London.

Pitt-Rivers, J. (1965), 'Honour and Shame', in Peristiany, J.G. (ed.), *Honour and Shame*, Weidenfeld and Nicolson, London, pp.21-39.

Poggi, G. (1972), *Images of Society: Essays on the Sociological Theories of Tocqueville, Marx and Durkheim*, Oxford University Press, London.

301

Poggi, G. (1978), *The Development of the Modern State: A Sociological Introduction*, Hutchinson, London.

Poggi, G. (1983), *Calvinism and the Capitalist Spirit: Max Weber's Protestant Ethic*, Macmillan, London/Basingstoke.

Poggi, G. (1988), 'Max Weber's Conceptual Portrait of Feudalism', *The British Journal of Sociology*, vol. 39, no. 2, pp.211-27.

Polanyi, K. (1944), *The Great Transformation*, Rinehart and Co., New York/Toronto.

Polanyi, K. (1957), 'The Economy as Instituted Process', in Polanyi, K. et al. (eds), *Trade and Market in the Early Empires*, Free Press, New York, pp.243-70.

Polsby, N.W. (1980), *Community Power and Political Theory: A Further Look at Problems of Evidence and Inference*, 2nd enlarged edn, Yale University Press, New Haven/London.

Portis, E.B. (1978), 'Max Weber's Theory of Personality', *Sociological Inquiry*, vol. 48, pp.113-20.

Portis, E.B. (1979), 'Political Action and Social Science: Max Weber's Two Arguments for Objectivity', *Polity*, vol. 12, pp.409-27.

Portis, E.B. (1986), *Max Weber and Political Commitment: Science, Politics and Personality*, Temple University Press, Philadelphia.

Poulantzas, N. (1978), *Political Power and Social Classes*, O'Hagan, T. (trans.), Verso, London.

Prager, J. (1981), 'Moral Integration and Political Inclusion: A Comparison of Durkheim's and Weber's Theories of Democracy', *Social Forces*, vol. 59, no. 4, pp.918-50.

Rasmussen, D.M. (1973), 'Between Autonomy and Sociality', *Cultural Hermeneutics*, vol. 1, no. 1, pp.3-45.

Rex, J. (1970), *Key Problems of Sociological Theory*, Routledge and Kegan Paul, London.

Rex, J. (1971), 'Typology and Objectivity: A Comment on Weber's Four Sociological Methods', in Sahay, A. (ed.), *Max Weber and Modern Sociology*, Routledge and Kegan Paul, London, pp.17-36.

Rheinstein, M. (1954), 'Introduction', in Weber, M., *Max Weber on Law in Economy and Society*, Harvard University Press, Cambridge, Mass., pp.xxv-lxxii.

Riesebrodt, M. (1989), 'From Patriarchalism to Capitalism: The Theoretical Context of Max Weber's Agrarian Studies (1892-93)', in Tribe, K. (ed.), *Reading Weber*, Routledge, London, pp.131-57.

Rose, A.M. (1967), *The Power Structure: Political Process in American Society*, Oxford University Press, New York.

Rossi, P. (1971), 'Discussion on Value-Freedom and Objectivity', in O. Stammer (ed.), *Max Weber and Sociology Today*, Basil Blackwell, Oxford, pp.71-8.

302

Rossides, D.W. (1972), 'The Legacy of Max Weber: A Non-Metaphysical Politics', *Sociological Inquiry*, vol. 42, no. 3-4, pp.183-210.

Rossides, D.W. (1976), *The American Class System: An Introduction to Social Stratification*, Houghton Mifflin, Boston.

Roth, G. (1963), *The Social Democrats in Imperial Germany: A Study in Working-Class Isolation and National Integration*, The Bedminster Press, Totowa, New Jersey.

Roth, G. (1965), 'Political Critiques of Max Weber: Some Implications for Political Sociology', *American Sociological Review*, vol. 30, pp.213-23.

Roth, G. (1971), 'The Historical Relationship to Marxism', in Bendix, R. and Roth, G. (eds), *Scholarship and Partisanship: Essays on Max Weber*, University of California Press, Berkeley, pp.227-52.

Roth, G. (1976), 'History and Sociology in the Work of Max Weber', *The British Journal of Sociology*, vol. 27, no. 3, pp.306-18.

Roth, G. (1978), 'Introduction', in Weber, M., *Economy and Society*, Vol. I, University of California Press, Berkeley, pp.xxxiii-cx.

Roth, G. (1984), 'Max Weber's Ethics and the Peace Movement Today', *Theory and Society*, vol. 13, no. 4, pp.49-511.

Roth, G. (1992), 'Interpreting and Translating Max Weber', *International Sociology*, vol. 7, no. 4, pp.449-59.

Rubery, J. (1982), 'Structured Labour Markets, Worker Organisation, and Low Pay', in Giddens, A. and Held, D. (eds), *Classes, Power and Conflict: Classical and Contemporary Debates*, Macmillan, London/Basingstoke, pp.330-48.

Runciman, W.G. (1968), 'Class, Status and Power', in Jackson, J.A. (ed.), *Social Stratification*, Cambridge University Press, Cambridge, pp.25-61.

Runciman, W.G. (1972), *A Critique of Max Weber's Philosophy of Social Science*, Cambridge University Press, Cambridge.

Sadri, M. (1983), 'Reconstruction of Max Weber's Notion of Rationality: An Immanent Model', *Social Research*, vol. 49, no. 3, pp.616-33.

Sahay, A. (1972), 'Weber's Ideas on the Analysis of Rationality and its Effect on Modern Society', in Sahay, A., *Sociological Analysis*, Routledge and Kegan Paul, London, pp.17-48.

Sahay, A. (1974), 'Weber's Definition of Capitalism: History and Sociology', *Sociological Analysis and Theory*, vol. 4, no. 1, pp.25-40.

Sayer, D. (1991), *Captialism and Modernity: An Excursus on Marx and Weber*, Routledge, London/New York.

Scaff, L.A. (1981), 'Max Weber and Robert Michels', *American Journal of Sociology*, vol. 86, no. 6, pp.1269-86.

Scaff, L.A. (1988), 'Weber, Simmel and the Sociology of Culture', *The Sociological Review*, vol. 36, no. 1, pp.1-30.

Scaff, L.A. (1991), *Fleeing the Iron Cage: Culture, Politics, and Modernity in the Thought of Max Weber*, University of California Press, Berkeley.

Scaff, L.A. and Arnold, T.C. (1985), 'Class and the Theory of History: Marx on France and Weber on Russia', in Antonio, R.J. and Glassman, G.M. (eds), *A Weber-Marx Dialogue*, University Press of Kansas, Lawrence, Kansas, pp.190-214.

Schermerhorn, R.A. (1961), *Society and Power*, Random House, New York.

Schluchter, W. (1979a), 'Value-Neutrality and the Ethic of Responsibility', in Roth, G. and Schluchter, W., *Max Weber's Vision of History: Ethics and Methods*, University of California Press, Berkeley, pp.65-116.

Schluchter, W. (1979b), 'The Paradox of Rationalization: On the Relation of Ethics and World', in Roth, G. and Schluchter, W., *Max Weber's Vision of History: Ethics and Methods*, University of California Press, Berkeley, pp.11-64.

Schluchter, W. (1981), *The Rise of Western Rationalism: Max Weber's Development History*, Roth, G. (trans.), University of California Press, Berkeley.

Schmidt, G. (1976), 'Max Weber and Modern Industrial Sociology: A Comment on Some Recent Anglo-Saxon Interpretations', *Sociological Analysis and Theory*, vol. 6, no. 1, pp.47-73.

Schumpeter, J.A. (1976), *Capitalism, Socialism and Democracy*, 5th edn, Allen and Unwin, London.

Schwarz, W. (1964), 'The Right of Resistance', *Ethics*, vol. 74, pp.126-34.

Seidman, S. and Gruber, M. (1977), 'Capitalism and Individuation in the Sociology of Max Weber', *The British Journal of Sociology*, vol. 28, no. 4, pp.498-508.

Sennett, R. (1978), *The Fall of Public Man: On the Social Psychology of Capitalism*, Vintage Books, New York.

Sewart, J. (1978), '"*Verstehen*" and Dialectic: Epistemology and Methodology in Weber and Lukács', *Philosophy and Social Criticism*, vol. 5, no. 3-4, pp.319-66.

Sharp, G. (1964), 'Ethics and Responsibility in Politics', *Inquiry*, vol. 7, pp.304-17.

Sharp, G. (1973), *Power and Struggle*, Porter Sargent, Boston.

Shils, D. (1968), 'Deference', in Jackson, J.A. (ed.), *Social Stratification*, Cambridge University Press, Cambridge, pp.104-32.

Sica, A. (1990), *Weber, Irrationality, and Social Order*, University of California Press, Berkeley.

Sica, A. (1993), 'Who Now Speaks for Weber? A Response to Burger', *Theory and Society*, vol. 22, no. 6, pp.837-43.

Simey, T.S. (1965), 'Weber's Sociological Theory of Value: An Appraizal in Mid-Century', *The Sociological Review*, vol. 13, no. 1, pp.45-64.

Simey, T.S. (1966), 'Max Weber: Man of Affairs or Theoretical Sociologist', *The Sociological Review*, vol. 14, no. 3, pp.303-27.

Smith, M.J. (1986), *Realist Thought from Weber to Kissinger*, Louisiana State University Press, Baton Rouge/London.

Southern, R.W. (1953), *The Making of the Middle Ages*, Hutchinson, London.

Speier, H. (1952), 'Honor and Social Structure', in Speier, H., *Social Order and the Risks of War*, George W. Stewart, New York, pp.36-52.

Spencer, M.E. (1970), 'Weber on Legitimate Norms and Authority', *The British Journal of Sociology*, vol. 21, pp.123-34.

Spencer, M.E. (1973), 'What is Charisma?', *The British Journal of Sociology*, vol. 24, pp.341-54.

Spencer, M.E. (1977), 'History and Sociology: An Analysis of Weber's "The City"', *Sociology*, vol. 11, no. 3, pp.507-25.

Stark, D. (1982), 'Class Struggle and the Transformation of the Labour Process: A Relational Approach', in Giddens, A. and Held, D. (eds), *Classes, Power, and Conflict: Classical and Contemporary Debates*, Macmillan, London/Basingstoke, pp.310-29.

Stark, W. (1967), 'Max Weber and the Heterogony of Purposes', *Social Research*, vol. 34, no. 2, pp.249-64.

Stark, W. (1968), 'The Agony of Righteousness? Max Weber's Moral Philosophy', *Thought*, vol. 43, pp.380-92.

Strauss, L. (1953), 'Natural Right and the Distinction Between Facts and Values', in Strauss, L., *Natural Right and History*, University of Chicago Press, Chicago/London, pp.35-80.

Strayer, J.R. (1968), 'Feudalism in Western Europe', in Cheyette, F.L. (ed.), *Lordship and Community in Medieval Europe*, Holt, Rinehart and Winston, New York, pp.12-21.

Struve, W. (1973), *Elites Against Democracy: Leadership Ideals in Bourgeois Political Thought in Germany 1890-1933*, Princeton University Press, Princeton, New Jersey.

Swatos, W.H. (1984), 'Revolution and Charisma in a Rationalized World: Weber Revisited and Extended', in Glassman, R.M. and Murvar, V. (eds), *Max Weber's Political Sociology: A Pessimistic Vision of a Rationalized World*, Greenwood Press, London/Westport, Connecticut, pp.201-15.

Tausky, C. (1965), 'Parsons on Stratification: An Analysis and Critique', *The Sociological Quarterly*, vol. 6, no. 2, pp.128-38.

Taylor, F.W. (1912), *Shop Management*, Harper and Brothers, New York/London.

Therborn, G. (1980a), *Science, Class and Society: On the Formation of Sociology and Historical Materialism*, Verso, London.

Therborn, G. (1980b), *What Does the Ruling Class Do When It Rules?: State Apparatuses and State Power under Feudalism, Capitalism and Socialism*, Verso, London.

Thomas, J.J.R. (1984), 'Weber and Direct Democracy', *The British Journal of Sociology*, vol. 35, no. 2, pp.216-40.

Thompson, E.P. (1982), 'Time, Work-Discipline, and Industrial Capitalism', in Giddens A. and Held, D. (eds), *Classes, Power, and Conflict: Classical and Contemporary Debates*, Macmillan, London/Basingstoke, pp.299-309.

Tiryakian, E.A. (1981), 'The Sociological Import of a Metaphor: Tracking the Source of Max Weber's "Iron Cage"', *Sociological Inquiry*, vol. 51, no. 1, pp.27-33.

Tocqueville, A. de (1954), *Democracy in America*, Vol. II, Vintage Books, New York.

Toennies, F. (1967), 'Estates and Classes', in Bendix, R. and Lipset, S.M. (eds), *Class, Status, and Power: Social Stratification in Comparative Perspective*, Routledge and Kegan Paul, London, pp.12-21.

Torrance, J. (1974), 'Max Weber: Methods and the Man', *European Journal of Sociology*, vol. 15, pp.127-65.

Touraine, A. (1977), *The Self-Production of Society*, Coltman, D. (trans.), University of Chicago Press, Chicago/London.

Treiman, D.J. (1975), 'The Process of Status Attainment in the United States and Great Britain', *American Journal of Sociology*, vol. 81, no. 3, pp.563-83.

Treiman, D.J. and Terrell, K. (1975), 'Sex and the Process of Status Attainment: A Comparison of Working Women and Men', *American Sociological Review*, vol. 40, no. 2, pp.174-200.

Treitschke, H. von (1978), *Politics*, Vol. I, Dugdale, B. and De Bille, T. (trs), AMS Press, New York.

Tribe, K. (1983), 'Prussian Agriculture - German Politics: Max Weber 1892-97', *Economy and Society*, vol. 12, no. 2, pp.181-226.

Trubek, D.M. (1972), 'Max Weber on Law and the Rise of Capitalism', *Wisconsin Law Review*, vol. 3, pp.720-53.

Turner, B.S. (1977), 'The Structuralist Critique of Weber's Sociology', *The British Journal of Sociology*, vol. 28, no. 1, pp.1-16.

Turner, B.S. (1981), *For Weber: Essays on the Sociology of Fate*, Routledge and Kegan Paul, London.

Turner, B.S. (1982), 'Nietzsche, Weber and the Devaluation of Politics: The Problem of State Legitimacy', *The Sociological Review*, vol. 30, no. 3, pp.367-91.

Turner, B.S. (1986), *Citizenship and Capitalism*, Allen and Unwin, London.

Turner, B.S. (1987), 'Marx, Weber, and the Coherence of Capitalism', in Wiley, N. (ed.), *The Marx-Weber Debate*, Sage, London, pp.169-204.

Turner, B.S. (1988), *Status*, Open University Press, Milton Keynes.

Turner, B.S. (1992), *Max Weber: From History To Modernity*, Routledge, London.

Turner, C. (1992), *Modernity and Politics in the Work of Max Weber*, Routledge, London.

Turner, S.-P. (1982), 'Bunyan's Cage and Weber's Casing', *Sociological Inquiry*, vol. 52, no. 1, pp.84-7.

Turner, S.-P. (1983), 'Weber on Action', *American Sociological Review*, vol. 48, pp.506-19.

Turner, S.-P. and Factor, R.A. (1981), 'Objective Possibility and Adequate Causation in Weber's Methodological Writings', *The Sociological Review*, vol. 29, no. 1, pp.5-28.

Turner, S.-P. and Factor, R.A. (1984), *Max Weber and the Dispute over Reason and Value: A Study in Philosophy, Ethics and Politics*, Routledge and Kegan Paul, London.

Turner, S.-P. and Factor, R.A. (1994), *Max Weber: The Lawyer as Social Thinker*, Routledge, London/New York.

Udéhn, L. (1981), 'The Conflict between Methodology and Rationalization in the Work of Max Weber', *Acta Sociologica*, vol. 24, pp.131-47.

Valentine, J. (1972), 'Weberian and Broader Concepts of Class in the Sociology of Culture', *Sociological Analysis, Sheffield*, vol. 2, pp.64-8.

Veblen, T. (1970), *The Theory of the Leisure Class: An Economic Study of Institutions*, Unwin Books, London.

Voegelin, E. (1952), *The New Science of Politics: An Introduction*, University of Chicago Press, Chicago.

Wallace, W.L. (1989), 'Max Weber's Two Spirits of Capitalism', *Telos*, vol. 81, pp.86-90.

Wallerstein, I. (1979), *The Capitalist World-Economy*, Cambridge University Press/Editions de la Maison des Sciences de l'homme, Cambridge.

Wallimann, I. et al. (1980), 'Misreading Weber: The Concept of *"Macht"*', *Sociology*, vol. 14, no. 2, pp.261-75.

Walton, P. (1971), 'Ideology and the Middle Class in Marx and Weber', *Sociology*, vol. 5, pp.389-94.

Ward, J.O. (1985), 'Feudalism: Interpretative Category or Framework of Life in the Medieval West?', in Leach, E. et al. (eds), *Feudalism: Comparative Studies*, Sydney Association for Studies in Society and Culture, Sydney, pp.40-67.

Warriner, C.K. (1969), 'Social Action, Behaviour and *Verstehen*', *The Sociological Quarterly*, vol. 10, pp.501-11.

Watkins, J.W.N. (1953), 'Ideal Types and Historical Explanation', in Feigl, H. and Brodbeck, M. (eds), *Readings in the Philosophy of Science*, Appleton-Century-Crofts, New York, pp.723-43.

Weber, M. (1988), *Max Weber: A Biography*, Zohn, H. (trans.), Transaction Books, New Brunswick.

307

Weights, A. (1978), 'Weber and "Legitimate Domination": A Theoretical Critique of Weber's Conceptualization of "Relations of Domination"', *Economy and Society*, vol. 7, no. 1, pp.56-73.

Weiss, J. (1985), 'On the Marxist Reception and Critique of Max Weber in Eastern Europe', in Antonio, R.J. and Glassman, G.M. (eds), *A Weber-Marx Dialogue*, University Press of Kansas, Lawrence, Kansas, pp.117-31.

Weiss, J. (1986), *Weber and the Marxist World*, King-Utz, E. and King, M.J. (trs), Routledge and Kegan Paul, New York.

Wells, G.C. (1986), 'The Reich President', *Social Research*, vol. 53, no. 1, pp.125-8.

Wells, G.C. and Baehr, P. (1995), 'Editors' Introduction', in Weber, M., *The Russian Revolutions*, Wells, G.C. and Baehr, P. (trs and eds), Polity Press, Cambridge, pp.1-39.

Wenger, M.G. (1980), 'The Transmutation of Weber's *Stand* in American Sociology and its Social Roots', *Current Perspectives in Social Theory*, vol. 1, pp.357-78.

Wenger, M.G. (1987), 'Class Closure and the Historical/Structural Limits of the Marx-Weber Convergence', in Wiley, N. (ed.), *The Marx-Weber Debate*, Sage, London, pp.31-64.

Wesolowski, W. (1979), *Classes, Strata and Power*, Kolankiewicz, G. (trans.), Routledge and Kegan Paul, London.

Whimster, S. (1980), 'The Profession of History in the Work of Max Weber: Its Origins and Limitations', *The British Journal of Sociology*, vol. 31, no. 3, pp.352-76.

Wiener, J.M. (1982), 'Max Weber's Marxism: Theory and Method in "The Agrarian Sociology of Ancient Civilizations"', *Theory and Society*, vol. 11, no. 3, pp.389-401.

Wild, R.A. (1971), 'Social Stratification or Statistical Exercises?', *Politics*, vol. 6, no. 2, pp.169-77.

Wild, R.A. (1978a), *Bradstow: A Study of Status, Class and Power in a Small Australian Town*, rev. and expanded edn, Angus and Robertson, London.

Wild, R.A. (1978b), *Social Stratification in Australia*, Allen and Unwin, Sydney.

Wiley, N. (1967), 'America's Unique Class Politics: The Interplay of the Labor, Credit, and Commodity Markets', *American Sociological Review*, vol. 32, no. 4, pp.529-41.

Wiley, N. (1983), 'The Congruence of Weber and Keynes', *Sociological Theory*, vol. 1, pp.30-57.

Willer, D.E. (1967), 'Max Weber's Missing Authority Type', *Sociological Inquiry*, vol. 37, no. 2, pp.231-9.

Williams, R. (1976), *Keywords: A Vocabulary of Culture and Society*, Fontana/Croom Helm, London.

Wilson, H.T. (1976), 'Reading Weber: The Limits of Sociology', *Sociology*, vol. 10, pp.297-315.

Wolfinger, R.E. (1970), 'Reputation and Reality in the Study of "Community Power"', *American Sociological Review*, vol. 25, pp.636-44.

Wolpe, H. (1968), 'A Critical Analysis of Some Aspects of Charisma', *The Sociological Review*, vol. 16, pp.305-18.

Wright, E.O. (1974-75), 'To Control or to Smash Bureaucracy: Weber and Lenin on Politics, the State, and Bureaucracy', *Berkeley Journal of Sociology*, vol. 19, pp.69-108.

Wrong, D. (1979), *Power: Its Forms, Bases and Uses*, Basil Blackwell, Oxford.

Wuthnow, R. (1987), 'Rethinking Weber's View of Ideology', *Theory and Society*, vol. 16, no. 1, pp.123-37.

Zaret, D. (1980), 'From Weber to Parsons and Schutz: The Eclipse of History in Modern Social Theory', *American Journal of Sociology*, vol. 85, no. 5, pp.1180-1201.

Zeitlin, M. (1960), 'Max Weber on the Sociology of the Feudal Order', *The Sociological Review*, vol. 8, pp.203-8.

Index

311

Burris, V. 154n34, 159n80
Bush, M.L. 213n51, 215n73, 217n93
Butts, S. 33n21

C

Calvert, P. 265n56
capital accumulation, in Western
  feudalism 184-185
capital-labour, relationships 122
capitalism
  class action 145-147
  as cultural phenomenon 12-14
  and discipline 86
  and economic rationalism 46,
    104-111
  and freedom 60, 65
  modern industrial 21
  international character 128
  power inequalities 73
  and Protestantism 61-62
Castoriadis, C. 159n83
causality 61-63
cause-effect 19
Cavalli, L. 267n73
charismatic action 48
charismatic authority 222-224,
  251, 253
charismatic domination 25
  by a plebiscitary leader 243
  defined 25, 81, 90
charismatic leaders 26
  as a counter to
    bureaucratization 251-252
  in the modern nation-state,
    legitimation of, 242
  of political parties 236-237
  as a solution to value-conflict 31
  and value-rationality 50
  see also personality
charters, in Western feudalism
  193-194, 202

Chinoy, E. 159n83
Christianity
  and discipline 85-86
  and economic rationalism 46
  citizenship, as a political force
    248-249
  city states 199-202
civil society 1-2, 6n1
Clarke, S. 67n17
class
  action
    capitalist 145-147
    collective 141
    socialist 147
    wage labourers 36, 117
    of wage labourers 140-145
  in antiquity 118-119
  capitalist 119
  in civil society 2
  consciousness, preconditions
    140-145
  and economic power 104-111
  as a function of marketable
    skills 115-116
  and power 71, 73
  and property/lack of property
    111-128
  slaves 118
  and status groups 235-236
  typology 115-119
Cohen, I.J. 148n1,3, 264n46,
  267n74
Cohen, J. 33n20, 100n25, 102n46,
  54n38
collective action 42-44, 255-258
  and class 141
collective responsibilities, ethics
  255, 258
collectivities 55
Collins, R. 101n37, 102n47,
  148n1, 157n62,67, 261n20
communal relationships 146, 255,
  258

316

318

defined 226-231
and value-free social science
29-30
and violence in the modern
nation-state 227
political dictatorship 244-245
political emancipation, in the
modern nation-state 249-258
political freedom 252-255
political leadership 227-232
in the modern nation-state 218-232
political parties
in the modern nation-state
232-240
relationship with classes and
status groups 235-236
political power
of bureaucracy in the modern
state 225
in the modern nation-state
126-128
in Western feudalism 168
warfare and litigation 193
in Wilhelmine Germany 225-226
Polsby, N.W. 98n6,10
Portis, E.B. 33n14,23, 35n40,
68n25, 262n30, 270n97
Poulantzas, N. 98n7, 100n24
power
in American stratification theory
4, 74
of classes 2
of consumers 123-124
control and disposal 111-115
de facto 89
defined 72
disciplinary 86-87, 93
and wage labourers 129-130
economic 104-111, 119-121
and structural compulsion
121-122
in feudal city states 198-199
Herrschaft as 22, 24, 25

international 127-128
political 76, 126-128, 234-236,
244
property ownership as 111-128
and resistance 71-78
state 125-128
and value-free social science 29
in Western feudalism 168
see also domination
power bases in modern society 2-3
power-political interests, in the
German nation-state 230, 233, 241
powerlessness of citizens in the
German nation-state 248
Prager, J. 69n36, 264n46
press, power of 237
pressure groups *see* interest
organizations
propaganda, as a political tool 237,
243
property, forms of 112-115
property rights, and classes
115-119
property/lack of property,
implications of 111-128
Protestant ethic, key to modern
capitalism 40, 132
Protestantism
and human rights 59
and individual responsibility 247
key to modern capitalism 61-62
psychological motives 41
Puritanism, rationalization in 54,
57, 220

R

Rasmussen, D.M. 68n25,26
rational capital accounting *see*
economic rationalism
rationality
as a cultural value 52

320

traditional domination 25, 81,
90-91, 165-166
feudalism 168, 176-177,
202-203
traditional law, in Western
feudalism 188-196
Treiman, D.J. 211n39
Tribe, K. 262n25
Trubek, D.M. 149n7,8, 156n56,
260n13
truth
as a cultural value 18
and value-freedom 26-27
Turner, B.S. 67n8, 100n25,
102n40,43,46, 206n3, 214n66,
260n11,14, 269n81
Turner, S.-P. 33n20, 35n38,
66n4,6, 67n16, 68n20,25,
70n41, 149n7

characteristics 54
in political leadership 227, 243
and power-political interests 231
value-rational authority 81
value-relevance 8-20, 11-12
values
common 74-76
shared, and legitimacy 82
see also cultural values
vassalage, as an honourable estate
167
Veblen, T. 213n55
violence
legitimation in the modern
nation-state 219, 220, 226-227
and political leadership, in the
modern nation-state 230
Voegelin, E. 33n20
voters *see* electoral masses

U

Udéhn, L. 66n6, 70n45, 155n41,
159n79, 270n87
uncertainty, and rational action 40
unconscious motives, and
means-end rational action 51
utopian perspectives in social
theory 256-257

V

Valentine, J. 153n29
valuation 75
value-conflict 30-31, 82
value-freedom, methodological
principle of 26-32, 65
value-judgements, in social
-scientific knowledge 10-11, 19,
26-29
value-rational action 25, 48-50, 52,
81-83

W

wage-labourers
bureaucratic organization of
133-137
as a capitalist class 119
class consciousness,
preconditions 141-144
Wallace, W.L. 158n75
Wallerstein, I. 157n62
Wallimann, I. 97n2, 100n25,
102n46
Walton, P. 153n29
Ward, J.O. 206n4
warfare
in feudal politics 193
and modern nation-states 220,
234
threat of atomic 255
Watkins, J.W.N. 34n32
Weber, M. 34n25,27,33, 158n69,
159n84, 160n89, 262n26

Weiss, J. 32n3, 33n7,19, 34n24,28
Wells, G.C. 161n100
Wenger, M.G. 7n7, 154n34,
  160n92, 206n2
Wertbeziehung see value-relevance
wertrational action *see* value-
  rational action
Wertung see valuation
Wesolowski, W. 98n11
Western feudalism
  as cultural phenomenon 12,
    165-170
  economy 178-185
  social structure 165-170
Whimster, S. 34n32
Wiener, J.M. 150n11
Wild, R.A. 98n9, 265n54
Wiley, N. 156n50
will 41
Willer, D.E. 100n25
Williams, R. 206n1
Wilson, H.T. 34n28, 68n26,
  101n36
Wolfinger, R.E. 98n6
Wolpe, H. 262n32, 267n72
women's experience 6
workers *see* wage labourers
Wright, E.O. 261n23, 263n37
Wrong, D. 100n25

Z

Zaret, D. 70n41
Zeitlin, 207n15
zweckrational action *see*
  means-end rational action